Health and Disease in Tribal Societies

The Ciba Foundation for the promotion of international cooperation in medical and chemical research is a scientific and educational charity established by CIBA Limited – now CIBA-GEIGY Limited – of Basle. The Foundation operates independently in London under English trust law.

Ciba Foundation Symposia are published in collaboration with Elsevier Scientific Publishing Company, Excerpta Medica, North-Holland Publishing Company, in Amsterdam.

Elsevier/Excerpta Medica/North-Holland, P.O. Box 211, Amsterdam

Health and Disease in Tribal Societies

Ciba Foundation Symposium 49 (new series)

1977

Elsevier · Excerpta Medica · North-Holland

Amsterdam · Oxford · New York

Science
RA
652
S98
1976

ISBN 0-444-15271-7

Published in August 1977 by Elsevier/Excerpta Medica/North-Holland, P.O. Box 211, Amsterdam and Elsevier North-Holland, Inc., 52 Vanderbilt Avenue, New York, N.Y. 10017.

Suggested series entry for library catalogues: Ciba Foundation Symposia.
Suggested publisher's entry for library catalogues: Elsevier/Excerpta Medica/North-Holland

Ciba Foundation Symposium 49 (new series)
352 pages, 46 figures, 38 tables

Library of Congress Cataloging in Publication Data

Symposium on Health and Disease in Tribal Societies, London, 1976.
  Health and disease in tribal societies.

  (Ciba Foundation symposium; new ser., 49)
  Bibliography: p.
  Includes indexes.
  1. Man, Primitive–Diseases–Congresses. 2. Epidemiology–Congresses. 3. Medical anthropology–Congresses. I. Title. II. Series: Ciba Foundation. Symposium; new ser., 49.
[DNLM: 1. Medicine, primitive–Congresses. 2. Acculturation–Congresses. 3. Ethnic groups–Congresses. 4. Communicable diseases–Congresses. C161F v. 49 / WZ309 S992h 1976]
RA652.S98 1976   614.4   77-9478
ISBN 0-444-15271-7

Printed in The Netherlands by Mouton, The Hague.

Contents

Participants

Symposium on *Health and Disease in Tribal Societies*, held at the Ciba Foundation, London, 28th–30th September 1976

Chairman: P. HUGH-JONES Chest Unit, King's College Hospital Medical School, Denmark Hill, London SE5 8RX

R. G. BARUZZI Department of Preventive Medicine, Escola Paulista de Medicina, Rua Botucatú 720, CEP 04023, São Paulo, Brazil

F. L. BLACK Department of Epidemiology and Public Health, Yale University School of Medicine, 60 College Street, New Haven, Connecticut 06510, USA

T. A. COCKBURN Paleopathology Association, 18655 Parkside, Detroit, Michigan 48221, USA

N. COHEN Department of Clinical Epidemiology and Social Medicine, Royal Free Hospital School of Medicine, 21 Pond Street, London NW3 2PN

D. C. GAJDUSEK National Institute of Neurological and Communicative Disorders and Stroke, Building 36, Room 5B25, National Institutes of Health, Bethesda, Maryland 20014, USA

P. J. S. HAMILTON PAHO/WHO Caribbean Epidemiology Centre (CAREC), PO Box 164, Port-of-Spain, Trinidad

S. HARALDSON Scandinavian School of Public Health, S-413 46 Göteborg, Sweden

G. A. HARRISON Department of Biological Anthropology, University of Oxford, 58 Banbury Road, Oxford OX2 6QS

A. D. JONES Department of Social Psychology, London School of Economics and Political Science, Houghton Street, London WC2A 2AE

G. A. LEWIS Department of Social Anthropology, Downing Street, University of Cambridge, Cambridge CB2 3DZ

S. L. LIGHTMAN   Survival International, 36 Craven Street, London WC2N 5NG *and* Department of Medicine, Middlesex Hospital, Mortimer Street, London W1P 7PN

BETSY LOZOFF   Division of Geographic Medicine, Case Western Reserve University, Wearn Research Building, University Hospitals, Cleveland, Ohio 44106, USA

FRANÇOISE MORIN   Institut des Sciences Sociales, Université de Toulouse-Le Mirail, 109 Bis rue Vauquelin, 31076 Toulouse-Cedex, France

J. V. NEEL   Department of Human Genetics, University of Michigan Medical School, 1137 Catherine Street, Ann Arbor, Michigan 48104, USA

H. OHLMAN   Educational Communication Systems, Division of Health Manpower Development, World Health Organization, Avenue Appia, 1211 Geneva 27, Switzerland

MARGUERITE S. PEREIRA   Virus Reference Laboratory, Central Public Health Laboratory, Colindale Avenue, London NW9 5HT

Sir GEORGE PICKERING   5 Horwood Close, Headington, Oxford OX3 7RF

I. V. POLUNIN   Department of Social Medicine and Public Health, University of Singapore Faculty of Medicine, Outram Hill, Singapore 3

A. G. SHAPER   Department of Clinical Epidemiology and Social Medicine, Royal Free Hospital School of Medicine, 21 Pond Street, London NW3 2PN

FIONA STANLEY   University Department of Medicine, Perth Medical Centre, Shenton Park, Western Australia 6008

A. S. TRUSWELL   Department of Nutrition and Food Science, Queen Elizabeth College, University of London, Atkins Buildings, Campden Hill, London W8 7AH

D. A. J. TYRRELL   Division of Communicable Diseases, MRC Clinical Research Centre, Northwick Park Hospital, Watford Road, Harrow, Middlesex HA1 3UJ

J. S. WEINER   MRC Environmental Physiology Unit, London School of Hygiene and Tropical Medicine, Keppel Street, Gower Street, London WC1E 7HT

ISOBEL M. WHITE   20, Blackbutt street, O'Connor A. C. T. 2601, Australia

J. C. WOODBURN   Department of Anthropology, London School of Economics and Political Science, Houghton Street, London WC2A 2AE

Editors: KATHERINE ELLIOTT *(Organizer)* and JULIE WHELAN

Introduction

PHILIP HUGH-JONES

King's College Hospital Medical School, London

It may be interesting, as an introduction, to describe how this symposium came about and what we who planned it thought we might achieve by it. The original germ of the symposium happened ten years ago when I was on the Royal Society and Royal Geographical Society expedition to the Xingu River in Brazil. At that time there was good reason to suppose that the well-known Brazilian explorers, the Villas Boas brothers, might make contact with the Kren-Akorore, who remained an unknown, isolated, Stone Age group. My particular interest was to be there, as Orlando Villas Boas had kindly agreed, at the time of (or very soon after) primary contact, and then to try to obtain blood samples, in order to measure their viral and bacterial antibody content.

I spent three extremely interesting months waiting for contact to be made but then had to return to London. As Dr Baruzzi will describe, contact subsequently took place. Although many interesting records were made the studies I had in mind were never done. I felt sad about this, especially as about ten years previously I had similarly hoped that the Motilone Indians would be contacted on the Colombia–Venezuela border. Again, no evidence on viral antibodies was obtained when these people were finally contacted.

I had a strong feeling, after the Xingu expedition, that although we now have a method for preserving blood in field conditions for up to four months in solid carbon dioxide (Secord 1972) there may no longer be any people who are sufficiently isolated on whom such studies could be made. I don't know whether that's true and whether there are still isolated Stone Age people, perhaps in South America, perhaps in the Andaman islands, perhaps in Indonesian New Guinea; but I doubt it.

It was important to know about the virus and bacterial antibody content in the blood of primitive man, not only to try to help protect him from the effects of contact with civilization—past experience even with groups such as the

1

Txukarramãe and the Kren-Akorore who have been befriended and helped after contact has shown that up to 50% of any such group may die soon after primary contact because they are not immune to introduced respiratory pathogens—but also in order to understand the evolution and mutation of respiratory viruses which produce our own illnesses.

Whether we shall now ever be able to make such studies in immunology or not, it is certain that primitive man is now being assimilated or destroyed at a rapid rate and not nearly enough is being done to record crucial features of his social and physical state before they are lost for ever. Of course, much good work has been done in recording the life of such people, and television film may, in future, represent the modern equivalent of Samuel Pepys!

These ideas were those of an interested amateur and nothing more, and I felt it was time that experts met to discuss the problem of recording essential information for the future; that sociologists met anthropologists and doctors. I therefore approached the Ciba Foundation through whose generosity scientific workers from different disciplines can meet and discuss mutual problems.

When a group met to think about the proposed symposium it seemed that the subject had much wider possibilities than the one aspect of what to record and how to achieve the optimum information at early contact with primitive people. We felt that there was little excuse for searching out isolated peoples, but if we knew their whereabouts we might be able to save them from the disasters which have befallen them in the past and, at the same time, gain much for ourselves when they were visited, as they surely would be. So three questions emerged: first, how can one protect primitive people? Secondly, what would the study of primitive people do to help us, the so-called civilized societies, in relation to the ills of modern man? And, thirdly, what could (or should) we do about the assimilation of such people into our society?

In protection, we are obviously not only interested in the physical efforts to prevent actual killing of people and to minimize effects of the introduced disease, but also in the effects of despoliation of their environment and of the cultural shock. In fact the psychosocial effects of contact and loss of identity thereafter can be much more permanently destructive than either violence or disease. Examples are numerous: the Aborigines of Australia, the Indians of North America, or more specifically and recently the proud and feared Xavante studied by Maybury-Lewis (1967) barely 15 years ago, are now represented by a few beggars in the town of Xavantina; only their name is preserved.

Apart from the ethics of helping primitive man we, ourselves, should have much to gain by anthropological study. Consider the ills of modern man, such as (1) the problem of world population and how to regulate it; (2) the problems of violence and war in modern communities; (3) the problems of psychoneurosis which, as a physician in a London hospital, I find are extreme; and finally (4) physical illnesses, like hypertension, atherosclerosis and so on. It seems that the study of primitive people might help us in all these areas. It is of great interest to know how primitive people do maintain a population balance between themselves and their environment. As far as problems of violence go, there is the work of Konrad Lorenz and other ethologists to suggest that man is like an aggressive, territorial, acquisitive ape, whereas others believe that this aggressiveness is not fundamental in man's nature and is acquired and passed on in upbringing. Fundamentally, how aggressive are primitive people?

The psychoneuroses of modern man are of great interest. I find that when I go to South America, the Far East, or Africa, what I see in medicine are problems like malnutrition, parasitic diseases, and bacterial infections. At King's College Hospital in London I am cynical enough to say to students that I only need to make three diagnoses to cover many of the illnesses one sees in the medical wards. These diagnoses are overeating, oversmoking and psychological dependency, and I think the last is the most important. When you come to think of it, these diagnoses cover bronchitis, lung cancer and diabetes, and probably hypertension, coronary artery disease, and so on. The need to overeat and oversmoke appears to arise from psychological dependency. At King's a survey of the taking of drug overdoses in attempted suicide (Greer *et al.* 1966; Greer & Gunn 1966) showed that something like 90% of cases arise from dependency problems. It is of great interest to know why, in our society, we have got into that state. What happens in primitive society? On the physical side there are obvious illnesses such as atherosclerosis and hypertension and we are intrigued to know how primitive man escapes—if indeed he does escape from these ills.

Finally, there is the question of assimilation. When one looks at what has happened to primitive people and the dire results of contact with modern so-called civilization, how should assimilation be done? One can't keep human beings in zoos; one can't stop the march of progress; one can't stop assimilation. But how can one minimize its bad effects? And what should be the aim?

I hope, in this symposium, that we may formulate ideas about working with primitive people, where to look in order to find them, how to protect them when we go there, what information we ought to collect, how to collect and record it and why to preserve these people (not only ethically, because that is obvious), but because there is much to be gained for ourselves.

References

GREER, S., GUNN, J. C. & KOLLER, K. M. (1966) Aetiological factors in attempted suicide. *Br. Med. J.* 2, 1352–1355

GREER, S. & GUNN, J. C. (1966) Attempted suicides from intact and broken parental homes. *Br. Med. J. 2*, 1355–1357

MAYBURY-LEWIS, D. (1967) *Akwe-Shavante Society*, Oxford University Press, London

SECORD, C. (1972) in Hugh-Jones, P. *et al*. Medical studies among Indians of the Upper Xingu. *Br. J. Hosp. Med. 3*, 317–334

Some characteristics of tribal peoples

IVAN POLUNIN

Department of Social Medicine and Public Health, University of Singapore

Abstract The study of health and disease in distinctive human groups is an important source of knowledge, and ultimately of understanding. Tribal societies are at the polar extreme from modernized communities. However, with the breakdown of isolation this distinctiveness is being eroded, slowly for genes, more rapidly for ideas and behaviour, and fastest for infective agents of disease. Though contemporary tribal men cannot be equated with prehistoric men, they resemble them more than do modernized men. Therefore the study of tribal peoples not only widens the range of circumstances in which human adaptability is observed, it throws some light on the evolution of human diseases. This is particularly the case with regard to the study of 'diseases of modern life'.

Tribal life is characterized by comparative physical and cultural isolation, simplicity, small group size, low population density and closeness to nature, both physically and conceptually. In spite of rapid change, which itself needs study, there are still situations where what is studied has shown little recent change.

In a world where dissatisfaction with life and medicine grows in spite of unparalleled technical success, we should look again at tribal men. There is much to learn from each other's successes and failures.

The reasons for the medical study of tribal peoples largely reside in their differences from other groups. In this paper I shall attempt to describe some of the characteristics of tribal peoples and the ways in which they differ from advanced peoples.

I do not think that we should worry too much about who should be called 'tribal'. In the past we all used the word 'primitive'. But that word carries unacceptable evolutionary implications and can arouse resentment. 'Tribal' implies common origin and group solidarity, but it has always had political implications and may include urban peoples (Lewis 1968). I suggest for our purposes that we use the word for those isolated breeding populations whose differences from mainstream cultures make them worth discussing at this symposium.

ISOLATION: A DEFINITIVE CHARACTERISTIC

Because of their isolation, change in tribal groups has at least the appearance of being largely due to forces arising within the group and its environment. This isolation may be geographic, and may also be significantly determined by the attitudes of both the people themselves and their neighbours. Effective isolation between two groups exists where there is no flow or transmission between them. This is true whether we are dealing with the flow of living organisms, of culture or of genes, though what constitutes 'effective isolation' depends very much on what is being transmitted.

Some living organisms, including microbial and helminthic agents of disease or their vectors and useful or weed species of plants or animals, are freely transmissible under conditions of minimum contact. They may spread to an isolated community through a series of intermediaries, before the first investigator reaches the people. The spread of culture may also be rapid and easy, as where superior steel tools are involved, or slow and difficult, where innovations are felt to be threatening.

Genes can only be incorporated into a breeding population at a comparatively slow rate, and significant gene flow usually requires considerable friendly contact. It is practically impossible to find communities which are microbially and culturally uninfluenced from outside. It is easier to find communities with little or no evidence for recent gene flow, but the extent of earlier contact cannot be determined (Neel & Salzano 1964).

With the rapid disappearance of the tribal state, studies relating the tribal way of life to health and disease become urgent. Postponement diminishes their value. This is also true of studies of change itself, as baseline studies are needed before rapid change begins, if the situation is to be well understood.

The group studying 'Methods of Geographical Pathology' (1959) wrote: 'The primary objective of studies in geographical pathology is to increase knowledge of the incidence of specific diseases in population groups living in different environments and having varying habitats, customs and working conditions ...'

Tribal peoples should be especially rewarding because they are at the opposite end of the scale to the highly developed 'modernized' populations which are the subject of most epidemiological studies.

HUMAN HISTORY AND MODERN TRIBAL MAN

It used to be believed that human communities evolved through rather definite states of culture, from hunter-gatherers to agriculturalists to modern men. If this were true we could equate ancient with modern hunter-gatherers. But the idea is a gross over-simplification, and there are many reasons why modern tribal groups are unique (Geddes 1963).

There are always human influences from outside the group. Of these the most subtle is the influence of tribal neighbours. There are also the more obvious influences of settlers, traders, officials, missionaries, tourists and others. These include scientists who will deliberately influence the people by gifts and medical care in the discharge of their social obligations. Almost everywhere, some artefacts and exotic microbial agents will have been introduced.

Contemporary tribal people differ from early humans in that all the species interacting in the human ecosystem will have evolved since early times, and there will also have been global changes in the environment.

However, I think that we would all agree with the idea which has often been expressed that tribal societies are the contemporary societies which most closely resemble communities of early man. To quote the WHO Expert Committee on Research in Population Genetics in Primitive Groups (1964):

'Such groups present both in their size and level of economy, the closest approximation one can find to the conditions under which man has lived for the greater part of his existence. It is probable that much of the genetic endowment of modern man has been shaped by the action of natural selection and other evolutionary processes at these cultural levels.'

I do not think that there are diagnostic features of tribal societies. They are distinguished from modernized societies by a pattern of characters which are

TABLE 1

Some characteristics commonly found in tribal societies which may help to distinguish them from modern societies, which usually have contrasting characteristics

(A) *Distribution*
    (1) Lower overall population density
    (2) Smaller settlements and social groups
    (3) Greater settlement mobility; shorter range individual movements
(B) *Isolation*
    (4) Greater settlement isolation (related to 1 & 9)
    (5) More contact with fewer people (related to 2 & 4)
(C) *Stability*
    (6) Greater resistance to 'spontaneous' changes
    (7) Greater vulnerability to external influences
(D) *Simplicity*
    (8) Fewer formal roles and occupations (related to 9)
    (9) Simpler arts and technology (related to 8)
(E) *Ecology*
    (10) Closer to nature and the subsistence system (related to 9 & 11)
    (11) Less degradation of ecosystem (related to 1 & 9)

usually present. Some of these characters are listed in Table 1, and are to be compared with contrasting characters found in most modernized societies.

POPULATION DENSITY

If the smallest residence groups of a population, the households, were evenly and sparsely spaced through the territory, we might think of them as 'islands' in a 'sea' of climax vegetation, such as forest. We might expect their environmental impact to be proportional to the population density. However, with increasing density, a linear relation no longer holds. As population density increases, the proportion of relatively unaffected land diminishes, and is cut into smaller and smaller pieces and finally disappears (Fig. 1). Animal, vegetal and

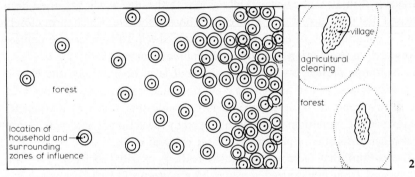

FIG. 1. Diagram showing the effect of population density on dispersed households. Zones of influence are shown by concentric circles.
FIG. 2. Effect of grouping households into settlements. There is a smaller area of more intensely affected land and a larger area of relatively unaffected land, in large parcels.

soil resources are exploited more rapidly than they can be renewed, leading to environmental deterioration, with consequences for human subsistence and health. To the extent that these changes begin to become serious at a particular population density, we can speak of the carrying capacity of an ecosystem exploited in a particular way.

Such a crude island model of settlement takes no account of the duration of environmental effects. Thus shifting cultivators make new clearings every year, which are soon abandoned and slowly revert to forest (Fig. 3). The effects of this are very prolonged for large mammals and forest trees because of slow reproduction and maturation, and brief for small forms of life. They are long for species dependent on climax vegetation and shorter for opportunists colonizing the man-modified areas.

The influence of a human group can be thought of as a series of concentric

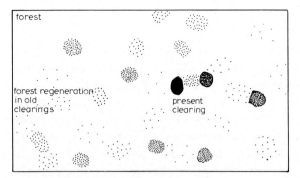

FIG. 3. Effects of one family of shifting cultivators on forest over the last 30 years (schematic). The closeness of the dots indicates the intensity of environmental modification.

zones of progressively diminishing influence surrounding the house. That such zones of influence can be significant determinants of health and diseases is suggested by Dunn (1972), on which Fig. 4 is based.

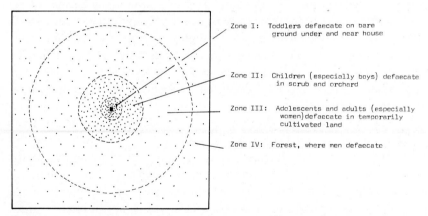

FIG. 4. Zones of vegetation surround a West Malaysian aboriginal house. Faeces are represented by dots. (Freely adapted from Dunn 1972.)

SETTLEMENT SIZE

Households are usually grouped into settlements, as in Fig. 2. Compared with the same density of households evenly distributed, grouping produces a smaller area with still more intensely altered conditions, while a greater area is left with climax vegetation, in large parcels. Inside the village there will be a greater concentration of parasitic disseminules, and the group in close contact is larger.

POPULATION DENSITY AND DISEASES

Classical observations and experiments on the effects of population density on health have shown that crowding of hosts leads to crowding of parasites and increased morbidity, which was ascribed to an increased load of infection (Wilson & Miles 1955). The belief is growing that crowding also affects health by sociosomatic means. Cassel (1974) supposed that 'the social process linking high population density to enhanced disease susceptibility is not crowding *per se* but the disordered relationships that are the inevitable results of such crowding'. Tribal people are often crowded in their little houses and settlements, but their groupings are small and generally well ordered, so harmful social effects of overcrowding are probably unimportant.

SMALL POPULATIONS

Settlements are usually small among tribal peoples, for economic, techno-logical and social reasons. The minimum size of a group may be that of an effective hunting team. At the other extreme a ceiling is approached above which the distance from the settlement to the food supply becomes so great that it takes too long to reach. This varies under different circumstances, and is smaller for hunter-gatherers than for cultivators. Larger populations tend to lack unity and to split, while small groups may amalgamate. Such changes usually involve kinsfolk (Neel 1970).

Any small series of people is likely to lack some alleles, especially rare ones, even if they are unrelated. Their offspring are likely to lose further alleles by chance. Small isolated breeding populations will further increase homozygosity through inbreeding. Homozygosity at a locus is a stable state in a genetically isolated population, and diseases due to recessive genes are likely to be commoner than in a larger population. Besides selection, a variety of often 'chance' events has been important in determining the ancestry of small isolated groups (Gajdusek 1964).

An analogous situation exists for culturally transmitted characteristics, such as inventions. Where the population is small, the cultural pool is small and there is a severe limitation on the amount of cultural variation that can be transmitted and maintained in a population. We also have a situation which might loosely be called 'cultural inbreeding' where variation is minimized because of the common ancestry of ideas and the development of cultural uniformity in a close-knit group.

Where parasitic agents have no non-human reservoir, the size of the pool of susceptibles is important. The smaller the population the greater the chance that the parasite is absent. If it is present, and if conditions for the parasite are favourable, the prevalence will become and remain high if infection confers no immunity. Thus we would expect such isolated small groups to show a mosaic of high and zero prevalence rates (Polunin 1963).

Where infection confers sufficient immunity, the introduction of the infective agent tends to lead to massive spread followed by its disappearance because the susceptibles are used up. But this is a subject for discussion later in the symposium.

To generalize, characteristics occurring at low prevalence rates are likely to be absent in small populations for most of the time. If present, their frequency is likely to show wide fluctuations due to chance. If an absent characteristic is self-replicating and needs to be transmitted, it is likely to stay absent because of isolation. If present, drift (exemplified by genetic drift) is likely to be rapid. This may proceed to the more stable state of complete absence, or to a high prevalence rate.

MOBILITY OF RESIDENCE

Though individual movements tend to be limited, tribal people are less likely to have fixed settlements than modern men. The hunter-gatherers (Fig. 5)

FIG. 5. A Lanoh Negrito lean-to, Upper Perak, Peninsular Malaysia. Such a temporary home provides a minimal barrier to the external environment.

FIG. 6. Homes and shifting cultivation of Semai-Senoi families, Pahang, Peninsular Malaysia.

usually stay briefly in an area as they exploit its resources before moving on. The shifting cultivator (Fig. 6) exhausts his garden after a season or so and has little incentive to stay in his old house unless he has invested heavily in it. In contrast to this, permanent agriculture and industry make for permanent settlements.

Population movements are important determinants of microbial disease, especially when they lead to an infection being introduced for the first time. On the other hand, an infection present in neighbouring settled peoples may be diminished if the people move fast enough. For this to occur there must be a stage in the life history of the parasitic agent which has a non-human reservoir which cannot migrate with the host population. If the parasite has insufficient time to complete its non-migrating stage and infect people before they have moved on, and if the people are adequately separated from infected neighbours, they will be free of infection. De Zulueta (1956) thought that the reason for the comparative freedom from malaria of the nomadic Punan of Sarawak was that they did not stay long enough in one place for vector mosquitoes to become infective.

Infrequent moves may be sufficient to discourage *Ascaris* infection. If the duration of stay approximates to the length of life of adult worms, and if the eggs can survive in soil for longer, infrequent moves may prevent the build-up of sufficient soil infection to allow heavy infection. This may account for the low *Ascaris* prevalence rates found in some shifting cultivators (Polunin 1963; Dunn 1972).

In tribal society a person only has a small number of contacts, but the frequency and intensity of contact is likely to be very great. At the other extreme, in city life one person may have more contacts in a week than a tribesman has in his whole lifetime, but most of these are fleeting and ineffective.

STABILITY IN TRIBAL GROUPS: SOME TENABLE ECOLOGICAL ANALOGIES?

There seems to be a paradox here. On the one hand, the isolation of the tribal people limits outside influences. The conservative tribal people resist change, while the neighbouring peoples have often put up barriers against assimilation. The picture is one of relative stability.

On the other hand the tribal people are often those whose lives are being most drastically interfered with, and who may be in danger of depopulation or even extinction. Or if they survive the depopulation which follows contact, most of their culture will disappear in the course of their making 'the great adaptation'.

Perhaps this extreme vulnerability is not so surprising after all. We may look on the tribal people as much more isolated than others, but this is partly an illusion due to our outside viewpoint. The difference that is important for some purposes is that between minimal contact and no contact at all. For a particular virus, contact which introduces it is more important than many more obvious later contacts. Of course, other very obvious influences, like environmental disruption, social pressures or hostilities, are sometimes important (Price 1950).

The situation appears to be one of considerable stability in the face of change generated within the tribe and its environment, and great instability in the face of obviously outside influences. I think that there is an analogy between the stability of the tribal peoples and that of the tropical rain forest that supports many of them. Tropical rain forest has great stability and is believed to have persisted in its general form for over 100 million years. It can regenerate freely

after storm, lightning strike and flood. But in the face of massive external influences like modern logging, prolonged cultivatioñ or repeated burning, it is
utterly vulnerable.

We know that the introduction of species is particularly disruptive of island
ecosystems where there are many unfilled ecological niches. Is this analogy
relevant to the breakdown of isolation in a tribal group? I think it is, to the
limited extent to which we can equate different human technological groups with
species, and ecosystems with economic systems. The outsiders with their diversity of technologies can outperform the original inhabitants in specific ways.
The consequences of traditional tribal roles becoming unviable in the new situation are very serious, as the whole basis of subsistence is undermined. In an
island the introduction of new species is dangerous because of the absence of a
control system (of predators and parasites). New introductions, such as alcohol
and guns, can be disastrous if social controls are not developed.

Depopulation has been one of the most serious and common sequels of
contact. The excess of deaths over births has usually been ascribed to high
death rates due to diseases, especially newly introduced infections. But a
decrease of births has sometimes been the most striking feature (Scragg 1957;
Polunin 1959).

Rivers (1922) supposed that 'loss of the will to live' was the cause of depopulation in Melanesia, but this was not widely accepted at the time, as it did not
seem to be an adequate cause of death. Nowadays, however, more attention
is paid to the multiple and remote determinants of disease. I do not think it is
difficult to see how economic stress and cultural breakdown can affect personal
hygiene, the sanitary state of the environment and the care of the sick (Polunin
1967), leading to an excess of deaths from conventional causes.

THE SIMPLICITY OF SOCIAL ROLES AND TECHNOLOGY

In tribal societies, most economic roles are directed towards subsistance. The
role of any member is largely determined by age and sex and, looking at the
whole lifespan, we could say that there are two occupations, that of the male
and the female. Special roles, of leader, medico-religious practitioner, midwife
or smith occupy only a part of a person's time. This makes for simplicity of
description.

ENVIRONMENTAL MODIFICATION AND CLOSENESS TO NATURE

There are three major types of environment, according to the extent to which
they are modified by man. In wilderness and near-wilderness, man-made change
is limited to the minor effects of hunting and gathering. In the countryside,

much or all of the climax vegetation has been removed. Useful biota are encouraged, and competitors are discouraged as 'weeds' or 'pests'. In the urban areas, humans and artefacts dominate.

All hunter-gatherers of suitable age participate in subsistence activities, in close contact with the natural environment. Barriers are minimal. They may lack the protection of clothing, and small flimsy houses offer little protection against environmental stresses (Fig. 5, p. 11). At the other extreme, the townsman is far removed from his subsistence base, and is cocooned against the natural environment. Clothing, impervious buildings with artificial climate and lighting, and all the measures of environmental sanitation are deliberate attempts at protection from the hazardous world outside. In comparison with this, tribal man has to be largely content with his simpler technology and with magico-religious manipulation.

The physical closeness to the natural environment and the life support system must also influence the people's outlook and thought processes. Hallpike (1976) has pointed out that nature is full of symbolic potential, with analogies to human life processes, but is not easily broken down to component elements, unlike machines. The hunter-gatherer tends to conserve the forest which is his home and his subsistence base (Turnbull 1965) while settled villagers, whose subsistence comes from their farms, often try to destroy the forest which they fear.

Ecological modification and parasites

The more favourable an environment, the more species it contains, and complexity reaches its peak in tropical rain forests, with a very large number of plant and animal species present at low density.

Dunn (1968) argued that as hunter-gatherers are part of the ecosystem with little or no buffering from other species, the number of species of parasitic helminths and protozoa they support should vary with the environmental complexity. He found that hunter-gathering communities of the African and Malaysian rain forest each harboured more than twice as many parasite species as Bushmen and Australian Aborigines from habitats poor in species. 'Closeness to nature' would lead us to expect that 'sylvatic' infections would be more likely to affect hunter-gatherers. It is interesting that three out of the thirteen species of animal helminths in man reported in West Malaysia by Sandosham & Mohamed Noordin (1967) have been found in the little studied and numerically insignificant Aborigines only.

Interference with tropical rain forest tends to discourage species with specialized environmental requirements and encourage opportunistic species. In

general the effect of interference is to reduce the number of species and increase
the population for those species which remain. Audy & Harrison (1951) showed
this for rats and trombiculid mites in West Malaysia. The number of tree species
may be reduced from over one hundred to very few (Corner 1940). Dunn (1972)
found that hunter-gatherer Negritoes in Malaya harboured more species of
parasites than shifting-cultivators, who spend less time in the forest. Whether a
medically interesting species is discouraged or encouraged depends of course
on its particular environmental requirements. Thus shifting cultivation, by
letting in sunlight, encourages the multiplication of *Anopheles maculatus*, the
principal vector of malaria in interior Peninsular Malaysia (Polunin 1963).

Disease patterns in tribal peoples

Dunn (1968) has discussed the situation in hunter-gatherers. The picture is one
of considerable variation between groups. Tribal people suffer from the same
diseases as other peoples with the marked preponderance of infective over
degenerative diseases which is typical of the traditional human lot. Fatal
disease and socially induced mortality is fairly frequent at all ages, leaving few
old people. In general the precontact situation appeared to be one of adapted-
ness with intermediate morbidity and mortality (Neel 1970), with a worsening
following disruption from outside.

There are few diseases limited to tribal peoples because of special circumstances. The classic tribal disease is kuru, because of its unusual mode of
transmission, and the distribution of the agent (Gajdusek 1973). There must,
however, be many examples of allergies and intoxications due to species limited
to tribal territories.

There are some diseases which are characteristic of tribal peoples, though
by no means confined to them. Yaws is so easy to treat that it is only found in
groups receiving little medical treatment. Therefore it is particularly liable to
persist in tribal groups.

Or a disease may be prevalent because of the higher susceptibility of tribal
people. Tinea imbricata, due to *Trichophyton concentricum*, is difficult to cure.
It is strikingly localized in South-East Asia and New Guinea although apparently it was once much commoner in other peoples (Polunin 1952). Schofield *et al.*
(1963) found that it was usually acquired during a period of general undernutrition. This suggests that the frequency of episodes conferring lowered
resistance was responsible for its distribution.

Endemic goitre is particularly prevalent among many tribal groups. This is
because their usually inland environment is often deficient in iodine, and they
are remote from iodine-rich sea foods. Other single-nutrient deficiency states

are unlikely to be important where hunting and gathering are major subsistence activities because of the greater variety of foodstuffs with different nutrient contents, while their naturally occurring food supply is less likely to fail than that of the cultivators. They are liable to general undernutrition, but even today their nourishment is sometimes so good that they have been described as the 'original affluent society' (Sahlins 1974).

Chronic degenerative diseases contribute only a small proportion of morbidity because of the shorter life expectancy and the lack of risk-raising features in the people's lives. Some of these diseases, like myocardial infarction and essential hypertension, which have reached epidemic proportions in modernized societies, are virtually absent from some tribal groups. The simpler, more uniform circumstances of tribal life should make further aetiological studies rewarding, particularly if tribal groups can be found with high rates of these diseases.

Disease patterns are often characterized by a high prevalence of several chronic infections, which accounts for most of the morbidity present in the population. This has important implications for health care, as tribal people with limited training and a few drugs can treat most of the sick. The contrast between affected and unaffected persons in a group seems surprising in view of the apparent uniformity of the environmental circumstances. Follow-up studies of healthy birth cohorts could provide clues as to why some people do not become sick. Because of the high rates, small groups could provide useful results. Conversely, small population size makes tribal groups unsuitable for the study of rare conditions.

Two main themes regarding the general health of tribal groups recur. One is that they are reasonably healthy until they are subjected to outside influences. This might be called the 'healthy savage' idea, with contact representing a sort of fall from the Garden of Eden. The other 'progressivist' idea of tribal people recalls the 'benighted heathen' view of the missionaries, and points to the duty to provide modern health services for those who lack them. There is something to be said for both views, each in its own context. While isolation lasted, the people were not exposed to certain hazards, but once isolation breaks down, effective health measures and adaptations are needed to protect against new hazards. There has been considerable variation in the success with which tribal groups have adapted, and we need to know more about the reasons for this.

TRIBAL MEDICINE

I believe that the study of tribal medicine can contribute to the health of mankind, but not just because of the likelihood of further enrichment of modern materia medica. Modern medicine is so rich in diagnostic, therapeutic and bureaucratic practices that the patient's point of view tends to be ignored. The more successful medicine becomes, the less it seems to satisfy people. I suggest that tribal medical systems are sufficiently simple for us to understand the ways by which they satisfy human needs, and sufficiently different from ours to provide new insights. Let me recount one small experience and show how it helped my understanding.

One afternoon I had to make a quick and exhausting walk to reach a settlement of the Jah Hut people in Malaysia. Later that night I felt nauseated. My assistant, himself a traditional healer, offered to make a therapeutic incantation, which of course I accepted. I was surprised by the great effect his ministration had in inducing a feeling of mental well-being in me. I had a strong intuition that this was because he showed me that somebody cared, in a situation where I felt isolated and helpless. I learned from this something I had scarcely been aware of: that an important part of the therapeutic situation is the social support it can provide.

Modern medicine has largely been judged by criteria of objective therapeutic effectiveness, and subjective effects have been ignored. But, independent of this, medicine has other social functions. Besides social support, medicine, to quote Katz & Wallace (1974) 'provides much of the confidence that holds societies together ... where this knowledge is challenged and too precipitately cast aside, an unwanted side effect is the decay of many social institutions'. Besides this, the medical system resolves the problem of what to do and hence removes anxiety.

Studies of the medical system of a tribal group are of obvious use in devising modern health services suited to that group. The medical system of simpler societies must be satisfying human needs in circumstances very different to those of our own system. The finding of recurring patterns in tribal medicine would point to widely felt human needs, and might help in the planning of more satisfying modern health services.

This of course is but a small part of what can be usefully learned from tribal peoples. They at least have in hunting and gathering what is, to quote Lee & De Vore (1968) 'the most successful and persistent adaptation man has ever achieved'.

Tribal people have shown the widest variation in their bio-social response to modern life, varying from extinction and social disappearance to successful adaptation. If we could understand the reasons for this not only would we be able to help tribal people make their adaptations, but the knowledge would be valuable to the whole human species in its responses to ever more rapidly changing circumstances.

References

AUDY, J. R. & HARRISON, J. L. (1951) A review of investigations on mite typhus in Burma and Malaya, 1945–1950. *Trans. R. Soc. Trop Med. Hyg.* 44, 371–404

CASSEL, J. (1974) An epidemiological perspective of psychosocial factors in disease etiology. *Am. J. Public Health 64*, 1040–1043

CORNER, E.J.H. (1940) *Wayside Trees of Malaya*, vol. 1, p. 1, Government Printing Office, Singapore

DE ZULUETA, J. (1956) Malaria in Sarawak and Brunei. *Bull. W.H.O. 15*, 651

DUNN, F. L. (1968) Epidemiological factors: health and disease in hunter-gatherers, in *Man the Hunter* (Lee, R. B. & De Vore, I., eds.), pp. 221–228, Aldine, Chicago

DUNN, F.L. (1972) Intestinal parasites in Malayan Aborigines (Orang Asli). *Bull W.H.O. 46*, 99–113

GAJDUSEK, D.C. (1964) Factors governing the genetics of primitive human populations. *Cold Spring Harbor Symp. Quant. Biol. 29*, 121–135

GAJDUSEK, D.C. (1973) Kuru in the New Guinea Highlands, in *Tropical Neurology* (Spillane, J.D., ed.), Oxford University Press, London

GEDDES, W.R. (1963) The human background, in *Proceedings of the UNESCO Symposium on the Impact of Man on Humid Tropics Vegetation*, Goroka, Territory of Papua–New Guinea, 1960, pp. 42–56, Commonwealth Government Printer, Canberra

HALLPIKE, C.R. (1976) Is there a primitive mentality? *Man 11*, 253–270

KATZ, S.H. & WALLACE, A.F.C. (1974) An anthropological perspective on behavior and disease. *Am. J. Public Health 64*, 1050–1052

LEE, R.B. & DE VORE, I. (1968) Problems in the study of hunters and gatherers, in *Man the Hunter* (Lee, R.B. & De Vore, I., eds.), Aldine, Chicago

LEWIS, I.M. (1968) Tribal society, in *International Encyclopedia of the Social Sciences*, Macmillan, New York

Methods of Geographical Pathology (1959) Report of the Study Group convened by the Council for International Organizations of Medical Sciences, Springfield, Thomas. Quoted by Mann, I. (1961) Climate, culture and eye disease. *Trans. Ophthalmol. Soc. N.Z. 81*, 261–282

NEEL, J.V. (1970) Lessons from a 'primitive' people. *Science (Wash. D.C.) 150*, 815–822

NEEL, J.V. & SALZANO, F.M. (1964) A prospectus for genetic studies of the American Indian. *Cold Spring Harbor Symp. Quant. Biol. 29*, 85–95

POLUNIN, I. (1952) Tinea imbricata in Malaya. *Br. J. Dermatol. 64*, 378–384

POLUNIN, I. (1959) The Muruts of North Borneo and their declining population. *Trans. R. Soc. Trop. Med. Hyg. 53*, 312–326

POLUNIN, I. (1963) The effects of shifting agriculture on human health and disease, in *Proceedings of the UNESCO Symposium on the Impact of Man on Humid Tropics Vegetation*, Goroka, Territory of Papua–New Guinea, 1960, pp. 388–393. Commonwealth Government Printer, Canberra

POLUNIN, I. (1967) Health and disease in contemporary primitive societies, in *Diseases in Antiquity* (Brothwell, D. & Sandison, A.T., eds.), Thomas, Springfield, Ill.

PRICE, A.G. (1950) *White Settlers and Native Peoples*, Georgian House, Melbourne

RIVERS, W.H.R. (1922) *Essays on the Depopulation of Melanesia*, Cambridge University Press, London

SAHLINS, M.D. (1974) *Stone Age Economics*, Tavistock Press, London

SANDOSHAM, A.A. & MOHAMED NOORDIN BIN KELING (1967) Animal parasites of animals which affect man in Malaysia. *Med. J. Malaya 22*, 16–25

SCHOFIELD, F.D., PARKINSON, A.D. & JEFFREY, D. (1963) Observations on the epidemiology, effects and treatment of Tinea imbricata. *Trans. R. Soc. Trop. Med. Hyg. 57*, 214

SCRAGG, R.F.R. (1957) Depopulation in New Ireland, a study of demography and fertility.

M.D. Thesis, University of Adelaide. Port Moresby, Administration of Papua and New Guinea

Turnbull, C.M. (1965) The Mbuti Pygmies of the Congo, in *Peoples of Africa* (Gibbs, J.L., ed.), Holt, Rinehart & Winston, New York

W.H.O. Expert Committee on Research in Population Genetics of Primitive Groups (1964) *W.H.O. Tech. Rep. Ser.* no. 279

Wilson, G.S. & Miles, A.A. (1955) *The Principles of Bacteriology and Immunity*, 4th edn, Arnold, London

Discussion

Gajdusek: I wonder whether tribal people in the absence of civilization always do respect their environment and not destroy it. Some centuries before civilized people entered the Highlands of New Guinea, the sweet potato plant was introduced there and replaced taro as the staple food. There followed a population explosion which ended in the cutting of the forests of the Highlands and the denuding of the broad high valleys. There seems no way to account for the disappearance of the forest except by the human activity of slash and burn gardening. The habit of burning off the *kunai* grass-covered slopes in the hunting of small rodents and snakes and to keep the height of the grass down also inhibited regrowth of the forests. When the first European arrived in the 1920s the valleys were denuded of trees; warfare between villages included raiding, chasing the enemy away, and ringing all their trees so that there would be no firewood when the people returned. Today, after the reforestation programmes of the Australian government, many Highland valleys are wooded again. We hear a lot about equilibrium in and balance with their environment and respect for nature by primitive and tribal groups. There was little sign of this when civilized man entered the Stone Age cultures in the Highlands of New Guinea earlier this century (Robbins 1963).

Lightman: It is certainly a common misconception that tribal man is by nature conservationist, and a respecter of his environment. The environment itself, however, can certainly colour and sometimes govern the attitudes that a society holds towards its cohabitant flora and fauna. Thus tribal groups that live in marginal environments, with their particularly fragile ecological balance, develop a necessary respect for their environment that is rarely seen in areas of plenty. It is these marginal areas, where a large proportion of our remaining tribal people now live, which are so sensitive to the drastic ecological changes brought about by the advent of industrial man. The ecological ravishing of the Amazon jungle, for instance, is well on its way to producing a new and even greater dust bowl.

Haraldson: This is particularly true if we consider nomads, and the majority of tribal people in the world today are nomadic. Such people are found in over 100 countries but predominantly in about 25 very poor countries, characterized by being land-locked and having few natural resources, extreme climates, and frequent natural disasters; and also by having scattered populations. There is a certain ecological balance when numbers are few, but nomad populations are increasing all over the world and so are their cattle. There is often no longer any balance. When numbers are small there is no destruction of nature but where nomads are multiplying, as the Masai and their cattle have done by a factor of three over the past 40 years, there is land erosion. Again in the Sahel (desert) area of Africa, the goat is definitely not in ecological balance with its environment; the goat eradicates the entire vegetation and thus contributes to the 'desert creep'.

Lozoff: Hunter–gatherers probably should not be grouped with agriculturalists and pastoralists in this respect. The impact of the human species on the environment was minimal over the more than one million years of hunting and gathering. In contrast, the 10 000 years of agriculture and the 200–300 years of industry have devastated environmental resources.

White: Most hunter–gatherers, as compared with the cultivators in particular, have an ideology of conservation: the Australian Aborigines do, and also the Kalahari Bushmen (Silberbauer 1972, p. 321). Both have a religious belief that the land is in trust to them and they must pass it on to their children in the state in which they found it. This may not have a vast effect on their treatment of the land, but it has some. They know that complete destruction of the natural vegetation is against what the gods told them to do, whereas we do not seem to find any such concept in the religion of the cultivators: the forest is regarded as bad.

Polunin: For the fixed cultivators, that is so. Most shifting cultivators, at least in South-East Asia, know well who really owns the forest and are very careful to propitiate the supernatural owners! But there are also shifting cultivators, such as the Ibans described by Freeman (1955), who live in a conceptual world where there is always more forest to move on to. Benjamin (1967) mentions that the ideal settlement of the Temiar forest-dwelling shifting cultivators of West Malaysia has as large a treeless area around the houses as possible.

Stanley: Among American Indians who are shifting cultivators there is the same religious approach to the land, that they must not damage it—and they accuse the white man of doing just this.

Woodburn: We simply cannot generalize about the attitudes of tribal man to conservation of the environment: there is too much variation from one society to another. Even among hunters and gatherers, who depend on wild foods for their sustenance, the evidence certainly does not support the idea that they usually have a conservationist ideology. I did research for some years with a hunting and gathering group in East Africa, the Hadza, who are remarkably non-conservationist in their attitude to the land and the wild animals and plants they use. When they are gathering berries they quite happily on occasion cut down the trees and carry home the berry-bearing branches rather than picking the berries on the spot; in hunting animals they are not concerned to hunt selectively, avoiding pregnant and lactating female animals and their young; in digging up wild tubers they do not trouble to replant any portion. Their non-conservationist attitude may be connected with the fact that they are living at a low population density in a relatively prolific environment and can afford to be unconcerned. As far as one can tell without very detailed evidence, they are not threatening their own future food supply by these practices. (For additional information, see Woodburn 1968.)

Ohlman: The idea of animals in the wild being as destructive as some of these tribes are, or as modern man is, seems incomprehensible. In a very crowded situation animals will attack each other but in a normal situation they are essentially conservationist.

Hugh-Jones: Professor Weiner, since man has existed as a species for about 250 000 years, how far do you think that present-day tribal people who have only been contacted recently represent what has happened in human history?

Weiner: I don't think one can really know how far to extrapolate from the present to the past. Something Dr Polunin said has a bearing on this. I had the impression from him that he thinks in general that tribal people are impoverished not only materially but culturally; he said that they 'held and transmitted' rather little knowledge. However, although the material endowment per person is small, on the non-material side, modern primitive groups, like Pleistocene man perhaps, have quite a rich, complicated life; they know a great deal about their environment, and if you take into account the way they reify their kinship relationships, their detailed knowledge and practice of ritual, and their interest in music and dancing, compared to the average modern man in the street, I wonder if there is any difference in the intensity of cultural experience. If one looks at tools over this long period of time one sees a great deal of sophistication at that level too.

Polunin: You are looking at the individual; I was looking at the group, specifically the very small group. If one considers a large group, like all the people living in England, the amount of variation with regard to, say, religion is enormous. I was not implying that the *individual* tribesman is a poor fellow with an impoverished knowledge. As you say, he tends to be an all-rounder.

Jones: You made a point about the conservatism and resistance to change of tribal people. One can think of examples where there certainly has been strong resistance to change. A lot of efforts were made to stop some tribal people being polygynous, with no success: in some parts of Africa the polygyny rate has increased. On the other hand, some things have changed rapidly. For example, it took about two years, between 1932 and 1934, for the plough to be introduced over a large area of what is now Southern Zambia. They continued to use the traditional hoe but began to use the plough. It seems that, if one is looking for an underlying principle, in the short-run where innovations work they tend to be adopted and there is not much resistance to the change; where they don't work well, there will be resistance. (Polygyny seems to work: why give it up?)

Some things change even without attempts to make them change. The building of round huts in that part of Africa was found to be dying out and the numbers of square huts was increasing, but nobody had tried to get people to build square huts. It simply happened because the local people learnt to make sun-baked bricks, and presumably found it easier to build square rather than round huts with these bricks.

You also spoke about the ways in which traditional medicine satisfies human needs (p. 18). Evidently it gives some meaning to life for people living in a group; it defines the person and gives him his identity as someone with certain characteristics, including his illnesses and his feelings of pain or anguish. Traditional medicine seems to enable people to take on an identity, to define it and to understand it in such a way that it becomes easier for them to live with it.

Harrison: Dr Polunin implied to me that in some way or other we can measure the mental health or, perhaps more subjectively, the contentment and happiness of peoples in tribal societies and show it to be in some way 'better' than that of people in modern industrial societies. This seems a reasonable hypothesis that one can make a good theoretical case for, and perhaps subjectively that is one's assessment of the situation, but there is very little if any hard evidence in favour of this view. Such evidence as there is points in the opposite direction, for example studies by Leighton & Lambo (1963) and Srole *et al.* (1962). They found essentially the same frequency of psychological illness among Yoruba villagers in Nigeria as in mid-town Manhattan. So one has to be careful about this.

Hugh-Jones: Perhaps it's the type of psychological disturbance that differs. Whereas anxiety and depression seem to be a phenomenon of western life, hysteria seems to be more appropriate to other societies. But I am not sure if that is well-documented.

References

BENJAMIN, G. (1967) Temiar Religion, Ph.D. Thesis, Cambridge University

FREEMAN, J.D. (1955) *Iban Agriculture; a report on the shifting cultivation of hill rice by the Iban of Sarawak* (Colonial Office, Colonial Research Studies No. 18), HMSO, London

LEIGHTON, A.H. & LAMBO, T.A. (1963) *Psychiatric Disorder among the Yoruba*, Cornell University Press, New York

ROBBINS, R.G. (1963) The anthropogenic grasslands of Papua and New Guinea, in *Proceedings of the UNESCO Symposium on the Impact of Man on Humid Tropics Vegetation*, Goroka, 1960, pp. 313–329, UNESCO

SILBERBAUER, G.B. (1972) The G/wi Bushmen, in *Hunters and Gatherers Today* (Bicchieri, M.G., ed.), chapter 7, Holt, Rinehart & Winston, New York

SROLE, L., LANGNER, T.S., MICHAEL, S.T., OPLER, M.K. & RENNIE, T.A.C. (1975) *Mental Health in the Metropolis: the Midtown Manhattan Study*, Harper & Row, New York

WOODBURN, J.C. (1968) An introduction to Hadza ecology, in *Man the Hunter* (Lee, R.B. & DeVore, I., eds.), pp. 49–55, Aldine, Chicago

First contact with a tribal society*

HERBERT OHLMAN

Educational Communication Systems, Health Manpower Development Division, World Health Organization, Geneva

Abstract The first contact with a tribal society is probably the most important event that takes place in any exploration. It is likely to limit what we are able to find out about them, as well as how they react to us. It may even set the society on an irreversible course towards survival, integration, or—as has happened so often—destruction. Is it possible to plan new first contacts so as to maximize the information obtained while minimizing such disintegrative effects?

More specifically, what can we do *before* physical contact with an unknown tribe? To help answer this question, we need to study the findings of past explorations and try to derive general principles of first contact. In addition to the written record, there exist the unique resources of the anthropological film. We can also consider the vast literature of the imagination common to all societies for clues to behaviour during first contact. Even the recent work on communication with extra-terrestrial intelligence may offer relevant insights.

We can also consider the question: what are the possibilities of locating an unknown tribe in an unexplored region before sending in a ground expedition? Here, recently developed remote-sensing technologies may help. The broadest look is made possible by earth resources technology satellites, but only gross changes can be detected at the resolutions available, changes least likely to have been accomplished by a primitive society. Therefore, the more detailed look provided by balloon- or aircraft-based sensors is essential.

By old wisdom combining with new technology we may hope to prevent the errors of the past in attempts at first contact.

This paper is concerned with how to make 'first contact'† with a tribal society. This occasion is probably the most important, the most significant—and the most dangerous—event that has ever taken place in the tribe's history. It is

---

* The views expressed in this paper are those of the author alone, and are not necessarily those of the World Health Organization.
† I use quotation marks around certain words and phrases to remind us how ethnocentric our usage is.

also these things to us, but sensible precautions have not always been observed, and both the tribe and its 'discoverers' are often the losers.

I am not an anthropologist, but a technologist; however, to gain full understanding of 'first contact' situations, both human and technical elements must be considered. I hope therefore that I shall be excused in the first part of this paper for what amounts to an amateur's attempt to formulate some guidelines for the human aspects of first contact.

In the second part, I shall attempt to show how recently developed advances in the technology of remote sensing may enable us to locate and analyse tribal settlements *before* the critical event of 'first contact'.

It is my hope that by combining age-old wisdom with new technology we may be able to forestall some of the hazards of 'first contact' situations while there may yet remain a few 'undiscovered' tribes.

HUMAN ASPECTS OF FIRST CONTACT

Imagine yourself in a strange city for the first time. You can't understand what anybody is saying; you can't even read the signs. You could find yourself in this situation just by travelling from Western to Eastern Europe. Consider then, how much you still have in *common* with the people—they appear and are dressed about the same way as you are; their food is not too different, and is served to you in a restaurant; the buildings are generally constructed in the same way—in fact, there is a great deal of shared experience stemming from a common cultural background.

Another way to understand this situation is to consider the words others apply to us when we are far from home—alien, foreigner, stranger—none of which have pleasant connotations. They remind us of the difficulties we have with everyday life and, if our visit must be prolonged, the painful and expensive period of adaptation we must go through.

The impact we have on 'primitive' people is profound and lasting, and the results are unpredictable. Three Fuegians had been taken to England by Robert FitzRoy, captain of the *Beagle*, in the late 1820s to be 'civilized'. He made them into model 'ladies and gentlemen', and then took them back to Tierra del Fuego during 1832–1833, so that they could in turn 'civilize' their own people. The disastrous results should have been predictable:

'When the *Beagle* returned a year later the camp was derelict. York Minster and Fuegia had long since decamped with Jemmy's goods and had joined the wild Fuegians. Jemmy himself remained, but he had cast civilization away as though he had never known it existed; his European clothes had been replaced with a loincloth, he was terribly thin, and his once sleek hair fell in a coarse mat about his painted face ... Harm rather than good had been done by taking the Fuegians to England; their brief peep at civilization had merely made it more difficult for them to live in their own country ... By the end of the nineteenth century the three Fuegian tribes were almost extinct. The Alacalufes, canoe people of the Western channels, numbered ten thousand at the time of Darwin's visit; by 1960 there were hardly a hundred.' (Moorehead 1969).*

One hundred and forty years later, we have learned a little more about 'first contact'. Certainly the experience with the Tasaday of the Philippines, described by John Nance (1975), is a great improvement over the well-intentioned but inevitably destructive Fuegian 'experiment' (see p. 29 below). Yet one wonders whether the Tasaday will fare any better as a unique people and culture in the long run.

It may also may be helpful in understanding 'first contact' situations to look at our literature of the imagination. For example, every culture has myths about voyages to strange places and encounters with alien situations and people. Today's expression of myth is often found in the form of fantastic and science-fiction stories (Nicholson 1948; Radford 1976). Such tales allow a free run of our imaginations over space and time, and the situations described may have useful parallels to those which actually occur in dealing with 'primitive' societies (as well as with our society, regarded as 'primitive' by an advanced race from another world). Stableford (1976) has categorized science fiction into three broad areas of what he terms ideative investigation: the speculative exploration of the man/machine confrontation, the man/alien confrontation, and the man/environment confrontation. There has even been a textbook published which uses science-fiction stories as case studies for an introductory psychology course (Katz et al. 1974). Perhaps it is not too far-fetched to imagine that we may appear as aliens from another world to a previously 'undiscovered' tribe on 'first contact'.

Beyond fiction, there has been much recent work on the problem of communication with extra-terrestrial intelligence (often abbreviated CETI) which may provide many useful insights into problems of communication with a tribe whose language we do not speak (Wilson & Gordon 1972). There have been searches for messages broadcast from outside the solar system (Sagan & Drake 1975; Bracewell 1975), as well as attempts to broadcast messages from earth

---

* Darwin (1839) was more optimistic about Jemmy's chances; a fuller account of the Fuegian experiment was published by FitzRoy (1839).

(Sagan *et al.* 1972). There have even been attempts to ban such efforts, as potentially dangerous to our independent survival (Sullivan 1976).

Using as a basis all these strains—past experience with actual 'first contacts', myth, science-fiction, attempts to communicate with extra-terrestrial intelligence —we can try to formulate a few do's and don't's. Table 1 lists ten possible guidelines for 'first contact'. In later discussion, we may refine these. Certainly, I do not intend to offer immutable principles, and more—or stronger, but fewer— guidelines may emerge from our discussions.

TABLE 1
Tentative guidelines for 'first contacts'

---

1. Don't drop 'out of space' (e.g. by helicopter) unless you want to be worshipped!
2. Try to fit in with the local situation: don't bring in lots of elaborate equipment (cameras, tape recorders, canned foodstuffs, highly coloured tents, etc.); rather, try to live off the land as much as possible
3. Try not to offer gifts, such as knives, beads, etc. to the tribe, which will inevitably change life-styles (cargo cult, etc.)
4. Try not to take or buy artifacts from the tribe; this also changes life-styles, and often violates taboos
5. Try to observe and communicate without an elaborate entourage of porters, interpreters, cameramen; limit first contact to two or three people on each side
6. Try to prepare yourself not to be surprised or shocked at what you find; gaming and role-playing exercises, and observing films of previous contacts, may help in sensitizing yourself
7. Do what you can to prepare primitive people for others to come who may not be sensitive to the situation, particularly media people, and those with commercial interests
8. Don't leave the debris of civilization behind; do what you can with local authorities to limit visits, control destructive changes, and to set up a reserve area
9. Be perceptive; be receptive; and be willing to learn. There are many things which you will be completely blind to initially; however, if you persist and try to observe on many levels of consciousness, you may attain a truer understanding of the people
10. Above all, take your time; don't hurry ahead according to some schedule imposed from the outside, but let things unfold at their own pace

---

It may be useful to illustrate some of these points by examples. For instance, Carpenter (1976), in his book *Oh, What a Blow That Phantom Gave Me!*, illustrates the unforeseen power of modern media (Point 2 in Table 1):

'In New Guinea, when villagers ignore their leader, the government may tape-record his orders. The next day the assembled community hears his voice coming to them from a radio he holds in his own hand. They obey him.'' (p. 11.)

A newspaper article (Charlton 1975), 'Putting "Primitive" Civilization on Film', which describes the work of Richard Sorensen and the National Anthropological Film Center (see Sorensen 1974), shows our surprise at seeing our own cultural taboos violated (Point 6):

'In most "civilized" societies, for example, the sight of a very small boy playing with a large sharp knife would prompt the nearest adult to take the knife from the child. But among the Fore people of New Guinea, even the child's mother is unruffled. Fore children play freely with knives and machetes, and with fire ... (but) never cut or burn themselves.

Is there, perhaps, a connection between this ability and their upbringing, which is in Western terms totally indulgent? Fore children are in constant contact with their mother's bodies, they are never punished, never refused, never frustrated. And yet, the result seems to be not dependence, but an extraordinary self-sufficiency'.

And, from the same article, Sorensen comments on how limited our view may be of our own potential (Point 9):

'Humankind ... has extraordinary potential for adaptation. But we have only studied our own children, our own cultures. This has deprived us ... of full knowledge of the alternative ways in which humans have adapted their behavior to their surroundings and to each other ... we are on the verge of losing that knowledge for all time. Within 10 more years it will be gone'.

In his popular but highly detailed account of the Tasaday tribe in the Mindanao rain forest, Nance (1975) shows that gift-giving may lead to difficulties in trying to learn how a people has existed before contact (Point 3):

'The Tasaday revealed three ... fragments of metal ... : part of a knife ...; an awl made of wire; and a short metal rod ... Questioning ... eventually disclosed all ... had not been handed down by ancestors or acquired through trade, but had been supplied by Dafal [a hunter from another tribe who had apparently "discovered" the tribe ten years before this account] ... [who] emerged as the dominant figure in their technical history'. (p. 22.)

Points 1, 2, 5 and 10 are all illustrated in the following:

'I was eager to get some idea of what was going on inside their minds ... "How do they feel about what has happened to them over the last few weeks? What are their feelings about all the new things and new people they have seen?" ... "It is like lightning ... it has come to us without warning," Balayam said [Balayam was the most outgoing and articulate member of the tribe] ... For a moment the simple power and eloquence of his response befuddled me. I realized he had said in four words a stunning amount, more than I had expected—perhaps more than I wanted to know. I became aware of a nagging apprehension ... What right had we ... to inflict ourselves on these gentle people, peer at them, poke our cameras at them?' (Nance 1975, p. 52.)

There are many other illustrations of one or more of the ten points in this fascinating account; however, I also want to talk about the potential of modern technology to aid us in first contact situations. As a lead-in, one could not do better than to quote from Lindbergh's eloquent foreword to Nance's book:

'Somehow I must strike a balance between the civilized and primitive ... a balance that both the Tasaday and I were seeking from opposite directions ... I did not want to renounce my civilization, and they did not want to renounce their cave-centered culture ... Years before, the search for this balance had diverted my attention from the progress of aviation to the plight of primitive life ... an exponential breakdown in our environment was taking place; and ... my profession of aviation was a major factor in that breakdown. Aircraft had opened every spot on earth to exploitation, carried developers into wildernesses that had been inaccessible before. I realized that the future of aviation ... depended less on the perfection of aircraft than on preserving the epoch-evolved environment of life, and that this was true of all technological progress ... This volume ... describes the interaction of the ultraprimitive and ultracivilized under circumstances unique to our time. It captures the wonders and emotions of the first meeting on the forest's edge—the stone axe on one side, the helicopter on the other.' (Nance 1975, pp. x-xi.)

It is my hope that another technological offspring of aviation, space technology, can help us to minimize the adverse affects of 'first contact'.

REMOTE SENSING

Although the words 'first contact' usually bring to mind only person-to-person contact, for more than a century we have had other, technologically mediated capabilities for what is termed *remote sensing*. This range of technologies includes not only remote imaging, which uses photo-optical or electro-optical sensors, but also systems which gather data (and can even take action based on this data) without human intervention. Ordinary photography is designed to match the response capabilities of the human eye as closely as possible. However, the portion of the electromagnetic spectrum to which the eye is sensitive is only a tiny fraction of a range of wavelengths of more than 20 orders of magnitude which includes long- and short-wave radio, microwaves, infrared, ultraviolet, X-rays, gamma rays and cosmic rays. Remote-sensing systems may utilize one or more of these types of radiation.

Furthermore, other types of sensors may be used to detect other phenomena to which humans are insensitive, such as magnetic field, micro-vibrations, and gravitational anomalies. Some remote-sensing systems are active, in which case the system itself generates the energy to be detected. Examples are the use of visible and infrared laser beams, and microwaves generated by radar systems. Other remote sensors are passive, depending upon energy emitted from objects to be sensed, such as infrared from people and other organisms, and their activities; or upon the sun's energy reflected from the earth.

Data gathered remotely can be transmitted, processed, and displayed by a variety of analogue and digital techniques. Remote sensors may be placed at fixed locations, or they may be mobile, as in vehicles, balloons, rockets, and satellites.

The means at our disposal today for remote sensing are infinitely more varied and powerful than Nadar, the first aerial photographer, could have dreamed when, in 1858, he photographed Paris from a captive balloon half a kilometre in the air. Nadar had to carry his darkroom aboard, because the wet collodion process then used required that plates be coated and sensitized just before exposure, and developed immediately afterwards (Scharf 1975). Slightly more than a century has gone by, but our current sensorimotor capabilities enable us to observe and manipulate the Martian environment at a distance of 373 million kilometres.

However, the question that should interest this symposium most is: how can

TABLE 2

Capabilities of remote-sensing systems for earth

Vehicle and sensor	Distance from earth (km)	Coverage (km²)	Resolution
Apollo cameras[a] at moon (1967–1975)	384 000	2.5×10^8 [c]	50 to 100 km
Landsat multi-spectral scanner[a] (mid-1972 to date)	900	3.5×10^4	down to 100 m
Skylab cameras[a] (mid-1973)	100	2.5×10^3	down to 10 m
High-altitude aircraft cameras[b]	up to 20	several 100 to several 1000	down to 3 m
Low-altitude aircraft cameras[b]	up to 10	50 to several 100	0.3 to 1 m
Tethered balloon or ground-based cameras[b]	up to 2	from 1 to several 100	less than 1 m

[a] NASA programmes.
[b] Aircraft, balloon, and ground-based cameras often increase coverage by taking oblique views, at the expense of distortion and lower resolution.
[c] Assuming that the earth's disc occupies only about 10% of the camera's field of view.

This table is similar to but not derived from Plevin (1974).

we put remote sensing to use in locating and analysing people and objects here on earth? Table 2 summarizes the capabilities of such systems, which complement rather than compete with each other. Of these systems, only two are capable of incorporating a synoptic view in sufficient detail for our purposes—Skylab and Landsat.

The Earth Resources Technology Satellite Program (Landsat)

Although the photographs taken by the Skylab astronauts come closest to matching our requirements, they are available only for 1973, and their coverage was very selective, rather than comprehensive. On the other hand, Landsats tirelessly scan most of the earth's surface repetitively.

NASA (the National Aeronautics and Space Administration) launched the first Landsat (originally called ERTS, for Earth Resources Technology Satellite) on July 23, 1972. It was placed into a near-polar orbit 910 kilometres from earth, so that the entire world between 80 degrees north and 80 degrees south is viewed once every 18 days. Furthermore, this orbit is sun-synchronous, so that there is a consistent balance of light and shade in all images; the satellite passes across the equator at 9.42 a.m. local time each day. On January 22, 1975, NASA

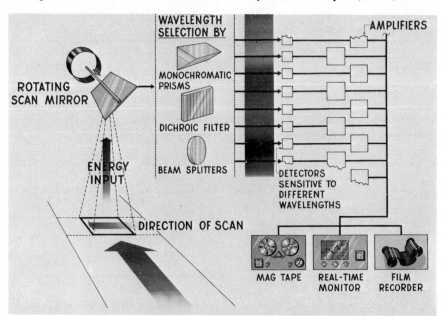

FIG. 1. Schematic diagram of multispectral scanner system. This is a general-purpose diagram; details of particular scanners will differ in aircraft, satellite, and ground-based use. (Reproduced by courtesy of NASA, Houston.)

launched Landsat 2, which together with Landsat 1 provides coverage of the earth once every nine days.

The remote sensors in both Landsats sweep out a path over the earth 100 minutes of arc (100 nautical miles, or 185 km) wide. The type of sensor used is called a multispectral scanner. In this scanner, an oscillating mirror directs reflected spectral energy through optical band-pass filters onto arrays of photo-sensitive detectors (see Fig. 1).

In Landsat 1, there are four bands which together record the four scenes which make up each image:

Band 4: 0.5 to 0.6 μm (green-yellow)
Band 5: 0.6 to 0.7 μm (red-orange)
Band 6: 0.7 to 0.8 μm (red-near infrared)
Band 7: 0.8 to 1.1 μm (near infrared)

Band 4 may be used to determine the depth and turbidity of standing bodies of water; band 5 for showing topographical and cultural features; band 6 for land-use practices; and band 7 for distinguishing land from water. To extract the maximum amount of information from Landsat images, all four bands should be used; however, if only a single band is employed, the best compromise seems to be band 5 (see Fig. 2).

The photo-optical detectors convert the energy in each band into a stream of electrical signals, which are stored on-board for later transmission to ground stations on command. The tonal value of each picture element (called pixel for short), and data about its location, the date of the exposure, the band used, etc., must all be encoded and stored.

Each scene is composed of 7.6 million pixels; therefore each image requires 7.6 × 4, or over 30 million pixels. Furthermore, to encode the tonal value of each pixel into 128 grey levels requires 7 bits per pixel. Therefore, complete digitalization of one Landsat image requires more than 200 million bits, which must be transmitted sequentially to a ground station before an output that can be used by man is obtained. The telemetry system currently in operation can transmit 15 million bits per second, or one image every 13 seconds. Theoretically, at this rate each Landsat could transmit 13 536 images every 18 days, which would require ground facilities capable of processing five trillion bits during this period. And, in actuality, more than three-quarters of the land masses and coastal areas of the world have been imaged under cloud-free conditions at least once by Landsat 1. However, the ground facilities in the United States could not cope with such a volume of data if transmitted in real time, and a tape-recorder failure on board Landsat 1 has diminished its ability to store images for delayed transmission (Giddings 1976).

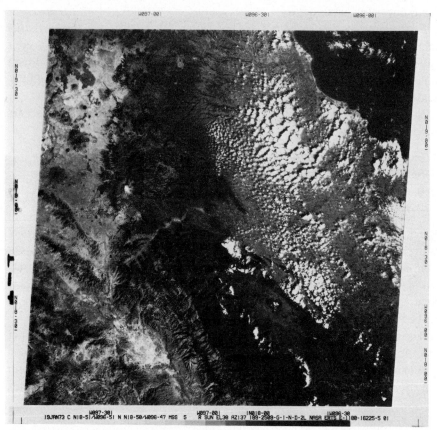

FIG. 2. System-corrected image showing Mexico test site for joint NASA—Comision Nacional del Espacio Exterior (CONEE) project (scene E-1180-16225-5, 19 January 1973, by courtesy of NASA, Houston.)

Ground processing facilities

Any country may establish its own ground stations to receive data from Landsats. At present such stations exist in the continental United States, Alaska, Canada, Brazil, and Italy. Also, late in 1976, the Council of the European Space Agency (ESA) approved a new programme called Earthnet, which will centralize and coordinate European earth resources satellite data reception, pre-processing, distribution, and archiving. Initially, Earthnet will include the existing reception and pre-processing facilities at Fucino, and utilize ESA's computer facility at Frascati (both near Rome). During 1978, a ground station at Kiruna, Sweden, above the Arctic Circle, will be added. Other countries are building their own Landsat stations, including Iran, Zaire and Chile.

For the United States, there are three Landsat ground stations: Fairbanks, Alaska; Goldstone, California; and Greenbelt, Maryland. However, only in Greenbelt, at the Goddard Space Flight Center (GSFC), can the data be processed. There, the NASA Data Processing Facility (NDPF) can handle up to 1300 scenes per week. Received bit streams are converted into System-Corrected Images (SYCI) on 70-mm wide film at a scale of 1 : 3 369 000. Selected SYCI may be further processed to become Scene-Corrected Images (SCII) by matching them to ground control points. SCII are at a scale of 1 : 1 000 000, and equivalent to maps on an orthographic projection; they may be combined to form colour composites. Each Landsat image covers an area of 10 000 square nautical miles (34 225 square kilometres), or $8^1/_2$ million acres (3.4 million hectares). Reproducible masters are sent to the Earth Resources Observation Systems (EROS) Data Center at Sioux Falls, South Dakota, which is under the direction of the US Department of Interior. Copies of images are in the public domain, and may be ordered from EROS by any individual or institution in any country for the cost of reproduction, plus handling and postal charges. This is an unprecedented degree of open access to government-owned information. Principal investigators are also welcome to contact the Landsat User Services at GSFC directly.

Data are transmitted from a Landsat only upon command from a ground station, and the period of transmission is limited to the time of passage of the satellites from horizon to horizon at a particular location. While each Landsat completes 14 orbits every day, only two of these orbits will be within range of a station, and the satellite will be within sight for only about 10 minutes per orbit. Therefore, the maximum number of images a ground station can receive from both Landsats is less than two hundred per day.

The several conversions required to transform digital data streams into analogue images inevitably degrade the spatial and tonal resolution of which Landsat MSS are capable. For Landsat, the best analogue resolution is about 80 to 100 metres across (certain *linear* features, such as rivers and roads, can be detected even though they may be as little as 10 metres across). However, for a small percentage of images, digital versions are available as computer-compatible tapes (CCT). These provide resolution down to 70 metres across, equivalent to a single pixel 0.45 hectare (1.1 acre) in area.

Applications of Landsat

With this background on the technical capabilities of Landsat, we may consider its applications. A cost-benefit study made early in the earth resources satellite programme predicted that major applications would be found in agriculture, health, oceanography, resource management, and geography. A total net annual benefit of almost US $ 60 thousand million was projected, with an estimated 50 000 lives and six thousand million sick days saved (Thiel 1972, p. 48). (For comparison, NASA's total expenditure so far on Landsats 1 and 2 is estimated to be only US $ 200 million.)

It is interesting to note that most of the applications anticipated have been the ones actually made. For example, COSPAR, a cooperative programme of the International Council of Scientific Unions devoted to rocket and satellite research, recently reported applications to agriculture, mineral exploration, road planning, water and air pollution, and demography, in such diverse countries as France, Poland, Iran, Kenya, India, South America, and the United States (COSPAR 1976).

Demographic applications, including the location and measurement of the extent of small-scale human settlements, and the estimation of their populations, should be of particular interest to this symposium.

Remote sensing for anthropology

Although on the limit of resolution of present Landsat capabilities, villages as small as five hectares in area (250 metres in diameter) have been identified in 1 : 1 000 000 scale images, using cues of reflection, location, and contrast. The best time for finding villages is during dry seasons; particular features looked for are shade trees (band 5), and thatched roofs, manure piles, and debris (band 7). Also, cultivated fields as small as 10 hectares can be located during the growing season (band 5). This work has been done by Reining (1974*a*, *b*, 1975).

More quantitative work can be done with the aid of computer-compatible tapes, using powerful analytic tools such as the Image 100 System (General Electric Space Division 1975). Using the Image 100 system, Reining & Egbert (1975) found Sonrai villages in Niger ranging in size from 45 hectares (100 pixels) down to less than one hectare (only a few pixels). However, it is not certain that all existing villages were found with this technique.

The Image 100 system and other digital processing systems depend for their working upon the fact that different objects reflect different portions of the sun's spectrum in different ways. That is, they have unique 'spectral signatures'. The processing system must be informed about features of interest, such as water, soil, or vegetation, and can be trained to remember them by their spectral signatures (see Fig. 3). The system then can classify an entire image or its computer-compatible tape equivalent pixel by pixel, testing the signature of

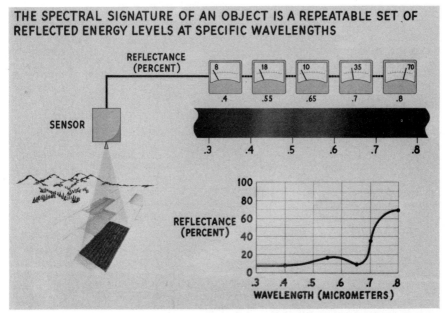

THE SPECTRAL SIGNATURE OF AN OBJECT IS A REPEATABLE SET OF
REFLECTED ENERGY LEVELS AT SPECIFIC WAVELENGTHS

FIG. 3. Schematic diagram of the spectral signature concept. This is a general-purpose diagram of a system using five bands in the visible region; particular systems may use other bands in (or outside) the visible spectrum, depending on the purpose of the remote-sensing system. (Reproduced by courtesy of NASA, Houston.)

each pixel against those of features of interest. The resulting 'thematic map' may be displayed on a colour monitor (see Fig. 4), or printed out in single-colour sections.

Landsat Follow-On

NASA has made plans to follow the present, experimental phase of the Landsat programme with an operational system, to be called Landsat Follow-On (NASA 1976a). Late in the 1970s, two advanced spacecraft are expected to be launched. Each will have two remote-sensing instruments, a Multispectral Scanner with 80-metre resolution, and a Thematic Mapper with 30-metre resolution.

Thus, the coverage of each pixel in the Thematic Mapper will be less than 0.1 hectare (better than $^1/_4$ acre), an improvement which, coupled to the increased number of bands, improved pointing accuracy, and much greater data-handling capability, should greatly increase Landsat's usefulness in anthropology.

FIG. 4. Part of an ERTS image made from computer-compatible tape using false colours to show up special features of interest; each square is one pixel. (In original, fresh water is represented by olive-green, salt water by light blue, and effluent plume by very light blue.) (From image E-1126-16201, 20 November 1972, by courtesy of NASA, Houston.)

The six spectral bands sensed by the Thematic Mapper have been chosen to discriminate among different types of vegetation, while avoiding the absorption bands of atmospheric water vapour.

The Thematic Mapper will share one data link with the Multispectral Scanner. This data link is designed to transmit data directly to suitably equipped ground stations at any place on earth. In addition, the Thematic Mapper will have a separate data link which transmits via a Tracking and Data Relay Satellite System. This satellite system, in stationary orbit, will relay data to a receiving station, which transmits the data via a domestic communications satellite to a central data-processing facility which, in turn, relays the processed data to any local data distribution centre. The basic data-transmission rate for all links is 135 million bits per second, which is nine times faster than present Landsat transmissions.

This new combination of capabilities should enable the Landsat Follow-On System to deliver data within 48–96 hours after imaging. This will make practical a high-resolution tool for such users as agricultural analysts, health workers, hydrologists, disaster-relief workers, pollution monitors, and others who require close to real-time monitoring of the earth's surface. A detailed manual of the transfer of aerospace technology to nineteen different areas of application may be obtained from the Denver Research Institute (1976). The applications of remote sensing to the conservation of the ecology of tropical regions are discussed in NASA (1976*b*); to disaster relief management, in Rush *et al.* (n.d.); and to the eradication of the screwworm fly, in Barnes & Forsberg (1976).

CONCLUSION

We have explored the notion of 'first contact' from the extreme of a micro-basis (individual-to-individual) to a cosmic basis (remote sensing from 900-km orbits). However, it should be emphasized that there is a continuum of observational possibilities which supplement each other. For example, it may be awkward in 'first contact' situations to begin with a face-to-face encounter; this stage may be eased by group contacts. At the other extreme, the synoptic view afforded by Landsat needs to be supplemented by aircraft-based remote sensors to check on likely locations, and to provide the maximum amount of information possible before personal contacts are made.

Also, although this paper has emphasized 'first contact', it is equally important to continue both direct and remote observations at periodic intervals to check on the human and environmental changes which inevitably result. In this way, we can hope to alleviate our impact on the few unique tribal communities which remain on earth.

ACKNOWLEDGEMENTS

This paper had its beginning in discussions with Dr Philip Hugh–Jones, Chairman of the symposium, without whom it would never have been written. My original interest in earth resources satellite technology was stimulated by Dr Charles M. Barnes of NASA, Houston, Texas, who has provided me with a continuing stream of useful documentation. Miss Priscilla Reining of the American Association for the Advancement of Science, Washington, D.C., has shown what can be done to locate and make censuses of villages using Landsat. Mr Colin

Lester of the Science Fiction Foundation helped me to identify stories dealing with alien contact. I would also like to express special thanks to Dr Katherine Elliott and Mrs Julie Whelan of the Ciba Foundation, and to staff members of the World Health Organization for their help and advice: Dr Andrew Arata, Mrs Barbara Campling, Mrs Judith Dahl–Hansen, Dr M. A. C. Dowling, Dr Ferdinand Littaua, Dr Pierre Mansourian and Dr Jack Marshall. Many other people have provided advice and documentation, including Dr Lester F. Eastwood, Jr and Dr Robert P. Morgan of Washington University, St Louis, Missouri; Mr J. A. Howard, Food and Agriculture Organization, Rome; Mr Paul A. Tessar, South Dakota State Planning Bureau, Pierre; Mr Robert W. Towles, General Electric Space Division, Daytona Beach, Florida; Dr Marjorie Rush and Dr Alfonso Holguin, The University of Texas, Houston; Dr George Jacobs, NASA Goddard Space Flight Center, Greenbelt, Maryland; Mr Norman Scotney, African Medical and Research Foundation, Nairobi, Kenya; and Mr J. Plevin, European Space Agency, Paris.

I would like to thank the authors and publishers who have given permission to reproduce excerpts, including John Nance and Harcourt, Brace Jovanovich, Inc., and the Sterling Lord Agency, Inc.; Edmund Carpenter and Paladin Books/Granada Publishing Ltd.; Alan Moorehead and Hamish Hamilton Ltd; L. Charlton and the *International Herald Tribune*; and the Lyndon B. Johnson Space Center, National Aeronautics and Space Administration.

References

BARNES, C.M. & FORSBERG, F.C. (1976) *An overview of the development of remote sensing techniques for the Screwworm Eradication Program*, paper presented at the Earth Resources Survey Symposium, June 1975; originally printed as part of NASA TMX-58168; also available as document LEC-6244 from Lockheed Electronics Company, Inc., Aerospace Systems Division, Houston, Texas, February 1976

BRACEWELL, R.L. (1975) *The Galactic Club: Intelligent Life in Outer Space*, Freeman, San Francisco

CARPENTER, E. (1976) *Oh, What a Blow That Phantom Gave Me!*, Paladin, London

CHARLTON, L. (1975) Putting 'primitive' civilization on film. *International Herald Tribune*, 27 November 1975

COSPAR (1976) *Nineteenth Plenary Meeting, Five Symposia and Open Sessions, Program/ Abstracts, Philadelphia, Pa., 9–19 June 1976*, COSPAR Secretariat, Paris (in particular, see Open Meeting of W.G. 6, Latest Results of Earth Surveys, pp. 411–417)

DARWIN, C. (1839) *Narrative of the Surveying Voyages of Her Majesty's Ships* Adventure *and* Beagle *Between the Years 1826 and 1836*, vol. III: *Journal and Remarks*, London (Later editions were published in 1845 and 1860; the edition referred to is that in the Everyman's Library series, published by J.M. Dent & Sons, London, 1906, under the title *The Voyage of the Beagle*. In particular, see Chapter 10, Tierra del Fuego, pp. 194–240)

DENVER RESEARCH INSTITUTE (1976) *Space Benefits: the Secondary Application of Aerospace Technology in Other Sectors of the Economy* (inside title: *NASA Benefits Briefing Notebook*), prepared for the Technology Utilization Office, Code KT, NASA by the Program for Transfer Research and Impact Studies, Industrial Economics Division, Denver Research Institute, University of Denver, Colorado, May 1976

FITZROY, R. (1839) *Narrative of the Surveying Voyages of Her Majesty's Ships* Adventure *and* Beagle *Between the Years 1826 and 1836*, vols. II & III, London

GENERAL ELECTRIC SPACE DIVISION (1975) *Image 100: Interactive Multispectral Image Analysis System; System Description*, Ground Systems Department, Space Division, General Electric Company, Daytona Beach, Florida (Document No. 717001SD) March 1975, revised December 1975

GIDDINGS, L.E. (1976) *Technical Memorandum: Satellites for Life Sciences*, prepared for the

Health Applications Office, Life Sciences Directorate, Lyndon B. Johnson Space Center, Houston, by Life Sciences Applications Department, Lockheed Electronics Company, Inc. Aerospace Systems Division, Houston, under contract NAS 9-12200 (LEC-7737; JSC-10856) January 1976

KATZ, H.A., WARRICK, P. & GREENBERG, M. H. (eds.) (1974) *Introductory Psychology Through Science Fiction*, Rand McNally, Chicago (reviewed by Radford, J. (1976) *Foundation 10*, 121–123)

MOOREHEAD, A. (1969) *Darwin and the Beagle*, Hamish Hamilton, London

NANCE, J. (1975) *The Gentle Tasaday: a Stone Age People in the Philippine Rain Forest*, Harcourt Brace Jovanovich, New York

NASA (1976a) *Landsat Follow-On* (folder), National Aeronautics and Space Administration, Washington, D.C.

NASA (1976b) *Technical Memorandum: First Concept for a Tropical Area Monitoring Project*, Health Applications Group, Life Sciences Directorate, NASA, Lyndon B. Johnson Space Center, Houston, Texas, July 1976

NICHOLSON, M.H. (1948) *Voyages to the Moon* (Macmillan Paperbacks edn, New York, 1960)

PLEVIN, J. (1974) Remote sensing of earth resources: a European point of view, *Impact of Science on Society 24*, 247–259 (In particular, Table 3, Different types of platforms, p. 254)

RADFORD, J. (1976) Science fiction as myth. *Foundation: the Review of Science Fiction 10*, 28–44

REINING, P. (1974a) Human settlement patterns in relation to resources of less developed countries, COSPAR Seminar on Space Applications of Direct Interest to Developing Countries, São Jose dos Campos, Brazil, 21 June 1974

REINING, P. (1974b) Earth Resources Technology Satellite-1 (ERTS-1) data and anthropology: use of these data in carrying capacity estimates for sites in Upper Volta and Niger, American Anthropological Association meeting, Mexico City, 24 November 1974

REINING, P. (1975) The demographic potential of ERTS-1 data, American Association for the Advancement of Science, 141st Annual Meeting, New York, 29 January 1975

REINING, P. & EGBERT, D. (1975) Interactive multi-spectral analysis of more than one Sonrai village in Niger, West Africa, in *Proceedings of the NASA Earth Resources Survey Symposium*, NASA TM X-58168, L.B. Johnson Space Center, Houston, Texas, 8–12 June 1975

RUSH, M., HOLGUIN, A. & VERNON, S. (n.d.) *Potential Role of Remote Sensing in Disaster Relief Management*, University of Texas Health Science Center at Houston (document published either 1975 or 1976)

SAGAN, C. & DRAKE, F. (1975) The search for extraterrestrial intelligence. *Sci. Am. 226* (5), 80–89

SAGAN, C., SAGAN, L.S. & DRAKE, F. (1972) A message from Earth. *Science (Wash. D.C.) 175*, 881–884

SCHARF, A. (1975) *Pioneers of Photography: an Album of Pictures and Words*, British Broadcasting Corporation, London

SORENSON, R.E. (1974) Anthropological film: a scientific and humanistic resource. *Science (Wash. D.C.) 186*, 1079–1085

STABLEFORD, B.M. (1976) The prizewinners (reviews of Logan, C. *Shipwreck*, and Boyce, C. *Catchworld*). *Foundation 10*, 77–80

SULLIVAN, W. (1976) From other civilizations: NASA to seek outer-space signals. *International Herald Tribune*, 5 November, 1976 (reprinted from *New York Times*, with inset: Briton, fearing invasion of earth, asks ban on signals to space)

THIEL, A.K. (1972) Requirements and technology for observations from space, in *Remote Sensing of Earth Resources*, pp. 43–81, U.S. House of Representatives, Committee on Science and Astronautics, U.S. Government Printing Office, Washington, D.C.

WILSON, A.G. & GORDON, T.J. (1972) Requirements for communications to a naive recipient, in *Ahead of Time* (Harrison, H. & Gordon, T. J., eds.), pp. 68–83, Doubleday, New York

Discussion

Hamilton: If you need over-flying as a follow-up to make Landsat particularly useful, what is the specificity of the technique?

Ohlman: The satellite 'sees' everything but not everything is processed. As far as being able to see detail goes, the resolution simply isn't there; it will be better in the third satellite, which has been designed to have a resolution down to 30 metres.

Black: Would it be practical, and should it not be done, to use these techniques to survey, say, the Transamazonic Highway network area in Brazil so as to avoid unnecessary disruption of the Indians, and to anticipate and minimize the disruption that is going to occur? There are still a few uncontacted tribes that we know about; there may be others.

Ohlman: We tried to do something like this at WHO. Dr Guy Lavoipierre, an epidemiologist, was working in the Sudan. We wrote to NASA, telling them that in order to make a series of medical surveys in the Rahad area (some 300 km south-east of Khartoum), we wanted to locate the villages and make a full population census from which to sample the population to be medically examined. Such a census is being done, but the area is poorly mapped and the villages are scattered. We thought that satellite images would help in checking the accuracy of our ground enumerations. The photograph we received was not of much use. The extensive canal system of the Gezira was apparent, but even large towns were hard to find without reference to a map. Perhaps more trained eyes might have found smaller habitations or, if we had had the time, money, and inclination, we could have asked to work with a computer-compatible tape (CCT, p. 35) of this image.

Neel: If we are interested in using remote sensing to locate people, we should have a representative of the military of any number of countries at the symposium! There are now standard techniques by which to locate guerilla groups.

Ohlman: This technology is probably the most important spin-off of all our space activities. The potential for doing censuses is there, even though the resolutions aren't yet what they could be, but probably this has been a deliberate decision by NASA. As resolution improves, Landsat images will become more accepted and more useful to governments. Many governments have now built their own ground stations to receive this information directly—for example, Brazil—so that they can process it themselves.

White: It is all very well if one assumes that people are 'discovered' by others who are benevolent, but in the experience of the world, tribal peoples have been contacted first by explorers, by missionaries, by people who have wanted PhD's, by the military, or by governments interested in counter-insurgency. I therefore find the whole thing distasteful.

Shaper: I echo that, because one feels that there is nowhere to hide any more.

Ohlman: It is really not altogether so distasteful. As an example from agriculture, you can see individual farms, different crops can be identified, and crop diseases can be found. It is a question of how to use this technique for the benefit, rather than the destruction, of life.

Cohen: However, the Landsat technique is apparently no help in picking up the few small groups of people who remain virtually unknown to us. Nor can it be used for census purposes (which could be a useful application in some of the poorer countries) without some idea from sample survey data of how many people on average make up the families that live in any of the huts or settlements that one can identify. Most of the remaining possible uses seem to be military or paramilitary ones—or maybe for the coming race of super-bureaucrats! I can see scope for low-flying expeditions in which one might follow nomadic movements or look at the spatial distribution of habitations, but I have not gathered how this technique can help us with the problems that relate directly to this symposium.

Ohlman: There has been a considerable amount of work by an anthropologist, Priscilla Reining. As I mentioned (p. 36), she has studied settlement patterns in relation to the resources of less-developed countries and has made capacity estimates for sites in Upper Volta and Niger. The potential of the technique obviously has to be explored before it can be applied reliably.

Lightman: To turn to the first part of your paper, the problem with your ten principles for primary contact is that although they might be applicable to the single intended visit of the starship Enterprise to an alien world in space, they are totally unrealistic in terms of the vast majority, if not all, of tribal groups on our own globe. To be more specific, these people are inevitably going to be contacted—and not just on a short-term basis; thus changes are equally inevitable. Moreover, I would deny your contention that change *per se* is 'wrong' in such a situation, although control of the process of contact should, one hopes, prevent the medical and social disintegration of the newly contacted group.

On your antipathy to the offer of gifts at first contact, I again feel that you are on, at best, shaky ground. The exchange of gifts is basic to many tribal societies. In addition, it is often the only way to gain the confidence of people you might be seeking to contact.

Another of your suggestions is that gifts of metal axes and other Iron Age implements should be avoided, since once people possess such implements they are unable to return to their own 'Stone Age'. The imperative question is: *who* wants them to return to the Stone Age, and why? I am sure *they* would not, and, unless you believe in the preservation of human zoos, I can see no reason why *we* should. The use of iron can and does make a considerable difference to the quality of life.

Finally, in relation to the search for and contact with unknown settlements, I think it is very questionable in most cases whether we *should* want to find them at all. Unless some development is already planned on their land, our experience must surely teach us that contact can only be destructive to the welfare of an isolated group, so that deliberate contact must be only in the selfish self-interest of those making the contact.

Hugh-Jones: Perhaps what matters is the rate of contact, as well as the actual contact? On the point of whether one should try to make contact, perhaps we should not make an effort to do so; but, if somebody is going to contact them, for example if a road is being driven through their territory, then we wish to make sure that the proper information is collected and that the right rate of change of their physical and psychological environment is regulated.

Lightman: If a road is to be built, that is true, but the idea of looking for people with the sole purpose of contacting them is to me ethically questionable.

Ohlman: Inevitably, such people will be found. The question is whether they are found sooner or later. Inevitably, they will change—but we would like to see them change as little as possible, at least while we are trying to understand them. I am particularly struck by the tribe called the Tasaday, a Stone Age people in the Philippine rain forest. I derived a lot of the ten principles from a book about them (Nance 1975), more than from science fiction.

Lightman: You have unfortunately chosen a rather unrepresentative group, since their population only amounted to about 30.

Haraldson: Anthropologists clearly have to use special techniques when approaching tribal societies. In my own work, in the field of health planning, it has been a question of short visits to many tribal groups (Haraldson 1972). We always try to find someone in the health services who originates from the particular tribe we are going to visit. If possible he goes with us and will explain to the local people what sort of people we are, what we are doing, and what we are aiming at. This works well and saves much time.

Mr Ohlman mentioned that one should go on foot. I agree. You should also walk on their tracks, and you should carry your luggage yourself. You should take your time and stay overnight. On the second day, normal life begins again, whereas on the first day everything stops in the village. As soon as the people know you have accepted their culture, their food, their sleeping techniques, the next day you are fully accepted and there is no problem in any culture. There are other small points which are nevertheless important and very easy to apply: you can admire their handicraft and techniques; you can learn from them; and what to my mind is very important is to come with your wife. This changes the whole situation.

Baruzzi: I would like to comment on the problem of gifts. If making contact with an isolated tribe became necessary, for various reasons, such as the opening of a new road, one must make the initial approach carefully and slowly. There is always the risk of an aggressive response from the indigenous group or the possibility of their disappearing into the jungle in order to avoid contact. We must first be able to show them our friendly intentions. The lack of knowledge of their language is an obstacle to communication, and the use of gifts as a symbolic language can be very useful. For example, we can be encouraged to go on with the attempt to make contact when the people begin to take away our gifts and to replace them with their own.

Ohlman: The problem is that if you want to know how the tribe was before you arrive, which is the idea of first contact, giving gifts is going to change it.

Lozoff: Your very presence changes the situation!

Ohlman: Of course, but we want to minimize the changes, at least at first; this is the whole idea of the ten principles.

Baruzzi: The main purpose of the work of 'approach' is to preserve such people from indiscriminate contact in the near future. This is more relevant than the possible changes caused in tribal life by the introduction of a few tools or things given as gifts to attract them for the first contact. Even the process of approaching them has repercussions in the tribal culture.

Ohlman: In his book *Oh, What a Blow that Phantom Gave Me!* Edmund Carpenter (1976) has a chapter entitled 'Misanthropology' which concerns American Indians. He says that 'What disturbed most was the feeling that when their dances and tales were filmed, taped and written down, they were stolen from them as surely as their lands and furs were taken away. When they saw their sacred treasures under glass, heard their songs on radio, watched their dances on TV, they [the Indians] not only objected to errors they spotted, they felt robbed. None of this had anything to do with them. They felt used. And they were'. (Carpenter 1976, p. 168.)

Gajdusek: I disagree with all the ten principles. Today, there isn't much left of 'first contact' to be made, but in the last 40 years there have still been many hundreds of thousands of people who did not know that there were two sexes to civilized man, that aeroplanes didn't have jaws and teeth, and who were still in the Stone Age and did not know of metals, ceramics, grain crops or of the existence of oceans or salt seawater. Most of the New Guinea Highlanders did not know man was a species able to swim. I am not exaggerating the isolation and restricted horizons of the East New Guinea Highlanders. The Australian government established peaceful administration rapidly, often arriving sudden-

ly, even by aeroplane or helicopter. They extended their administration, the
Pax Australica, and rule of law as *rapidly* as possible, with the aim of making
sure that no remote cultural or linguistic group, of which there were several
hundreds, was left out of the political process which they knew was shortly
going to be in the hands of the indigenous populations, and now is. Their attempt was a laudatory one: there is now no outside European or Asian government running Papua New Guinea. They ensured that no indigenous group was
left out of the political process by quickly establishing courts, Medical Aid
Posts, and schools in the most remote regions. At times they quickly eradicated
yaws and reduced tropical ulcers to a rare phenomenon—previously, lasting
scourges to these populations. Medical aid, cessation of warfare, the opening
of trails and roads between villages that had been at war for generations, came
to most groups in a matter of months or a few years. In no case did the Australians meet with lasting hostility, and there was very little direct conflict and
loss of life. This very rapid change in culture affected over a million people in
Stone Age cultures; it has happened in the past 40 years and we shall not see any
new contacts with primitive cultures of this magnitude again.

Hugh-Jones: The amount of information lost must have been unbelievable!

Gajdusek: Was it better to lose that, or to have inflicted prolonged protective
reservations and colonial status, or self-government by an élite selected solely
from a few cultural and linguistic groups which had been placed under administrative control early, leaving out all the rest of the peoples from participation in their own government?

Ohlman: This is all from our aspect, not from theirs. Consider the American
Indians. There were hundreds of tribes, each with its own culture and language.
Many have been wiped out completely. This also in a similar 'laudatory'
process; we were 'developing' the country.

Gajdusek: In the past two decades economic development in Papua New
Guinea was rapid and the direction of the future of their country was left in the
hands of an elected government of New Guinea from every province of the
country. There are no absentee land owners, and very little land is owned by
persons not born in New Guinea.

Woodburn: I want to stress the unreality of Mr Ohlman's view that uncontacted groups should be located using satellite photographs and contacted
using his extraordinary ten principles. There are now virtually *no* uncontacted
groups left in the world. Even contacted but very isolated groups are extraordinarily rare. Recent research among Bushmen in Botswana suggests that a
very tiny proportion of the small minority still living their traditional way of
life did, until recently, keep themselves out of contact, or almost out of contact,
with outsiders. But I don't think such groups persisted so long anywhere else in

Africa. In Australia the last few uncontacted or really isolated Aborigines —probably the Bindibu or Pintubi—were contacted several years ago. There are perhaps four or five other places in the world where uncontacted tiny groups—like the Tasaday—may well remain. But it would be rather surprising if any group remained with a population as large as 1000 people—a few dozen people is more plausible. If we are going to make programmatic statements about how to contact groups of a few dozen people the programme has to be totally different from the one outlined.

Jones: I think James Woodburn is wrong; in the Bangwela swamps, in Zambia, for example, there probably are some uncontacted people. Do you, Mr Ohlman, by using these satellite techniques, know any place in the world where you are fairly certain that there are people who have *not* yet been contacted? I wonder if you could point the satellite at the Bangwela swamp system in the middle of Africa and see if there is anybody there.

Ohlman: It has been pointed there; two satellites go over it every 18 days, so there could be plenty of photographs to which you could get access. If you decided there was something interesting there, you would have to analyse the pictures further by one of the available techniques. Landsat photographs can be taken only by permission of the government in question, however.

As far as your first point goes, apparently the Tasaday referred to two other peoples (The Tasafeng and the Sanduka) but I don't know whether they have been contacted in that mountain forest area; so there may be some undiscovered people.

Gajdusek: There is an example of how such aerial photography has been used profitably. The 1943 aerial survey of New Guinea prepared during World War II by the military was used in 1973 to check the old peoples' stories about where their villages were located, how much garden area they had, and so on. The people were first 'contacted' in the 1950s. The anthropologists had from the older aerial surveys pictures of the villages and gardens from a period when they had not yet been visited (Sorenson & Kenmore 1974). Ethnic history and childhood memory has been vindicated from a study of the early aerial photographs, and with their aid it has been possible to ask specific questions about earlier village and garden sites and to thus assess the reliability of amnestic reporting. Memory was jogged by the use of the photographs and events were then reported that people had previously 'forgotten'.

References

CARPENTER, E. (1966) *Oh, What a Blow That Phantom Gave Me!*, pp. 168–169, Paladin, London
HARALDSON, S.R.S. (1972) Health services among scattered populations. *Acta Socio-Medica Scand.*, Suppl. 6

NANCE, J. (1975) *The Gentle Tasaday: A Stone Age People in the Philippine Rain Forest*, Harcourt Brace Jovanovich, New York

SORENSON, E.R. & KENMORE, P.E. (1974) Proto-agricultural movement in the Eastern Highlands of New Guinea. *Curr. Anthropol. 15*, 67–73

Field methods for the assessment of health and disease in pre-agricultural societies

BETSY LOZOFF and GARY M. BRITTENHAM

Divisions of Geographic Medicine and Hematology, Departments of Pediatrics, Medicine and Anthropology, Case Western Reserve University, Cleveland, Ohio

Abstract   The few surviving pre-agricultural societies preserve the best available indication of human adaptation during more than 99% of the species' history. The field methods described allow collection of data that may explain why hunters and gatherers are physically small in the face of apparent plenty, what causes their death and how they control population growth. Observations of daily life, especially family, food and work, provide the context within which biological data can be interpreted. Computer-compatible event-recording systems make possible the collection and encoding of quantitative behavioural observations. A careful census permits characterization of fertility and mortality. Physical assessment, by medical history, physical examination and anthropometry, establishes the patterns of growth and development in the population and the prevalence of clinically recognizable diseases and nutritional disorders. If blood, urine or faeces can be collected, lightweight portable field-proven equipment and techniques are available for the collection, analysis and preservation of specimens for biochemical, nutritional, haematological and genetic determinations.

The field methods described here have been chosen on the basis of their usefulness in resolving specific issues involving the health of hunters and gatherers. Three apparent contradictions in the available data on nutrition, mortality and fertility in these populations will be considered.

NUTRITION

Quantitative studies among contemporary hunter–gatherers have suggested that a nutritionally adequate diet may be consistently obtained with modest effort, 2–5 hours a day (Lee 1968, 1973; McCarthy & McArthur 1960; Wehmeyer *et al.* 1969). A substantial reserve in both environmental resource and human energy remains. Even less effort may have been required in societies not displaced from their traditional environments (Sahlins 1972). Most of this diet comes from varied vegetable sources although nearly all pre-agricultural populations derive at least 20% of their food from the hunting of mammals (Angel 1975; Callen 1973; Isaac 1975; Lee 1968).

Human nutritional requirements may be considered the product of the species' adaptation during its evolutionary history. Humans were hunter–gatherers for over 99% of this time; the diet of foragers, combining a diversity of vegetable foods with animal protein, is therefore theoretically unlikely to result in nutritional deficiency. Empirically, it is those agricultural and industrial populations whose diets consist mainly of high-carbohydrate grains with little or no animal protein or fresh vegetables that suffer from the common deficiency states: protein-energy malnutrition, beriberi, scurvy, pellagra, ariboflavinosis, and folic acid and iron deficiency. These deficiencies are rare or absent among the few contemporary pre-agricultural groups which have been surveyed (Dunn 1968).

However, the stature and weight of contemporary hunter–gatherers and those estimated for Palaeolithic foragers are substantially below the 'standards of reference' derived from the taller, heavier populations which have appeared in industrialized countries over the past century (Barnicot et al. 1972; Neel et al. 1964; Truswell & Hansen 1968; Truswell et al. 1972). Some have argued that the smaller size of hunter–gatherers is 'optimal' and that increases in height and weight are the result of 'overnutrition' which in turn is associated with a variety of cardiovascular, digestive and neoplastic disorders (Esche & Lee 1975; Stini 1975). In general, however, it has been assumed that smaller size in a population, in the absence of a genetic cause, constitutes evidence of undernutrition. Thus, the first paradox in the data on pre-agricultural populations is: *if hunter–gatherers have a plentiful, nutritionally adequate diet, why are they physically small?*

MORTALITY

Hunter–gatherers generally seem to be physically fit and relatively disease-free, both to anthropologists and to the few physicians who have made systematic examination (Dunn 1958). Many of the major causes of mortality and morbidity in industrial and agricultural societies are absent or infrequent among hunter–gatherers. Nutritional deficiency is apparently a rare cause of death. Many of the leading causes of mortality in industrialized countries have been attributed to deviations from the dietary patterns of pre-agricultural populations. Thus, high-calorie, low-residue diets with large amounts of saturated fats, refined carbohydrates and salt have been said to be associated with an astonishing variety of diseases, such as atherosclerotic, cardiovascular and cerebrovascular disease, obesity, diabetes mellitus, many digestive tract disorders (appendicitis, diverticulitis, ulcerative colitis, gallstones) and a number of neoplasms (gastrointestinal malignancies and the 'hormone-related' cancers of breast, pancreas, ovary, uterus, testicle and prostate) (Armstrong & Doll 1975; Burkitt 1973; Carroll & Khor 1975; Weinhouse 1975). All are uncommon among hunter–gatherers.

Many major epidemic diseases are not found among foraging societies. Measles, influenza, diphtheria, smallpox and poliomyelitis are self-perpetuating only in the larger populations which appeared after the origin of agriculture (Bennett *et al.* 1973; Black 1975; Black *et al.* 1974; Neel *et al.* 1968). Some pre-agricultural groups were also free of tuberculosis and syphilis until contact with non-foraging cultures (Black 1975). In Africa, at least, hyperendemic malaria may have arisen only after the displacement of hunter–gatherers from the forest by agriculturalists (Wiesenfeld 1967). For many parasitic diseases, such as schistosomiasis, hookworm and ascariasis, the small mobile foraging populations were unlikely to have accumulated the heavy parasite burdens which produce disease manifestations. Finally, predation, trauma and 'social' causes of death must vary greatly in importance from group to group (Dunn 1968).

However, the same pre-agricultural societies characterized as fit and healthy are also reported to have high mortality rates. Short life expectancies are described for both contemporary and Palaeolithic populations. Weiss (1973*a*), reviewing the available data, estimates a life expectancy at birth of 19–25 years for Palaeolithic hunter–gatherers and of 22–29 years among 'living primitives'; furthermore, both juvenile and adult mortality rates seem to be high. Thus, a second paradox is: *if hunter–gatherers are relatively disease-free, what explains their high mortality rates?*

FERTILITY

Mortality rates among many contemporary subsistence agriculturalists and impoverished urban peoples are as high as those described for hunter–gatherers (Dunn 1968). Whereas these agricultural and urban populations are typically rapidly increasing in size and exceeding their resources, the pre-agricultural societies are characteristically stable or very slow growing and maintain a relatively constant relation to the environment (Dumond 1975; Hassan 1975). The mechanisms which preserve this balance are unknown, in spite of the variety of hypotheses advanced. Thus, a third paradox is: *if the size of hunter–gatherer populations is balanced with environmental resources, how is population growth controlled?*

The field methods described here are particularly useful for the collection of quantitative data relevant to the resolution of these three apparent paradoxes. It is assumed that the investigations are to be conducted among small groups living in relative isolation by a few primary field-workers (2–3 persons) who spend long periods of time in the field and become thoroughly familiar with the foraging society. Specialist consultation is expected only on brief visits and comprehensive laboratory facilities are assumed to be distant. The techniques may be grouped into those of interview and observation, direct physical assessment, and laboratory evaluation.

INTERVIEW AND OBSERVATION

Ethnographic observations

A basic ethnographic description of the daily patterns of family life, work and food is a prerequisite for any medical undertaking. Indigenous concepts of health and disease must be understood so that a description of the investigations allows members of a society to become fully active and voluntary participants. Social and cultural considerations may also explain otherwise puzzling phenomena; for example, food distribution may depend on kinship relations, the spread of infection may follow lines of social contact, fertility patterns may be influenced by sexual customs and marriage rules.

Event-recording systems

In the past, the restrictions of available recording systems—pen and paper, film, audio and videotape—have hindered the collection of quantitative data on nutrition, mortality and fertility. Many of these problems may be solved with the introduction of field-proven computer-compatible methods for collecting, encoding and transcribing (for subsequent automated analysis) large numbers of quantitative behavioural observations. The application of one such system to health issues will be briefly described here.

The SSR system is an event-recording system that encodes the incidence, duration, coincidence and sequence of entries in real time on to magnetic tape for subsequent high-speed computerized transcription (Stephenson et al. 1975). It consists of a lightweight, battery-powered keyboard (Fig. 1) utilizing a conservating encoding and multiplexing circuitry for sampling a set of 48 alphanumeric and other characters 20 times a second. The encoding signal is recorded on an audio tape-recorder; a supplementary vocal record may be simultaneously made on a parallel tract. At some later time, a small computer decodes the data tape into binary form, transcribing one hour of data in 7.5

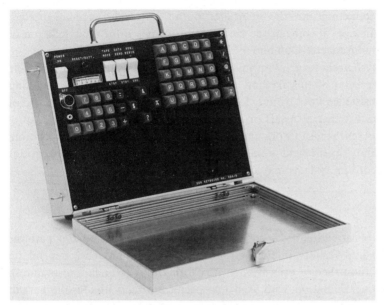

FIG. 1. The SSR system keyboard (12 inches × 9 inches × 3 inches; 7 lb.)

minutes. Additional programmes organize the data into a timed manuscript of lines, permit editing and error correction, and allow temporal synchronization with cine or video material, the records of multiple observers or any other temporally registered process. The character set and functions are entirely software-defined and may be altered at any time in the field. The completely open format and the flexibility of the software grammars allow definition of subjects, actions, objects and other contextual information in whatever form the user requires; several different applications may be made during a single field trip.

We have recently used the SSR system in the study of mother-infant interaction (B. Lozoff & G. Brittenham, unpublished work). Systematic observations were made on all children less than two years of age in a village; the type and duration of interaction with the infants, by person, was recorded. Special emphasis was given to physical and visual contact, the frequency and duration of breast-feeding, and the frequency and amount of solid foods. The particular programme used allowed recording and timing of up to 100 individuals performing as many as 625 actions; these figures could be easily altered with other programmes. Our observations in this group, which until recently depended on hunting and gathering, suggested that older siblings are major caregivers and carriers of infants and that solid foods, modified by crushing and added water, are early introductions into the infant diet. Both these results were unexpected, particularly in view of some of the mechanisms proposed for the regulation of fertility among foragers (Dumond 1975).

The SSR system shows great promise for use in nutritional investigations. The increased precision of this method makes possible both a second-by-second record of subsistence work by individual and a mouthful-by-mouthful record of consumption, whether at meals or nibbling. Combined with energy measurements for different kinds of work and biochemical analyses of food composition, a 'balance study' in the field is thus possible. A number of other applications for event-recording systems may be envisioned.

Demography

Considerable attention has been given to problems of characterizing patterns of mortality and fertility in hunter–gatherers. Most approaches depend on stable population theory, even though its assumptions (population infinite in size, without net migration, with fixed age-specific mortality and fertility) are of necessity only approximated in the field (Coale 1972; Keyfitz & Flieger 1971; Lotka 1956; Shyrock & Siegel 1971). Practical problems of data collection are formidable under the best of circumstances and are especially so in pre-agricultural populations where the incidence of abortions, stillbirths and early infant deaths is difficult to determine and ages are typically unknown and of little concern. Fieldworkers are generally unable to tell people's ages by appearance alone and no satisfactory objective methods of determining age exist at present. The best available technique of age estimation is to combine construction of a local event calender with a compilation of relative age rank (Howell 1973).

Census data may be used directly to give estimates of mortality rates (Stolnitz 1956); procedures for estimating age-specific fertility rates have also been proposed (Weiss 1973b). A more powerful technique, especially with relatively complete data, is the use of computer simulation to interrelate demographic information with ethnographic, genealogical, linguistic and genetic data in dynamic models of the features of populations over time (Dyke & MacCluer 1973; MacCluer et al. 1971; Neel & Weiss 1974). Another procedure, of special value with incomplete or fragmentary data, utilizes the model life-tables devised by Weiss (1973a) specifically for use in populations of 'anthropological interest'. These are designed so that an appropriate model synthetic cohort abridged life table can be chosen on the basis of any one or a combination of measures realistically obtainable in the field, such as completed family size, mean family size, various proportions of the population, or average age. These tables, in addition to supplying usable models, aid in assessing the reasonableness and internal consistency of the field data.

PHYSICAL AND LABORATORY EXAMINATION

The resolution of issues of nutrition, mortality and fertility will almost always require that the information obtained by interview and observation be supplemented with the results of physical assessment and laboratory examination. Such investigations have been made in only a very few pre-agricultural populations and nearly all those have been limited to short-term cross-sectional prevalence surveys. In the remaining foraging societies, the single most urgent need is for carefully designed and executed longitudinal incidence studies. Substantial periods of continuous observation would greatly augment the value of such an undertaking by increasing their diagnostic accuracy. Longitudinal incidence studies are notoriously difficult; the characteristic small size and mobility of hunter–gatherer cultures introduce even further complications. The population itself is likely to be the unit of study; if it is so large as to require sampling, the choice of representative groups for complete study is a more feasible technique than attempting a sample of members of all the groups. Careful statistical guidance in sampling methods is required in order that the results obtained be interpretable.

The serial data to be collected will be considered in two categories: physical assessment and specialized laboratory examinations.

Physical assessment

For the efficient examination of a large number of people in a short time it is advantageous to use a 'line of flow' technique with several staff members operating a series of distinct stations through which individuals move and undergo separate examinations. However, in the circumstances of a hunting and gathering society, complete examinations by one or two investigators over an extended period in the community may be more advisable. The identifying information should allow the unambiguous re-identification of the individual and collation of the examinations with the ethnographic, demographic and nutritional data. Checklist forms make it possible to indicate quickly and clearly if each item was examined, found normal, abnormal or variant and, if either of the latter two, specifically describe the finding; the forms should be designed for easy transcription for computerized analysis.

The tools required for the physical examination are simple and readily obtainable; they include a physician's common diagnostic instruments (mercury sphygmomanometer, stethoscope, ophthalmoscope, otoscope, tuning forks and reflex hammer) and the devices for anthropometric measurements (portable beam balance weighing scale, flexible steel or fibreglass centimetre tape, infant length board, Martin anthropometer and Harpenden skinfold calipers, both the latter preferably with digital read-out). The insertion type of tape introduced by Zerfas (1975) is convenient for circumference measurements. Portable scales are the most unsatisfactory item in this list; no truly lightweight, reliable and easily transportable model is at present available although Homs, Avery or Morgan scales are usable (Burgess & Burgess 1975).

The techniques for blood pressure determination and for anthropometric measurements may be found in the recommendations for the International Biological Programme (Weiner & Lourie 1969). The minimum set of measurements required for ascertaining nutritional status are weight, height, triceps skinfold thickness and circumference of the left midupper arm; in children chest and head circumference are valuable additions (Buzina & Uemura 1974). Body composition and proportions can be estimated more accurately if more detailed anthropometric measurements are made on at least a sample of the population; the 'basic' list of the International Biological Programme is the recommended minimum (Weiner & Lourie 1969).

The physicians who conduct the examinations should have special training in anthropometry and some clinical experience both in nutritional assessment and in the type of problems specific to the area. A standard clinical examination, adapted as required by field circumstance, should be made. Physical examination has an immediate usefulness in allowing estimation of the prevalence of clinically recognizable illnesses; it provides the sole practical means of identifying many of these conditions, and only with clinical observation will it be possible unequivocally to identify factors responsible for mortality in hunting and gathering populations. The clinical signs of nutritional disorders are especially valuable; in the interests of uniformity of terminology and standardization of results the definitions proposed by Jelliffe (1966) should be adopted. Even though most of these signs are non-specific and give but an approximate indication of the true prevalence of deficiency states, they may provide clues to problems which can be accurately diagnosed with the use of laboratory procedures. In some communities, however, the acute physical signs suggestive of nutritional disturbances may be uncommon and the existence of malnutrition must be demonstrated by anthropometry; thus somatic measurements are of the greatest importance. With detailed information on body composition and proportions from all age groups in the population it may be possible to define the causes for the small size reported for hunter–gatherers and to resolve the issue of whether this represents an optimal adaptation or evidence of undernutrition.

Laboratory examinations

Laboratory examinations will almost inevitably be required to establish with accuracy the factors responsible for the patterns of fertility, mortality and nutrition found in a population. Some procedures must be performed almost immediately while others require complex facilities found only in research centres. For many techniques a choice may be made between doing tests at a base established in the field or preserving specimens for later examination. Either choice requires the introduction of more complex equipment and often the provision of a power source. Battery-powered models of many types of laboratory apparatus are now available. Even if only alternating-current-requiring versions exist, these may still be powered from battery sources by the use of a square-wave inverter to convert direct current to a suitable wave form. Portable refrigeration or freezing equipment is available which utilizes liquid nitrogen and dry ice (Secord 1972) or is powered by batteries, or gas (propane or butane). For samples to be examined outside the field it is recommended that investigators not personally experienced in the conduct of the procedures involved should make prior collaborative arrangements with reference laboratories for the processing of the specimens.

We have had experience with a Bausch and Lomb Spectronic mini 20 portable spectrophotometer, the size of a pocket calculator, which makes possible accurate field determination of a wide variety of biochemical measurements dependent on spectrophotometric measurements; it is powered by rechargeable nickel-cadmium batteries. We have also used a Nikon Model H-3 portable microscope, the size of a 35mm camera, with 10X, 40X and oil immersion lenses. An International Equipment Company Model TE Clinette centrifuge with a single head containing positions for both microhaematocrit tubes and test tubes ranging from 2 to 15 millilitres in size has been very useful; it requires alternating current but may be powered from a battery with the use of a square wave inverter. A Bernzomatic portable refrigerator (17 lbs; $12^1/_2$ inches $\times$ $13^1/_2$ inches $\times$ $14^1/_2$ inches) may be operated from either alternating current or a battery. These instruments (Fig. 2) were readily obtainable in the United States; European alternatives are also available.

The selection of laboratory tests for assessing nutritional status has been widely discussed and recommendations for the methods of choice have recently been made elsewhere (King & Faulkner 1973). The collection and preservation of blood or urine samples is required for most; the use of hair for protein-calorie assessment or for detecting trace-metal deficiency has also been attempted.

Laboratory examinations will further establish the factors responsible for the

FIG. 2. Portable laboratory equipment for field use.
Top: Bernzomatic refrigerator, IEC model TE Clinette centrifuge.
Bottom: Bausch & Lomb mini 20 spectrophotometer, Nikon Model H-3 microscope. (Scale bar 15 inches.)

mortality and morbidity encountered in the population. Infectious causes have received the most attention. The collection of blood specimens allows one to study the immune status of the population to a wide variety of viral, bacterial and parasitic agents. Algorithms summarizing the best available methods for diagnosing many infections in non-industrialized societies have appeared serially and will soon be published in book form (Warren & Mahmoud 1975, 1976). Other laboratory examinations relating to causes of morbidity and mortality would be dictated by the long-term clinical findings of physicians working with the population (blood sugars, lipid studies, radiological examinations, electro-cardiograms, and so on).

Techniques for the detection of genetic polymorphisms are still increasing in sophistication; anthropometric measures and dermatoglyphics continue to be used but blood specimens provide the broadest range of information. Even if only finger puncture specimens are collected, preservation in haematocrit tubes or in filter paper allows the satisfactory detection of a variety of serum proteins and red cell enzymes (Saha & Kirk 1973); however, filter paper preservation of samples for detecting haemoglobinopathies may not be as reliable as first thought (Schmidt *et al.* 1976). If blood samples are collected by venepuncture, preservation by refrigeration or freezing is adequate for many polymorphisms, but for some, liquid nitrogen must be used. All of these techniques have been successfully applied in field studies.

Considerable refinement in laboratory assessment of the control of fertility promises to improve our understanding of its regulation in pre-agricultural societies. It has now become possible more precisely to quantify the balance of hormonal factors involved in ovulation and lactation (Abraham *et al.* 1974; Schmidt-Gollwitzer & Saxena 1975). Reliable means exist for detecting pregnancy from urine samples in the field (Porres 1975); used serially in a defined group, more accurate determinations of rate of conception, abortion, infanticide and infant mortality are feasible.

The field methods described allow collection of data that may help explain why hunter–gatherers are physically small in the face of apparent plenty, what causes their death, and how they control population growth. The use of any of these procedures requires communication between very different societies. Small stable groups, conservative of their environment over millennia, meet large rapidly expanding populations, which seem inevitably destructive of the environment essential for the others' survival. In spite of our concern for the health of hunters and gatherers, our sensitivity to their understanding of our purpose, our eagerness to attempt solutions to their problems and our determination that their self-sufficiency be maintained, our investigations are likely to record their disintegration as much as their previous adaptation.

ACKNOWLEDGEMENTS

We are deeply indebted to P.K. Misra, Ph.D., Anthropological Survey of India, whose comments have caused us to reconsider the significance of medical studies for the investigated society as well as the investigating one. The field testing of the equipment described has been made possible by the support of the Rockefeller Foundation and the encouragement of John W. Harris, M.D. (Division of Hematology), Kenneth S. Warren, M.D. (Division of Geographic Medicine), Department of Medicine and Marshall H. Klaus, M.D., Department of Pediatrics, Case Western Reserve University. All the unnamed people who have agreed to be observed and examined deserve thanks that cannot be adequately expressed.

References

ABRAHAM, G.E., MAROULIS, G.B. & MARSHALL, J.R. (1974) Evaluation of ovulation and corpus luteum function using measurements of plasma progesterone. *Obstet. Gynecol.* 44, 522–525.

ANGEL, L.J. (1975) Paleoecology, paleodemography and health, in *Population, Ecology, and Social Evolution* (Polgar, S., ed.), pp. 167–190, Mouton, The Hague

ARMSTRONG, B. & DOLL, R. (1975) Environmental factors and cancer incidence and mortality in different countries, with special reference to dietary practices. *Int. J. Cancer 15*, 617–631

BARNICOT, N.A., BENNETT, F.J., WOODBURN, J.C., PILKINGTON, T.R.E. & the late ANTONIS, A. (1972) Blood pressure and serum cholesterol in the Hadza of Tanzania. *Hum. Biol. 44*, 87–116

BENNETT, F.J., BARNICOT, N.A., WOODBURN, J.C., PEREIRA, M.S. & HENDERSON, B.E. (1973) Studies on viral, bacterial, rickettsial and treponemal diseases in the Hadza of Tanzania and a note on injuries. *Hum. Biol. 45*, 243–272

BLACK, F.L. (1975) Infectious diseases in primitive societies. *Science (Wash. D.C.) 187*, 515–518

BLACK, F.L., HIERHOLZER, W.J., PINHEIRO, F. deP., EVANS, A.S., WOODALL, J.P., OPTON, E. M., EMMONS, J.E., WEST, B.S., EDSALL, G., DOWNS, W.G. & WALLACE, G.D. (1974) Evidence for persistence of infectious agents in isolated human populations. *Am. J. Epidemiol. 100*, 230–250

BURGESS, H.J.L. & BURGESS, A. (1975) A field worker's guide to a nutritional status survey. *Am. J. Clin. Nutr. 28*, 1299–1321

BURKITT, D.P. (1973) Some diseases characteristic of modern western civilization. *Clin. Radiol. 24*, 271–280

BUZINA, R. & UEMURA, K. (1974) Selection of the minimum anthropometric characteristics to assess nutritional status, in *Nutrition and Malnutrition* (Roche, A.F. & Falkner, F., eds.), pp. 271–285, Plenum Press, New York & London

CALLEN, E.O. (1973) Dietary patterns in Mexico between 6500 BC and 1580 AD, in *Man and His Foods* (Smith, C.E., Jr., ed.), The University of Alabama Press, Alabama

CARROLL, K.K. & KHOR, H.T. (1975) Dietary fat in relation to tumorigenesis. *Prog. Biochem. Pharmacol. 10*, 308–353

COALE, A.J. (1972) *The Growth and Structure of Human Populations: a Mathematical Investigation*, Princeton University Press, Princeton, New Jersey

DUMOND, D.E. (1975) The limitation of human population: a natural history. *Science (Wash. D.C.) 187*, 713–721

DUNN, F.L. (1968) Epidemiological factors: health and disease in hunter-gatherers, in *Man the Hunter* (Lee, R.B. & DeVore, I., eds.), pp. 221–228, Aldine, Chicago

DYKE, B. & MacCLUER, J.W. (eds.) (1973) *Computer Simulation in Human Population Studies*, Academic Press, New York & London

ESCHE, H.I.D. & LEE, R.B. (1975) Is maximal optimal? Reflections on overnutrition, under-development, and the size of human beings. Paper presented at American Anthropological Association Annual Meetings, San Francisco, California

HASSAN, F.A. (1975) Determination of the size, density, and growth rate of hunting-gathering populations, in *Population, Ecology, and Social Evolution* (Polgar, S., ed.), pp. 27–49, Mouton, The Hague

HOWELL, N. (1973) An empirical perspective on simulation models of human population, in *Computer Simulation in Human Population Studies* (Dyke, B. & MacCluer, J.W., eds.), pp. 43–57, Academic Press, New York & London

ISAAC, G. (1975) The diet of early man: aspects of archaeological evidence from lower and middle pleistocene sites in Africa. *World Archeol. 2*, 278–299

JELLIFFE, D.B. (1966) The assessment of the nutritional status of the community. *W.H.O. Monogr. Ser.* No. 53

KEYFITZ, N. & FLIEGER, W. (1971) *Population: Facts and Methods of Demography*, University of Chicago Press, Chicago

KING, J.W. & FAULKNER, W.R. (eds.) (1973) Laboratory tests for the assessment of nutritional status. *CRC Crit. Rev. Clin. Lab. Sci. 4*, 215–340

LEE, R.B. (1968) What hunters do for a living, or, How to make out on scarce resources, in *Man the Hunter* (Lee, R.B. & DeVore, I., eds.), pp. 30–48, Aldine, Chicago

LEE, R.B. (1973) Mongongo: the ethnography of a major wild food resource. *Ecology of Food and Nutrition 2*, 307–321

LOTKA, A.J. (1956, orig. 1924) *Elements of Mathematical Biology*, Dover, New York

MCCARTHY, D. & MCARTHUR, M. (1960) The food quest and the time factor in aboriginal economic life, in *Records of the Australian-American Expedition to Arnhem Land*, vol. 2: *Anthropology and Nutrition* (Mountford, C.P., ed.), Melbourne University Press, Melbourne

MACCLUER, J.W., NEEL, J.V. & CHAGNON, N.A. (1971) Demographic structure of a primitive population: a simulation. *Am. J. Phys. Anthropol. 35*, 193–208

NEEL, J.V. & WEISS, K.M. (1974) The genetic structure of a tribal population, the Yanomama Indians. *Am. J. Phys. Anthropol. 42*, 25–52

NEEL, J.V., SALZANO, F.M., JUNQUEIRA, P.C., KEITER, F. & MAYBURY-LEWIS, D. (1964) Studies on the Xavante Indians of the Brazilian Mato Grosso. *Hum. Genet. 16*, 52–140

NEEL, J.V., ANDRADE, A.H.P., BROWN, G.E., EVELAND, W.E., GOOBER, J., SODEMAN, W.A., Jr, STOLLERMAN, G.H., WEINSTEIN, E.D. & WHEELER, A.H. (1968) Further studies of the Xavante Indians. IX. Immunologic status with respect to various diseases and organisms. *Am. J. Trop. Med. Hyg. 17*, 486–498

PORRES, J.M., D'AMBRA, C., LORD, D. & GARRITY, F. (1975) Comparison of eight kits for the diagnosis of pregnancy. *Am. J. Clin. Pathol. 64*, 452–463

SAHA, N. & KIRK, R.L. (1973) A simple technique for collecting blood for population studies of enzyme polymorphisms and haemoglobins. *Hum. Hered. 23*, 182–187

SAHLINS, M. (1972) *Stone Age Economics*, Aldine, Chicago

SCHMIDT, R.M., BROSIOUS, G.M., HOLLAND, S., WRIGHT, J.M. & SERGEANT, G.R. (1976) The use of blood specimens collected on filter paper in screening for abnormal hemoglobins. *Clin. Chem. 22*, 685–687

SCHMIDT-GOLLWITZER, M. & SAXENA, B.B. (1975) Radioimmunoassay of human prolactin (PRL). *Acta Endocrinol. 80*, 262–274

SECORD, C. (1972) in Hugh-Jones, P. *et al.* Medical studies among Indians of the Upper Xingu. *Br. J. Hosp. Med. 3*, 317–334

SHYROCK, H.S. & SIEGEL, J.S. (1971) *The Methods and Materials of Demography*, 2 vols., U.S. Bureau of the Census, Government Printing Office, Washington, D.C.

STEPHENSON, G.R., SMITH, D.P.B. & ROBERTS, T.W. (1975) The SSR system: an open format event recording system with computerized transcription. *Behav. Res. Methods Inst. 7*, 497–515

STINI, W.A. (1975) The limits of human adaptability and how to exceed them with the best of intentions. Paper presented at American Anthropological Association Annual Meetings, San Francisco, California

STOLNITZ, G.J. (1956) *Life Tables from Limited Data: A Demographic Approach*, Princeton University Press, Princeton, New Jersey

TRUSWELL, A.S. & HANSEN, J.D.L. (1968) Medical and nutritional studies of !Kung Bushmen in North-West Botswana: a preliminary report. *S. Afr. Med. J. 42*, 1338–1339

TRUSWELL, A.S., KENNELLY, B.M., HANSEN, J.D.L. & LEE, R.G. (1972) Blood pressures of !Kung bushmen in Northern Botswana. *Am. Heart J. 84*, 5–12

WARREN, K.S. & MAHMOUD, A.A.F. (1975 & 1976) Algorithms in the diagnosis and management of exotic diseases I-XX. *J. Infect. Dis. 131–134*

WEHMEYER, A.S., LEE, R.B. & WHITING, M. (1969) The nutrient composition and dietary importance of some vegetable foods eaten by the !Kung Bushmen. *S. Afr. Med. J. 43*, 1529–1532

WEINER, J.S. & LOURIE, J.A. (1969) *Human Biology: A Guide to Field Methods*, Davis, Philadelphia

Weinhouse, S. (ed.) (1975) Symposium: nutrition in the causation of cancer. *Cancer Res. 35* (11), part 2

Weiss, K.M. (1973a) *Demographic Models for Anthropology* (Memoirs of the Society for American Archaeology, No. 27) *American Antiquity 38*, 1–88

Weiss, K.M. (1973b) A method for approximating age-specific fertility in the construction of life tables for anthropological populations. *Hum. Biol. 45*, 195–210

Wiesenfeld, S.L. (1967) Sickle cell trait in human biological and cultural evolution. *Science (Wash. D.C.) 157*, 1134–1140

Zerfas, A.J. (1975) The insertion tape: a new circumference tape for use in nutritional assessment. *Am. J. Clin. Nutr. 28*, 782–787

Discussion

Weiner: It is good to hear about these technical developments in recording systems. They represent a substantial advance over what we could recommend in the International Biological Programme (Weiner & Lourie 1969). Do you have anything in the way of a really portable X-ray machine yet? This would help greatly in determining the ages of children, for example.

Lozoff: We have not used portable X-ray equipment.

Polunin: Can you tell us more about the sort of observations you have made?

Lozoff: We are interested in developing techniques for the comprehensive assessment of the health of isolated populations. We have collected behavioural, demographic, nutritional, genetic and haematological data with the equipment I described. The SSR system has been used to study mother–infant interaction and infant-feeding practices; we are relating these behavioural observations to demographic and nutritional patterns (B. Lozoff & G. Brittenham, unpublished work 1976). The portable laboratory apparatus has made possible the investigation of nutritional anaemias and the haematological manifestations of haemoglobinopathies, as well as the preservation of specimens for subsequent detailed analysis (Brittenham *et al.* 1977).

Neel: It is a problem in such studies to decide how much to do in the field and how much to do in the base laboratory later. Something that is simple to do in a good laboratory can become very difficult in the field. We have rather adopted the opposite strategy to you, Dr Lozoff, and have concentrated on getting our specimens out of the area by light plane and bringing them home as rapidly as possible. As an example, doing histocompatibility typing in the field presented a lot of problems but we have now established that one can do it by harvesting the buffy coat from a blood specimen treated with an anticoagulant, up to five days after collecting the blood. We therefore did the histocompatibility typing in Ann Arbor, not up the Amazon!

Lozoff: Three considerations lead us to do studies in the field. First, certain critical haematological determinations must be done promptly if they are to be accurate. Second, such determinations make possible the immediate diagnosis and treatment of some common medical problems. Finally, individuals who require more extensive investigations can be identified and evaluated without delay.

Harrison: You mentioned briefly the problem of measuring energy expenditure. It seems to me that for the three problems that you identified and, indeed, in any type of situation where you are attempting to obtain a holistic view of the ecology of a human group, you need to know about energy expenditure in detail. Are you dealing with this problem?

Lozoff: Not yet.

Weiner: Measurements of energy expenditure are crucial in answering many of these questions, and for this we want more than a job analysis, such as you can achieve with your SSR system. What is also required is a really reliable portable technique to measure oxygen consumption in the field, with a job analysis, because you will have of course to calibrate the energy cost of jobs to obtain a daily energy total. That breakthrough on oxygen consumption is now on the horizon. Heinz Wolff of the Bioengineering Laboratory at the Clinical Research Centre in the UK has developed the paramagnetic method for oxygen determination built into the mouthpiece of a spirometer so one can make a continuous recording of oxygen consumption, almost breath by breath. Other methods for measuring oxygen utilization by sampling from the mouthpiece are cumbersome and slow.

Woodburn: Don't pulse-rate recording devices give a reasonably accurate figure?

Weiner: They are not as reliable as one would like, although the one now in general use (the Miniature Analog Tape Recorder, Oxford Instrument Co.) is better; but that too has to be calibrated in order to convert total pulse rate into energy consumption, which depends on the person's physique and training. I would prefer the direct method of monitoring the job in terms of oxygen consumed.

Harrison: To turn to a more theoretical point, I would just question the assumption that hunter–gatherers in general are characteristically small in size. I suppose this may be true of Africa now, but it certainly wasn't true of the Upper Palaeolithic period, and it isn't true of the Eskimo or the Plains Indian, or the Australian Aborigines.

Lozoff: I would like to emphasize that hunters and gatherers seem to be small only in relation to the heavier, taller populations which have appeared in industrialized societies in the past century. This recently increased stature has generally been thought to reflect human genetic potential for growth, given good nutrition and freedom from infection. If the diet of hunter–gatherers has been truly adequate, then why did they not also realize this growth potential?

Woodburn: There is a real issue here. If we look at Africa and India and South-East Asia, where there are contiguous populations of hunters and gatherers and non-hunting populations, it does seem to be true that in a striking number of instances the hunters and gatherers are smaller in stature and lighter in weight. In the other areas mentioned, Australia and the Arctic, the hunting and gathering populations were not, before the intervention of Europeans, in general in close contact with agricultural populations and so one doesn't have the same obvious basis for comparison. The issue needs close and careful investigation and the possible selective advantages of short stature and light weight for hunting and gathering should be considered.

Truswell: I agree with Dr Harrison; I don't think that all hunter–gatherers have necessarily always been small; some have been of medium height. Certainly they haven't been as tall as present-day Americans or Swedes, but then nobody ever has been!

Lozoff: That is the critical point.

Weiner: I would add that although it is a well-balanced diet in terms of proteins, it is also a precarious diet in terms of calories and is highly dependent on the game supply, which can be affected by drought in an unpredictable way.

Woodburn: If one were talking only about hunters and gatherers living in temperate and polar climates that might be so, but most of the studies of tropical and sub-tropical hunters and gatherers give an opposite picture (see, for example, Lee & DeVore 1968). Moreover, we are bound to find plenty of variation in food availability and nutritional status between hunting and gathering groups as more research is done. But it is unlikely that we shall find very many in which the overall food supply is precarious at any time of the year. The present evidence suggests that periodic famine is far more characteristic of agricultural and pastoral societies than it is of hunters and gatherers.

Truswell: P. V. Tobias in Johannesburg has been investigating the secular change in the height of the Kalahari Bushmen. There has been an increase in height for the last two generations (Tobias 1975), if not more (Tobias 1962). One problem is that the earlier physical anthropologists were inclined, if they saw someone rather tall, to say that he was obviously not a pure-bred Bushman, and therefore not to measure him, but we hope this can be sorted out now that we know the populations better. I certainly saw exceptional individuals at least as tall as I am (5ft 9in). At the same time, there are other populations in other parts of the world (not hunter–gatherers) whose height appears to be decreasing (Tobias 1975). So it is important to consider the date when you examine people.

Lozoff: Almost all studies of pre-agricultural populations have been short-term prevalence studies; carefully designed long-term incidence studies are urgently needed.

Woodburn: There is an acute practical difficulty of who you measure in such studies. In a hunting and gathering group, do you include immigrants from agricultural societies who are now contributing to the gene pool and are likely to stay with the group, or do you omit them because their ancestry is different? Different investigators work in different ways and the trouble is in getting data that can be compared. It seems to be particularly true of Pygmy groups that there has been a tendency in the studies to leave out people who didn't fit the paradigm of being short in stature. Even when the paradigms are shed, we have to decide clearly in each instance whether to measure the breeding population including immigrants, whether to search out and exclude known immigrants, or whether to go even further and to exclude all those with any known immigrant ancestry.

Hamilton: Longitudinal studies measuring multiple variables with different distributions which may or may not be discrete, according to how variables or groups are defined, create major difficulties in repeatability and quality control for data collection. How have you approached these problems?

Lozoff: Formal estimates of both intra-observer and inter-observer reliability are obviously essential if observations with any system like SSR are to be trustworthy, and we are making these estimates.

White: Dr Lozoff has talked about the portability of her recording equipment; I want to say something about the portability of babies! There seems to be evidence that in some societies where mothers carry their babies constantly these children are below optimal weight between the ages of nine months and about $2^1/_2$ years, though I would not claim direct causal connection. Australian Aboriginal babies have birth weights on average below those of European babies (Parsons 1964); they catch up by six or seven months but after that they tend to fall seriously behind again (Kirke 1974, pp. 86–87). As I shall discuss further in my paper (pp. 269–292), when white nursing sisters try to teach the Aboriginal mothers how to wean and feed their babies, and show the larger white babies to them, the Aboriginal mothers have asked 'but how would we carry them?' I think this is where their babies get their bad start in life; at these ages before they are walking when the mothers have to carry them everywhere, the increase in the baby's weight must take into account the pressure on the mother. We have observed that the mothers do not give their infants and toddlers as much food as the health educators advise, and I believe that paediatricians and dieticians should keep portability in mind when planning and recommending infant diets for societies that do not use wheels to move children around.

Stanley: This has not been my experience, also working with Australian Aboriginal people. I have always associated the falling-off of weight at 6–9 months with the decrease in the mother's breast milk and even the coming of another child at the end of the first year. A lot of the old practices which controlled fertility have changed and the mothers are now having pregnancies almost every year instead of every 2–3 years (Moodie 1973). The infants succumb to infections as soon as they come off the breast, and then their weight curves begin to fall, by comparison with white Australian growth curves (Kettle 1966). I have never heard a mother complain about the weight of a child.

Black: We have been measuring the weight of Kayapo Amerindian infants (Black *et al.* 1976). They seem to be small up to six months, but they gain weight, so that by 2–3 years they approach Caucasian standards. This is the reverse of what you are saying for the Australian Aborigines.

Stanley: Not really, because the Aborigines are small but have the same growth pattern as the Whites; then their growth falls off, so the graphs diverge. They are smaller-for-dates, if you like, than the white babies.

Black: The adult Kayapo may be up to six feet tall, and the average while less than the average Caucasian seems to be much *taller* than the more acculturated Indians.

Haraldson: We have a nomadic population in northern-most Scandinavia, the Lapps, who are smaller than the other Scandinavians by about ten centimetres; the newborn are 1–2 cm shorter than newborn Swedish babies. If they are put on a Swedish diet from childhood they will be about the same size as other Swedes by the time they grow up. We know that the food in Lapp societies is perfect for protein but we don't know about the rest of the diet, although they are known to have plenty of calories all year round. But there must be something about their diet that we don't understand. One should add that there are *no* pure races any longer; the Lapps are not genetically a pure race, but a considerable mixture. Fewer than 25% of them are pure.

Harrison: I was impressed by the way Dr Lozoff posed her three questions, and then discussed how one might go about answering them. It is vital that asking the question comes first, and that what you measure and on whom you measure it follows from that. With populations that are in danger of not surviving, one rightly tends to collect as much information as possible without any particular question in mind. But in general I think it vital that one has a question first, which dictates the technology used and who you measure.

Lozoff: In these small societies this is even *more* important, because if a question can be answered elsewhere, one should do it elsewhere; these disrupted communities have enough problems without the addition of inessential research.

References

BLACK, F.L., HIERHOLZER, W.J., BLACK, D.P., LAMM, S.H. & LUCAS, L. (1976) Nutritional status of Brazilian Kayapo Indians. *Hum. Biol.*, in press

BRITTENHAM, G., LOZOFF, B., HARRIS, J.W. & NARASIMHAN, S. (1977) Sickle cell anemia and trait in a population of southern India. *Am. J. Hematol. 2*, 25–32

KETTLE, E.S. (1966) Weight and height curves for Australian Aboriginal infants and children. *Med. J. Aust. 1*, 972–977

KIRKE, D.K. (1974) The traditionally oriented community, in *Better Health for Aborigines* (Hetzel, B.S., Dobbin, M., Lippmann, L. & Eggleston, E., eds.) (Report of a National Seminar at Monash University), University of Queensland Press, Brisbane

LEE, R.B. & DEVORE, I. (eds.) (1968) *Man the Hunter*, Aldine, Chicago

MOODIE, P.M. (1973) *Aboriginal Health*, pp. 26–39, Australian National University Press, Canberra

PARSONS, P.A. (1964) Birth-weights in the Pitjantjatjara tribe of the Australian Aborigine. *Oceania 35*, 144–146

TOBIAS, P.V. (1962) On the increasing stature of the Bushmen. *Anthropos 57*, 801–810

TOBIAS, P.V. (1975) Stature and secular trend among southern African Negroes and San (Bushmen). *S. Afr. J. Med. Sci. 40*, 145–164

WEINER, J.S. & LOURIE, J.A. (1969) *Human Biology: a Guide to Field Methods*, International Biological Programme (IBP) Handbook No. 9, Blackwell Scientific Publications, Oxford

Urgent opportunistic observations: the study of changing, transient and disappearing phenomena of medical interest in disrupted primitive human communities

D. CARLETON GAJDUSEK

National Institutes of Health, Bethesda, Maryland

Abstract Two newly identified foci of usually rare disease occurring in high incidence in isolated primitive populations of West New Guinea are discussed as examples of medical problems that demand immediate intensive investigation because the unique naturally occurring experiments they represent are soon likely to be altered. These are: (1) amyotrophic lateral sclerosis, Parkinsonism, and dementia syndromes in a small population of Auyu and Jakai peoples in the Lowlands, and (2) an epidemic of burns from cysticercosis epilepsy from newly introduced *Taenia solium* in pigs in the Ekari people of the Wissel Lakes in the Highlands. A third new example is a focus of male pseudohermaphroditism among the Simbari Anga in the Highlands of Papua New Guinea. These are presented along with a series of eleven further examples of the kind of problems that require urgent opportunistic observation because of the extreme changes that investigation and therapeutic and preventive efforts themselves, as well as the inevitable effects of acculturation, will evoke from the moment an investigator or other outsider from a technologically advanced culture enters the previously isolated community.

There are no longer primitive peoples or tribal societies unaware of the existence of the 'civilized world'; the passage overhead of aeroplanes and the appearance of manufactured items by trade routes have already brought at least some awareness of the cosmopolitan world to all bands of hunter–gatherers or fisherfolk, or hoe and digging-stick agriculturists, who have been truly isolated into modern times. Many, such as the Guayaki of Paraguay and the Dem of West New Guinea Highlands, have had extensive intimate contact with Europeans in their past only to lose the knowledge of this experience from their tribal memory—in the case of the Guayaki in Jesuit 'reducciones' in the seventeenth century, and in the case of the Dem with a huge Dutch military and anthropological expedition a half-century ago.

Present-day isolation rarely implies similar isolation over past centuries, even for what are now the most primitive groups. In fact, there are many examples of groups becoming hunter–gatherers from peoples who were previously settled agriculturalists and of populations with extremely primitive material cultures who were derived from technologically more advanced groups. Illiterate cultures have developed from peoples who were once highly literate even in the last several centuries of western history, as in the case of some small groups of Europeans settled in remote regions of both the North and South American continents. Thus, 'primitiveness' today may not always imply a similar technologically impoverished or unadvanced culture in the distant past. Moreover, no isolated group or band of mankind of which we have learned has been cut off from all gene flow from the outside for many centuries.

Then again, the culture and world view of any primitive group is disrupted severely by the very nature of our medical and anthropological inquiries with the appearance among them of men (including investigators) who do not belong to the group and who represent so obviously a different level of technological development, an observation which the primitive people make immediately. Even if these brief and strange contacts do not outwardly disrupt culture and traditional practices, they instantly tell the young members of the society that there are men in the world whose behaviour is not comprehended and whose skills and abilities are not understood by their elders. The beliefs of their people and their 'tribal vision' have been proved to them to be inadequate.

A changing way of life may not affect greatly or quickly the possibility of studying many problems of medical interest in 'tribal' or primitive cultures, particularly the genetic structure of the population, which can often be studied as well a decade after early contact as in the first year of contact. Medical problems most worthy of immediate attention are those most vulnerable to the changes brought in, through loss of isolation, by government, mission and commercial influences as well as by the investigators themselves.

I cite a few examples of such phenomena which must be studied early, often while they are changing, if at all:

1. Virginal status with respect to certain pathogenic microorganisms which are nearly universal in more cosmopolitan cultures, such as total 'virgin soil' susceptibility to measles, mumps, rubella, tuberculosis, influenza, or adenovirus infections. This may include discovery of 'partial virginal status'—a nominally contradictory designation—by which we mean complete susceptibility to a specific organism in all persons of ages from infancy through some age in adolescence or adult life, but not in still older people in groups which may in the past have had experience with the given virus or other infectious agent, but have not encountered it again for many years (Adels & Gajdusek 1963; Brown *et al.* 1969*a*). Studies of the antibody response to vaccine in such virginal populations give confirmation of their virginal status and data on the response of the people to live viruses with attenuated virus vaccines and to killed virus antigens with other vaccines (Brown *et al.* 1965; Brown *et al.* 1969*b*).

2. Extreme deficiency of sodium and near toxic levels of potassium in the diet in inland salt-poor populations and the adrenal cortical and renal function shifts made to compensate for such low sodium, high potassium intakes by extreme sodium-sparing in urine, sweat, and faeces, and during lactation (Gajdusek 1970).

3. Specific forms of culturally patterned hysteria and other psychiatric disorders which change in form and content soon after new social influences are introduced. A specific example: Melanesian village 'wild man' or 'longlong' behaviour (Gajdusek & Meyer 1977) is rapidly replaced by westernized schizophrenic reactions soon after the early phases of 'westernization'.

4. Odd psychosexual patterns and adjustments which are promptly altered with mission and government influence. Thus, in many Highland New Guinea cultures men never slept in the houses of their wife or wives, and restricted sexual intercourse to daylight in the privacy of forest-enclosed gardens, themselves sleeping in men's houses at night. Some New Guinea cultures practised extremely promiscuous heterosexual activity even at prepubertal ages; in others, such as the Fore and many Sepik and Western Highland groups, long sexual abstinence extending far into or through adolescence and practised for long periods in married life was instead the rule. Marriages in some New Guinea cultures were consummated in very early puberty, for girls in some groups, such as the Chimbu, and for boys in others, such as the adjacent Awa and Gimi. Yet others, such as the Etoro and the Anga, institutionalized an active long-lasting homosexuality for all male youths who all adjust later to an arranged marriage, often based on sister exchange with the companions of their men's house days (Gajdusek 1964a). With the introduction of schools and Christian mission and government intervention, all these patterns are rapidly replaced by a more western family residence style of life and the complex psychosexual practices and adjustments of the precontact period can no longer be investigated (Gajdusek 1959–1977).

5. Psychosocial reactions to natural catastrophe, such as the destruction of homeland which has just (1976) resulted from a severe earthquake totally destroying villages and all gardening areas in the Eipomek valley of West New Guinea's Central Highlands (W. Schiefenhoeval, personal communication 1977); or the loss of traditional land in volcanic action, as among the group around Mount Lamington in Papua; or the Tongariki–Tongoa Shepherd Island cataclysm of several centuries ago (Gajdusek et al. 1967; Espirat et al. 1973); or the destruction by typhoon of the entire coral island as a habitable place for the community, as that which recently struck Merir in the Western Caroline Islands, leaving it a deserted island.

6. The social responses to epidemics and plagues of disease need to be studied

quickly. Specific examples of these are the more than decimation of a population
by a chronic degenerative disease such as kuru in the Eastern Highlands of
New Guinea (Gajdusek 1973, 1976; Gajdusek & Zigas 1957, 1959; Zigas &
Gajdusek 1957) or the intense foci of motor neuron disease, or of congenital
deaf-mutism with feeble-mindedness (Gajdusek & Garruto 1975); sudden
severe outbreaks of so-called virgin soil epidemics of measles, rubella, cholera
or influenza; the explosive de-populating effects of the introduction of venereal
disease in peculiar cultural settings, such as that of donovanosis in the Goilala
of Papua (Zigas 1971), or lymphogranuloma venereum to the Marind Anim
(Kooijman *et al.* 1958; van Baal 1966), or of gonorrhoea on Rennell and Bellona
Islands (Simmons & Gajdusek 1966).

7. The variation from culture to culture in violence, homicide, and suicide,
and the role these play in a culture are worthy of study. Other psychosocial
phenomena requiring urgent study, since cultural change soon alters their pattern, are the culturally stereotyped hysterical equivalent reactions or mass hys-
terias, on the one hand involving single individuals, in such patterns as those of
running amok or falling into latah, trance states, ritual clowning, or convulsive
seizures of lulu (Rodrique 1963) or, on the other hand, involving whole groups
of many members in patterned mass attacks of tremors or dancing or laughing
manias, and cargo cults or Messianic movements.

8. Alternative forms of cognitive style, including different modes of per-
ception, which change quickly on contact with such civilization. Such changes
are occasioned by the introduction of a verbal numbers system to people
who do not use language to count, or who do not calculate using writing or even
verbal numbers. Such rapid changes in cognitive style can also be brought about
by suddenly bringing a primitive people into familiarity with pictures and photographs, with the principle of the wheel and screw, or with the sudden accustoming
of the people to planar surfaces and right angles in manufactured articles of the
civilized world, and in the construction of dwellings with such planes and right
angles. In but the past several decades there were still many cultures which did
not draw on planar surfaces and were without such preferred use of the hori-
zontal or vertical in observing pictured material; which were without knowledge
of the wheel or screw, or without experience with the preferred use of planes
and right angles in construction or manufacture. Few such people are left. Thus,
such phenomena as learning to study pictures and to read with the work page
or pictures at any orientation to the visual field, even upside down, as usually
occurs early after contact, are rapidly corrected into a conventional 'established'
manner of viewing and using the picture or work page. The system of nonverbal
computation and number memory without a verbal counting system, and the
methods of pattern recognition and of learning where verbal transformation and

other 'modelling' are not given high preference as they are in western schools, are difficult matters to study and they change rapidly during the period of any such study (Gajdusek 1964c, 1969; Rubinstein & Gajdusek 1970).

9. Extreme iodine deficiency causing cretinoid defects in the central nervous system and deaf-mutism in areas of endemic goitre, and the presence of asymptomatic iodine deficiency in other 'pregoitrous' populations which make them very vulnerable to minor further iodine depletions (Gajdusek & Garruto 1975). An example in case is that of the explosive epidemic appearance of endemic goitre and cretinism with European entry into the Jimi River Valley in Papua New Guinea caused by the replacement with uniodized European trade salt of the traditional salt from mineral springs, which had been the only source of iodine for the already severely depleted, but still asymptomatic populace (Pharoah 1971).

10. Odd deficiencies and excesses in diet resulting from feasting and fasting, or near starvation occasioned by the vicissitudes of fortune in the hunting and gathering band, or from the sequential ripening of wild or cultivated crops among the primitive agriculturalists. These may include such phenomena as diastasis recti in toddlers and the resulting mid-epigastric herniae and lipomata of adults, occasioned by the necessary stuffing which is required when meals are infrequent and composed of high carbohydrate bulky foods low in fat and protein (Sorenson & Gajdusek 1966), and other problems, such as metabolic balance and work efficiency associated with low fat, protein and salt intake and low body weight (Gajdusek 1970).

11. Unusual toxic exposure from drug usage or pica (dirt eating) or specific environmental toxins in the diet or drinking water, as occur with kava in its excessive cult use in Tanna and Tongariki in the New Hebrides (Gajdusek 1967), or with intoxicating snuff by the South American Indians, or toxic bean poisoning or toxic limbun poisoning in New Guinea, or goitrogens in the diet in many parts of the world. Such intoxications may be found also in the domestic or wild animals, as well as in man. As a corollary of this, the ethnozoological and ethnobotanical and, especially, the ethnopharmacological lore of the people should be scrupulously recorded in detail, with the relevant wild or cultivated species collected and identified.

I will now provide three examples of medical situations which have provoked my own urgent opportunistic investigation in recent years: (1) amyotrophic lateral sclerosis, Parkinsonism, and dementia syndromes occurring in high incidence in a small isolated Lowland population of West New Guinea; (2) the epidemic occurrence of burns from cysticercosis-induced epilepsy as the result of the new introduction of *Taenia solium* into the pigs in the Central Highlands of West New Guinea; and (3) male pseudohermaphroditism with ambiguity

of the external genitalia in high incidence and the associated problems of sex
role indentification in a culture with prolonged homosexual activity in their
male child-rearing rituals and practices in the Papua New Guinea Highlands.

FOCUS OF HIGH INCIDENCE OF AMYOTROPHIC LATERAL SCLEROSIS
ASSOCIATED WITH A HIGH INCIDENCE OF PARKINSONISM AND DEMENTIA
SYNDROMES IN A SMALL POPULATION OF AUYU AND JAKAI WEST NEW
GUINEANS

I have encountered an extraordinarily high incidence of classical amyotrophic
lateral sclerosis (ALS; motor neuron disease) in a population of under 5000 Auyu
and Jakai people living in small communities along rivers in the flat inland
jungles of southern West New Guinea (Irian Jaya), Indonesia. This discovery
of twenty-four current typical cases of rapidly progressive motor neuron disease
in this small Auyu population on surveys in 1974 and 1976, with a history of at

TABLE 1

Amyotrophic lateral sclerosis, Parkinsonism and myoclonic dementia: patients currently
active at time of chronic neurological disease survey in Edera and Obaa Districts, West New
Guinea, April–May 1974 and March 1976

No.	Name	Sex/age	Village	Linguistic group	River	Population
Amyotrophic lateral sclerosis						
1.	Ka	M/35	Yagatsu		Paru	300
2.	A.G.	M/28	Gauda		Passue	300
3.	U.	M/30	Taim		Passue	150
4.	Is	M/30	Gaiyu (Gaime)		Mappi	150
5.	Un.	M/30	Yare (from Namun)		Mappi	300
6.	Te	F/37	Yare (from Namun)		Mappi	
7.	F.W.	F/34	Taigaimon (from Konebi)		Mappi	300
8.	A.A.G.	F/35	Yeloba		Bangi	250
9.	P.A.	M/30	Yeloba		Bangi	
10.	J.N.	M/35	Asset		Ia	300
11.	Ha	M/40	Osso		Ia	250
12.	Ya	M/45	Osso		Ia	
13.	Bu	F/50	Bosuma	Auyu	Ia	250
14.	Ke	M/60	Bosuma		Ia	
15.	S.A.	F/30	Bosuma		Ia	
16.	Ba	M/35	Bosuma		Ia	
17.	Unk.	F/Ad	Ogorito		Ia	200
18.	C.M.	F/28	Siyen		Dumut	300
19.	At	F/35	Siyen		Dumut	
20.	Ko	F/45	Muya		Dumut	180
21.	D.W.	M/40	Muya		Dumut	
22.	Ye	F/35	Sagapikia		Edera	200
23.	M.K.	F/25	Gogoia (Khogoya)		Edera	200
24.	Ga	M/45	Maki (Harapan)		Edera	150

TABLE 1, *continued*

Parkinsonism						
1.	B.B.	F/60	Geturki	⎫	Ia	250
2.	B.W.	M/45	Asset	⎬ Auyu	Ia	300
3.	Ba	M/45	Muya	⎮	Dumut	180
4.	D.D.	M/48	Siyen	⎭	Dumut	300
Myoclonic dementia						
1.	J.Y.	M/45	Yatan	Jakai	Obaa	300

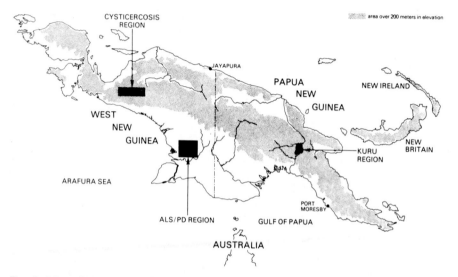

FIG. 1. Map of New Guinea showing the location of three areas of epidemic neurological diseases under investigation. These are, from west to east:

The focus of epidemic burns and epilepsy caused by cysticercosis from the new introduction of *Taenia solium* into their pigs (the area is inhabited by the Ekari and Moni people around the Wissel Lakes area of the West New Guinea Highland).

The area of high incidence of amyotrophic lateral sclerosis, Parkinsonism and dementia syndromes among the Auyu and Jakai people in the West New Guinea Lowlands.

The kuru region in the Eastern Highlands of Papua New Guinea.

least a similarly high prevalence over the past decade, confirms and extends the preliminary observations made fifteen years ago of a high incidence of motor neuron disease (ALS) in Jakai and Auyu-speaking peoples in this same area (Gajdusek 1963). It has now been possible to determine the precise limits of this small focus, since no other case of ALS has been found in the surrounding population of over 45 000 indigenous New Guineans of the same and related Auyu and of other cultural and linguistic groups after extensive search for

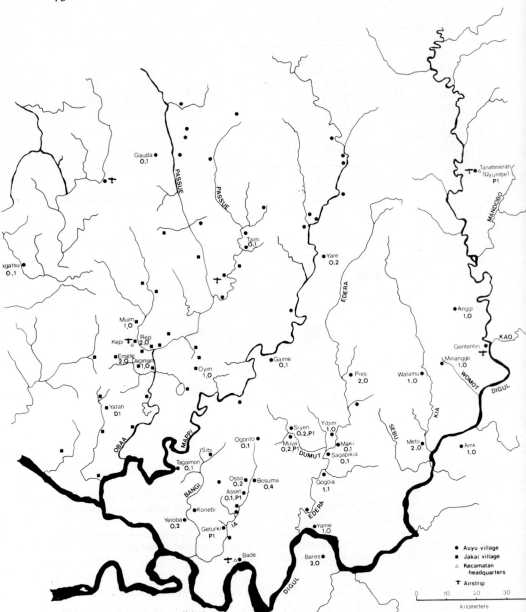

FIG. 2. Distribution of amyotrophic lateral sclerosis, Parkinsonism and bradykinetic dementia patients in the Obaa and Edera Districts of southern West New Guinea. There were 17 ALS patients in the 1962 survey and 24 in the 1974 and 1976 survey; and a total of five Parkinsonism and one dementia patients. Auyu villages are shown as black circles, Jakai villages as black squares. District administration centres at Bade, Kepi, Tanahmerah and Gententiri are shown.

→

neurological disease conducted with the same intensity as that pursued in the affected area (see Table 1).

In the population affected with ALS I also found in 1974 four cases of Parkinsonism, in which it was impossible to make a concomitant diagnosis of ALS (Table 1). Several of the ALS patients, however, did demonstrate rest tremors, rigidity and other basal gangliar symptoms, and two showed marked bradykinesis with progressive dementia, reminiscent of the Parkinsonism-dementia syndrome (Mulder *et al.* 1954; Hirano *et al.* 1961) in the focus of high incidence ALS in Chamorro Micronesians on the islands of Guam and Rota (Arnold *et al.* 1953; Kurland & Mulder 1954; Reed & Brody 1975; Reed *et al.* 1975). These additional neurological degenerative syndromes were also not encountered even sporadically in the large surrounding population free of ALS.

A summary of the locations and other data on the 24 patients with ALS, four with Parkinsonism, and one with a progressive dementia with myoclonus, whom I found during my surveys in April and May 1974 and in March 1976 of neurological diseases in the Edera and Obaa Districts of West New Guinea, is presented in the maps (Figs. 1 and 2) and in Table 1. Patients 11, 18, 19 and 22 are illustrated in Figs. 3–5. On the map in Fig. 2 we have tabulated the villages of residence of these patients as well as of the 20 ALS and one Parkinsonism patients from our 1962 survey.

All cases have occurred in Auyu and Jakai villages, but only in a small portion of the total number of villages which comprise each of these cultural and linguistic groups. In fact, the disease has been seen only in 27 Auyu villages with only about 6000 total inhabitants, and in six Jakai villages, which are larger than the Auyu villages and contain a total of about 2500 people. On some of the river drainages, however, such as the Bangi, Ia, Edera, Dumut, Kia, Womut, and lower Mappi, most villages are affected. All cases are from the drainages of rivers which flow into the Digul from the north, with the exception of Yagatsu, whose river drains northward to the Eilanden and Amk, Bares, and Uyumbe, which are just to the east and south of the Digul (see map, Fig. 2).

All of the affected Jakai villages and the Auyu village of Yagatsu lie in the Obaa District of Indonesian-administered Irian Jaya, which has a total population of about 10 000. All other Auyu villages lie in the Edera District, where the

---

←

Only villages in which patients with ALS, Parkinsonism and dementia have been found are named. Sibi and Konebi on the Kali Bangi and Yodom on the Kali Digul had no patients in either of my surveys but reported patients who had died before 1962 and between the two surveys. The number of patients found are listed according to the following code:

Number before the comma: number of ALS patients in 1962
Number after the comma: number of ALS patients in 1974 & 1976
Number after the P: number of Parkinsonism patients (both surveys)
Number after the D: number of dementia patients in 1974 & 1976

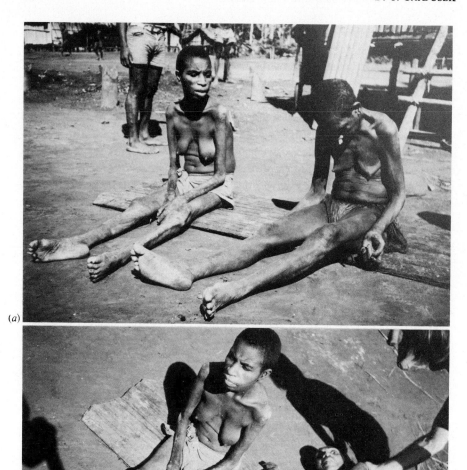

(a)

(b)

FIG. 3. Two Auyu women with advanced ALS in 1974 in the village of Siyen on the Kali Dumut, both living in the same household. Neither patient could walk without extensive support and the woman on the right with head drop could not maintain a sitting posture without falling over (b) (below). Both showed muscular fasciculations, pareses, atrophy and severe dysarthria; the woman on the right had marked hyperreflexia of deep tendon jerks and moderate mental slowing. They had been ill for 4 and 4¹/₂ years, respectively, and they both died in 1976.

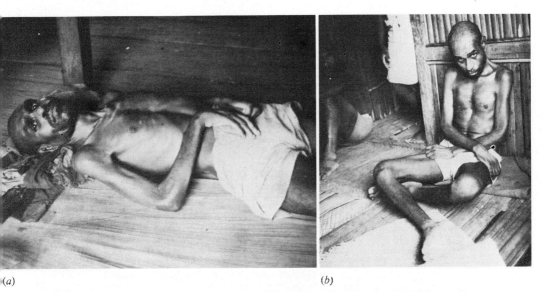

FIG. 4. An Auyu man with advanced ALS in 1974 from the Asset village on the Kali Ia. He had been ill for two years and showed severe fasciculation, marked muscular weakness and atrophy, hyperreflexia of deep tendon jerks, and dysarthria but no dementia. In the picture on the left (a) his arms, forearms and hands show severe muscular atrophy and in the view on the right (b), while sitting, he shows head drop and atrophy of his shoulder girdle muscles.

total population is about 7500. Kepi is the administrative centre and mission headquarters of the Obaa District, and Bade of the Edera District. Both are towns with about 1000 inhabitants. The whole area is low tidal sago swampland and the villages are built on low sandy hills which rise from ten to sixty feet above the level of the high tides. The villages in the Edera District, although on the shores of tidal streams, are mostly over one hundred river miles from the sea.

On numerous expeditions over the past fifteen years through all the surrounding groups, including all the Auyu and Asmat-related groups between the sea coast and the upper reaches of the Becking, Mappi, and Digul River drainages (Mandobo, Jaiir, Wanbom, Wangom, Kombai, Jakai, Kayagar, Sauwi, Atohwaem, Asmat, Tjitak cultural and linguistic groups), I have not seen any sporadic cases of ALS or Parkinsonism.

In the affected area the diet of the people does not differ in any recognizable way from that of much larger surrounding populations who are free of these degenerative disorders, and there is nothing we have detected that is unique to the ecology or culture of the affected peoples. The people still live a primitive life of subsistence farming, fishing, sago-making and food-gathering. They have had only a few decades of contact with the outside world.

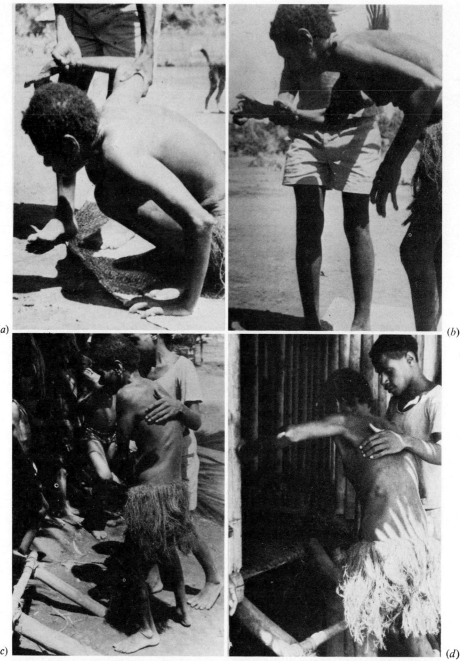

FIG. 5. An Auyu woman with advanced ALS in 1974 from the village of Sagapikia on the Kali Edera, who had been ill for $3^{1}/_{2}$ years and could no longer arise from sitting or climb into her home without assistance. Sequential views of her arising and entering her house show her severe muscular atrophy and weakness. She had marked fasciculations, hyperreactive deep tendon jerks, and severe dysarthria but no dementia. She died in 1976.

Detailed anamnesis has been difficult. With the assistance of Father Ben van Oers of the Sacred Heart Mission, who speaks the local Auyu language and has worked extensively in the area for many years, it has been possible to obtain clinical histories (confirmed by cross-checking with independent informants) of the same disease in at least the current high incidence over the past two decades in some villages. In others, the Auyu people resist giving any information about the past and we have no information, rather than negative reports. In a few instances it has been possible to obtain reports of cases linking the present survey with the more cursory survey of 1962, in which I discovered 13 cases of ALS from the same Auyu area, without visiting all the villages now studied. Information in 1962 indicated that the river basins where we now found cases in 1974 and 1976 were also affected at the time of the earlier, 1962, survey. At that time we also found seven patients from the Jakai Linguistic Group which is directly adjacent to the affected Auyu groups. These patients were from five Jakai villages: Muim, Rep, Emete, Dagiman, and Oyim villages.

Data on past experience with this easily described and recognized syndrome from patients and their relatives, and from other villagers, adds a few further villages to the list of those affected. Reports from the Catholic priests who have been resident in the region for several decades, and who have watched me examine the patients, confirm the occurrence of many past cases which I did not see, but which are reported by the Auyu and Jakai people. From the accounts of Fathers Schieperein and Dongen we have knowledge of the past occurrence of the disease in the villages of Sibi and Konebi on the Kali Banggi, the Digul tributary just west of the Kali Ia, and from the Jakai village of Yodom on the Kali Digul near Bade.

Even if the total population of the Edera and Obaa administrative districts (kecamatan) is taken as a baseline, including many villages not known ever to have been affected, the incidence rates are extraordinarily high. For the year 1974 prevalence in the affected villages was over 500 per 100 000 population, or about ten times that among the Chamorro people of Guam, or 1000 times that found in most other populations.

We now know that in the focus of ALS in southern West New Guinea new cases of ALS have continued to appear in about the same frequency throughout a period of over fifteen years, since I first reported this high incidence focus. The presence of Parkinsonian rigidity and Parkinsonism-like tremors in many of the ALS patients, and also of Parkinsonism without signs of associated motor neuron disease in the same villages affected by ALS, presents us once again with the simultaneous occurrence of both ALS and basal gangliar symptoms, together in the same patients or separately, in a single focus of high incidence of ALS. There is, however, no true Parkinsonism-dementia, such as we see on

Guam (Gibbs & Gajdusek 1972). This third geographic and ethnic isolate of high incidence motor neuron disease should thus be added to those we now know of among the Chamorro people on Guam (Mulder *et al.* 1954), and in Japanese on the Kii Peninsula (Yase *et al.* 1968).

Intensive investigations in the two latter foci for over two decades have failed to produce any solution to the ALS problem. Intensive clinical and laboratory investigations are more readily possible in the latter two foci than in West New Guinea, but continued surveillance of the situation in these remote Auyu and Jakai villages of West New Guinea is surely indicated.

EPIDEMIC OF BURNS FROM CYSTICERCUS EPILEPSY *(Taenia solium)* IN THE EKARI PEOPLE OF THE WISSEL LAKES

In 1974 two Indonesian physicians, Dr L. R. Tumada and Dr D. B. Subianto, working with the Ekari people who live in an area surrounding the Wissel Lakes in the Central Highlands of West New Guinea, were astonished at an epidemic of severe burns among older children and adults who were arriving for treatment at the Enarotali hospital on Lake Paniai. During the two previous years they had seen 75 patients with severe burns, 29 in 1972, and 46 in 1973. In 1971 they had seen only eight patients with such severe burns, and in earlier years they and their predecessors, Dutch physicians before 1961 and Indonesian physicians thereafter, had not seen more than a half-dozen such patients in any given year. The Catholic Mission Fathers and nursing Sisters, with several decades of perspective in the region, were similarly impressed by the epidemic proportions that the severe burns had assumed. In fact, many of their adult patients in 1972 and 1973 had burns of such severity that amputation of extremities was required. Burns of similar severity in previously healthy adults had not been seen earlier.

Most of the burns occurred at night when patients fell into the house fires in their traditional Ekari houses. Nights in these hamlets at 5000 feet elevation are cold and the people sleep beside their house fires. The physicians slowly realized that most of the severe burns were the result of grand mal epileptic seizures during which the unconscious patient was unable to withdraw from the house fire into which he rolled. Healthy sleepers who were burned could normally withdraw from the fire quickly enough so that their burns were less serious. Very few of these convulsing patients had a previous history of epilepsy. The physicians thus became aware that an epidemic of the new appearance of epilepsy in previously healthy adults was in progress.

While attending the convalescent burn patients in their hospital, observation of further convulsions in many of them and the appearance of subcutaneous

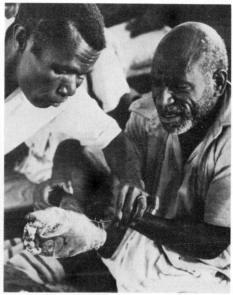

(a)   (b)

FIG. 6. Two Ekari patients with severe burns of their feet resulting from grand mal seizures at night while they were sleeping huddled close to their house fires. The Ekari people live at about 2000 metres elevation, near to the Wissel Lakes in the West New Guinea Highlands, and they sleep near to house fires during the cold nights. Neither victim was known to have had convulsions previously; both developed cutaneous cysticercosis during convalescence from their burns at the Enarotali Hospital. (Photograph courtesy of Father J. Donkers.)

nodules in some led Dr Tumada and Dr Subianto to the suspicion that cysticercosis from the larval form of *Taenia solium*, which had been newly introduced into the Wissel Lakes area of West New Guinea in 1971 by pigs imported from the more western Indonesian islands, was responsible for the epilepsy. (See Figs. 6–8.)

There had been no previous reports of *Taenia solium* intestinal infection in man, or of cysticercosis in man or pigs in West New Guinea, or in Papua New Guinea, although numerous studies have identified tapeworms and cysticercosi elsewhere in Indonesia (Bone 1940; Hausman *et al.* 1950; van der Hoeven & Rijpstra 1957; Adnijana & Djojopranoto 1961; Soebruto *et al.* 1960; Kow En Hoa & Jo Kian Tjay 1965; Hadidjaja 1971; Hadidjaja *et al.* 1971). Numerous surveys for ova and parasites in stools had been done, particularly in Papua New Guinea, and the failure to observe taeniasis was not the result of insufficient or uninformed search. During the period of Dutch administration of West New Guinea, van der Hoeven & Rijpstra (1957) reported the investigation of intestinal parasites in 98 persons. In 30 patients in the Enarotali hospital they found *Ascaris lumbricoides* in 13 persons (43%), hookworm in 20 (67%),

Trichinella trichiura in 23 (77%), and *Opisthorchis vermicularis* in three persons. Among school children they found 90% infected with the first three parasites. The study was initiated because of the high incidence of *Balantidium coli* in the mucus of stool samples in Enarotali. In 1959, Kleevans & de Haas reported a case of *Hymenolepsis nana* infection in Manokwari, on the north coast of West New Guinea. This was the only previous report of a tapeworm infection in man in the country. On the eastern side of the island in Papua New Guinea, more extensive search for intestinal parasites had confirmed the absence of taeniasis and recognized the presence of *H. nana* in the highlands (Bearup & Lawrence 1950; Kelly & Vines 1966).

Thus, when in 1973 Tumada and Margono reported their first survey for intestinal helminthic infection in the Paniai highlands, they were surprised to find *Taenia* proglottids in 9% and *H. nana* in 8% of the 170 patients in the Enarotali hospital and each parasite in 8% of 74 additional out-patients at Enarotali. In 78 persons from the Moni linguistic group in the Dogondora valley to the east they found no tape-worm. These findings were consistent with the observation of a new appearance in 1972 of *Cysticercus cellulosae* cysts in the pigs which were slaughtered in the Enarotali region. The Ekari people, as all New Guinea Highlanders, are a pig-breeding culture, the pig and dog being their only traditional domestic animals. All Ekari men regularly slaughter and butcher their own pigs and it was these Stone Age Highland Melanesians who first noted the appearance in the pig flesh of strange cysts, which they had never seen before, and brought this to the attention of the doctors, missionaries and administrators. They themselves had associated this infection with the introduction of new pigs, a gift from the Indonesian government in Java, since they had first seen the cysts in the flesh of new pigs and such cysts had appeared later in their own pigs. The Veterinary Pathology Institute in Bogor confirmed the identification of the parasite in the cysts as *Cysticercus cellulosae*, the larval stage of *Taenia solium*.

During 1972 the first appearance of such 'measly pork' was noted by the natives in an expanding region around the Lake Paniai shores and spread to the pigs of the Ekari around Lake Tigi to the south and later to the Mappi areas, also inhabited by Ekari to the west. By 1973 the pigs were found to be infected as far west as the Western Dani area around Mulia and continued medical and veterinary surveillance throughout the West New Guinea Highlands has established that the infection is absent in pigs elsewhere, except where the new introduction was noted. In 1975 an Ekari teacher brought pigs from the Ekari area as far west as Oxsybil by small plane and the cysts were later noted in his pigs and those of his neighbours. All of the surrounding pigs were killed and burned, and it is hoped that the new focus has been eradicated.

After noting this appearance of cysticercosis in the pigs, Dr Tumada first noted intestinal taeniasis in man; yet later during 1972 his attention was brought to the appearance of subcutaneous nodules in the Ekari people, a phenomenon they had not previously experienced. After surgical removal of these subcutaneous nodules, histopathological examination revealed *Cysticercus cellulosae*. Dr Tumada then instituted a search for cysticercosis patients and reported (Tumada & Margono 1973*a, b*) the clinical findings in 13 cases confirmed by biopsy, analysing the location of palpable cysticercus nodules and the other associated symptoms: headache and dizziness in nine persons, epileptic seizures

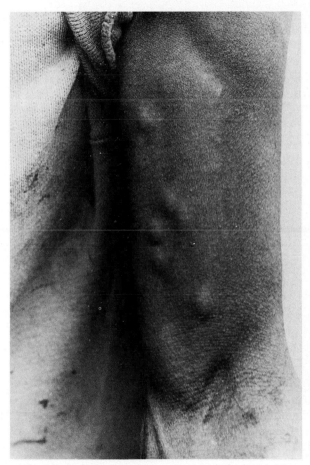

Fig. 7. Subcutaneous cysticercosis nodules seen on the inner aspect of the arm of an Ekari youth. These nodules were first noted by the Ekari patients themselves as a phenomenon totally new to them. They themselves associated them with the nodules which they found were recently introduced into their pigs by pigs imported from Java. (Photograph courtesy of Father J. Donkers.)

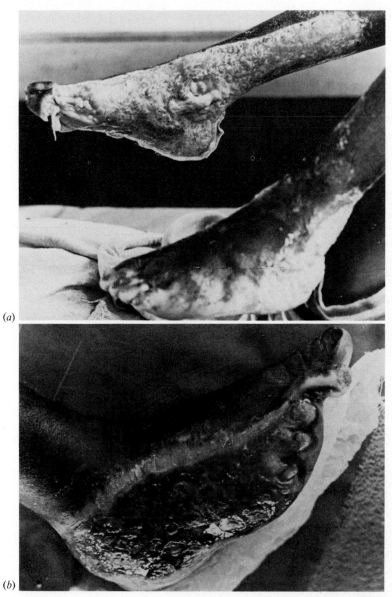

(a)

(b)

FIG. 8. Severe burns on the feet of two youths who failed to withdraw their feet from house fires because they were in post-convulsive coma. They were not previously epileptic and subsequently they were both found to have cysticercosis, which was newly introduced into their homeland with pigs from Western Indonesia. (Photographs courtesy of Father J. Donkers.)

in seven, eye complaints (blurred vision, photophobia or diplopia) in six, epigastric or abdominal pain in five, and personality changes and lethargy each in two. Two of the seven who had developed epileptic seizures were severely burned, and three of these patients had themselves first noted their subcutaneous nodules (Fig. 7). In a later study (Tumada & Subianto 1974) of 75 burn patients, only eight cases (13%) were in infants and caused by parental neglect. About 60% had a history of recently acquired seizures and the remainder could well have had seizures unrecognized by themselves or their family.

During 1973 Dr Subianto and Dr Tumada made further surveys in 2051 persons in the Enarotali population for the appearance of the cysticerci. They found that 87 (4.2%) had developed cysticercosis, with the incidence increasing with age, and no children under eleven years of age affected. Stool examination of 74 of these subjects revealed *Taenia solium* ova in about 8%. During the last two years the incidence of intestinal infection has increased, particularly in school children in and around Enarotali, to about 20%. The incidence of cysticercosis has increased and both taeniasis and cysticercosis have spread

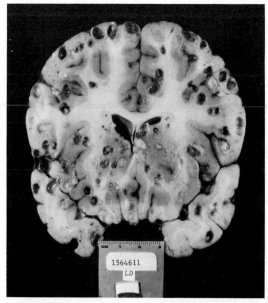

FIG. 9. Brain of a 13-year-old Ekari girl who deteriorated progressively after her initial convulsions and burns and died in coma one year later. Coronal section showing multiple cysts measuring about 4 mm in diameter with an internal nodule measuring 2.5 mm in diameter. The estimated total number of such cysts in the whole brain would exceed 2000. On microscopic examination most cysts contained identifiable organisms which occasionally included hooklets from invaginated scolices of *Taenia solium* larvae: *Cysticercus cellulosae*. No calcifications were present. (Courtesy of Dr S. C. Bauserman, Washington, D.C.)

throughout the Ekari population to as far west as the Mappi area and eastward into the Moni people living adjacent to the Ekari at Pogapa.

The appearance of convulsions in adults who have not been previously epileptic and who only later developed subcutaneous nodules suggests that the seizures are a result of primary CNS invasion and not of the calcification of and inflammatory reaction around old lesions. X-ray examination of several dozen such epileptic patients has failed to reveal any intracerebral calcification. Most patients have had only a few or no further grand mal seizures after the first, and this is contrary to expectations from the available literature. Thus, the careful neurological follow-up of patients has promise of providing new data on the natural history, symptomatology and prognosis of cysticercosis with CNS invasion. In the current situation we can estimate the earliest possible date of infection in newly infected areas, and this is not usually the case with cysticercosis patients.

Only one of the burned patients has come to autopsy, an adolescent girl who developed, after her initial convulsions and burns, progressive neurological incapacities with a wide variety of motor and mental symptoms, progressing to stupor, coma and opisthotonos, in which state she died after a lingering course of one year. Her brain, studied neuropathologically by Dr S. C. Bauserman, was filled with thousands of small cysticercus cysts and some larger ones (see Fig. 9).

MALE PSEUDOHERMAPHRODITISM AMONG SIMBARI ANGA IN THE HIGHLANDS OF PAPUA NEW GUINEA

Male pseudohermaphroditism with ambiguity of the external genitalia occurs in high incidence in small inbred 'clans' among the forest-dwelling, hunting, food-gathering and hoe and digging-stick primitive agriculturists of the Dunkwi, Simbari and Malari groups of southwestern-most Anga (Kukukuku) peoples of mountainous interior of Papua New Guinea. The populations concerned belong to the Simbari–Anga Language Group of about 1800 people, who are named for the largest group, the Simbari, who speak this one of the eleven languages belonging to the Anga linguistic family. The Simbari–Anga comprise seven local groups living in different valleys: Dunkwi, Muniri, Simbari, Malari, Iatwia, Bulakia and Iambananye (Gajdusek 1964b; Gajdusek et al. 1972; Mbaginta'o 1971, 1972, 1976).

Among the Simbari–Anga there are seven individuals with male pseudohermaphroditism personally known to me and two further recounted individuals who died years ago. All have been members of a few closely related inbred 'clans' in small hamlets comprising under one hundred persons each.

The natives recognize that the defect is inborn and usually accept those boys with malformed external genitalia as males, at an early age, often in infancy, whereas I, myself, found it difficult to be sure of the biological sex on examination of the subjects in infancy. They show small testes, often difficult to palpate, in bilateral scrotal folds, which may be difficult to distinguish from labia. There is a rudimentary clitoris-like penis, which is hardly evident before puberty, with only a 'foreskin' formed as a small fold above the urethral orifice, and two scrotal flaps resembling labia enclosing the testes on either side. In small children with this defect there is a blind pouch, resembling a vagina, but only about one centimetre deep, between the labia, just below the hypospadic urethral orifice. There have been no herniae and the anus is normal.

The studied patients have lived a normal life, accepted as members of the male sex, and three are now adults who have married. The people have a term for these boys with ambiguous external genitalia, namely, *kwalatmala*. The Simbari–Anga have a creation myth in which the progenitress of their people planted sugar cane from which sprang males who proved to be unsatisfactory consorts for her; these were all *kwalatmala*. She then planted a red variety of sugar cane from which sprang real men with large penises. Two of the *kwalatmala* who were reported and not observed by me have died; they were married and both had children. In one case the villagers attribute the offspring to other males in the community, whereas in the other case the villagers claim they were the patient's own children who resembled him, and attribute his fertility to artificial insemination by hand.

In the southern Simbari and Malari valleys, however, patients have not been recognized as boys at birth or in infancy and have been reared as girls into puberty and marriageable age. At puberty there is a rapid enlargement of the clitoris-like rudimentary penis which becomes erectile and normal testicular enlargement which causes distension and descent of the bifurcated scrotum, which previously resembled female labia, and a masculine voice, beard and habitus develop along with this other virilization. At the time of marriage these 'girls' were thus found to be boys, and a switch of sexual roles has been instituted. This is particularly remarkable since these Simbari–Anga, like many Anga groups, are a society practising extreme sex segregation with a complicated sex-segregated pattern of age grades and ritual, prolonged, and universal homosexual practices (Gajdusek 1959–1977, 1964a). Yet, in a culture with the most secret and far-reaching sexual segregation and ceremonial taboos relating to sexuality of all in Melanesia, these people have confronted the problem of a 'biological trick' played upon them as if they were rational empiricists, and after debating the necessity of killing the sex-changed 'girls', they have rejected this need and decided simply to let them assume the role of young adult males.

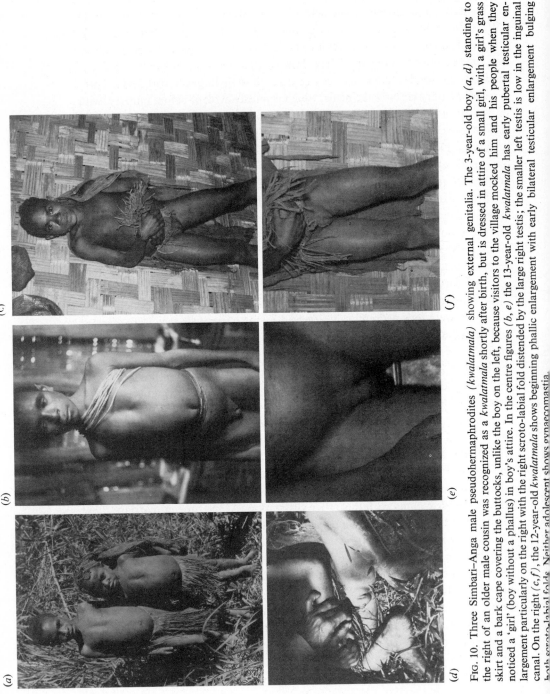

FIG. 10. Three Simbari-Anga male pseudohermaphrodites (*kwalatmala*) showing external genitalia. The 3-year-old boy (*a, d*) standing to the right of an older male cousin was recognized as a *kwalatmala* shortly after birth, but is dressed in attire of a small girl, with a girl's grass skirt and a bark cape covering the buttocks, unlike the boy on the left, because visitors to the village mocked him and his people when they noticed a 'girl' (boy without a phallus) in boy's attire. In the centre figures (*b, e*) the 13-year-old *kwalatmala* has early pubertal testicular enlargement particularly on the right with the right scroto-labial fold distended by the large right testis; the smaller left testis is low in the inguinal canal. On the right (*c, f*), the 12-year-old *kwalatmala* shows beginning phallic enlargement with early bilateral testicular enlargement bulging both scroto-labial folds. Neither adolescent shows gynaecomastia.

Faced with the awkwardness of trying to reconstruct an elaborate four-stage age grade initiation, they have rationally decided to abandon it in these exceptional cases and simply to explain the whole ceremonies of the first three grades to these youths, already too old to start with the first and second of these elaborate ceremonies.

I have found one additional case of male pseudohermaphroditism in an adult Anga in the village of Wako, of the Amdei group of Baruya-speaking Anga. This is just upstream from the Simbari speakers in the Ipmaiyaiga River valley. There is no known marriage contract between this group of Anga and the affected villages of Simbari speakers.

Two cases of a similar male pseudohermaphroditism have been reported in the kuru region from the adjacent Fore linguistic group that numbers some 12 000 individuals. In these cases a rudimentary penis has been evident and the subjects have married and fathered families. They are not Klinefelter-like hypogenital syndromes.

Peterson, Imperato-McGinley and their colleagues (Imperato-McGinley *et al.* 1974, 1975; Peterson *et al.* 1977) have described an inherited form of male pseudohermaphroditism secondary to a decrease in steroid $\Delta 4$–5α-reductase activity in 24 families with 38 affected males, who are all located in four villages in the south-western Dominican Republic. The affected males (46XY) have at birth a clitoral-like phallus, bifid scrotum, and urogenital sinus. The testes are in the inguinal canals or labial-scrotal folds. The Wolffian structures are normally differentiated; there are no Mullerian structures. At puberty they develop a muscular male habitus with growth of the phallus and scrotum, voice change and no gynaecomastia. They have erections, ejaculations and the libido directed towards females. They have decreased body hair and scant to absent beard, no temporal hairline recession, and small prostate. Our patients differ from these only in the presence of normal beard and body hair after puberty. Biochemical studies to determine the nature of the defect, which clinically more closely resembles that found in the Dominican Republic cases than any of the biogenetic defects with deficiency of testosterone production, in view of the sudden quick virilization at puberty and lack of gynaecomastia, are in progress in collaboration with Peterson and Imperato-McGinley in New York.

ACKNOWLEDGEMENTS

The studies in West New Guinea have been possible only through the cooperation and collaboration of my colleagues in Indonesia: Dr Julie Sulianti Saroso, Director of the National Institutes of Health, Jakarta, and Dr Suriadi Gunawan, Director of the Provincial Health Service, Jayapura, Irian Jaya. I am grateful to Bishop Alphonse Sowada, O.S.C. of the Crosier Mission, Agats, and Fathers H. Weytens and C. Van Halen, Superiors of the Sacred Heart

Mission, Kepi, and the Missions' staffs for their hospitality and assistance. For field assistance in 1974 in Irian Jaya, I am indebted to my colleagues, Dr L. R. Tumada and Dr D. B. Subianto, and to Fathers Ben van Oers of Arere, C. Schipperyna of Kepi, and F. W. van Dongen of Bade. I thank Dr S. C. Bauserman of the Armed Forces Institute of Pathology, Washington, D.C. for his neuropathological help; and for photographs of cysticercosis patients, Father Jos Donkers, of Enarotali, Irian Jaya.

References

ADELS, B.R. & GAJDUSEK, D.C. (1963) Survey of measles patterns in New Guinea, Micronesia and Australia. With a report of new virgin soil epidemics and the demonstration of susceptible primitive populations by serology. *Am. J. Hyg. 77*, 317–343

ADNIJANA, I.C.N.P. & DJOJOPRANOTO, M. (1961) Cysticercosis dibawah kulit Pada manusia. *Majalah Kedokteran Indonesia 11*, 188

ARNOLD, A., EDGREN, D. & PALADINO, V. (1953) Amyotrophic lateral sclerosis: fifty cases observed on Guam. *J. Nerv. Ment. Dis. 117*, 135–139

BEARUP, A.J. & LAWRENCE, J.J. (1950) A parasitological survey of five New Guinea villages. *Med. J. Aust. 1*, 724

BONE, C. (1940) De lintwormen van den mensch in Indië [The tape-worms of man in the Dutch East Indies]. *Geneesk. Tijdschr. voor Nederl. Indië 80*, 2376–2384

BROWN, P., BASNIGHT, M. & GAJDUSEK, D.C. (1965) Response to live attenuated measles vaccine in susceptible island populations in Micronesia. *Am. J. Epidemiol. 82*, 115–122

BROWN, P., GAJDUSEK, D.C. & MORRIS, J.A. (1969a) Virus of the 1918 influenza pandemic era: new evidence about its antigenic character. *Science (Wash. D.C.) 166*, 117–119

BROWN, P., GAJDUSEK, D.C. & MORRIS, J.A. (1969b) Antigenic response to influenza virus in man. I. Neutralizing antibody response to inactivated monovalent A2 vaccine as related to prior influenza exposure. *Am. J. Epidemiol. 90*, 327–335

ESPIRAT, J.-J., GUIART, J., LAGRANGE, M.-S. & RENAUD, M. (1973) *Système des titres dans les Nouvelles-Hébrides Centrales d'Efate aux Iles Shepherd*, Institut d'Ethnologie, Musée de l'Homme, Paris

GAJDUSEK, D.C. (1959–1977) *Journals 1956–76*, twenty-one vols., published in limited edition, National Institutes of Health, Bethesda, Maryland

GAJDUSEK, D.C. (1963) Motor-neuron disease in natives of New Guinea. *New Engl. J. Med. 268*, 474–476

GAJDUSEK, D.C. (1964a) Sex avoidance and pederasty with juvenile fellatio as traditional homosexuality among bisexual southwestern Kukukuku people in New Guinea. Program and Abstracts, 74th Annual Meeting, American Pediatric Society, Seattle, June 16–18, abstr. 127, pp. 137–138

GAJDUSEK, D.C. (1964b) Congenital absence of the penis in Muniri and Simbari Kukukuku people of New Guinea. Program and Abstracts, 74th Annual Meeting, American Pediatric Society, Seattle, June 16–18, abstr. 128, p. 138

GAJDUSEK, D.C. (1964c) The composition of musics for man. Or decoding from primitive cultures the scores for human behavior. *Pediatrics 34*, 84–91

GAJDUSEK, D.C. (1967) Recent observations on the use of kava in the New Hebrides, in *Ethnopharmacologic Search for Psychoactive Drugs* (Efron, D.H., editor-in-chief; D. Holmstedt & N.S. Kline, coauthors), PHS Publication no. 1645, pp. 119–125, National Institute of Mental Health, Washington, D.C.

GAJDUSEK, D.C. (1969) Drawings by children in primitive cultures: elucidating cultural patterning of symbolic representation and cognitive style—or—the pattern of symbolic representation as determined by patterns of culture. Program and Abstracts, 39th Annual Meeting, Society for Pediatric Research, Atlantic City, May 2–3, p. 78

GAJDUSEK, D.C. (1970) Physiological and psychological characteristics of Stone Age man. Conference on Biological Bases of Human Behavior, California Institute of Technology, March 16, Pasadena, in *Engin. Sci. 33*, 26–33 and 56–62

GAJDUSEK, D.C. (1973) Kuru in the New Guinea Highlands. in *Tropical Neurology* (Spillane, J.D., ed.), pp. 376–383, Oxford University Press, New York

GAJDUSEK, D.C. (ed.) (1976) Correspondence on the discovery and original investigations of kuru, Smadel-Gajdusek Correspondence 1956–1950, National Institutes of Health, Bethesda, Maryland

GAJDUSEK, D.C. & GARRUTO, R.M. (1975) The focus of hyperendemic goiter, cretinism and associated deaf-mutism in Western New Guinea, in *Biosocial Interrelations in Population Adaptation* (Watts, E.W., Johnston, F.E. & Lasker, G.W., eds.), pp. 267–285, Mouton, The Hague

GAJDUSEK, D.C., GUIART, J., KIRK, R.L., CARRELL, R.W., IRVINE, D., KYNOCH, P.A.M. & LEHMANN, H. (1967) Haemoglobin J Tongariki (α115 alanine → aspartic acid): the first new haemoglobin variant found in a Pacific (Melanesian) population. *J. Med. Genet. 4*, 1–6

GAJDUSEK, D.C. & MEYER, J. (1977) Longlong behavior. Ritual clowning as a socially accepted pattern of behavior disorder. A film study

GAJDUSEK, D.C. & ZIGAS, V. (1957) Degenerative disease of the central nervous system in New Guinea. The endemic occurrence of 'kuru' in the native population. *New Engl. J. Med. 257*, 974–978

GAJDUSEK, D.C. & ZIGAS, V. (1959) Kuru: clinical, pathological and epidemiological study of an acute progressive degenerative disease of the central nervous system among natives of the Eastern Highlands of New Guinea. *Am. J. Med. 26*, 442–469

GAJDUSEK, D.C., FETCHKO, P., VAN WYK, N.J. & ONO, S.G. (1972) Annotated Anga (Kukukuku) Bibliography, National Institutes of Health, Bethesda, Maryland

GIBBS, C.J., Jr & GAJDUSEK, D.C. (1972) Amyotrophic lateral sclerosis, Parkinson's disease, and the amyotrophic lateral sclerosis-Parkinsonism-dementia complex on Guam: a review and summary of attempts to demonstrate infection as the etiology. *J. Clin. Pathol. 25*, Suppl. *(R. Coll. Pathol.)*, 132–140

HADIDJAJA, P. (1971) Beberapa Kasus taeniasis di Jakarta. Cara diagnosa dan pengobatan. *Majalah Kedokteran Indonesia 21*, 173–179

HADIDJAJA, P., RUKMON, B., SJAMSUHIDAJAT, & HIMAWAN, S. (1971) Another case of cysticercosis in Djakarta. *Majalah Kedokteran Indonesia 21*, 461

HAUSMAN, R., LIONA, YOE TJIN & FOSSEN, A. (1950) Een geval van cysticercose met enkele aantekeningen over taeniasis in Indonesia [A case of cysticercosis with some notes on taeniasis in Indonesia]. *Doc. Neerl. Indones. Morb. Trop. 2*, 50

HIRANO, A., KURLAND, L.T., KROOTH, R.S. *et al.* (1961) Parkinsonism-dementia complex, an endemic disease on the island of Guam. I. Clinical features. *Brain 84*, 642–661

HOEVEN, J.A. VAN DER & RIJPSTRA, A.C. (1957) Intestinal parasites in the Central Mountains District of Netherlands New Guinea. An important focus of *Balantidium coli. Doc. Med. Geogr. Trop. 9*, 225–228

IMPERATO-MCGINLEY, J., GUERRERO, L., GAUTIER, T. & PETERSON, R.E. (1974) Steroid 5α-reductase deficiency in man: an inherited form of male pseudohermaphroditism. *Science (Wash. D.C.) 186*, 1213–1215

IMPERATO-MCGINLEY, J., GUERRERO, L., GAUTIER, T., GERMAN, J.L. & PETERSON, R.E. (1975) Steroid 5α-reductase deficiency in man. An inherited form of male pseudohermaphroditism, in *Genetic Forum on Hypogonadism* (Bergsma, D., ed.) *Birth Defects 11*, 91–102

KELLY, A. & VINES, A.P. (1966) Highland region survey of intestinal parasites. *Med. J. Aust. 2*, 635–640

KLEEVENS, J.W.L. & HAAS, R.A. DE (1959) A case of *Hymenolepis nana* in Netherlands New Guinea. *Trop. Geogr. Med. 11*, 376–377

KOOIJMAN, S., DORREN, M., VEEGER, L., VERSCHUEREN, J. & LUYKEN, R. (1958) Report of the

Investigation into the Problem of Depopulation among the Marind-Anim of Netherlands New Guinea 1953–1954. South Pacific Commission, Population Studies, Noumea

Kow En Hoa & Jo Kian Tjay (1965) A case report of *Hymenolepis diminuta* infection in Medan. *Paediatr. Indones. 5*, 24–27

Kurland, L.T. & Mulder, D.W. (1954) Epidemiologic investigations of amyotrophic lateral sclerosis. I. Preliminary report on geographic distribution, with special reference to the Mariana Islands, including clinical and pathological observations. *Neurology 4*, 355–378 and 438–448

Mbaginta'o, I.G. (1971) The Anga initiations. *Journal de la Société des Océanistes 27*, 285–294

Mbaginta'o, I.G. (1972) Les esprits guérisseurs chez les Dunkwi Anga. *Journal de la Société des Océanistes 28*, 337–343

Mbaginta'o, I.G. (1976) Medicine practice and funeral ceremony of the Dunkwi Anga. *Journal de la Société des Océanistes 32*

Mulder, D.W., Kurland, L.T. & Iriarte, L.L.G. (1954) Neurological diseases on Island of Guam. *U.S. Armed Forces Med. J. 5*, 1724–1739

Peterson, R.E., Imperato-McGinley, J., Gautier, T. & Sturla, E. (1977) Male pseudo-hermaphroditism due to steroid 5α-reductase deficiency. *Am. J. Med. 62*, 170–191

Pharoah, P.O.D. (1971) Epidemiological studies of endemic cretinism in the Jimi River Valley in New Guinea, in *Endemic Cretinism* (Hetzel, B.S. & Pharoah, P.O.D., eds.), pp. 109–116, Institute of Human Biology, Papua New Guinea

Reed, D.M. & Brody, J.A. (1975) Amyotrophic lateral sclerosis and Parkinsonism-dementia on Guam, 1945–1972. I. Descriptive epidemiology. *Am. J. Epidemiol. 101*, 287–301

Reed, D.M., Torres, J.M. & Brody, J.A. (1975) Amyotrophic lateral sclerosis and Parkinsonism-dementia on Guam, 1945–1972. II. Familial and genetic studies. *Am. J. Epidemiol. 101*, 302–310

Rodrique, R. (1963) A report on a widespread psychological disorder called lulu seen among the Huli linguistic group in Papua. *Oceania 33* (4), 273–279

Rubinstein, D. & Gajdusek, D.C. (1970) A study in nascent literacy. Neo-melanesian correspondence from a Fore, New Guinea youth. Section of Child Growth and Development and Disease Patterns in Primitive Cultures, NINCDS, National Institutes of Health, Bethesda, Maryland

Simmons, R.T. & Gajdusek, D.C. (1966) A blood group genetic survey of children of Bellona and Rennell Islands (BSIP) and certain northern New Hebridean Islands. *Archaeol. Phys. Anthropol. in Oceania 1*, 155–174

Soebruto, F.K., Njoo Tjing Haw & Djojopranoto, M. (1960) Cysticercosis dibawah kulit pada manusia. *Majalah Kedokteran Indonesia 10*, 460–462

Sorenson, E.R. & Gajdusek, D.C. (1966) The study of child behavior and development in primitive cultures. A research archive for ethnopediatric film investigations of styles in the patterning of the nervous system. *Pediatrics 37*, 149–243

Tumada, L.R. & Margono, S.S. (1973a) Cysticercosis in the area of the Wissel Lakes, West Irian. *S.E. Asian J. Trop. Med. Publ. Health 49*, 371–376

Tumada, L.R. & Margono, S.S. (1973b) Intestinal helminthic infection in the Paniai Highlands, with special reference to *Taenia* and *Hymenolepis nana*. *Majalah Kedokteran Indonesia 7–8*, 103–107

Tumada, L.R. & Subianto, D.B. (1974) Combustio epidemic in the Wissel Lakes. Mimeographed report, 1974, 3 pp., Department of Public Health, Jayapura, West Irian

van Baal, J. (1966) *Dema. Description and analysis of Marind-anim culture*, Mouton, The Hague

Yase, Y., Matsumoto, N., Yoskimasu, F., Handa, Y. & Kumamoto, T. (1968) Motor neuron disease in the Kii Peninsula, Japan. *Proc. Aust. Assoc. Neurol. 5*, 335–339

Zigas, V. (1971) A donovanosis project in Goilala. *Papua New Guinea Med. J. 14*, 148

Zigas, V. & Gajdusek, D.C. (1957) Kuru: clinical study of a new syndrome resembling paralysis agitans in natives of the Eastern Highlands of Australian New Guinea. *Med. J. Aust. 2*, 745–754

Discussion

Stanley: What was the effect of kuru on the Fore people?

Gajdusek: Since the boys moved at an early age into the men's community, where men did not usually take part in the cannibalism of kuru victims, they escaped further chances of infection with kuru. The incidence of kuru among male children was nearly that among female children, unlike the situation among adults with more than 10 women affected for every male affected. As a result of kuru the sex ratio of males to females reached 3:1 in some South Fore hamlets and, for persons of marriageable age, even higher than this. This must have posed a very severe problem to a polygamous community. They were dying at a rate of 1–3% of the population per year, in some villages, a rate which more than decimated the village in a decade. At this rate of loss of adults of reproductive age and of children before reproductive age they could not survive.

We could find no genetic advantage associated with kuru. Girls were married before puberty usually to older men. There was a conscious effort to have children from the girls before they died of kuru. Since kuru accounted for far more than half the adult female deaths of the South Fore people over the first 10 years of observation, and over 90% of female deaths in the reproductive age in some villages, the Fore were correct in fearing that their wives would die before they left a sufficient number of offspring for survival as a people. They tried successfully to compensate for this by marrying the girls early and having pregnancies in quick succession. They determined who were the offending sorcerers—always males—by divination and often murdered them in reprisal by a ritual murder, called *tukabu*. This helped to restore the sex ratio toward normal.

Some groups of Fore had many bachelors and these restless unmarried youths crossed to the neighbouring, usually hostile, unaffected areas and ingratiated themselves with these kuru-free groups, eventually adopting large numbers of children and marrying into these groups. They succeeded in 'Forenizing' these neighbours, grafting even their language on to some of them, thus effectively saving themselves from extinction from kuru by colonization.

The disappearance of the disease has been remarkable and progressive. It first disappeared from the 5–9-year-old children then, about five years later, from the 10–14-year-old age group, and about five years later from the 15–19-year age group. It appears that it will soon be gone as a disease of those under 25 years of age. No one born in an area after cannibalism of dead kinsmen ceased has ever developed kuru. We have, in the progressive disappearance of kuru from the lowest ages upward, strong evidence against transplacental transmission or any vector or reservoir in nature (see Fig. 1).

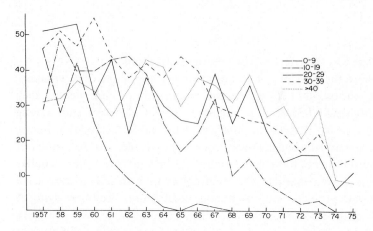

F<small>IG</small>. 1 (Gajdusek). The disappearance of kuru in different age groups of the Fore people. *Ordinate:* number of cases of kuru per year during the period 1957–1975.

Lightman: In your discussion of cysticercosis among the Ekari you did not mention the epidemiological importance of their method of cooking. They cook their food by wrapping it in leaves and placing it on hot stones that have just been removed from a fire. Although this gentle baking process produces tender succulent pork, the temperature achieved during the cooking is often insufficient to kill all the cysticerci. These will be eaten and develop into adult tapeworms within the human gut where they will present a further potential source of cysticercosis infection from faecal–oral contamination, or retroperistalsis during some temporary bowel disorder.

Gajdusek: Yes. However, the control measures they employ have been more severe than a change in cuisine! I did not believe one could convince the Ekari people to throw away and bury affected pig. Their horror at the new appearance of epilepsy, associated severe burns, and the necessity of amputating burned limbs has, in fact, led to their discarding affected pig meat. They were convinced that their own subcutaneous cysts were the same as those they saw in their pigs. They readily accepted the fact that they were contaminating themselves with eggs in their own faeces, having looked at the proglottids through the microscope and having seen the adult worms passed in their stools after treatment with atabrine. This led to a craze for digging enormously deep pit latrines, 3–5 metres deep. They are also becoming rather strict with their children, in trying to control their defaecation in the gardens and village areas.

Lightman: Are they being encouraged to change their cooking methods?

Gajdusek: They have been told to cook the meat more thoroughly but it is impossible for them to achieve temperatures high enough, with their steam cooking at high altitudes, to kill all the larvae. They do not cook pork as thoroughly as the Chinese do. Around the stations they are beginning to fry in grease and to use pots and pans; the missions are encouraging this. The real problem is that the intestinal taeniasis is not a very serious disease and it is difficult to bring everyone infected with taenia to atabrine treatment. You cannot treat cysticercosis; there is no effective drug.

Weiner: Dr Gajdusek, you are extremely familiar with this particular geographical area where you have made very thorough studies; one wonders if, for example, amyotrophic lateral sclerosis would be encountered with such frequency in Africa if it was as intensively looked for.

Gajdusek: There has been a widespread search for other foci of neurological degenerative diseases in Africa as well as in the Pacific. Studies have been made in Australia, Taiwan, Israel, South America, throughout the Pacific, and in Fiji, New Zealand and Japan. We have searched intensively for motor neuron disease throughout New Guinea and we do encounter cases of it sporadically. We have made a vast survey of neurological disease in many parts of the South Pacific, including whole populations of the Western Caroline Islands and of the Banks and Torres Islands and the Shepherd Islands in the New Hebrides (Gajdusek 1975), of the Southern and Eastern Solomon Islands and in selected sites in New Britain and East and West New Guinea, and found only the one focus of motor neuron disease which I described here. In the process we have found foci of great interest of other neurological diseases, all of which are under study: familial periodic paralysis on Tongariki Island (Gajdusek *et al.* 1964); a distal type of progressive muscular dystrophy in the Sentani Region of West New Guinea (see Gajdusek 1959–1977); pseudohypertrophic muscular dystrophy of Duchenne in New Britain; *puriripiram* or the western kuru-like syndrome (Wilson *et al.* 1969); *kogaisantamba*, or the Auyana tremor syndrome (Gajdusek & Zigas 1959; Zigas 1971). ALS is a major world problem and the foci on Guam, in Japan, and in West New Guinea must contain the solution if we are only shrewd enough to see it.

Lewis: You have described a number of most unusual disease patterns from New Guinea, yet there are only three million or so people in New Guinea. Despite this small total population, New Guinea has an extraordinary proportion of the world's languages (Wurm & Laycock [1961] estimate between 700 and 1000 languages—that is, between a fifth and a seventh of the world total); its peoples show great variety in the customary behaviours they accept as normal; social groups are small and lead relatively isolated and independent lives. Is the variety of rare disease patterns you have been able to find in New Guinea connected with this remarkable diversity in culture?

Gajdusek: We do expect that in the high inbreeding and/or in the phenomena of different social practices and restricted environment, dietary styles and so on we may be able to find the answer to the high incidence of the diverse neurological and many other non-neurological diseases we have found in concentrated foci in isolated populations in Melanesia.

The comparable situation in Europe is the diversity and high incidence of degenerative and familial neurological diseases reported from Swedish and Finnish Baltic Island populations, many with specific, local 'sub-forms' or varieties of classical neurological syndromes. The Scandinavian experience somewhat parallels the work on the island populations off the Carolina coast in the USA, and Victor McKusick's work among the Amish and Hutterites.

Truswell: What is the present state of the cycad disease?

Gajdusek: This disease is not the same as ALS but is a real entity. Cycad (tree fern) was used as an emergency food during periods of food shortage on Guam in World War II. There is a neurotoxin in some Caribbean cycads producing a motor neuron disease in cattle in the Dominican Republic. There is also cycad poisoning in Australian cattle in Queensland and in Papua New Guinea. No one has been able to link the use of cycad to ALS on Guam. (See Whiting 1965.)

Cohen: You described a hermaphrodite condition in the New Guinea area that you studied and suggested that it was due to an enzyme deficiency, presumably determined by a specific gene. If that is so, how do you account for the apparently high prevalence of such a disadvantageous gene? Or is it like the situation with curare and curare-like derivatives where fast or slow inactivation is determined by differing levels of the same enzyme whose setting is determined genetically for each individual? There, are of course, plenty of other examples of differing enzyme levels among homozygotes and heterozygotes.

Gajdusek: We have only encountered some 9 cases of male pseudohermaphroditism in the total population of about 1800 Simbari–Anga people. One village complex in the Dominican Republic is the only other place where a similar defect has been found. There the incidence is considerably higher than with the Simbari–Anga. The defect appears to be an autosomal recessive trait in both the Caribbean and in New Guinea and the familiar effect of random genetic drift and historical accident in small groups could easily account for these accumulations of cases without the trait itself having any genetic advantage.

Hugh-Jones: You mentioned periodic paralysis: this is not associated with adrenal tumours, is it?

Gajdusek: Presumably not. We know of three cases, all of whom died on the island of Tongariki, during their hypokalaemic attacks of periodic paralysis. In one patient whom I reported (Gajdusek *et al.* 1964) there was a total heart block with a heart rate of only 20–30/minute. Attacks seem to be precipitated by rapid hydration after dehydration. We expect the disease to develop in family members whom we have now under observation; there are no cases alive at the moment. There is also a high incidence of familial periodic paralysis among the Chinese on Taiwan.

Truswell: Is the separation of the rectus abdominus muscle confined to one group of New Guineans?

Gajdusek: No, it is found widely, and is very common in some other Melanesian islands. In some villages a third or half the men have mid-epigastric herniae or lipomata. In New Guinea it is less often found in the people of the Lowlands than in the Highlanders. I became aware in the early 1960s that all the toddlers of some groups have such a split rectus abdominus muscle in early childhood, presumably from severe abdominal distension during the regular stuffing at the one real meal a day, made up largely of bulky carbohydrates.

Polunin: Divarication of the recti is common in Malayan tribal people, affecting 20% of people. I think it is associated with pot belly. Epigastric hernia was rare, although a fatty roll often projected in the midline between the recti when they were tensed. This was not a hernia.

Gajdusek: In the feeding pattern found in much of New Guinea children regularly fill themselves with bulky staples (taro, sweet potato, plantain, green leaves) to such abnormal abdominal distention that they have tight tympanic abdominal walls. They stuff themselves to capacity at the one ample meal a day. Their meals come irregularly and they have to eat an enormous bulk because their high carbohydrate diets consist of foods containing so much waste and roughage.

Hamilton: Dr Gajdusek, you have collected a vast amount of information over a long period of time. In considering the problem of what information should be collected, would you comment on the value of your data banks to you (excluding those variables you have followed to test a specific hypothesis from the start)?

Gajdusek: Our research orientation is admittedly not entirely directed to the primitive population. We are interested in iodine and testosterone metabolism; in many kinds of infectious disease; in immunological problems; and in slow viruses. On the other hand, our long-term longitudinal observations in primitive and isolated groups have slowly made us aware of unusual situations that were staring us in the face yet unrecognized for years, or others that have only slowly been uncovered. I had visited the community in four successive years before becoming aware that there was more than one pseudohermaphrodite; it took another five annual visits before I realized the importance of thorough genealogical survey for this trait, with specific inquiry in this direction; and only later still did I start to investigate the cause. Only over decades of observation have we learned what are the long-term effects of various causes of death in the populations. We have villages in the kuru region where kuru is rare and the first cause of death, instead, is found to be snake bite. In others drowning or suicide has been a major cause of death over many years. On one island the loss of many closely related kinsmen with two lost canoes has had a greater effect on the population structure over a period of the last 30 years than all the diseases we have studied there combined.

Only long-continued record-keeping and close familiarity with the population have revealed these findings to us. Recently many young men died all on one day, shortly after a bean feast, from hydrocyanic acid poisoning from *Phasaeola* sp., the native New Guinea bean, which in certain odd growing conditions accumulates toxic levels of HCN. Over many years, for some very primitive villages, a major cause of death, even though the families at home were still at Stone Age level, has been road and plane accidents of young men while away as labourers or students. Our long-continued data-keeping has taught us how very different the history and disease experience of each village may be even in a given language group.

Another interesting by-product related to what Dr Neel has been demonstrating has been the interesting findings in our work with Robert Kirk, where occasionally the discovery of family- or tribe-specific new genetic pleomorphisms has given an unexpected and dramatic anthropological perspective. We found on Tongariki a new haemoglobin, the first α-chain haemoglobin variant, now called haemoglobin J Tongariki, which was sequenced in Cambridge (Gajdusek *et al.* 1967). A few years later we brought in sera from the surrounding islands and only people of the Banks and Torres Islands in the northern New Hebrides had this specific haemoglobin marker. The Banks and Torres Islands had never before been associated anthropologically or linguistically with the Shepherd Islands. It was also later found in the islands off the north coast of New Britain and yet later on Manam island off the northern coast of New Guinea near Madang. This arc of islands matches one of the hypothetical lines of migration of people into the New Hebrides from South-East Asia. The linguists are now looking into this, as a result of the work on this genetic marker.

A further example: peptidase B PepB[6] allele, first found only in Australian Aborigines on the coast of north-east Arnhem Land, we later found, after wide screening of stored frozen sera from New Guinea, in several coastal villages of the Asmat people far across the Arafura sea (Blake *et al.* 1970; Gajdusek *et al.* 1977). There had never previously been any suggestion of common origin, common contacts or mixing between these widely separated peoples. More recently the rare PepB[6] allele has also been found in Aborigines in Malaysia. Such findings are by-products of having a huge frozen serum bank and associated genealogical and travel and other anthropological data.

Another by-product of such work is the possibility of screening such stored and well-documented specimens for antibodies to new viruses not even yet discovered at the time of the collection of the sera. We have done this with dramatic discoveries on several occasions. Most recently we have used such old sera from our own and Dr Frank Black's files for a world-wide screening for antibody to the newly discovered JC human papovavirus, the cause of progressive multifocal leucoencephalopathy, and the newly identified human BK papovavirus. We discovered the only known populations free of the JC virus and yet affected by the BK virus, and the reverse situation as well, in very isolated American Indian and South Pacific groups. These findings have strongly influenced our thinking on the epidemiology and biological cycles of these important and still little-understood virus infections (Brown *et al.* 1975). Similarly, we have made significant studies on the epidemiology of cytomegalovirus and Epstein-Barr virus infections using sera collected from remote isolated populations long before the techniques of estimating antibodies to these viruses were developed (Lang *et al.* 1977).

References

BLAKE, N.M., KIRK, R.L., LEWIS, W.H.P. & HARRIS, H. (1970) Some further peptidase B phenotypes. *Ann. Hum. Genet. 33*, 301–305

BROWN, P., TSAI, T. & GAJDUSEK, D.C. (1975) Seroepidemiology of human papovaviruses: discovery of virgin populations and some unusual patterns of antibody prevalence among remote peoples of the world. *Am. J. Epidemiol. 102*, 331–340

GAJDUSEK, D.C. (1959–1977) *Journals 1956–76*, twenty-one vols., published in limited edition, National Institutes of Health, Bethesda, Maryland

GAJDUSEK, D.C. (1975) Medical and population genetic survey of the Banks and Torres Islands of the New Hebrides, and the southern islands of the British Solomon Islands Protectorate, in *R/V Alpha Helix Research Program, 1972–1974*, pp. 25–32, Scripps Institution of Oceanography, University of California, San Diego

GAJDUSEK, D.C. & ZIGAS, V. (1959) Kuru: clinical, pathological and epidemiological study of an acute progressive degenerative disease of the central nervous system among natives of the Eastern Highlands of New Guinea. *Am. J. Med. 26*, 442–469

GAJDUSEK, D.C., KIRK, R.L. & GUIART, J. (1964) Familial periodic paralysis with complete heart block in a family of New Hebridean (Melanesian)–Australian aboriginal crossing. First report in aboriginal Australasians. Program and Abstracts, 74th Annual Meeting, American Pediatric Society, Seattle, June 16–18, abstr. 126, p. 137

GAJDUSEK, D.C., GUIART, J., KIRK, R.L., CARRELL, R.W., IRVINE, D., KYNOCH, P.A.M. & LEHMANN, H. (1967) Haemoglobin J Tongariki (α115 alanine $\rightarrow$ aspartic acid): the first new haemoglobin variant found in a Pacific (Melanesian) population. *J. Med. Genet. 4*, 1–6

GAJDUSEK, D.C., LEYSHON, W.C., KIRK, R.L., BLAKE, N.M., KEATS, B. & McDERMID, E.M. (1977) Genetic differentiation among populations in Western New Guinea. *Am. J. Phys. Anthropol.*, in press

LANG, D., GARRUTO, R.M. & GAJDUSEK, D.C. (1977) Early acquisition of cytomegalovirus and Epstein–Barr virus antibody in several isolated Melanesian populations. *Am. J. Epidemiol.*, in press

WHITING, M.G. (ed.) (1965) *Conference on the Toxicity of Cycads (fourth)*, National Institutes of Health, Bethesda, Maryland

WILSON, K., ZIGAS, V. & GAJDUSEK, D.C. (1959) New tremor syndromes occurring sporadically in natives of the Wabag–Laiagam–Kundep region of the Western Highlands of Australian New Guinea. *Lancet 2*, 699–702

WURM, S.A. & LAYCOCK, D.C. (1961) The question of language and dialect in New Guinea. *Oceania 32*, 128–143

ZIGAS, V. (1971) Auyana head nodders. (Letter.) *Papua and New Guinea Med. J. 14*, 39

Where did our infectious diseases come from?
The evolution of infectious disease

AIDAN COCKBURN

Paleopathology Association, Detroit, Michigan and Division of Physical Anthropology, Smithsonian Institution, Washington D.C.

Abstract Infectious diseases have been evolving from the earliest days of life on earth. Major factors influencing their developments include the splitting of continents (continental drift), the radiation of early primates into present-day forms, migrations of man around the world, the ending of the Ice Age, the invention of agriculture, the domestication of animals, the increase in populations, and the urbanization of societies. The impact of such basic changes on infectious diseases is reviewed.

To understand fully the steps by which infectious diseases were created and assumed their modern forms, one must take the long view and go back to the primitive earth and the origin of life. For it was then that the first cells, bacteria and, possibly, viruses, were created, and afterwards that early forms of commensalism and parasitism developed. In the beginning, the earth's atmosphere was anaerobic and free oxygen did not exist. However, a discussion of these stages is beyond the bounds of this paper. We shall begin at the period when much of the earth's land mass was concentrated into one super-continent. At this time, mammals and primates existed on it and it can be assumed that they had parasites. Then movements of the earth's crust split the one continent and, as Wegener put it, the present-day continents began drifting away from one another (Runcorn 1962).

CONTINENTAL DRIFT

Some time about one or two hundred million years ago a great crack split the super-continent where the Mid-Atlantic Ridge is today. Our present-day New and Old Worlds started moving apart at the rate of a few centimetres a year, taking with them all the parasites and their hosts, as well as the insects, intermediate hosts and so on that existed at that time. This must have had a profound

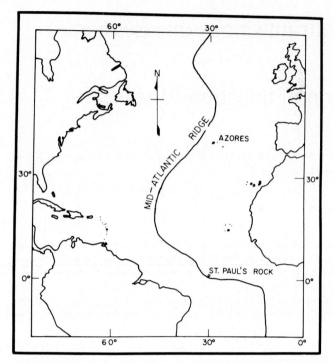

Fig. 1. The New and Old Worlds and the Mid-Atlantic Ridge.

effect on present-day infections and evidence of this effect is demonstrable (Fig. 1).

Two great groups of parasites that most probably existed before the separation are the leishmanias and the trypanosomes. Those of South America and Africa must certainly have been derived from common ancestors; their locations today, divided by the wide Atlantic, are difficult to explain except on the grounds of their existence before continental drift began. All other explanations, such as carriage over the oceans by birds, fish, insects, or winds, are not satisfying.

Hoare (1972) has suggested that the trypanosomes of horses and cattle were introduced into America within the past two or three centuries, and with this I have no disagreement. However, whenever a species invades a new territory, it remains as a single entity for quite a long time: to radiate into many new species can be quite a lengthy process. In South America, the forms and distributions of trypanosomes are so diverse that they could not have evolved within a couple of centuries: organisms which are morphologically indistinguishable from *Trypanosoma cruzi* of man are found in many species of animals, of at least seven orders (Lumsden 1976). They are obviously ancient infections of that continent.

With the leishmanias, we are on more secure ground. The peoples of Chile and Peru, long before Columbus, made clay pots in the shape of people, some of whom where depicted as having cutaway upper lips. This condition persists even to the present, and has been identified as cutaneous leishmaniasis. The name 'uta' had been given by the Incas both to the disease and the sandflies that transmit it (Herrer & Christensen 1975). The infection could not have been carried there by man via Siberia and Alaska and so must have been there before man arrived in South America.

Interestingly enough, the vector of African trypanosomiasis, the tsetse fly *Glossina*, once existed in the New World, although it is no longer found there, and four excellent specimens have been discovered in the Florissant shales near Denver, Colorado. Perhaps African trypanosomiasis was once present in America but died out after the continental drift began (Cockerill 1908).

INFECTIONS OF THE PRIMATE RADIATION

When the primitive ancestral primate groups were split into two halves, they evolved in two directions. Those in the New World remained largely tree dwellers with prehensile tails, while those in present-day Africa lived to a great extent on the ground. Some of these, in time, developed into the early men who were our ancestors.

It is a well-established concept in biology that when a species splits into separate groups which eventually become species themselves, the parasites from the original ancestor are passed to all its descendants. The aphorism 'like hosts have like parasites' is more than a hundred years old and was first expounded by Von Thering at the turn of the century (Kellogg 1913; Harrison 1914).

If we apply this concept to the primate radiation, it would seem that the parasites of the original primate ancestor would be passed on to all primates, while those acquired by a more recent ancestor, such as that of man and the apes, would be limited to just those hosts. Occasionally, an animal would lose a parasite by changes in its ecology inimical to the transmission of the particular parasite (Fig. 2.)

Twenty years ago, I studied the intestinal protozoa reported in the literature (Cockburn 1963) and found that of the twelve common ones of man, no less than eleven had been found in monkeys. The exception, *Iodamoeba williamsi*, had only one report from captive monkeys in China, and could have been acquired in captivity. Cross-infection of parasites between man and monkey undoubtedly happens: in many parts of the tropics, people defaecate in their fields among their crops and monkeys raiding those same crops can easily be contaminated. But it is difficult to conceive how monkeys in different parts of

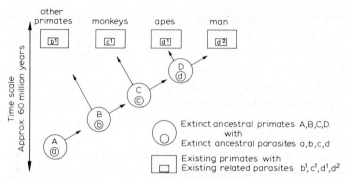

FIG. 2. Parallel phylogenies of hosts and parasites.

the world happened to pick up the same eleven protozoa. It is more logical to conclude that over millions of years they were passed down to monkeys, apes, and man from the one ancestor.

The same applies to helminths. Of 34 genera of parasitic helminths in the Hominoidea, man is known to be host to 20, *Pan* to 26, *Pongo* to 13, and *Hylobates* to 14. Seven genera, *Trichuris, Filaria* and *Bertiella,* have been reported from all four primate genera (Dunn 1966). The distribution of helminths is apparently related to the phylogenetic relationships of the primate hosts.

Yellow fever and malaria are two arthropod-borne infections of man, ape, and monkey and it is difficult to avoid concluding that they both evolved over millions of years in common with those primates. Herpes simplex of man is closely related to a similar one in monkeys. Infectious hepatitis virus is found in nature only in apes and man. The virus has been difficult to isolate and grow, but its presence in apes became obvious when so many zoo keepers and others handling them became ill with the disease.

In 1963, I argued by this kind of reasoning that the treponemal infections such as yaws and syphilis might be present in the apes of Africa. Three years later Fribourg-Blanc & Mollaret (1968) showed the baboons to be infected. It is now known that chimpanzees and gorillas are also hosts to treponemes. The ape treponemes are identical with those of yaws, and the areas of the two in Africa coincide.

These are all examples of parasites that could have been in association with primates for many millions of years. Their distribution in the Order Primates largely follow their phylogenetic relationships.

EARLY MAN

That man evolved in Africa and migrated from there around the world is an

FIG. 3. Dispersal of *Homo sapiens* from an Asian focus.

accepted concept today. In Africa, he had a host of infections, but many of them were left behind when he drifted away. All those needing special vectors or inter-mediate hosts not found in his new homes failed to survive. These would include schistosomes, trypanosomes, tick-transmitted infections, arboviruses, and so on. Temperature variation would affect malaria and yellow fever. Only those that belonged directly to man could go with him. These would include the intestinal protozoa, pinworm, whipworm, the treponemes, lice, and mites like *Acarus* (Fig. 3).

On arriving at a new location, man would find a host of parasites already established in the animals and some would infect him also. In the Far East, there would be new schistosomes, *Paragonimus* (the lung fluke), and new arboviruses. Much later, on arriving in areas such as America and Australia, he would find completely new fauna and would acquire some of their infections. In South America, for example, there would be the *Leishmania* of the west coast, and the *Trypanosoma* of Brazil.

Wanderings in northern climates would clear the immigrant populations of all parasites with specific temperature requirements. For example, malaria could not have been carried to America via Siberia and Alaska.

AGRICULTURE AND THE DOMESTICATION OF ANIMALS

Two events resulted from the ending of the Ice Age: the invention of agriculture and the domestication of animals. The immediate effect of these was an abundance of food and a resulting increase in populations.

The anchoring of man to his fields led many animals to move in beside him —not only those which he domesticated, such as the cow, pig, sheep, cat, dog and goat, but many that were unwanted such as the rat and mouse, English sparrow, tick, flea and mosquito. Later, man tamed a number of birds, such as pigeon, jungle fowl, duck and goose, and they also joined the community centred on man's habitation.

Each of these animals would be infected with its own collection of pathogens. The community living in which they participated would ensure that these pathogens would be spread readily among all members, so man would receive samples of all of them. Among them would be all the intestinal bacteria, protozoa, helminths, viruses, and most of the parasites from other tracts of the body. Many of these would be unable to make a successful invasion, but occasionally one would succeed. Then, if this one could be transmitted from man to man, the stage would be set for the evolution of a new specifically human pathogen.

SURVIVAL OF AN INFECTION IS RELATED TO THE SIZE OF THE HOST POPULATION

I suggest that for every purely human infection there is a minimal host population required; if the population falls below the required threshold, then the infection becomes extinct. In small populations, only chronic infections such as typhoid, amoebic dysentery, trachoma or leprosy will survive, while the more acute and transient the infection, the larger is the population that will be needed to support it (Cockburn 1967).

The earliest study to show this pattern is the classic work of Panum (1940) on measles in the Faroe Islands in 1846. At that time, a disastrous epidemic struck the people of the islands, who numbered 7 782, and Panum found that about 95% were attacked. In three months it was gone. The same pattern had appeared before, in 1781, with a severe epidemic, then the disappearance of the disease for 65 years, until it was introduced again in 1846 by a carpenter from Denmark. The explanation is that since measles has no animal reservoir and does not create infectious carriers, it cannot survive in so small a population once it has either killed or immunized a high proportion of the population.

In more recent times we have a similar story with measles in Greenland. That country, with its population of 30 000 persons, had been protected against infection because the time of sea travel from Denmark exceeded the incubation period of measles. However in 1951, a sailor exposed in Denmark had an unusually long incubation period and landed in Greenland in an infectious state. Again, almost everyone became ill, only a few escaping, and then the disease disappeared (Bech 1962). Apparently the country's population of 30 000 cannot support measles as an endemic infection, although, with the opening of air travel, introduced infections have now become more common.

The first person I discovered who wrote on this matter of population size was Hamer in 1906. After a severe epidemic of influenza in London he wrote 'It is important to observe that the capacity for smouldering depends upon the existence of a large population densely aggregated. It may be roughly stated that in London, with its 5 000 000 people, some million cases occur up to the time of maximum prevalence; there are after 13 weeks some 5000 cases a week; and a few cases still occur weekly even after six months. On this basis we see that in a population of say 5000 persons, the outbreak would have practically terminated after 13 weeks, and be altogether extinct before the end of half a year. In these considerations we may find explanation of the behaviour of influenza in Martinique, Reunion, or the Fiji Islands'.

The 'smouldering' of Hamer can only take place in a very large 'herd', which can provide enough susceptibles until a new crop of babies accumulates and another epidemic can take place. With measles, this usually occurs about every two or three years. The interesting question is what the minimum number might be to support measles indefinitely. It seemed to me to be in the region of a million, and this thought was in my mind when, in 1961, I took the position of Assistant Commissioner of Health in Cincinnati, Ohio. Cincinnati had a population of half a million, while the suburbs around provided altogether a total population of $1^1/_4$ million, so that the situation was ideal for a study of the threshold level. In 1961, the city was chosen as one of five in which to test out the newly developed measles vaccine, and for two years, in addition to directing the trials, it was possible for me to watch the incidence of measles fairly closely.

More than 1000 children took part in the experiment in which half were given vaccine and the other half, placebos (Guinee et al. 1963). The 500 unprotected children therefore could be regarded as 'sentinels' for the detection of measles virus.

The numbers of cases of measles reported to the Cincinnati Health Department in the past showed that as a rule there was a two-year cycle, with low levels for the years in between. In some of the years there had been very few cases reported for the months of August to December, only about one case or less per week.

In 1962, all cases reported to the Health Department during these months were investigated. Usually, a conversation was held with the reporting physician on the telephone. If the diagnosis seemed correct, a nurse was sent to make a home visit to inquire into the movements of the patient for the month before the onset of illness. Of the fifteen cases reported, four seemed unlikely to be measles; two were non-residents of the city who had been admitted to Cincinnati hospitals; two were Cincinnati residents who had been in contact with cases of measles in towns some distance away from Cincinnati; and one was a visitor to Cincinnati. The remaining six seemed to be genuine cases of measles indigenous to the city: none gave a history of being in contact with any known case of the disease. There were no true indigenous cases in the four months from mid-September 1962 to mid-January 1963. In 1964, there were eleven cases reported between August 14th and the end of the year, and a period of four months when no indigenous cases could be found.

Cincinnati, with its 108 000 children of school age, had an excellent school medical service, so the first notice of an epidemic usually came from the schools. Every child off sick for more than one day had to bring a medical certificate before re-admission. The City operated 22 infant welfare clinics with 92 000 attendances a year.

To summarize, in 1962 and again in 1964, between August and December there was no sign of indigenous measles in the city. The children in the vaccine tests, those in the schools and those in clinics all were free of measles so far as could be detected. Those cases with genuine measles proved to have been infected outside the city.

The conclusion I have drawn from this is that a population of $1^1/_4$ million is too small by itself to keep measles 'smouldering'.

Another example of an acute community infection is rubella. There were a number of outbreaks in Australia in the 19th century, but every time they died out until the infection was reintroduced from outside. The last time this happened was in 1917, and by all accounts the disease was unknown after that until 1938 when it reappeared as a great epidemic that affected many adults. It was during this epidemic that the relationship between rubella and congenital malformation was discovered.

Unfortunately, it is not possible to prove that rubella disappeared from Australia for the years mentioned, although the general impression is that it did. Rubella was not made a notifiable disease until 1953, so no statistics are available. Nevertheless, the great outbreak at the end of the 1930s seemed to affect all age groups, whereas in endemic areas it is primarily an infection of children. It would therefore seem that the impression reached by practising physicians was correct and that the infection was newly imported in 1938 (Lancaster 1967).

Australia in 1917 had a population of only five million. The towns and cities were scattered through vast areas, Sydney being the only one whose population even approached a million. This was in the days before air travel, so that the chances of rubella virus being carried from one city to another were not very great. If rubella did in fact become extinct for a period of years, this could well be explained on the basis that the peoples of the continent were too few in numbers to support it indefinitely by person-to-person spread. The sea voyage from England took two months, which reduced the chances of it spreading from Europe.

By 1938, the story was different. The population had risen to eight million; Sydney was over the million mark, and an excellent air service was now linking the cities together. Instead of a number of isolated communities, there was now a single nation in which infections could spread with ease, and enough people existed to support a virus like rubella indefinitely. London was brought closer by air travel, so there was plenty of opportunity for the importation of the virus.

I propose the example of rubella in Australia to illustrate the size of community needed to support an acute community infection indefinitely.

LATER DEVELOPMENTS

Acute community infections are those that are specific to man, with no animal hosts, do not form carrier states, and exist by rapid passage from one person to another. As argued above, they require huge populations, at least a million or more, and therefore could not have existed before approximately 5000 B.C. They probably arose from animal infections that became adapted to man after a few man-to-man passages and survived when the host population passed the required threshold.

Examples are measles virus, which probably came from dog distemper virus, and mumps, smallpox and influenza, which arose from related viruses in domestic animals and birds.

The roundworm *Ascaris* may have evolved at the same time. *Ascaris* has been recovered from eight locations in prehistoric Europe, always in association with the whipworm, *Trichuris*. The pinworm *Enterobius*, *Trichuris* and the hookworm *Ankylostoma* have all been found in the pre-Columbian New World and must have been carried there during the Ice Age, but *Ascaris* has not been found there. This suggests that *Ascaris* evolved in man after the Ice Age, probably from ascarids of the newly domesticated swine. Agricultural practices themselves led to the increase of selected parasites. It is impossible here even to summarize the various influences, but examples are the use of faeces as fertilizer in the East, which resulted in a huge increase in hookworm disease in China, irrigation with the spread of schistosomiasis in Egypt and the East, fish farming using human faeces, which increased the number of fluke infections, slash and burn farming that promoted malaria in Africa, and rice farming with its mosquitoes and arbovirus infections.

CODA

The period covered by this paper ends with the beginning of the historic period, with rapidly increasing populations, the spread of agriculture, improved communications, urbanization, mass movements of peoples and the coming of the industrial age. All these factors, however, simply accentuated those processes which were first established in the millennia preceding the era for which we have written records.

References

BECH, V. (1962) Measles epidemics in Greenland 1951–59. *Am. J. Dis. Child. 103*, 252

COCKBURN, T.A. (1963) *The Evolution and Eradication of Infectious Disease*, Johns Hopkins University Press, Baltimore

COCKBURN, T. A. (1967) *Infectious Diseases: their Evolution and Eradication*, Thomas, Springfield, Ill.

COCKERILL, T.D.A. (1908) Fossil insects from Florissant, Colo. *Bull. Am. Mus. Nat. Hist. 24*, 65–66

DUNN, F. L. (1966) Patterns of parasitism in primates. *Folia Primatologica 4*, 329–345

FRIBOURG-BLANC, A. & MOLLARET, H.H. (1968) Natural treponematosis of the African primate. *Primates in Medicine 3*, 110–118

GUINEE, V.P. *et al.* (1963) A collaborative study of measles vaccines in five United States communities. *Am. J. Public Health 53*, 645–651

HAMER, W.H. (1906) Epidemic diseases in England. *Lancet*, p. 735

HARRISON, L. (1914) The Mallophaga as a possible clue to bird phylogeny. *Aust. Zool. 1*, 7–11

HERRER, A. & CHRISTENSEN, H.A. (1975) Implication of *Phlebotomus* sandflies as vectors of bartonellosis and leishmaniasis as early as 1764. *Science (Wash. D.C.) 190*, 154–155

HOARE, C.A. (1972) *The Trypanosomes of Mammals*, Blackwell Scientific Publications, Oxford

KELLOGG, V.L. (1913) Distribution and species forming of ectoparasites. *Am. Naturalist 47*, 129–158

LANCASTER, H.O. (1967) The infections and population size in Australia. *Bull. Int. Statist. Inst. 42*, 459–471 (In a personal communication he added that measles died out several times from its first introduction to Australia in 1835)

LUMSDEN, W.H.R. (1976) Chagas' disease—a survey of the present position. *Trans. R. Soc. Trop. Med. Hyg. 50*, 121–122

PANUM, P.L. (1940) *Measles in the Faroe Islands*, Delta Omega Society, New York (American Public Health Association)

RUNCORN, S.K. (1962) *Continental Drift*, Academic Press, New York

Discussion

Black: You cited rubella as an example of a disease that requires a rather large population to keep itself in existence. However, rubella seems to be anomalous in that it has even died out from Taiwan, which has a population of more than 10 million. This is in spite of the fact that the virus does persist in cases of congenital rubella for long periods of time. There is something odd about the incidence of rubella.

As to the source of measles, I suggest that rinderpest virus should be considered as well as canine distemper.

Cockburn: There is a whole group of related animal viruses but I thought the dog, being so close to man, might provide the precursor of measles virus. The dog has lived with man since the Palaeolithic, hunting with him, sharing his food and habitat, and often even his bed. Dog viruses must often have infected man, but until man's population passed the critical threshold level, a human virus like that of distemper of dogs could not evolve and survive. Incidentally, in the US today, human measles vaccine is being used to protect dogs against distemper.

Truswell: How many dogs do you need to keep dog distemper going? If you need more than a million it would be rather difficult to envisage.

Black: Canine distemper killed two-thirds of the dogs of Tahiti in 1957 and persisted there afterwards for at least several years. I do not know the specific number of dogs involved, but it must have been much less than a million at that time, when there were 50 000 humans.

Cockburn: My work was done on measles of today; I do not know how dog distemper was maintained in the Palaeolithic. In the US today there are almost as many dogs as families, so there are adequate numbers of them to support the distemper virus.

Epidemiology of infectious disease: the example of measles

FRANCIS L. BLACK, FRANCISCO DE P. PINHEIRO*, WALTER J. HIERHOLZER** and RICHARD V. LEE+

Department of Epidemiology and Public Health, Yale University School of Medicine, New Haven, and Instituto Evandro Chagas, Brazilian Ministry of Health, Belém

Abstract The situation of unacculturated Brazilian Amazon tribes is described. The isolation of these populations has been sufficiently tight that they have been free of most epidemic diseases of the cosmopolitan world, although diseases associated with persistent infection have a high prevalence.

The history of measles epidemics in Amerind populations is reviewed and it is concluded that most deaths can be prevented by basic nursing care but that there is a residual excess mortality characteristic of these populations. Three Brazilian virgin-soil populations and one experienced tribe in Chile, the Mapuche, were vaccinated against measles. Elevated febrile responses were observed in the three virgin-soil populations relative to the fevers seen in the Mapuche and in cosmopolitan populations. Nutritional status, immunological experience, humoral immune response and genetic characters have been examined for an explanation of this phenomenon. The most pronounced correspondence detected so far is a high degree of homozygosity in HLA loci of the virgin populations.

TRIBES OF THE UPPER TRIBUTARIES OF THE AMAZON

The difficulty of ground travel in those parts of the Amazon–Orinoco basin where the rivers are not navigable, coupled with the relative uniformity of the flora and fauna, has led to the persistence there of cultures based on small independent social units. Chagnon (1974) has described the circumstances which determine the size of the social unit among the Yanomamo. Similar, though generally less violent, interpersonal relationships limit the size of social unit in

---

* Awardee of the Centro Nacionão da Pequisas, Brazil

** *Present address:* Program of Epidemiology, University of Iowa Hospitals and Clinics, Iowa City, Iowa

+ *Present address:* Department of Medicine, State University of New York School of Medicine, Buffalo, N.Y.

these parts of Brazil to between 100 and 400 people each. I shall refer to such groups as a 'tribe'. Although different 'tribes' may have cultural and historical affinities, they are politically and economically independent and often hostile toward one another. The populations, as long as their culture is unmodified by contact with the cosmopolitan world, live in isolation just as profound as that of people on the most remote islands of the oceans.

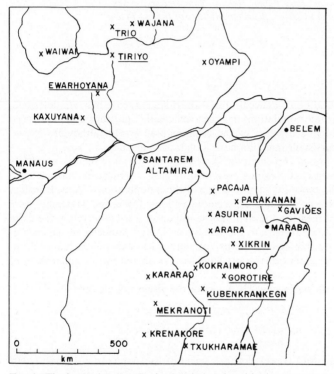

FIG. 1. The lower Amazon Basin showing major cities, ●, and unacculturated Indian tribes, ✕. Those tribes included in the study are underlined.

Fig. 1 shows tribes we have worked with and their known neighbours. The average distance to the nearest neighbour is 150 km, about a week's trek. Visits or raids between tribes usually occur less than once a year. A more important index of isolation for this study, however, is the absence of disease transmission from one tribe to another. In 1962 rubella was introduced to the Tiriyo from Surinam, but serological studies show that it did not reach the Ewarhoyana, their nearest neighbours to the south. The same year, measles was introduced to the Gorotire; it reached the Kuben Kran Kegn but did not spread to the Xikrin or Mekranoti. In 1964 a devastating measles epidemic hit the southern tribes of the Xingu Park, but it did not spread to the Txukàrramãe, in the northern part of the park (Nutels 1968).

EPIDEMIC PATTERNS IN ISOLATED POPULATIONS

Panum (1940) showed in his classic study of the Faroe Islanders, and it has been amply confirmed since, that epidemics in previously isolated communities are more intense than in partially immune populations. There is no dampening effect of preimmune persons, and the epidemic bursts forth with great intensity to reach almost the whole population in a very few cycles. Then, if the agent has no human or extra-human reservoir, it has nowhere to go and dies out completely.

Paul and his associates (1951) showed that serum collections from various age groups in an isolated community can be used to determine the history of these epidemics long after the event, if the disease agent elicits a lasting specific immune response. In sera collected in 1949 Paul found Type 2 poliovirus antibodies in most persons born before 1930 but not later; Type 1 only in persons

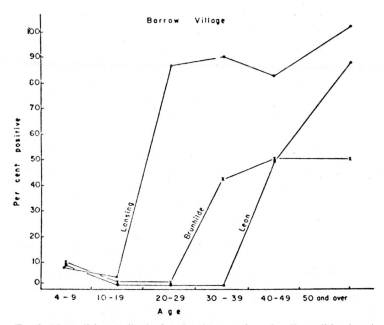

FIG. 2. Neutralizing antibody for the three strains of poliomyelitis virus in different age groups of the population of Barrow Village, Alaska in 1949. (Taken from Paul *et al.* 1951.)

born before 1915; and Type 3 in persons born before 1905. They suggested that these dates represented the last occasions on which the respectives viruses were present in the community and they were able to correlate two of these dates with histories of epidemic paralytic disease (Fig. 2).

TABLE 1

Classification of diseases in isolated populations by epidemiological patterns determined serologically

Infection of most persons at an early age	*Occasional infections occurring throughout life*	*Infections absent or occurring in intense epidemics with clear termination*
Herpes simplex 1	Yellow fever	Measles
Epstein-Barr virus (infectious mononucleosis)	Ilheus	Rubella
	Mayaro	Mumps
Cytomegalovirus	Malaria	BK Polyoma
Varicella	Toxoplasmosis	Parainfluenzas 1, 2 & 3
Hepatitis B	Tuberculosis	Influenza A & B
Amoebiasis		Poliomyelitis 1, 2 & 3
Treponemosis[a]		Smallpox

[a] Infections do not seem to begin until adulthood. The treponemal infections were limited to the Kayapo.

We have used this serological technique to reconstruct the history of infectious diseases in the Amazon tribes. In general, we find the age-specific antibody patterns (Black *et al.* 1974) fall into three categories (Table 1):

1. The endemic agents which regularly elicited antibodies at an early age. These we believe are agents which are continuously present in even these small communities. They include most of the viruses which establish chronic latent infections. In the Kayapo tribes a treponemal infection follows a similar pattern, although it only becomes prevalent at the age of puberty. Malaria may also persist in some tribes without mediation of any non-human reservoir (but, of course, with a mosquito vector).

2. The zoonoses which elicited a progressively higher prevalence of antibody with increasing age over an extended range. These are agents which occur frequently in the tribes, but never with sufficient intensity to affect the whole population at once. They prove to be agents that cycle primarily in a non-human reservoir.

3. Finally, there were the exogenous agents which fit the pattern described above in which either everybody, or nearly no one, above some specific age had

antibody. This group included most diseases that occur in epidemic form in populations.

MEASLES IN VIRGIN-SOIL POPULATIONS

None of the Mekranoti, and only three Xikrin and Tiriyo, had antibody to measles. All positive specimens were from adults who may have travelled outside the tribal boundaries. Knowing that measles antibodies, once acquired, usually persist for life in measurable titre, we can be quite sure that measles virus is exogenous to the tribes and had not been active within them during the lifetime of their eldest members. Furthermore, on the basis of historical and theoretical evidence, we believe that measles did not occur in the Americas before the Iberian conquests. It is tempting then to suppose that, if measles had visited these tribes neither before 1500 nor since 1890, it probably was also absent during the interval, a period when travel was more restricted than it has been recently. That is, we believe that when we find no antibody to this disease, there is a good possibility that there has been no experience with it for several millennia. Since we also believe that measles first appeared in the most densely populated parts of the world a few thousand years ago (Black 1966), we think these people may never have been exposed to it.

The supposition that these peoples have had no prior experience with measles is, of course, not novel. It originated as an explanation for historical accounts of high measles mortality in the first post-Columbian epidemics. The mortality data from these early epidemics is only qualitative and specific case fatality rates are nowhere available before 1951. Between 1951 and 1969 data were collected during a number of virgin-soil epidemics and they reveal a high but variable mortality rate (Table 2). Availability of medical care seems to be an important factor. Areas like Western Greenland which had a good medical infrastructure suffered relatively little from these epidemics, but this may also be because the Greenlander's genetic heritage by the time was a blend of Eskimo and European traits. Nevertheless, even in these most favourable circumstances the mortality was 15 times greater than in cosmopolitan populations. Four factors might account for this difference:

1. Differences in the age-specific attack rate.
2. Differences in the effects of secondary bacterial infections.
3. Problems associated with the breakdown of basic nursing services when much of the population was sick at once.
4. Population-wide differences in susceptibility to the effects of the virus.

In the virgin-soil epidemics in Greenland and Ungava the mortality rate

TABLE 2

Measles mortality in recent outbreaks

Locality	Year	Medical care	IgG given	No. of cases	Case rate fatality (%)	References
S.W. Greenland	1951	Yes	Yes	4320	1.8	Christensen *et al.* 1953
Ungava, Canada	1952	No	No	900	7.0	Peart & Nagler 1954
Baffin Island, Canada	1952	Yes	Yes	900	2.0	Peart & Nagler 1954
Xingu Park, Brazil	1954	No	No	298	27.0	Nutels 1968
Xingu Park, Brazil	1954	Yes	?	356	9.6	Nutels 1968
Jacobshaven, Greenland	1959	Yes	Yes	1178	0.3	Bech 1962*a*
Several towns, Greenland	1962	Yes	Yes	10 722	0.5	Bech 1962*b*
Yanomamo, Venezuela	1968	Yes	No	505	8.8	Neel *et al.* 1970
England and Wales	1961	Yes	Yes	764 000	0.02	Cited by Celers 1965

where it is lowest, in the 5- to 30-years-old group, was as high as in the least-favoured age groups in areas with past measles experience (Fig. 3). We do not believe, therefore, that the relatively high average age at infection in virgin-soil epidemics explains the mortality rates. In fact, postponing the majority of cases beyond the first few years of life might reduce mortality, by comparison with some cosmopolitan situations.

Many deaths associated with measles are due to secondary invaders, and since these are more responsive than the virus to therapy, higher death rates may be expected where medical services are lacking. In the virgin-soil epidemics that have been studied, however, many of the deaths occur very early in the course of the disease. In Greenland in 1951, for instance, 38% of all deaths in persons untreated with gammaglobulin occurred during the prodromal period (Christensen *et al.* 1953). These deaths, which by themselves occurred at a rate well above the total measles death rate of developed countries, could hardly be due to secondary invaders.

The data in Table 2 suggest that medical care does reduce mortality. During a virgin-soil epidemic, so many people may be sick at once that the most basic services often break down. Since there is no specific treatment for measles, other than gammaglobulin given early, the effect of the medical care may actually be exerted in ways as simple as supplying warmth and water. Yet even with this care there is an excess mortality and it is hard to see how nursing care could have much effect on the number of prodromal deaths.

This analysis shows, then, that factors other than unusual susceptibility of the population can account for much of the excess mortality, but it suggests that

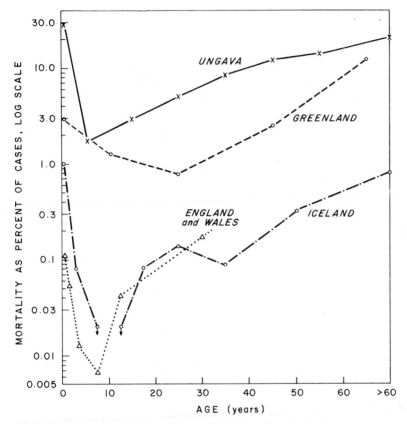

FIG. 3. Measles age-specific mortality rates in virgin-soil and endemic areas.

x———x   Ungava (Peart & Nagler 1954)
o - - - - o   Greenland (Christensen *et al.* 1953)
o—.—.—o   Iceland (Heilbrigdisskyrslur 1941–1950)
Δ.........Δ   England and Wales (Celers 1965)

there may also be a residual fraction of the mortality not accounted for by the other factors. It was enough to encourage us to look for specific evidence of susceptibility differences.

MEASLES VACCINE REACTIONS IN VIRGIN POPULATIONS

Attenuated live measles vaccine gives rise, in almost all respects, to a mild but complete set of measles symptoms. It causes rash, koplick spots, leucopenia and fever in a proportion of vaccinees, all in the same time sequence as has been observed after injection of wild virus. The only consistent difference seems to be the absence of neurological involvement. If the virgin-soil measles mortality were a reflection of some difference in individual susceptibility, one would expect to see the difference reproduced in the vaccine reaction. Here was a model of a natural disease which we could use with a clear conscience; indeed, delivery of this vaccine seemed an urgent component of good medical care. We used the Schwarz further-attenuated strain of vaccine in all studies.

In looking for a measure of the vaccine reaction, we found that these people with their dark, weathered skin did not manifest a recognizable rash, nor were daily finger pricks for white cell counts tolerated. Rectal or oral temperature measurements were not practical, but axillary measurement presented no problem and offered a quantitative index of the reaction. To make these temperatures comparable with data from studies in cosmopolitan areas, which usually utilized rectal temperatures, we have worked with the difference in body temperature between vaccinees and controls. This has been standardized to the difference between the maximum temperature recorded in vaccinees 7–14 days after vaccination and the maximum recorded in members of a control group over the same length of time.

TABLE 3

Febrile response to Schwarz measles vaccine in various populations. Difference between maximum temperature 6–13 days after vaccination and maximum in a similar control period

	Children			15 years and over			Age adjusted
	No.	*Elev.°C*	*± S.E.*	*No.*	*Elev.°C*	*± S.E.*	*Elev.°C*
Tiriyo	36	1.16	0.08	72	0.79	0.13	1.04 ⎫
Xirkin	50	0.97	0.14	60	0.52	0.12	0.80 ⎬ 0.904
Mekranoti	82	0.88	0.11	100	0.22	0.09	0.49 ⎭
Mapuche	35	0.35	0.11	—	—	—	0.39 ⎫
Chileno	21	0.21	0.15	—	—	—	0.26 ⎬ 0.419
WHO	372	0.54		—	—	—	0.43 ⎭

Temperatures adjusted for age effects to give values expected if all were five years old. (See Black *et al.* 1971.)

We have made these studies (Table 3) in three virgin-soil tribes (Black *et al.* 1969, 1971); in the Pedrogoso Mapuche of southern Chile; and in Chilenos of the same area. Standard data are also available from a coordinated WHO study in five countries of Europe and the Americas (Cockburn *et al.* 1966). In the virgin soil tribes the population was divided into two groups for vaccination at different times and each group served as temperature control for the other; in Chile, the controls were made up of preimmune persons vaccinated at the same time as the responders; and in the WHO series, control groups received placebo injections.

The results given in Table 3 indicate that the vaccine reaction was stronger in all three virgin-soil groups than in any of the more cosmopolitan populations. An exception is the adult Mekranoti who did not have as much fever as the children. Overall, the difference in height of maximum fever between the isolated and cosmopolitan populations was about 0.5°C. This may not seem very much, but it is as great as the difference in reaction between the Edmonston B and the further-attenuated measles vaccines, or the effect of concomitant gammaglobulin on the Edmonston B vaccine. It surprised us that the Mapuche reacted as a cosmopolitan population. The people of the area of our study had been reported by Etcheverry *et al.* (1967) to have only 5% European gene admixture, on the basis of the assumption that the original population was 100% blood group O. On the basis of the less well-defined HLA (histocompatibility) system, we estimated about 20% foreign genes. They had presumably been exposed to measles since it was first introduced to Chile about 16 generations ago.

We have done similar studies using a live rubella vaccine, but with it have seen no evidence of unusual reaction.

Three possible explanations of the measles vaccine results may be considered:

1. The virgin-soil populations, by virtue of isolation from infections, lack experience with very common antigens that cross-react with measles and provide some priming for the measles response.
2. The virgin-soil populations are poorly nourished and this leaves them ill-equipped to resist measles virus.
3. The virgin-soil populations lack certain genetic traits which have become common in other populations through prolonged selective pressure.

The difference in response to the vaccine observed in the Mekranoti children and adults could be most easily explained if only the adults had been previously exposed to some cross-reactive antigen. However, the only antigens which are known to cross-react with measles virus are rinderpest and canine distemper viruses. Rinderpest is not widely distributed throughout the world and canine distemper virus has no effect on measles antibody titres in man under natural conditions (Black & Rosen 1962). More generally, the pattern of acquisition of measles antibody titre after vaccination is neither quantitatively nor temporally inferior to that observed in Iceland, where the people had a long history of exposure to measles (Fig. 4). The range of titres in the Indians is a little greater but the mean titres are slightly higher, as might be expected in association with a greater febrile response.

Cellular defences are almost certainly essential in the elimination of measles virus (Utermohlen & Zabriskie 1973). We have no direct measure of this element of the immune reaction of the Indians but we have looked for anergy during the vaccine reaction period. Anergy is reported between 5 and 15 days after

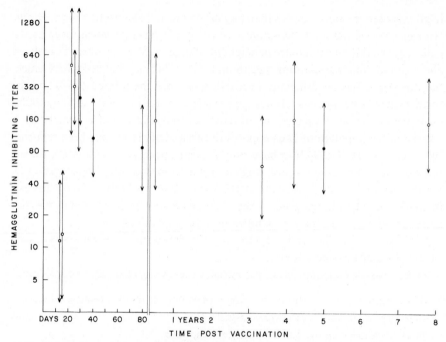

FIG. 4. Measles haemagglutinin inhibiting titres after vaccination with Schwarz further attenuated virus: titres in Icelanders and Brazilian Indians.
←O→, mean and standard deviation of titres in Icelanders.
←O→, mean and standard deviation of titres in virgin-soil Indian tribes.
A total of 241 Icelandic and 600 Brazilian serum specimens are included. Different time intervals represent different sub-populations in some instances.

measles vaccination (Brody & McAlister 1964) in cosmopolitan populations and for rather longer periods after natural measles. In the Xikrin we found no evidence of anergy to tuberculin 8–10 days after vaccination (Table 4), but there was partial reduction of sensitivity to *Candida* antigen in studies done with the Mekranoti.

We have collected data on weight for height, arm circumference, hair root diameter and serum albumin for the Xikrin, Mekranoti and Mapuche to test for evidence of malnutrition (Table 5) (Black *et al.* 1976). The Kayapo tribes reach or exceed international standards on all scores except hair root diameter. In this measurement they showed increasing size with increasing age, and the males had greater hair root diameters than females. Such a pattern is more suggestive of normal growth than malnutrition. Mid-arm muscle circumference values for the Kayapo were greater than in the Mapuche, who did not show an enhanced reaction to measles virus. Certainly, there is no evidence in the Kayapo

TABLE 4

Evidence of anergy in the measles vaccine reactions in virgin-soil populations

	Days after vaccination	No.	% positive	Mean[a] diameter	± S.E.
Tuberculin	8–10	47	25.6	13.8 mm	0.5
	21–22	50	42	14.6	0.6
Candida	0–1	21	76	8.2	1.5
	5–7	16	60	3.6	0.9
	12	19	89	9.0	1.4
	19	12	100	15.2	2.7

[a] Weal measured at 48 hours. The data on sensitivity to *Candida* antigen include both serial tests in the same individual and single tests at different times. No evidence was found of increased sensitization as a result of the serial testing.

of the kind of malnutrition associated with severe measles in Africa (Morley 1964).

GENETIC CONSIDERATIONS

Most marriages in the Brazilian Indian tribes are contracted within the village, or tribe, in the sense we have used the word. Although each tribe includes a few individuals who had entered from outside either voluntarily or as captives and although parallel cousin marriages are considered incestuous, the degree of inbreeding must be very high. Spielman *et al.* (1976) have estimated

TABLE 5

Nutritional status of Kayapo and Mapuche Indians

Age	Numbers tested for Wt/Ht & MMC		Weight as % of norm[a] for height		Mid-arm muscle circumference (MMC) % below U.S.[b] 15th percentile		Hair root bulb mean maximum diameter (μm)	Serum albumin (g/100ml)
	K[c]	Ma[d]	K	Ma	♂	Ma	K ± S.E.	K
< 5	89	40	96	103	1.5	3	100 ± 7	4.53
5–15	50	126	108	105	3	12	108 ± 3	4.07
♂ > 15	73	13	99	108	12	38	141 ± 7	4.02
♀ > 15	65	14	104	111	1.5	0	131 ± 6	4.28

[a] U.S. actuarial norms as published by Jelliffe (1966).
[b] U.S. standard as published by Frisancho (1974).
[c] Xikrin and Mekranoti combined.
[d] Mapuche of the Upper BioBio Valley.

the inbreeding frequency of the Yanomamo at 0.5. This value takes into account both the fact that the whole South American gene pool was twice constricted in passing the Bering Strait and the Isthmus of Panama and also the fact that nearly everyone in an isolated village is related in some way within the past three or four generations.

We have collaborated with Dr Salzano and others (Salzano *et al.* 1972*a, b*, 1974) in determining blood group antigens and enzymes in these populations. For the present purposes it is only necessary to state that they have very few genes characteristic of other races. In fact no foreign trait was found in the Xikrin, whom we shall consider in detail presently.

It is not surprising to find that the range of histocompatibility (HLA) polymorphisms in the isolated populations is very narrow. Only 9 or 10 of 31 commonly recognized types have been found with frequency in any isolated Eskimo or South American Indian populations and one type may predominate at each locus in any one tribe (Table 6 and Kissmeyer-Nielsen *et al.* 1973; Dossetor

TABLE 6

Distribution of major HLA types in two South American Indian populations

		Xikrin (N = 75)		Mapuche (N = 56)	
		% Phenotype	Gene frequency	% Phenotype	Gene frequency
HLA–	A1	0		12.5	0.65
	A2	69.3	0.446	48.2	0.280
	A9	10.7	0.055	25.0	0.134
	A11	0		3.6	0.018
	A28	4.0	0.020	48.2	0.280
	AW24	4.0	0.020		
	AW30	5.3	0.027	9.8	0.050
	AW32	16.0	0.084	9.8	0.050
	A blank (homozygous)		0.334		0.105
HLA–	B5	8.0	0.041	18.7	0.098
	B8	0		10.7	0.055
	B13	2.7	0.014	3.6	0.018
	BW15	66.7	0.423	7.1	0.036
	BW16	1.3	0.007	18.7	0.098
	BW21	0		5.4	0.027
	BW27	1.3	0.007	9.8	0.050
	BW35	34.7	0.190	43.8	0.250
	BW40	14.7	0.076	7.1	0.036
	B blank (homozygous)	—	0.222	—	0.231

Calculated by the formula $p = 1 - \sqrt{1 - f}$ where P is gene frequency and f the phenotypic frequency.

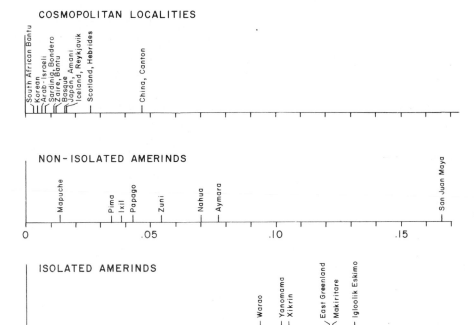

FIG. 5. Proportion of population estimated to be homozygous at both HLA loci on the assumption of free association between genes and absence of selective pressures. Calculated from data of several authors in *Histocompatability Testing, 1972* (1973, Munksgaard, Copenhagen); Yasuda *et al.* (1976); and data in Table 6 by the formula $H = (\Sigma F_A^2)(\Sigma F_B^2)$ where H is the fraction doubly homozygous and F_A and F_B are the frequencies of the individual alleles at the A and B loci respectively.

et al. 1973; Layrisse *et al.* 1973). This restriction is of special interest when considering disease response because the HLA loci are closely associated with a series of genes which control the breadth of the immune response (Ir genes) (Benacerraf & McDevitt 1972). If HLA polymorphisms are restricted, the range of Ir genes may be similarly limited. The small total number of different alleles and the local preponderance of individual alleles means that an unusually high proportion of the isolated tribes are homozygous for both HLA loci. This is evident when one assumes free association between the loci (Fig. 5), but is doubtless even more pronounced in actuality, because linkage would hold pairs together in an inbred population. The positive response Ir genes so far characterized are additive, and concentrated in a limited linkage group, so that homozygosity in this region could halve the number of potential responses. The larger South American Indian populations, as for example the Mapuche, generally have a much lower proportion of their population homozygous. This would be the result of reduced inbreeding; incorporation of some exogenously derived genes is usually also part of the pattern. The diversification process would have been greatly accelerated if, in addition, it were advantageous in the heavy selective pressure from infectious diseases, to which these larger Indian populations have been subject for a few hundred years.

As a preliminary look at this possibility we have examined the distribution of fevers after measles vaccine by HLA type. Information on the two characteristics is available for 56 of the Xikrin. This group was divided in half according to whether their fevers had been more or less than 1.4 degree-days over 37.2°C, in the axilla (Table 7). In this tabulation there is a negative correlation between

TABLE 7

Distribution of major HLA types by measles vaccine reaction group

	Post-vaccine fever-days[a]	
	> 1.4° C	< 1.4° C
A2	64%[b]	68%
A32	21	14
A blank or homozygous	89	61
B15	61	68
B35	11	46
B40	41	14
B blank or homozygous	75	46
A2, B15 only	29	7

[a] Sum of temperatures greater than 37.2 °C (axillary) during the 7th–13th days after vaccination.
[b] % of group exhibiting trait.

fever and HLA-B35 and a positive correlation with the proportion blank but, perhaps most relevant to the theory if not most significant statistically, 8 of 10 individuals who exhibited only A2 and B15 were in the group with the higher fevers. These two types occur together less frequently than would be expected by chance when the data are analysed by gene pairs, as if there had been a selection against the combination (Table 8).

We have said that an association of HLA type with severity of infection might be exerted through differences in immune response. We have already seen that the immune response in these populations is normal, except for a reduced degree of anergy. If this is the basis of the difference it must lie in the cellular response, perhaps in the availability of suppressor T lymphocytes.

We cannot ascribe probability values to these data because the hypotheses were formulated after the data were examined. In any case, confirmation in more than one tribe is needed. If, however, homozygosity of the HLA region is

TABLE 8

Haplotype frequency: D values of Mattuiz. Italicized values exceed twice the standard error (S.E.)

	A locus				
	2	9	32	Miscellaneous	Blank
B locus — 5	0.023	0.010	−0.008	0.008	−0.033
15	−0.120	0.001	0.035	0.036	0.007
35	0.019	0.019	0.007	0.001	0.006
40	−0.008	0	0.008	0.010	−0.015
Miscellaneous	−0.016	0.001	0.011	0.012	−0.008
Blank	0.056	0.019	−0.049	−0.054	0.044

associated with enhanced susceptibility to certain infectious diseases, these people will continue to require special medical consideration, by comparison with more diversified populations.

References

BECH, V. (1962a) Am. J. Dis. Child. 103, 252–253

BECH, V. (1962b) Arch. Ges. Virusforsch. 16, 53–56

BENECERRAF, B. & McDEVITT, H.O. (1972) Science (Wash. D.C.) 175, 273–279

BLACK, F.L. (1966) J. Theor. Biol. 11, 207–211

BLACK, F.L. & ROSEN, L. (1962) J. Immunol. 88, 725–731

BLACK, F.L., WOODALL, J.P. & PINHEIRO, F. deP. (1969 Am. J. Epidemiol. 89, 168–175

BLACK, F.L., HIERHOLZER, W.J., WOODALL, J.P. & PINHEIRO, F. deP. (1971) J. Infect. Dis. 124, 306–317

BLACK, F.L., HIERHOLZER, W.J., PINHEIRO, F. deP., EVANS, A.S., WOODALL, J.P., OPTON, E. M., EMMONS, J.E., WEST, B.S., EDSALL, G., DOWNS, W.G. & WALLACE, G.D. (1974) Am. J. Epidemiol. 100, 230–250

BLACK, F.L., HIERHOLZER, W.J., BLACK, D.P., LAMM, S.H. & LUCAS, L.A. (1976) Hum. Biol. 49, 139–153

BRODY, J. & McALISTER, R. (1964) Am. Rev. Resp. Dis. 90, 607–611

CELERS, J. (1965) Arch. Ges. Virusforsch. 16, 5–18

CHAGNON, N.A. (1974) Studying the Yanomamö, Holt Reinhart, Winston, New York

CHRISTENSEN, P.E., SCHMIDT, H., BANG, H.O., ANDERSEN, V., JORDAL, B. & JENSEN, O. (1953) Acta Med. Scand. 144, 430–449

COCKBURN, W.C., PEČENKA, S. & SUNDARSAN, T. (1966) Bull. W.H.O. 34, 223–231

DOSSETOR, J.B., HOWSON, W.T., SCHLAUT, J., McCONNACHIE, P.R., ALTON, J.D.M., LOCK-WOOD, B. & OLSON, L. (1973) Histocompatibility Testing, 1972, Munksgaard, Copenhagen

ETCHEVERRY, R., GUZMAN, C., HILLE, A., NAGEL, R., COVARRUBIAS, E., REGONESI, C., MU-RANDA, M., DURAN, N. & MONTENEGRO, A. (1967) Rev. Med. Chile 95, 599–604

FRISANCHO, A.A. (1974) Am. J. Clin. Nutr. 27, 1052–1058

HEILBRIGDISSKYRSLUR (1941–1950) Skrifstofu, Landlaeknis, Reykjavik

JELLIFFE, D.B. (1966) Assessment of the nutritional status of the community. W.H.O. Monogr. Ser. 53

KISSMEYER-NIELSEN, F., KJERBYE, K.E., LAMM, L.U., JØRGENSEN, J., PETERSEN, G.B. & GÜRT-LER, H. (1973) Histocompatibility Testing 1972, Munksgaard, Copenhagen

LAYRISSE, Z., TERASAKI, P., WILBERT, J., HEINEN, H.D., RODRIGUEZ, B., SOYANO, A., MITTAL, K. & LAYRISSE, M. (1973) *Histocompatibility Testing, 1972*, Munksgaard, Copenhagen
MORLEY, D. (1964) *Proc. R. Soc. Med. 57*, 846–849
NEEL, J.V., CENTERWALL, W.R., CHAGNON, N.A. & CASEY, H.L. (1970) *Am. J. Epidemiol. 91*, 418–429
NUTELS, N. (1968) in *Biomedical Challenges Presented by the American Indian (Pan Am. Health Org. Sci. Publ. 165)*, pp. 68–76, W.H.O., Washington, D.C.
PANUM, P.L. (1940) *Observations made during the epidemic of measles on the Faroe Islands in the year 1846*, American Publishing Association, New York
PAUL, J.R., RIORDAN, J.T. & MELNICK, J.L. (1951) *Am. J. Hyg. 54*, 275–285
PEART, A.F.W. & NAGLER, F.P. (1954) *Can. J. Public Health 45*, 146–157
SALZANO, F.M., GERSHOWITZ, H., JUNQUEIRA, P.C., WOODALL, J.P., BLACK, F.L. & HIERHOLZER, W. (1972a) *Am. J. Phys. Anthropol. 36*, 417–426
SALZANO, F.M., NEEL, J.V., WEITKAMP, L.R. & WOODALL, J.P. (1972b) *Hum. Biol. 44*, 443–458
SALZANO, F.M., WOODALL, J.P., BLACK, F.L., WEITKAMP, L.R. & FRANCO, M.H.L.P. (1974) *Hum. Biol. 46*, 81–87
SPIELMAN, R.S., NEEL, J.V. & LI, F. (1976) Cited by Neel, in *Johns Hopkins Med. J. 138*, 233–244
UTERMOHLEN, V. & ZABRISKIE, J.B. (1973) *J. Exp. Med. 138*, 1591–1596
YASUDA, N., TSUJI, K., ARIZAWA, M., ITAKURA, K., INOU, T., MATSUKURA, M., TOSHIDA T., FUKUNISHI, T., ORITA, K., NOMOTO, K. & ITO, M. (1976) *Am. J. Hum. Genet. 28*, 390–399

Discussion

Neel: May I congratulate you on a very cautious statement of the issue of genetic susceptibility! I believe you had to worry about the presence of an intercurrent undifferentiated respiratory illness in a couple of the villages?

Black: In the Tiriyo there was such an outbreak concurrent with half the reactions; in the others we did not encounter respiratory infection at the time.

Neel: The Tiriyo showed the greatest temperature response to the vaccine; perhaps concurrent infection played a role in that temperature response?

Black: Yes. Of course, it occurred in both the controls and in the vaccinees. It seemed to enhance the fever in the vaccinees somewhat more than in the controls.

Tyrrell: Would you not agree that the age distribution of cases *can* be important in determining the severity and the mortality of an infection? You referred (p. 117) to Paul's work on poliomyelitis in isolated communities. It was clear that many people died because these were first infections in adults. In the island which I shall be discussing later, Tristan da Cunha, they apparently had only one natural invasion by poliovirus, which in a group of a couple of hundred subjects produced one fatal case which was diagnosed as Landry paralysis, in an adult, whereas none of the children was severely affected (Taylor-Robinson & Tyrrell 1963).

Black: This is very true in polio. I think each disease has to be considered individually. In measles there was a U-shaped mortality curve and the greatest part of our populations are in the part of the curve with low mortality.

Truswell: When you were trying to explain why there were higher mortalities in some populations than others you examined all the possibilities and finally were left with genetic variability, but you hadn't at that stage mentioned nutrition. It was only when you came to the response to the vaccine that you included nutrition as a possible variable. I think one must include the possibility that nutrition can be responsible for differences in mortality from infectious disease, although I don't believe it would be, probably, in hunter–gatherers eating a mixed diet.

Black: Yes, I agree that it is just as relevant there as in the later considerations.

Gajdusek: How many of the reports of virgin-soil measles describe a high mortality in the early phase of the disease, such as was seen in Greenland? In many virgin-soil outbreaks in the Australian out-back and in isolated Pacific populations, mortality was mostly the result of secondary infections, especially bacterial complications of the measles (Adels & Gajdusek 1963).

Black: I have seen no other analysis in the literature. If you have data, it would be helpful.

Gajdusek: In many cases deaths have been attributed to diarrhoea which appeared *after* the rash. The near 100% morbidity produced such a breakdown of life in the community that food and drinking water supplies could not be maintained.

Black: Diarrhoea is certainly a problem associated with measles in some cosmopolitan areas.

Lozoff: Can you speculate further about the connection between the histocompatibility types and the vaccine response?

Black: The two histocompatibility (HLA) loci are separated by approximately 200 genes. In animals (it has not been studied to my knowledge in man) these 200 genes, and possibly others around them, include a number concerned with immune responses to specific antigens. This distance of 200 genes is only wide enough to permit recombination in about 1% of the generations. In a tribe like the Xikrin you would expect to get relatively few individuals with sequences different from the tribal founders. The immune response (Ir) genes may therefore behave as if they were an HLA gene in segregation, and yet operate by quite a different biochemical mechanism. Since we don't see any difference between people with different genes in their serum antibody responses, the genetic variation would have to be expressed in differences in cellular immunity. We have only done the one study on anergy to investigate this so far.

Tyrrell: May I make two comments on this topic of genetics in relation to resistance to disease? Firstly, it may be difficult to show an association between

HLA genes and the ability to make antibodies or some other kind of immune responses. For instance, we looked for an association between the presence of circulating antibodies against common respiratory viruses and the HLA types of the serum donors, and we found no such evidence (C. Williams, E. C. Lance & D. A. J. Tyrrell, unpublished). This does not mean that the association doesn't exist. Further studies are needed, such as testing the response to vaccines.

Black: I would think an association may be easier to find in a population like the Xikrin where the Ir gene will remain associated with a given HLA type, than it would be in an open population where you had opportunities for the various Ir genes to combine with various HLA genes.

Tyrrell: Secondly, I would be astonished if there was *not* an important genetic element in the way such isolated populations behave in response to infections of various sorts, because I can't believe that natural selection won't operate there as it does in many other realms. Looking at it in much broader terms, René Dubos assembled evidence that some of the differences in mortality from tuberculosis could best be explained by the prolonged effect of selection on urban populations and the absence of such selective processes in other places (see Dubos & Dubos 1952).

Black: This theory is an old one but it has been hard to get good supporting data for it. One would like to pin it down to specific populations and specific agents. We have looked at the response to rubella vaccine in two Indian populations and, unlike the measles vaccine response, we found no difference from the picture in cosmopolitan people, in spite of the fact that the Indians had never experienced rubella previously (Black *et al.* 1976).

Neel: In my paper (pp. 155–169) I shall be at some pains to challenge the theory that the apparently great susceptibility of primitive peoples to the infectious diseases of civilization is primarily genetic in origin.

Gajdusek: In the small-animal models used in the virus laboratory there are many examples of single autosomal recessive genes or single autosomal dominant genes which totally determine the response to a given virus: for arboviruses of group B, the Aleutian mink disease virus, the murine leukaemia viruses and others. Highly homozygous laboratory animals resulting from inbreeding may have very different susceptibility to a given virus from a wild-type mouse. We know of no similar situation in an inbred human population, although the increased susceptibility to all infections in children with genetic defects in the immune system, and in those with Chediak-Higashi disease, is well documented. Moreover, even with the animal models, I know of no case where the susceptibility has yet been explained on a molecular level, although with the Aleutian mink disease genetic control of susceptibility is traceable to the Chediak-Higashi lysosomal defect.

Cockburn: Albert Sabin (1952) had two strains of mice one of which was 100% susceptible to yellow fever and the other 100% resistant. This was found to be inherited in Mendelian fashion. Of course the Africans living in a yellow fever area are almost totally immune to it. It is not a question of antibodies but of genetic resistance. The African child infected for the first time develops antibodies but not the disease. The European living in the same area becomes ill and has a 50% chance of dying (Strode 1951).

Black: I would like to see data on that. There is always the problem of reporting differences. It's possibly true, but we lack numerical data to support it.

Tyrrell: In the animal models, although a biochemical explanation isn't available, differences have been discovered at the cellular level which explain some of the differences. For instance, the basis of the susceptibility to mouse hepatitis virus has been narrowed down to a difference in the susceptibility of the macrophages between the susceptible and insusceptible strains (Bang & Warwick 1960). So in several instances an explanation is available at the cellular level already, and one can go on from there and look for biochemical explanations.

Neel: Dr Black, are measles antibody titres related to HLA type in a manner analogous to the febrile responses, in your study of the Xikrin?

Black: There is a weak but consistent association between high fever and high measles antibody titre in all our vaccine studies. This association persists when these data are examined by HLA type; the higher measles titres have HLA frequencies similar to the higher fevers. This association is not strong enough for us to infer that titre is directly related to HLA; both may be related to fever.

Hamilton: You mentioned (Table 1, p. 118) yellow fever and Ilheus viruses as causing occasional infections throughout life in these groups. Do you have information on the prevalence of positive serological reactions to different viruses and particularly the clinical reactions to the arboviruses?

Black: Yes. Whereas some groups are totally devoid of each of the enterovirus and respiratory virus antibodies we have tested and others show sharp age cut-offs, all tribes had some group B arbovirus antibody and we found no distinct minimal age for this reaction.

The variety of arboviruses in these areas seems to be relatively restricted. There is a little in Venezuela in the north; there is none south of the Amazon River. There is quite a bit of yellow fever in the north and much less in the south, except in the Xikrin.

We have not studied the clinical effects of the group B viruses, but we hope to do so. There must be a low background of enteroviruses and respiratory viruses in these populations. With yellow fever vaccine as a model we should be able to determine if this—or genetics—modifies the reaction.

Hamilton: Have you found any rotaviruses (the viruses associated with diarrhoea in infants)?

Black: We have not looked for rotaviruses.

Cohen: Have we any idea of the death rate in the primary phase of measles among the Xingu Indians? The reports of very high death rates from measles are surprising and I wondered why the people died in the study made in Greenland. It runs so contrary to all that has come out from Africa and India about people dying in the secondary stages of measles.

Black: I think the mechanism in Africa and India is probably different. Nutrition is commonly blamed for a large part of the mortality there. Dr Baruzzi, do you know how many deaths were in the prodromal phase in the Xingu epidemic of measles? There was an overall mortality of 27% in 1954.

Baruzzi: I received some reports about the Xingu epidemic of measles in 1954. Deaths were mainly in the eruptive phase. During the epidemic the whole social life of the village was disrupted and disorganized; as a consequence they were short of food.

The same happened some years later among the Nhambiquara, an Indian tribe living in small groups in the jungle. At that time the effects of the measles epidemic were minimized by the prompt arrival of a medical team and also by food delivered by helicopters of the Brazilian Air Force. In this epidemic too the deaths were more frequent, even in children, in the eruptive phase than in the prodromal phase.

Neel: We were not aware of deaths in the pre-eruptive phase in the rubeola epidemic in the Yanomama.

Gajdusek: I have a suggestion: as has been done for live yellow fever vaccine, you might freeze down in liquid nitrogen serum specimens collected on the first, second, third and fourth days after vaccination and determine the level of viraemia. This would be a way of measuring the extent of virus replication in different individuals.

Black: That would be very relevant for yellow fever. Detecting measles viraemia after giving vaccine is very difficult.

Gajdusek: In measles, if you are proposing that Indian groups have a more severe response to the virus than do Whites, you might expect a greater viraemia in them than we are accustomed to seeing.

Woodburn: You have described three broad categories of infection, Professor Black: those which occur at early ages, occasional zoonotic infections occurring throughout life, and exogenous infections.

What is most likely to happen in the immediate postcontact situation? First, obviously, is the introduction of exogenous infections; the other consequence I want to stress springs not from contact as such but from the 'sedentarization' and the increased population density which often follows. Nomadic hunters and gatherers, typically living at very low population densities, may be encouraged or forced to settle in larger groups than their traditional ones. A recent instance in which hunters and gatherers in Surinam were settled almost immediately after the first recent contact is described by Geijskes (1970) and Schoen (1971). Such sedentarization (especially if conditions of hygiene are very poor, as they are likely to be) will, one must assume, probably result in an increase in such early-age infections as amoebiasis and hepatitis B and, perhaps, in reduced standards of health which will increase vulnerability to the new exogenous infections which follow from contact. I think it is important to distinguish between contact *as such* and the changes in size of group and frequency of movement which may or may not be associated with it. Am I right in assuming that in the Brazilian populations you studied, there was no great change in the system of residence?

Black: The Amerindian populations I have studied move every few years but not within the year, except to go out and come back to the original location. We studied them at a time when they had not stayed longer than was their previous habit at the given site, so I dont't think there had been much change in this respect when we collected our first specimens.

References

ADELS, B.R. & GAJDUSEK, D.C. (1963) Survey of measles patterns in New Guinea, Micronesia and Australia. With a report of new virgin soil epidemics and the demonstration of susceptible primitive populations by serology. *Am. J. Hyg. 77*, 317–343.

BANG, F.B. & WARWICK, A. (1960) Mouse macrophages as host cells for the mouse hepatitis virus and the genetic basis of their susceptibility. *Proc. Natl. Acad. Sci. U.S.A. 46*, 1065

BLACK, F.L., LAMM, S.H., EMMONS, J.E. & PINHEIRO, F.P. (1976) Reactions to rubella vaccine and persistence of antibody in virgin-soil populations after vaccination and wild virus immunization. *J. Infect. Dis. 133*, 393–398

DUBOS, R. & DUBOS, J. (1952) *The White Plague*, Little Brown, Boston

GEIJSKES, D.C. (1970) Documentary information about the Surinam Wama or Akurio Indians. *Nieuwe West-Indische Gids. 47* (3)

SABIN, A.B. (1952) Nature of inherited resistance to virus. *Proc. Natl. Acad. Sci. U.S.A. 38*, 540–546

SCHOEN, I.L. (1971) Report of the Emergency Trip made by the West Indies Mission to the Akoerio Indians, June 1971. Paramaribo (mimeographed)

STRODE, G.K. (1951) *Yellow Fever*, McGraw-Hill, New York

TAYLOR-ROBINSON, D. & TYRRELL, D.A.J. (1963) Virus diseases on Tristan da Cunha. *Trans. R. Soc. Trop. Med. Hyg. 57*, 19–22

Aspects of infection in isolated communities

D. A. J. TYRRELL

Clinical Research Centre, Harrow, Middlesex

Abstract Respiratory viruses are not generally carried by normal subjects and cannot persist in small isolated communities. When infection does occur epidemics are seen and the illness may be more severe than in the outside world. These points are illustrated by reference to studies on the island of Tristan da Cunha and stations of the British Antarctic Survey.

The tribal societies we are thinking about in this symposium often live in relatively remote and inaccessible places in villages or similar small agricultural or pre-agricultural communities which have no modern hygiene; each individual is thus in direct or indirect contact with some wild or domestic animals and with the relatively few human beings of his tribe; the tribe itself may have close contact between its members but is to a large extent cut off from contact with the rest of mankind. I wish to discuss the consequences this may have for the type and amount of infection from which the members of such communities suffer.

It is known that there are bacteria potentially harmful to man which are present in the faeces of many animals; examples are salmonellas which cause gastrointestinal infections and *Clostridium tetani* which causes tetanus; so the members of such tribes are likely to suffer infections caught from animal hosts with which they share the environment. However, many other bacteria are particular to man and although related bacterial species are found in animals they are not ordinarily infectious for man. Some of these organisms, such as *Staphylococcus aureus*, a cause of boils, can readily persist in man even though the individual seems well—a so-called normal carrier; these may persist in a very small group for a long time after they are introduced and reappear as a cause of disease if they encounter a suitable site for an infection, such as an injury. Some bacteria tend to be eliminated because the individual develops a specific immunity; they can only persist in a group in which they can pass from one individual to another without making everyone immune, and at such a rate that the number becoming immune does not exceed the number of susceptibles being added, by people being born, immigrating, or losing the immunity which they once had. It would not be surprising if organisms like this, such as pneumococci, disappeared from small groups, though sometimes causing an epidemic of chest infections as they pass around.

VIRUS INFECTIONS

However, I wish to discuss virus infection, which is my special field of study, and I should start by pointing out that the situation with viruses is rather different from that found with bacteria and parasites (Horsfall & Tamm 1965). Viruses rarely come to man from other species, although this is common with the Rickettsiae (several of the typhus fevers have reservoirs in ticks and are caught only from them) or Chlamydia (psittacosis is caught only from birds). There are, however, viruses of cattle and birds which are very similar to those which cause infections of the respiratory tract and gut of man, so we can assume that at some point in history an organism crossed from one species to another, but we practically never see this now. However, it is interesting that pigs and other animals apparently caught Hong Kong influenza A from man (Beare et al. 1972) while there was a small outbreak of a virus very like swine influenza in Fort Dix in the USA early in 1976 (Stuart-Harris 1976). In both these cases the viruses did not seem to become established in their new hosts, but there is no reason to doubt that this may happen from time to time and is the best explanation for the sudden antigenic 'shifts' which occur in the influenza A viruses which are circulating in man.

One would expect on general grounds that viruses of the herpes group would infect successfully in isolated groups, for they all produce life-long infection with periods of activity in which they are shed. The recurrent cold sore of herpes simplex is well known and the virus may lurk for a lifetime in the nervous system causing no symptoms at all and then become active and cause a skin lesion from which virus may be shed to infect other people. Herpes zoster, or shingles, common in old people, is a recurrence of infection with the chickenpox virus, and a case in an isolated village can start off an epidemic of chickenpox which will affect all the young people who have been born since the last such episode (Taylor-Robinson & Caunt 1972). Enteroviruses, on the other hand, could only survive in larger groups because although they may be shed in the faeces for weeks they do induce a solid immunity and are eliminated from the infected patient. Polioviruses are the best-studied members of this group and antibody surveys show that infection with all three serotypes occurs in all parts of the world; yet in very isolated spots, such as remote islands or Eskimo settlements, there may be no antibody to one, two or even all three serotypes (Paul et al. 1951).

Some viruses are shed only briefly and give solid immunity and can only survive by circulating in large populations; an excellent example is that of measles, and we have already heard about this from Dr Black (pp. 115–130) and Dr Cockburn (pp. 103–112). I wish to turn now to studies on a number of other viruses which, like measles, spread via the respiratory tract but which produce other syndromes and behave in rather different ways.

HOW ISOLATED IS ISOLATED?

It was a report on the isolated community of Spitzbergen (Paul & Freese 1933) which provided some of the best proof that colds were not due to bacteria, which they showed persisted while colds came and went, nor were they due to cold weather, which was intense in the winter when colds were absent and warm in the spring when they were common; they seemed indeed to be due to an infection brought in the spring when the ice broke up and the first ship arrived and broke the winter-long isolation of the small community.

In due course it became possible to study the viruses which cause colds and similar conditions (Table 1). Dr Taylor-Robinson carried out serological sur-

TABLE 1

Viruses which can cause common colds and related diseases in man

Rhinoviruses	— over 100 serotypes
Coronaviruses	— at least several serotypes
Parainfluenza viruses	— four serotypes; some can cause severe disease in children
Respiratory Syncytial Virus	— causes bronchiolitis in childhood also
Influenza B	— cold-like illnesses common
Influenza C	
Influenza A	— some infections resemble colds

veys on samples of blood collected from adults in various urban and isolated communities throughout the world. He found that in general they all had antibodies against the sort of virus likely to cause respiratory infections in children in the UK—for example, parainfluenza viruses—and also against a few representatives of the rhinoviruses, which are probably the commonest cause of common colds at all ages. By this sort of criterion there was no evidence that the degree of isolation of the Bushmen of the Kalahari Desert, or the Eskimos of Canada—or at least those who were bled for us—was enough to prevent the viruses of acute respiratory infections spreading to them (Table 2) (Brown & Taylor-Robinson 1966). These results are valid whatever means of spread the viruses usually employ, and although there has been recent stress on the possibil-

TABLE 2

Frequency of antibodies against respiratory viruses in the sera of members of isolated communities

Source of serum	No. tested	Percentage with antibody against		
		Rhinovirus 1A	Parainfluenza 3	Influenza A2
Hottentots	45	60	80	42
Eskimos	53	58	88	41
Micronesians	66	39	94	23
Tristan da Cunha (1961)	103–129	68[a]	48	0

[a] 19 sera tested.

ity that they may pass from person to person by fingers and fomites, it seems that they do not persist long in the environment and I still think droplet spread indoors is the main route of spread (Tyrrell 1967; Reed 1975). Subsequent research has confirmed our initial impression that the same viruses cause the same sort of acute respiratory illnesses in most parts of the world, but we followed up the interesting finding that there were relatively few antibodies in the sera collected on the Island of Tristan da Cunha. This is situated in the South Atlantic. The population is usually just over 200 and consists mainly of islanders who remain there all the year round. They are visited occasionally by ships, particularly a supply ship and fishing boats which come from Cape Town, South Africa and anchor off-shore, while passengers and goods are landed and loaded by small boats.

There were stories that the islanders only had colds when ships called, and then not if the ship had been at sea six weeks, long enough for any colds among those on board to have died out—for example, ships coming from South America. We were able to make an epidemiological study of this and other phenomena, and Fig. 1 shows a summary of the data on the arrival of ships and the occurrence of epidemics of colds. There was clinical and epidemiological evidence that different types of colds, presumably due to different organisms, were brought ashore. Close enquiry showed that the link between ship and shore might be quite slight—for example, a passenger had a drink with the cold-stricken captain in his cabin and then came ashore and developed a cold which spread via his family to the whole community. Sometimes the route ashore could not be traced at all. The association between the arrival of a ship and the occurrence is statistically significant. On one occasion we studied the effect of the arrival of an influenza A virus, the Hong Kong strain (Mantle & Tyrrell 1973). The islanders had little previous experience of influenza A and a severe

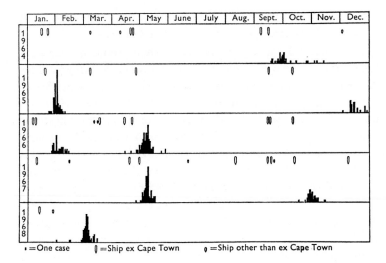

FIG. 1. The occurrence of colds on Tristan da Cunha and the arrival of ships (Shibli *et al.* 1971).

epidemic took place—two elderly islanders died and for a while the life of the community was brought to a halt. It was interesting also that there were instances of individuals having what seemed to be a second attack of influenza; this is reminiscent of the stories of the epidemic of 1918–1919, and could indicate a poor antibody response to the first attack, presumably due to lack of antigenic 'priming' by related viruses.

THE BREAKING OF GROUP ISOLATION

There are reports of whole communities being badly afflicted by infectious disease once they had been contacted by the outside world. We were able to observe this phenomenon in the Tristan da Cunha island community, for they had to be evacuated as a body to Britain when the volcano on their island home erupted. The evacuation ship called at Cape Town, and they were all suffering badly from respiratory infections by the time they reached Britain. They continued to suffer badly during the succeeding winter, although their living quarters were reasonable (Tyrrell *et al.* 1967). Serological studies showed that they were infected with viruses such as parainfluenza which cause infections early in life in Britain and no doubt with other viruses for which we were unable to test. They were vaccinated against influenza A and B but nevertheless some infections with these viruses were detected. However, they were not persistently immunized by this experience and, as Fig. 1 shows, the pattern of epidemics of colds returned soon after they repopulated the island, and they suffered severely from infection with the new Hong Kong serotype of influenza.

A similar type of natural experiment is made when Arctic or Antarctic stations are isolated during the winter and then are relieved each spring (Holmes & Allen 1973). We have made epidemiological records in stations of the British Antarctic Survey and have confirmed the reports that within a few weeks of the onset of isolation colds disappear (Allen 1973). We have proved that this is not due to an increase of resistance in the staff, because if they are experimentally exposed to typical respiratory viruses they become infected and may develop symptoms (Holmes *et al.* 1976). After certain infections the symptoms may indeed be more severe than expected. Very rarely a cold may appear in a group during the period of isolation; we think we have documented one of these (Allen 1973). Presumably some virus must have been carried by one of the group and then become active but none was cultured from the cases and more work is obviously needed.

It has been traditional among Antarctic explorers that when the bases are relieved in the spring and also when they themselves return to civilization they are likely to get particularly severe colds. This has also been studied by Allen, who has documented the outbreak of respiratory illness, which is often rather unpleasant. He showed also that the illnesses which occur on these occasions and on the journey home were more severe than those which occurred as they were entering isolation. The illnesses were not life-endangering—there were no cases of pneumonia—but there is some evidence that there was a rather general loss of resistance to infection of the respiratory tract in isolation. Holmes *et al.* (1976) and A. D. MacLeod (personal communication) have collected some evidence that there may be a decline in local secretory antibody production and this might provide an explanation. MacLeod (personal communication) has recently recovered viruses from colds occurring after isolation has been broken and it seems that coronaviruses may have been important in one outbreak, though a rhinovirus was also recovered.

ISOLATION AND GENETIC SELECTION

It has been suggested by Dubos that the severe consequences of introducing tuberculosis into some areas and racial groups have arisen mainly because the group had never been exposed in the past to the selective elimination of genetically susceptible individuals. I know of no evidence to support this from the study of viral respiratory disease in isolated tribal groups. We do have evidence that the possession of blood group A is associated with resistance to infection with influenza and some other viruses, though in the Tristan da Cunha islanders it seemed to be associated with increased susceptibility compared with the blood group O (Tyrrell *et al.* 1967).

CONCLUSIONS

If there are only a few contacts with the outside world each year it is likely that an isolated group will have less respiratory virus infection and less immunity to it than the rest of mankind. They may be expected to have unduly severe infections of this type and these may also be followed by bacterial infections such as pneumonia. Influenza infections are potentially serious and if an epidemic is active in the area it could be valuable to vaccinate those making contact and, if possible, the isolated group. If isolation has not been quite so severe the experience of respiratory tract infection is likely to be similar to that of the general population of adjoining areas.

References

ALLEN, T. (1973) Common colds in Antarctica. *J. Hyg. (Camb.)* 71, 649–656

BEARE, A.S., SCHILD, G.C. & HALL, T.S. (1972) Experimental infection of human volunteers with a swine influenza virus antigenically related to human A/Hong Kong/68 virus. *Bull. W.H.O.* 47, 493–495

BROWN, P.K. & TAYLOR-ROBINSON, D. (1966) Respiratory virus antibodies in sera of persons living in isolated communities. *Bull. W.H.O. 34*, 895–900

HOLMES, M.J. & ALLEN, T.R. (1973) Viral respiratory disease in isolated communities: a review. *Br. Antarct. Surv. Bull. 35*, 23–31

HOLMES, M.J., REED, S.E., STOTT, E.J. & TYRRELL, D.A.J. (1976) Studies on experimental rhinovirus type 2 infection in Polar isolation and in England. *J. Hyg. (Camb.) 76*, 379–393

HORSFALL, F.L., JR. & TAMM, I. (1965) *Viral and Rickettsial Infections of Man*, 4th edn, Lippincott, Philadelphia

MANTLE, J.P. & TYRRELL, D.A.J. (1973) An epidemic of influenza on Tristan da Cunha. *J. Hyg. (Camb.), 71*, 89–95

PAUL, J.H. & FREESE, H.L. (1933) Epidemiological and bacteriological study of common cold in an isolated Arctic community (Spitzbergen). *Am. J. Hyg. 17*, 517

PAUL, J.R., RIORDAN, J.T. & MELNICK, J.L. (1951) Antibodies to three different antigenic types of poliomyelitis virus in sera from North Alaskan Eskimos. *Am. J. Hyg. 54*, 275–285

REED, S.E. (1975) An investigation of the possible transmission of rhinovirus through direct contact. *J. Hyg. (Camb.), 75*, 249–258

SHIBLI, M., GOOCH, S., LEWIS, H.E. & TYRRELL, D.A.J. (1971) Common colds on Tristan da Cunha. *J. Hyg. (Camb.) 69*, 255–262

STUART-HARRIS, C.H. (1976) Swine influenza virus in man. Zoonosis or human pandemic? *Lancet 2*, 31–32

TAYLOR-ROBINSON, D. & CAUNT, A.E. (1972) Varicella virus. *Virology Monograph 12*, Springer-Verlag, Vienna

TYRRELL, D.A.J. (1967) The spread of viruses of the respiratory tract by the airborne route, in *Airborne Microbes* (Gregory, P.H. & Monteith, J.L., eds.) (Seventeeth Symposium of the Society for General Microbiology), pp. 216–306, Cambridge University Press, London

TYRRELL, D.A.J., PETO, M. & KING, N. (1967) Serological studies on infections by respiratory viruses of inhabitants of Tristan da Cunha. *J. Hyg. (Camb.) 65*, 327–341

Discussion

Hugh-Jones: In the Xingu Indians in Brazil as many as 50% of those in primary contact die from the *grippe*; one of the crucial questions is what it is exactly and whether it is a mixture of all these viruses.

Tyrrell: I have a suspicion of the answer from the results of our further studies on the scientists coming out of isolation in Antarctica; they are normally resident in Britain and so are well saturated with respiratory viruses before they go into isolation for eight or nine months. Yet they say that when their isolation is broken or they return from Antarctica their colds are worse than usual and seem clinically like influenza. This is one of the few groups where one can study the virology properly after isolation. We have just succeeded in isolating viruses from such cases; Dr MacLeod has found rhinovirus and coronaviruses, which in the UK cause a mild disease, but which seem to make these scientists quite ill. My guess therefore is that it isn't a *grippe*, a true influenza virus infection, but one of the other viruses which are around all the time causing mild colds but which can cause an influenza-like disease in a susceptible group.

Hugh-Jones: In fact a true viral pneumonia?

Tyrrell: Yes, some of the Tristan islanders develop this.

Neel: Earlier in the meeting (p. 132), Dr Tyrrell, you spoke rather strongly in favour of genetic susceptibility, and yet the Tristan da Cunha people, whose ancestors surely had all kinds of contact with respiratory infections, have reproduced the Indian picture almost completely. You have given a superb demonstration of the non-genetic basis of most of the response we see!

Tyrrell: I think the situation is complicated and we are not reproducing the whole of the Indian picture: the Tristan people do not *die* in these epidemics of colds; they have a lot of chronic respiratory infection but even so they do not die after these virus infections. This may reflect the modern medical care they receive, but it could also be partly because their ancestors were pre-selected to be resistant. No, I am not now saying that genetics has nothing to do with the response. It is all part of a larger picture. We did think about genetic causes and, as I said, we found some correlation between the occurrence of certain blood groups in Tristan islanders and the frequency with which people with those groups became infected (p. 142). This is to say nothing more than that something associated with a genetically determined factor like blood group was influencing how people reacted and how frequently they became infected when exposed to a lot of viruses.

Black: In the Xikrin Indians, where half the people died in a sequence of *grippes*, influenza was not one of the infections.

Woodburn: In talking about isolation, there is a complicating factor. The crews of the ships visiting these areas have themselves been isolated for some days beforehand. You mentioned the necessity for people visiting really isolated groups to have been vaccinated, but can we make recommendations about whether visitors should accept the responsibility of providing a measure of protection for the people they are to study by isolating themselves before they start work? How long would the period of self-isolation have to be?

Tyrrell: The evidence is not good and it is probably subject to much statistical fluctuation. It depends on what virus is on board, when you start, how many people are susceptible, and how severe the crowding is, because in some models of infection with a high frequency of contact there is a short, sharp epidemic and with a lower frequency of contact you have a long epidemic (Hammond & Tyrrell 1971). I can give a rough idea of the time, because on the ship going to Southampton, a three or four week journey, there were colds most of the time. Dr Hope Simpson did some (unpublished) work on weather ships in the Atlantic and found that colds lasted 3–4 weeks on those, in a totally isolated small group of people, before they died out. The Tristan da Cunha islanders say that people from South America never brought colds whereas those from South Africa did; the difference lies in the fact that it takes about 10 days to get from South Africa and three weeks or more from South America. This is why we obtained a correlation between visits of South African ships and the occurrence of epidemics. Thus several weeks would have to elapse, and the isolation must be total for that time. Even a quick drink with someone or just going into a hut to talk for a few minutes could be sufficient to pass on an infection.

Woodburn: Is the period shorter if you have only three or four people who are isolated than if you have 20 people?

Tyrrell: It is a matter of statistical fluctuation and depends on the composition of the group. All our mathematical modelling has been done on so-called deterministic models which treat people like molecules. Depending on the circumstances you may have a short sharp epidemic, a slow less intense one, or no epidemic at all. But these models may not apply, as we saw on Tristan, at the stage of an epidemic when only one or two people are infected. What happens then depends on the variability of individuals and on chance events. For example, people shed viruses for different periods of time; two people with clinically identical colds may be shedding ten or a million infectious particles one for a few days and the other for many days. It is not easy to predict what is likely to happen in small groups before the virus dies out.

Gajdusek: Even in the most isolated villages in New Guinea there is a visitor or so every week and therefore the antibody prevalence for enteric and respiratory viruses does not show evidence of a Tristan-like isolation. Probably the only places where isolation is still even more complete than Tristan are some of the most remote Polynesian, Melanesian and Micronesian islands in the South Pacific. These islands, such as the Banks and Torres Islands of the New Hebrides, Anuta in the Solomons and the Outer Islands of the Palau District in Micronesia, had, until recently, fewer ship visits each year than Tristan da Cunha: often a maximum of two or three brief calls a year with only a small shore-boat landing for a few hours. We have accurate accounts of what happened. Ship visits were followed by 'ship epidemics' of respiratory diseases, sometimes of xanthematous and diarrhoeal disease as well. For the last decade ships collect all the older children from the Micronesian outer islands and bring them to boarding schools. Most of the children first starting high school have never left their islands before. The students spend the whole school year away from home and return home in the summer for a three-month vacation. Of the new group of about a hundred coming into the Yap Outer Island High School on Ulithi Atoll in the Western Caroline Islands each year, most of the new students have repeated absences during their first few months at the school—they are ill much of the time with acute upper respiratory disease. The medical aides have learned to treat the children with depot penicillin before symptoms of bacterial complications appear. With such use of antibiotics they see fewer cases of secondary otitis media and other complications. They presume that the new students are often carrying many pathogenic bacteria, and they do not wait for complications before they initiate antibiotic prophylaxis. I would suggest that when you serve a primitive community, the moment you start having acute respiratory infections you should treat them with antibiotics prophylactically in an attempt to decrease the incidence of complications. We also found that with epidemic viral influenza the death rate on any island was inversely proportional to the amount of penicillin the health aides had used (Brown *et al.* 1969).

Tyrrell: To widen the examples of this, Thor Heyerdahl describes in *Aku-Aku* (1958) his journey to Easter island and how what the inhabitants call the *coconga* comes when the Chilean gun boat makes its annual administrative visit to the island. They bring what seems to be a respiratory infection, probably a perfectly ordinary one, but it seems to produce a severe disease in the islanders.

Lozoff: Are there comparable observations on individuals who develop infection after moving from a westernized environment to a more isolated community?

Tyrrell: This is not clearly understood. Certainly the business of getting to the community exposes one to infection on the way. I think this is multifactorial. We have an impression that stress and displacement might affect people's susceptibilities; it seems to affect some people and not others. In a study in volunteers at Salisbury it was found that mental stress seems to increase the symptoms produced by a common cold virus (Totman *et al.* 1977). Then we have received many refugees from Uganda in the UK and they have suffered a lot from tuberculosis. It looks as though they are catching tuberculosis after arrival. Something rather ill-defined is going on to which we can attach an immunological label, because Dr Cole has shown that their delayed hyper-sensitivity response against tuberculin is lower than that of people already living here and that this is due to a defect in their lymphocytes which is not found in local residents who get tuberculosis (P. J. Cole, personal communication). We are sufficiently ignorant still about the way immune responses are altered by general physiological factors for it to be possible that some other aspect of the immune mechanism which we can't define is depressed as a result of the stress of travelling.

White: You mentioned staphylococci. Medical personnel concerned with the desert Aborigines in Australia are having to treat staphylococcal infections after the initiation ceremonies such as circumcision. The Aborigines say that they never had that sort of infection until white people came, which suggests that staphylococcal infections were not known in the desert.

Tyrrell: As staphylococci are only carried by man and have no animal hosts, if a people had been sufficiently isolated it could be that the organisms had never entered their population; unfortunately, once introduced, they would be expected to persist. The chances of getting staphylococci *out* of the Aboriginal population now are very slim. It was shown in the Antarctic that they can be carried for long periods.

Hamilton: Streptococcal infection shows wide variations in different communities. What is the pattern of streptococcal infection in these small communities?

Tyrrell: We have no clinical evidence of streptococcal infections in the groups we have looked at closely, on Tristan da Cunha or in the Antarctic. That may be pure chance; I would have expected a mixed picture, since streptococcal carriers do exist, and they persist for months or years. On the other hand, the general story is that in a few weeks everybody eliminates the new serotypes of pneumococci as they arrive, so I would expect this to happen in a small group. What happened clinically might depend on the chance occurrence of a carrier in the group, but it will also be determined by how many people in a group became immune. Most people if exposed become immune to a particular serotype, and you would have to wait until the next serotype was introduced before seeing further clinical manifestations and therefore spread. If a carrier developed he could be detected by laboratory methods but it would probably not have much effect on the community's health.

Haraldson: We lived for about 15 years in the northernmost part of Lapp-land, north of the Arctic Circle, and every time we went on a train to Stockholm we caught a cold. When visitors came they had the same experience; if they stayed for a few days only, they did not get colds. We had the impression of a short-duration immunity which was lost in about two weeks in a very sparsely populated rural environment.

Tyrrell: That is extremely interesting, because it fits with something which has always been a paradox to me. When we follow what happens after infecting volunteers with respiratory viruses, they generally develop an infection and an immune response and the virus disappears. We also know that those who develop no symptoms can get an infection which is short-lived. But the rare outbreak I mentioned in the Antarctic, during winter time, suggests that there may be a few individuals who carry virus for a long time which cannot be detected by ordinary laboratory methods, and they shed the virus. If so, there may be one or two people in *your* community who are silently carrying virus infections. Carriers of colds have been hypothesized, because that has seemed the best explanation of why at a certain season of the year (in the northern hemisphere, in September or so), colds appear abundantly. That could be the result of virus being present at a low level but when the conditions for trans-mission are right, it would go up. But when these hypothetical carriers are looked for they are not found, and the situation may be similar to what is found with foot-and-mouth disease, which is caused by a virus very similar to a rhinovirus. Animals recover from foot-and-mouth disease (if they are not slaughtered) but until recently it was impossible to isolate virus from them. However, virus is present in the pharynx and if we bring recovered animals into contact with susceptible animals, these developed the disease. It could be an important part of the strategy of survival of the virus but we have not caught up with it yet. Your story suggests the existence of a virus being carried in this group.

Neel: To go back to the prostration of the Indians with respiratory infections, is it possible that they are simultaneously responding to three or four viruses, whereas usually we are responding to only one? This is a hypothesis that could be tested.

Tyrrell: It could be tested but it is intrinsically unlikely, I think, if you have extreme isolation. We have some evidence from the Tristan da Cunha islanders on this point because, since a whole shipload of people comes aboard in Cape Town, they may sometimes bring several viruses with them, and sometimes a number of them go ashore on Tristan. Bruce Hammond had problems with one or two of the curves in fitting the data to the simple model, namely that one infectious agent was going round. He found that they fitted beautifully if he re-wrote the programme to fit a model in which there were superimposed and overlapping epidemics due to two different viruses with different characteristics of infectiousness and so on. The problem is that we have never done any virology on Tristan to check whether this actually occurs and we probably never will, because of the lack of cooperation.

Gajdusek: Your comment on the rarity of virus-shedders and the extreme differences in the amount of virus shed by different virus-shedders could be important in explaining what happens in small groups. It was very disturbing for us to find very differing outcomes when one or two proved cases of influenza entered various New Guinea villages. In one village there were no secondary infections, in the second the whole village quickly became infected, and in the third only a small proportion of the people became ill. If the first cases were in individuals who were non-shedders, there would be no secondary cases; if one (or more) of the first cases was an extensive shedder, there would be a large number of secondary cases. The number of secondary cases also depends on the crowding, which is a function of the weather at the time. This fact that in small communities we could not predict in advance whether the introduction of the first few cases of influenza into the community would lead to an epidemic of high attack rate or to one with a very low attack rate, or even to no further cases, could be accounted for in this way (Garruto & Gajdusek 1975).

Tyrrell: Influenza may be an important exception to the rather simple model we have used. Bruce Hammond and I tried to fit the data from more-or-less isolated school outbreaks in the UK to this model and failed; yet we know that it can spread. We followed an epidemic of the 1968 Hong Kong serotype which reached Tristan da Cunha at the stage when the people had lost most of the antibodies that they had acquired by visiting Britain and by being vaccinated here (Mantle & Tyrrell 1973). There was a 100% incidence and two deaths, and some individuals almost certainly had double infections; although we haven't any proven case with serological confirmation of both attacks, it is difficult to believe that in this isolated community it was not the same infection. This could be the picture in people who are in some way deficient immunologically. We don't know how the virus got in, nor what are the necessary and sufficient conditions for the infection to get started in the island.

Lozoff: The focus so far has been on viruses; what is known about bacterial infections in similar populations?

Pereira: We did some work on serum samples provided by Dr Woodburn from the Hadza tribe in North-West Tanzania (Bennett *et al.* 1973). These are hunter–gatherers and when we undertook this study we thought they were extremely isolated, but it transpired that there had been some minimal contact with settlements.

The samples were tested for antibodies to a variety of viruses but also to bacteria, rickettsia and mycoplasma. Among the bacteria we included streptococci, *Bordetella pertussis*, *Brucella abortus* and salmonellae. There was serological evidence of the presence of streptococci, *Bordetella pertussis* and of some salmonellas of the types commonly carried by cattle and other animal species. Antibody was also frequent to tick typhus. However, no antibodies were found to typhoid or paratyphoid nor to *Brucella abortus* or to Q fever or psittacosis.

Of the viruses, antibodies to all the respiratory agents were found; and to mumps and measles in many including the youngest member tested, aged eight years. Antibodies to herpes simplex and Epstein-Barr viruses were almost universal.

Woodburn: This is a question of relative isolation. Among the Hadza there hasn't for at least the past two generations been a situation in any way comparable to Tristan da Cunha or the Antarctic scientific communities. They are simply relatively isolated in comparison with the neighbours. (See Bennett *et al.* 1970, p. 860.)

Pereira: Some blood samples were obtained by Dr Ross and Dr Juel-Jensen of Oxford when they were working in the Tigre Highlands of Northern Ethiopia among a very isolated community still living a medieval life without even the wheel and with very infrequent contacts with other people. It was found that of this group, even though they live in very primitive conditions, only about a third of the sera tested had antibody to herpes simplex virus. The numbers tested were small, as these people believe that if they lose blood they lose an essential part of life.

Dr Ross and Dr Juel-Jensen made some interesting points about these people. They have an enormous infant mortality, living as they do balanced on a knife-edge with their environment, and without any medical aid, as this was the first time that doctors had visited them. There is clearly much that could be done to help. But if the infant mortality is reduced and lives are saved, there is insufficient food available to maintain them. They felt that one should not interfere where people are in balance with their environment.

Tyrrell: Speaking of relative degrees of isolation, in retrospect we realized we had missed out something important on Tristan. We took much trouble to make sure that all the families cooperated and that everyone would record his or her colds on the same card in the same way, but we didn't pay equal attention to the events that took place when the islanders were contacted, when somebody arrived on the island, and so we have only a rather anecdotal account of what happened. It's certainly true that some of the contacts were apparently very trivial.

Woodburn: Using Dr Lozoff's equipment one could record actual individual interactions very precisely.

Weiner: Are there any results on the serum samples collected from Kalahari Bushmen?

Tyrrell: We had some sera from Bushmen and they were like the Hottentots; they had antibodies against almost every virus and bacterium that we tested for.

Harrison: In most field surveys it seems customary simply to examine whether or not an antibody is present. Is the technology too difficult or too time-consuming, or is it not thought worthwhile, to measure antibody titres?

Tyrrell: All our studies *are* done by measuring titres, but we simply condense the data into positives and negatives. Some of the titres are very interesting, in fact. The parainfluenza antibody titres of the Tristan da Cunha islanders, when they had these antibodies at all, were lower than we expected. We have repeated these measurements before and after a period of isolation and they were losing their antibodies, which is not what you would find in our sort of society where we get re-exposed and keep our antibodies against these so-called infantile viruses for long periods. While they were in Britain their titres of parainfluenza antibodies increased.

Woodburn: We have talked about the dangers in contacting isolated groups but another situation which is extremely common today is the forced sedentarization of nomadic populations including hunting and gathering groups. Some of what Dr Tyrrell has been saying is directly relevant to this situation. This policy of settling nomads is being put into effect by governments all over the world, of every political type (see e.g. Woodburn 1972). There seem to be three simultaneous effects on health. In the first place there is diminished isolation and increased exposure to exogenous infections. Coinciding with this is increased exposure to density-dependent diseases and to other diseases which affect nomadic populations less than sedentary ones because they leave their excreta behind when they move camp and are less likely to infect their sources of drinking water. Thirdly, considerable stress is inevitable if sedentarization is forced, and probable even if it is voluntary, and this too is likely to have health consequences. It is hardly surprising that after sedentarization, particularly in the subsequent six months, high mortality figures have often been reported. This situation is one we might focus on, rather than on the now exceptionally rare and perhaps less dangerous situation of first contact with a previously isolated group. Of course, the greatest dangers occur when first contact and forced sedentarization coincide.

Tyrrell: Not only does bringing groups into conditions of rather second-rate hygiene, close together, mean that there is increased infection by the faecal-oral route, but if you also provide buildings in which they are confined, when people sneeze and cough there is a higher probability of inhaling virus particles, so transmission of disease by the respiratory route is also increased. In Australia I believe that when some of the earlier groups of Aborigines were brought together there were terrible outbreaks of both gastrointestinal and respiratory disease.

Stanley: We now see much more chronic effects of settlement, with continuing high mortality and morbidity among the Aborigines (for far more than six months), because the diet also changes quite dramatically and this affects the response to infection. Also, Aborigines have high rates of alcoholism, venereal disease, diabetes, obesity and heart disease, all of which did not occur even 20 years ago.

Tyrrell: One could in theory try to handle the situation of bringing people together in settlements by making sure that there is education and satisfactory equipment so that the load of faecal–oral infections is reduced, and one can in theory also tide people over the respiratory infections by good medical care. What Dr Gajdusek said indicates that intrinsically many of these infections are not lethal or even severe, given what we would regard as ordinary nursing and medical care. The Tristan islanders, although many were ill with bronchitis, didn't die and after a period in Britain they were no longer much troubled by acute respiratory infections.

Stanley: My point was that there aren't any isolated groups now in Australia: they have all been contacted and our situation is a different one. The effects of settlement on health are much more chronic.

Haraldson: There is a time factor in transition. In the past, development took place as a slow evolution, which was a product of internal experience and inventions in the group, and rather limited external influences. Ideas and implements from outside were tested in the group during long periods, rejected, or accepted and adopted into the local culture without disrupting the general pattern. Today, transitional periods are short and impressions and ideas from outside are heaped upon tribal people, creating risk groups and risk periods which call for special attention. With the intensity and speed of communication the control and evaluation mechanism is switched off, and uncontrolled elements are integrated uninhibitedly, creating a gap between the traditional society and new ideas. This is a parallel to the generation gap in the western world.

Development curves are sensitive things to play with, and it looks as if a certain rate is physiological and healthy. Producing too steep development curves means acculturation, which may be seen as a social disease and a symptom of a brutal exposure to new systems, values and ideas. Disturbed hierarchies in tribes are often the result of rapid development.

The reasons given by governments for interference and for sedentarization programmes among tribal people have been various, and have included political integration (for reasons of loyalty and legal reasons); cultural integration; and the provision of social services (education and health), made possible by the improved accessibility.

References

BENNETT, F.J., KAGAN, I.G., BARNICOT, N.A. & WOODBURN, J.C. (1970) Helminth and protozoal parasites of the Hadza of Tanzania. *Trans. R. Soc. Trop. Med. Hyg. 64*, 857–880

BENNETT, F.J., BARNICOT, N.A., WOODBURN, J.C., PEREIRA, M.S. & HENDERSON, B.E. (1973) Studies on viral, bacterial, rickettsial and treponemal diseases in the Hadza of Tanzania and a note on injuries. *Hum. Biol. 45*, 243–272

BROWN, P., GAJDUSEK, D.C. & MORRIS, J.A. (1969) Antigenic response to influenza virus in man. I. Neutralizing antibody response to inactivated monovalent A2 vaccine as related to prior influenza exposure. *Am. J. Epidemiol. 90*, 327–335

GARRUTO, R. & GAJDUSEK, D.C. (1975) Unusual progression and shifting clinical severity, morbidity and mortality in the 1969 Hong Kong (A/New Guinea/1/69 H3N2) influenza epidemic in New Guinea. *Am. J. Phys. Anthropol. 42*, 302–303

HAMMOND, B.J. & TYRRELL, D.A.J. (1971) A mathematical model of common-cold epidemics on Tristan da Cunha. *J. Hyg. (Camb.) 69*, 365–377

HEYERDAHL, T. (1958) *Aku-Aku*, Allen & Unwin, London

MANTLE, J.P. & TYRRELL, D.A.J. (1973) An epidemic of influenza on Tristan da Cunha. *J. Hyg. (Camb.) 71*, 89–95

TOTMAN, R., REED, S.E. & CRAIG, J.W. (1977) Cognitive dissonance stress and virus-induced common colds. *J. Psychosom. Res. 21*, 55–63

WOODBURN, J.C. (1972) The future for hunting and gathering peoples. *!Kung: The Magazine of the London School of Economics Anthropology Society*, 1–3

Health and disease in unacculturated Amerindian populations

JAMES V. NEEL

Department of Human Genetics, University of Michigan Medical School, Ann Arbor, Michigan

Abstract The stereotype of uncontacted tribal populations is that they must reproduce at near capacity to maintain or slightly increase their numbers. This paper argues that the health of minimally contacted Amerindians, as judged by the results of physical examinations and life tables for the Yanomama of Southern Venezuela and Northern Brazil, is relatively good, with population control a feature of the Indian culture. It is further argued that the usual deterioration in health with contacts with western culture probably does not result so much from special innate susceptibilities to certain epidemic diseases and to the diets and 'stresses' of civilization as from the epidemiological characteristics of newly contacted peoples.

There are two commonly held beliefs about the health of tribally organized unacculturated populations which I wish to challenge in this brief presentation. The first is that the mortality pattern of such populations requires that they reproduce at near capacity simply to hold their numbers even. The second is that the well-documented collapse of their health, such as it is, which often follows contact with civilized populations results in large measure from genetically determined susceptibilities to the epidemic diseases of civilization to which they have not previously been exposed and to the 'stresses' of civilization. Instead, I will argue that the health of at least some newly contacted groups, when viewed on a scale that encompasses the health of a wide variety of human populations over the past several hundred years, is really pretty good. I will further suggest that the high morbidity and mortality of at least some of these groups when confronted with the infectious diseases of civilization is due much more to certain epidemiological characteristics of these populations than to innate, genetically determined susceptibilities. In order to set the stage for the appropriate discussion, I will quantify that generalization with the 'guesstimate' that at least 80% of the high mortality among some primitive groups from measles, smallpox, influenza, tuberculosis, and so on is the consequence of their socioeconomic and epidemiological structure, not their genes. A practical corollary of this is that with modern medical care, mortality in these groups from these diseases should be modest. Unfortunately, such groups are even now seldom in a position to receive modern medical care. My documentation will be largely based on personal experiences among Amerindian populations; these arguments will be familiar themes to some of you (Neel 1970, 1971). I hesitate to generalize to other types of newly contacted populations in the presence of such experts as we have at this symposium. Dunn (1968) has emphasized the dangers of over-easy generalizations.

THE HEALTH OF NEWLY CONTACTED AMERINDIANS

The definition of 'health' remains elusive, and so then does the evaluation of just how healthy a given population is. Our group has now conducted complete physical examinations of the inhabitants of entire villages among three Amerindian tribes (the Yanomama, Xavante and Makiritare) who, well past the stage of first contacts, may nevertheless be regarded as minimally acculturated at the time of our studies. By our usual medical standards, these groups have appeared relatively healthy, the average young man, in particular, exhibiting the physique of a trained athlete (Neel et al. 1964; Weinstein et al. 1967). However, these are cross-sectional studies, and leave open the possibility that these apparently healthy persons represent the relatively few survivors of a much larger birth cohort. We have therefore devoted a considerable effort to developing life tables for one of these groups, the Yanomama, not easy for a preliterate group where all ages must be estimated and it is considered dangerous to mention the names of one's departed ancestors, lest their spirits hear and be displeased (Neel & Weiss 1975). To this end, a sex-estimated age pyramid has been developed based on a census of 29 Yanomama villages. Age-specific pregnancy schedules have been generated by a combination of physical examinations and tests of urine for the presence of chorionic gonadotropins. Limited data are available on infanticide and infant and childhood deaths from histories from Indians and, for some villages, the observations of missionaries. From the unusual sex ratio among children under an estimated age of two we assume there is preferential female infanticide, to the extent that in addition to some 3–4% of infants of both sexes killed for such reasons as presence of congenital defect, an additional 25% of all females born are killed. We estimate that the average Yanomama woman between the ages of 15 and 40 has a liveborn child every three to four years, of which, averaging the sexes, some 85% are permitted to live. Some data are also available on the areal expansion of this group during the past 100 years, an expansion which with certain assumptions may be equated to population expansion. We take this growth rate to be approximately 0.7% per year. Our primary publication contains a full description of our concerns as to how these various data sets may have been influenced by post-Columbian developments.

The life tables which we developed are based on applying a series of 72 stationary (zero growth) model life tables to the Yanomama data, each modified for various possible growth rates between 0.5 and 1.0% per year, and determining, by means of an Index of Dissimilarity, which schedule gives the best fit (cf. Weiss 1973). Separate schedules have been developed for males and females. Our current best estimate of the life tables is given in Table 1. Several

TABLE 1

The most satisfactory male and female life tables for the Yanomama, after Neel & Weiss (1975). Q(X) is the mortality schedule, the chance that those who reach the age class will die before reaching the next age class. P(X) is the chance of surviving the age class, or $(1 - Q(X))$. l(X) is the number of survivors left at the beginning of the age class out of every 100 born

Age	Male			Female		
	Q(X)	P(X)	l(X)	Q(X)	P(X)	l(X)
0	0.267	0.733	100	0.430	0.570	100
1	0.160	0.840	73	0.118	0.882	57
5	0.110	0.890	62	0.066	0.934	50
10	0.088	0.912	55	0.042	0.958	47
15	0.148	0.852	50	0.130	0.870	45
20	0.152	0.848	43	0.134	0.866	39
25	0.156	0.844	36	0.137	0.863	34
30	0.160	0.840	30	0.140	0.860	29
35	0.164	0.836	26	0.143	0.857	25.2
40	0.168	0.832	21	0.147	0.853	21.6
45	0.173	0.827	18	0.150	0.850	18.4
50	0.177	0.823	15	0.154	0.846	15.6
55	0.213	0.786	12	0.188	0.812	13.2
60	0.282	0.718	10	0.251	0.749	10.8
65	0.362	0.638	7	0.327	0.673	8.1
70	0.470	0.530	4	0.432	0.568	5.4
75	0.612	0.388	2	0.570	0.430	3.1
80+	1.000	0.000	1	1.000	0.000	1.3

unusual features of these schedules should be noted. It is estimated that 27% of males die during the first year of life. However, because of the fact that we determine pregnancy rates rather than birth rates, and the fact that reliable figures on the frequency of infanticide cannot be obtained, this figure includes deaths from induced abortions, stillbirths, and infanticide. We believe that for males the infant death rate from natural causes does not exceed 20%. Note also the degree of male attrition during the years 15–40, relatively much higher than in our own life tables. We believe a large share of this to result from the pattern of incessant warfare and other forms of trauma (especially snake bite) rather than from 'natural causes'. With respect to the female life table, note the initial sharp dip, to which we believe preferential female infanticide contributes heavily, but note also the continuing, relatively high mortality during the reproductive years. Whereas we think we have at least a partial explanation for this phenomenon in the case of the males, we have no satisfactory insights in the case of the females. Fig. 1, a revision of an earlier figure (Neel 1970), contrasts the composite Yanomama life table, sexes combined, with comparable curves for India at the turn of the century and for modern Japan. Deaths from infanticide have been excluded. Infant mortality is approximately half that of India in 1900. While obviously in terms of modern expectation the Yanomama curve leaves much to be desired, nevertheless population numbers are currently increasing on a reproductive schedule which by no means taps the full reproductive capacity of the human female. In view of a comment to come later, it should be pointed out that whatever the motivation, the abortion and infanticide practiced by the Yanomama constitute a form of population regulation.

Stool examinations, antibody profiles, and clinical observation leave no doubt of the intimate and continuing exposure of the Indian to a wide variety of infectious agents (Neel et al. 1968a, b). We have suggested that one factor in the relatively good health record of the minimally contacted Amerindian might be a

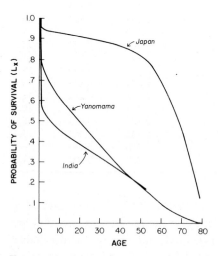

FIG. 1. A comparison of the life table for the Yanomama (sexes combined, infanticide excluded) with that for India at the turn of the century and Japan in the mid-60s.

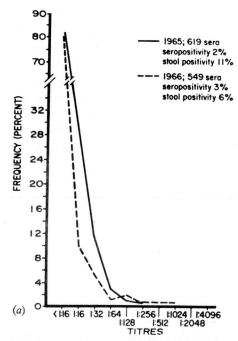

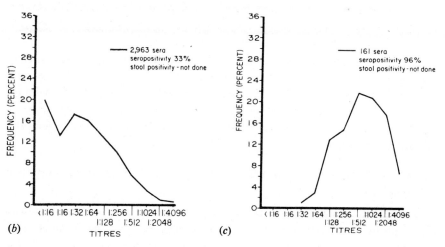

FIG. 2. A comparison of the frequency distribution of indirect haemagglutination test titres against *E. histolytica* in Cherokee Indian school children in the US (A), Colombian army recruits (B), and Yanomama of all ages (C), after Healey *et al.* (1970).

high passive transfer of immunity at birth, followed by a relatively smooth transition to a high level of active immunity with exposure to a variety of endemic pathogens (Neel *et al.* 1964). Globulin levels in several Amerindian tribes have been quite high (Cabannes *et al.* 1965; Neel *et al.* 1968*a*). Healey *et al.* (1970), in an examination of antibody titres to *Entamoeba histolytica* in sera from a variety of populations, were impressed by the unusual results with Yanomama samples, reproduced in Fig. 2, where they are contrasted with the most nearly comparable population examined by these investigators. It is conjectural to what extent this curve implies a relative, acquired immunity to this parasite, but I suspect most of us would believe that contamination of the water supply with *E. histolytica* cysts would be less of a health problem for the Yanomama than for ourselves. Studies of this type should be extended to other parasites and other populations.

I do not mean to imply that we really understand all aspects of the balance with pathogens which leads to these life tables. In this connection, let me discuss briefly the puzzling situation of onchocerciasis (and other filaria) among the Yanomama. After the discovery of this disease in several missionaries to the Yanomama, surveys among this tribe revealed a very high frequency of parasitization (refs. in Enrique Rassi *et al.* 1976). However, clinical manifestations were minimal, a fact we have also documented (Salzano & Neel 1976). The diagnosis seems secure, although other filaria are also prevalent in this region (Beaver *et al.* 1976). In view of the minimal physical findings, we have suggested that the appearance of the disease in such a high proportion of the population is a rather recent development (Salzano & Neel 1976), the source of the disease being still unknown, but an alternative explanation is that these Indians are in a better immunological balance with the parasite than those African populations from which our clinical picture of the disease has been derived. The general concept is that where the principal diseases are endemic rather than epidemic, and given the living conditions of these tribal populations, there develops an equilibrium with many agents of disease not characteristic of highly agricultural or industrialized societies.

CHANGES IN THE EPIDEMIOLOGICAL STRUCTURE OF AMERINDIANS AFTER CONTACT

What are the biomedical changes when the Indian comes in contact with representatives of western civilization? They may be categorized under three headings. Firstly, sooner or later these contacts result in an exposure to the epidemic, 'herd' diseases of civilization, diseases which cannot be maintained in widely dispersed populations in which there is not a suitable, constantly renewed proportion of susceptible individuals (cf. Black 1966, 1975). Secondly, the

Indian's culture is affected in ways relevant to his health and survival. For instance, infanticide, a common practice among tribal people all over the world, is invariably discouraged. Furthermore, as these contacts accelerate, there results a 'culture shock', as real as it is difficult to define. With particular reference to disease, a new set of psychosomatic factors enters the picture. Thirdly, then, the mobility of the Indian often decreases. Voluntarily or otherwise, he settles down, usually in larger-than-traditional aggregations, with depletion of the local game and soil, and deteriorating sanitary conditions. He comes into contact with refined carbohydrates, sometimes, as in the United States, in large amounts.

As we all know, these changes may occur rather rapidly. Obviously, by definition none of us has ever worked in a pre-contact population, and we must always be concerned about the degree to which the primeval picture has been altered before the situation comes under study. Even so, these three categories of changes are probably sufficiently elastic to cover what transpires from the first moments of direct *or indirect* contact.

SOME CASE STUDIES ON THE CONSEQUENCES OF THESE CHANGES

Against this brief background, let me present several attempts at an analysis of why the contacts and changes just mentioned can lead, even in the absence of any striking genetic susceptibilities, to the well-documented deterioration in Indian health.

1. *The unusual epidemiological characteristics of recently contacted groups, as illustrated by their response to measles*

Our group has had the experience of a total immersion in a measles epidemic in an Amerindian tribe, the Yanomama, in which the susceptibility approached 100%. We knew from previous serological profiles of this susceptibility and had with us, when we came in contact with the epidemic, 2000 doses of the Edmonston strain of measles vaccine plus the measles immune globulin then used to obtund the effect of the vaccine (vaccine, courtesy of Parke Davis and Co., Phillips Roxane Laboratories, and Lederle Laboratories; immune globulin, courtesy State of Michigan Department of Health). The details of our observations are summarized elsewhere (Neel *et al.* 1970). We felt that the response of the individual Indian either to the vaccine, with or without covering globulin, or to the disease itself, was not greatly different from that of his civilized Caucasoid or Black African counterpart. Febrile response to the vaccine was not notable. What was different was the complete collapse of village life with the high attack rates which characterized those villages not immunized sufficiently in advance of exposure, or not immunized at all. In this remote area, there was nothing approaching organized care of the sick, other than that provided by the few missionaries and ourselves, until late in the epidemic. In this culture mothers usually nurse their infants at least until age three; you can visualize the situation when in the tropics mother and nursing infant are both prostrate with measles and there is no one to bring water. The secondary complication of broncho-pneumonia was common, but we saw no case of the best known other complication, otitis media. We believe that the high incidence of bronchopneumonia is in part explained by the jack-knife position the ill Indian assumed in his hammock, there to await the death some very malevolent spirit was arranging. Our estimate of the case fatality rate was 9%. A small-scale serological follow-up some 11 months later revealed measles haemagglutination inhibition test titres in the vaccinated and in those who had experienced measles quite comparable to those reported in other populations. It is difficult in the face of these observations and those of Black (Black *et al.* 1969, this symposium, pp. 115–135) to maintain the myth of the great primary susceptibility of the individual Indian to measles.

This is the place to mention an important observation of the late Noel Nutels, who devoted his life to the medical problems of the interior of Brazil, and especially to tuberculosis. His principal observations deal with tribes of the Upper Xingu region of Brazil who, although they had intermittent contacts with *civilizados*, during the course of which they must have been exposed to tuberculosis, nevertheless retained their traditional, nomadic way of life. His conclusions regarding one of these tribes are at marked variance with conventional wisdom, namely: 'The X-rays presented here leave no doubt, in my view, that tuberculosis among these Indians, in its clinical, radiological, and even epidemiological aspects, can be equated with that of peoples with a long experience with BK' (Nutels 1968) (BK = *Mycobacterium tuberculosis*).

2. The retreat from population regulation, and its consequences for infant nutrition

Many Amerindian tribes recognize an intercourse taboo for roughly a year after the birth of child. This is a cause of village tension, since the taboo does not extend to the other man's wife. As noted, abortion and infanticide are both practiced by the Yanomama. In women lactation is almost continuous from the late teens into the forties. As noted earlier, we estimate that for these and possibly other reasons, the average Yanomama woman between the ages of 15 and 40 has a liveborn child every three to four years, of which, averaging the sexes, some 85% are permitted to live.

We are aware of no studies precisely similar to ours which are concerned with

Amerindians who are 30 or 40 years into the acculturation cycle. However, I believe it is a safe generalization that most representatives of western culture who come in contact with Amerindians tend to discourage those practices which help space children, with the result that the interval between births soon shortens rather appreciably. There really is no substitute in the jungle for mother's milk for a young child. Thus I would argue vigorously that the discouragement of these child-spacing practices at an early stage in the acculturation process almost surely results in a deterioration in maternal and child health.

3. The vicious cycle inherent in the rapid deterioration in the quality of their environment

Earlier I have briefly categorized in a qualitative fashion the kinds of changes which ensue with acculturation. Let us now attempt to be semi-quantitative. With the larger and more stable aggregations which contact encourages, both the soil and the game in the surrounding areas tend to deteriorate. Unless there is an abundance of fish nearby, protein suffers more than total calories. Even where an effort is made at compensatory changes in agronomy and animal husbandry, this takes time.

The consequences of these changes are sometimes obvious, sometimes more subtle. With respect to the obvious, let us discuss intestinal parasites. The recently contacted Indian usually is infected with hookworm, roundworm, and *E. histolytica* but parasite density seems moderate (Neel *et al.* 1968; I. G. Kagan & J. V. Neel, unpublished). One reason for this may be that although the Indian is not much given to the use of latrines, with small population sizes and the usual frequent changes in village location, the concentration of *Ascaris* or hookworm eggs or *E. histolytica* cysts in the soil (or water supply) does not build up. This changes with larger, more stable populations. If the intensity of parasitization increases at the same time as the quality of the diet is declining, health must suffer.

By now there are a number of other examples, from our experience and that of others, of how contact quickly alters the epidemiological characteristics of tribal populations. Space does not allow me to examine these here in any detail. There is, however, a situation emerging in my own country, the United States, which we must consider briefly, as a possible example of the full complexity of the genotype–environment interaction which in our view so confounds efforts to study primary susceptibilities in Amerindians. The very high frequency of such diseases as diabetes mellitus and cholelithiasis (gall stones) in the acculturated North American Indian, especially those of the Southwestern United States (Pima and Papago), is becoming well known (refs. in Miller *et al.* 1968;

Burch *et al.* 1968; Rushforth *et al.* 1971; Bennett *et al.* 1976). These are of course highly acculturated populations by any standards. The situation lends itself to the easy generalization that as these populations come into contact with western culture, they are exhibiting unusual susceptibilities. Some years ago I suggested that one explanation for the high frequency of diabetes mellitus in civilized populations might be that a 'thrifty genotype' of selective value in times of intermittent famine was in times of over-abundance and obesity no longer an asset but that the expected genetic adjustments had not yet occurred (Neel 1962).

In this context one could argue that with the adoption of western food habits and a more sedentary way of life, the Amerindian may exhibit marked genetically based responses to the selective pressures imposed by these changes, being asked in a few generations to make genetic adjustments to selective pressures which for the ancestors of most of us were spread over a much more extended period of time. In my opinion the discussions of these findings have failed to emphasize properly the possible role of the unusual degree of obesity encountered in these Indians. Although a treatment of obesity *per se* in this group has not yet appeared, numerous disease-oriented publications refer to the prevalence of obesity in these groups, beginning at an early age, a statement I can confirm from personal observation. Bennett *et al.* (1976) report that among Pima males aged 40 and over, the mean percentage desirable weight averaged 122%, and among females, 149%! The correlates of obesity are well known (Society of Actuaries 1959; U.S. Public Health Service 1966; Kannel *et al.* 1967; Rimm *et al.* 1972). Although Bennett *et al.* (1976) have emphasized the contribution obesity may make to the prevalence of these diseases in the Amerindian, they do not believe it is the only factor. I would like to go further: in my opinion, although special genetic susceptibilities cannot be excluded, it has not yet been demonstrated that the non-obese Pima or Papago is more susceptible to these 'diseases of civilization' than the average non-obese Caucasoid. There is the danger that in our thinking, these non-infectious diseases will become the counterpart of the epidemic diseases mentioned earlier, with the perpetuation of a myth of primary susceptibility which will be difficult to dislodge from the literature. Here may be another example of the care with which the question of innate, genetically determined susceptibilities must be approached.

HOW CAN WE APPORTION THE ROLES OF INNATE SUSCEPTIBILITY AND UNFAVOURABLE EPIDEMIOLOGICAL CIRCUMSTANCES IN HEALTH DETERIORATION?

As a professional geneticist, I am scarcely about to deny that there are genetically determined factors in disease resistance. These are well-documented for experimental mammals under both laboratory and 'natural' conditions (reviewed in Schull 1963). The specific evidence with reference to man is not voluminous, but at this point most of us would accept that the gene for sickle cell haemoglobin confers protection against *falciparum* malaria, although the exact mechanism is debatable. More recently, provocative evidence has been presented for the manner in which the Duffy (a-b-) trait confers protection against *Plasmodium vivax* malaria (Miller *et al.* 1975). And then, of course, there is the burgeoning literature on associations between histocompatibility (HLA) genotypes and particular diseases. However, these examples stand out against a background of unsuccessful efforts to demonstrate convincingly associations between genetic traits and susceptibilities to infectious disease, although it must be admitted that the small numbers involved in most of these efforts would only demonstrate rather striking associations. Be this as it may, the issue here is not whether there are genetically determined differences in disease susceptibilities in man, but to what extent are they responsible for the deterioration in Amerindian health after contact.

What is needed as the basis for any valid conclusions about Indian disease susceptibilities is a situation where Indian and non-Indian populations are living under comparable circumstances, and where accurate long-term records are being kept. To my knowledge this situation does not exist anywhere in the world today. But, in a setting where there is perhaps too much reliance on anecdote, I can perhaps add another. Most of our own field-work on Amerindian populations has been done in rather remote areas where the Indian is not in contact with any substantial number of nationals. However, this past summer (1976) in the Brazilian Amazonas I was involved in collaborative studies with Brazilian scientists of two rather acculturated but still little admixed groups, the Ticuna and the Cashinawa, both in juxtaposition with the neo-Brazilians of the interior. Our programme included physical examinations and immunizations of the Indians; under the conditions we acquiesced in the request that we devote some time to the local (*caboclo*) population. It is our impression that the novelty of our medical team evoked a rather complete turnout. We saw little difference in the state of health of the two groups, living under essentially comparable circumstances.

There is one respect in which I retreat from the iconoclastic position that there is little difference between the susceptibilities of Amerindians and ourselves. This is in relation to the viral respiratory infections. We all know the havoc an undifferentiated respiratory infection (URI) can inflict on a recently contacted group. Yet even here there are ambiguities. We civilized types come in contact with URI's from birth onwards, the effects of the first exposure perhaps being modulated by maternally derived antibody. The average Caucasoid experiences two or three URI's a year. Surely there is some immunity as well as cross-immunity, modulating the results of a URI in a Caucasoid aged 20, as contrasted to an Amerindian of the same age for whom this is a first experience. Furthermore, as I suggested earlier (p. 148), I am intrigued by the possibility that the newly contacted Indian may suffer from simultaneous infection by several respiratory viruses, whereas we civilized types seldom do.

SOME PRACTICAL IMPLICATIONS OF BELIEVING AMERINDIAN DISEASE SUSCEPTIBILITIES DO NOT GREATLY DIFFER FROM THOSE OF CAUCASOIDS

The practical implications of the foregoing for newly contacted Amerindians are obvious but not easily implemented (cf. Neel 1974). Obviously, an extensive programme of immunization is called for. Beyond this, the basic proposition is not to alter any important feature of tribal practice until provision has been made for the consequences of such alteration. This is of course more easily said than done. Those who criticize the efforts of governments in Latin America to meet the health needs of newly contacted peoples are often not aware of how sparsely inhabited the interiors of some of these countries are, and of the problems inherent in meeting the health needs of *all* the inhabitants of these regions.

So long as we believe in innate susceptibilities on the part of Amerindian populations, we can mentally justify poor medical statistics. These can be viewed as a selective bottleneck through which the Indian must pass in entering our civilization. The view which I take in this paper is much less conducive to complacency, especially on the part of health administrators in my own country. In the interior of such countries as Brazil, Venezuela, and Colombia, where governments are struggling to extend modern medical services to their citizens, one can scarcely be critical if the medical statistics for the relatively recently contacted Indian are somewhat inferior to those for the *caboclo* or *campestino*. The situation is very different in the United States, where 100 or so years ago we created neglected enclaves called reservations which by now in most parts of the country are surrounded by areas whose medical statistics match those of the rest of the US. The excess morbidity among these Indians from diarrhoeal diseases, otitis media, streptococcal pharyngitis and venereal diseases—in addition to the conditions just discussed—is well documented (U.S. Congress 1974). Data supplied by the National Center for Health Statistics indicate that life expectancy at birth, which is at best an imperfect indicator of the health status of a population, was 64.6 years for the Indian, but 71.3 years for the US white population in 1973. Much more is involved in the improvement of those statistics than the provision of more medical services of the traditional type. It will be difficult for us of the United States to be critical of the management of Amerindian health problems throughout the Americas as long as these figures persist.

ACKNOWLEDGEMENTS

The original studies described in this paper have been supported by the National Science Foundation and the Energy Research and Development Administration.

References

BEAVER, P.C., NEEL, J.V. & ORIHEL, T.C. (1976) *Dipetalonema perstans* and *Mansonella ozzardi* in Indians of Southern Venezuela. *Am. J. Trop. Med. Hyg. 25*, 263–265

BENNETT, P.H., RUSHFORTH, N.B., MILLER, M. & LECONTE, P.M. (1976) Epidemiologic studies of diabetes in the Pima Indians, in *Recent Progress in Hormone Research*, vol. 32 (Greep, R.O., ed.), pp. 333–376, Academic Press, New York

BLACK, F.L. (1966) Measles endemicity in insular populations: critical community size and its evolutionary implication. *J. Theoret. Biol. 11*, 207–211

BLACK, F.L. (1975) Infectious diseases in primitive societies. *Science (Wash. D.C.) 187*, 515–518

BLACK, F.L., WOODALL, J.P. & PINHEIRO, F. (1969) Measles vaccine reactions in a virgin population. *Am. J. Epidemiol. 89*, 168–175

BLACK, F.L., PINHEIRO, F. DE P., HIERHOLZER, W.J. & LEE, R. V. (1977) This volume, pp. 115–135

BURCH, T.A., COMERS, L.J. & BENNETT, P.H. (1968) The problem of gallbladder disease among Pima Indians, in *Biomedical Challenges Presented by the American Indian* (Publication No. 165), pp. 82–88, Pan American Health Organization, Washington, D.C.

CABANNES, R., BEURRIER, A. & MONNET, B. (1965) Studies of the proteins, haptoglobins and transferrins in Indians from French Guiana. (Études des protéines, des haptoglobulines et des transferrines chez les Indiens de Guyane française.) *Nouv. Rev. Fr. Hématol. 5*, 247–260

DUNN, F.L. (1968) Epidemiological factors: health and disease in hunter-gatherers, in *Man the Hunter* (Lee, R. B. & DeVore, I., eds.), pp. 221–228, Aldine, Chicago

ENRIQUE RASSI, B., LAURDA, N. & GUAIMARAES, J.A. (1976) Study of the area affected by onchocerciasis in Brasil: survey of local residents. *Bull. Pan Am. Health Organ. 10*, 33–45

HEALY, G.R., KAGAN, I.G. & GLEASON, N.N. (1970) Use of the indirect hemagglutination test in some studies of seroepidemiology of amebiasis in the Western Hemisphere. *Health Lab. Sci. 7*, 109–116

KANNEL, W.B., LE BAUER, E.J., DAWBER, T.R. & McNAMARA, P.M. (1967) Relation of body weight to development of coronary heart disease: the Framingham Study. *Circulation 35*, 734–744

MILLER, L.H., MASON, S.J., DVORAK, J.A., McGINNISS, M.H. & ROTHMAN, I.K. (1975) Erythrocyte receptors for *(Plasmodium knowlesi)* malaria: Duffy blood group determinants. *Science (Wash. D.C.) 189*, 561–563

MILLER, M., BENNETT, P.H. & BURCH, T.A. (1968) Hyperglycemia in Pima Indians: a preliminary appraisal of its significance, in *Biomedical Challenges Presented by the American Indian* (Publication No. 165), pp. 89–103, Pan American Health Organization, Washington, D.C.

NEEL, J.V. (1962) Diabetes mellitus: a 'thrifty' genotype rendered detrimental by 'progress'. *Am. J. Hum. Genet. 14*, 353–362

NEEL, J.V. (1970) Lessons from a 'primitive' people. *Science (Wash. D.C.) 170*, 815–822

NEEL, J.V. (1971) Genetic aspects of the ecology of disease in the American Indian, in *The Ongoing Evolution of Latin American Populations* (Salzano, F. M., ed.), pp. 561–590, Thomas, Springfield, Ill.

NEEL, J.V. (1974) Control of disease among Amerindians in cultural transition. *Bull. Pan Am. Health Organ. 8*, 205–211

NEEL, J.V. & WEISS, K.M. (1975) The genetic structure of a tribal population, the Yanomama Indians. XII. Biodemographic studies. *Am. J. Phys. Anthropol. 42*, 25–51

NEEL, J.V., SALZANO, F.M., JUNQUEIRA, P.C., KEITER, F. & MAYBURY-LEWIS, D. (1964) Studies on the Xavante Indians of the Brazilian Mato Grosso. *Am. J. Hum. Genet. 16*, 52–140

NEEL, J.V., ANDRADE, A.H.P., BROWN, G.E., EVELAND, W.E., GOOBAR, J., SODEMAN, W.A., STOLLERMAN, G.H., WEINSTEIN, E.D. & WHEELER, A.H. (1968a) Further studies of the Xavante Indians. IX. Immunologic status with respect to various diseases and organisms. *Am. J. Trop. Med. Hyg. 17*, 486–498

NEEL, J.V., MIKKELSEN, W.M., RUCKNAGEL, D.L., WEINSTEIN, E.D., GOYER, R.A. & ABADIE, S.H. (1968b) Further studies on the Xavante Indians. VIII. Some observations on blood, urine, and stool specimens. *Am. J. Trop. Med. Hyg. 17*, 474–485

NEEL, J.V., CENTERWALL, W.R., CHAGNON, N.A. & CASEY, H.L. (1970) Notes on the effect of measles and measles vaccine in a virgin-soil population of South American Indians. *Am. J. Epidemiol. 91*, 418–429

NUTELS, N. (1968) Medical problems of newly contacted Indian groups, in *Biomedical Challenges Presented by the American Indian* (Publication No. 165), pp. 68–76, Pan American Health Organization, Washington, D.C.

RIMM, A.A., WERNER, L.H., BERNSTEIN, R. & VAN YSERLOO, B. (1972) Disease and obesity in 73,532 women. *Obesity/Bariatric Med. 1*, 77–84

RUSHFORTH, N.B., BENNETT, P.H., STEINBERG, A.G., BURCH, T.A. & MILLER, M. (1971) Diabetes in the Pima Indians. *Diabetes 20*, 756–765

SALZANO, F.M. & NEEL, J.V. (1976) New data on the vision of South American Indians. *Bull. Pan Am. Health Organ. 10*, 1–8

SCHULL, W.J. (ed.) (1963) *Genetic Selection in Man* (Proceedings, Third Macy Conference on Genetics), University of Michigan Press, Ann Arbor, Michigan

Society of Actuaries (1959) *Build and Blood Pressure Study*, vols. I & II, pp. 268 & 240, Society of Actuaries, Chicago

U.S. CONGRESS, SENATE COMMITTEE ON GOVERNMENT OPERATIONS, SUBCOMMITTEE ON INVESTIGATIONS (1974) *Hearings on Indian Health Care*, Ninety-Third Congress, Second Session, 267 pp.

U.S. PUBLIC HEALTH SERVICE, DIVISION OF CHRONIC DISEASES (1966) *Obesity and Health: a Source Book of Current Information for Professional Health Personnel* (Public Health Service Publication No. 1485), U.S. Government Printing Office, Washington, D.C.

WEINSTEIN, E.D., NEEL, J.V. & SALZANO, F.M. (1967) Further studies on the Xavante Indians. VI. The physical status of the Xavantes of Simões Lopes. *Am. J. Hum. Genet. 19*, 532–542

WEISS, K.M. (1973) Demographic models for anthropology (Memoirs of the Society for American Archaeology, No. 27). *Am. Antiquity 38*, 1–186

Discussion

Hugh-Jones: Is it established that the filariae of onchocerciasis are antigenically the same in Africa and in South America?

Neel: Filariae don't seem to be highly antigenic, and there is also much cross-reactivity between the various species, so the serological approach has not been very useful. The evidence at present is entirely morphological, based on nodules excised from missionaries and the microfilariae in skin snips from the Indians.

Lozoff: A variety of related animal filariae have been used as sources of antigen for the immunological diagnosis of onchocerciasis and the other filariases. Grove *et al.* (1977) have shown in Bancroftian and Malayan filariasis that antigens prepared from *Brugia malayi* greatly improve the sensitivity and specificity of skin test reactions. Now that animal models for the various filariases are being developed, greater numbers of each human parasite will be available, and it is to be hoped that by fractionation and isolation of specific antigens the immunological diagnosis of these infections will be greatly facilitated.

Hamilton: The serology of the filariae has so far been disappointing as a neat epidemiological tool but clinical epidemiological studies in West Africa have shown marked differences in the manifestation of onchocerciasis between the savannah and the rain forest areas. These differences are not fully understood but may be associated with the biting habits of the flies and other environmental factors, rather than purely genetic ones (Anderson *et al.* 1974).

In Brazil some confusion has arisen over the identification of *Onchocerca volvulus* and *Mansonella ozzardi*, both of which are common. There is a real need for the use of standardized techniques, not only in identifying filariae but also in evaluating the clinical signs, in which very great variations were found in longitudinal studies in the Cameroons (Hamilton *et al.* 1974). I hope very much it will be possible for the standardized techniques developed in Africa to be applied in the Americas.

One major problem with the *Simulium damnosum* of Africa is that it is not a single species but a complex, and there is some evidence that the Simuliidae in Guyana and Brazil may also be a species complex (E. S. Tikasingh & A. J. Shelley, unpublished work 1976). Detailed studies of this are now being begun, since the opening of roads into the areas requires knowledge of this problem.

The apparently low density of infection and absence of severe complications so far reported from these isolated communities in Brazil support the concept of a newly introduced disease and it is intriguing therefore to wonder from where and how *Onchocerca volvulus* was introduced into these communities. The development of this disease and its control urgently require detailed studies of both the clinical and entomological aspects, and the collection of basic data in these isolated communities could be of great clinical and epidemiological interest.

Neel: We are indeed aware of the complexities of the situation, and I wish I had time enough to go into them all. We can attest to the presence of both *Mansonella* and *Dipetalonema* through the Upper Orinoco and Amazon basins.

So far the experts maintain that neither of these parasites is involved; the responsible organisms are more like *Onchocerca* than any other known filariae.

Cohen: You described the rather extraordinary population pyramid of the Yanomama, Professor Neel, and suggested that this was mainly due to preferential female infanticide. Do you see this unusual pyramid as a continuing phenomenon or was it just something that happened to affect one particular cohort, 10–30 years ago? I am not sure how you account for the similar numbers of males and females at the top of the pyramid. I would like to see that population pyramid in another 5–10 years' time, and I would like to know what the anthropologists said about it.

Neel: There are two peculiarities of the population pyramid. Firstly, we believe that the excess of males in the very young is due to preferential female infanticide. The anthropologists seem to agree on this. The difference in the numbers of males and females disappears about age 30 because of the much more dangerous life of the men. We don't think the sexual asymmetry we observed in the population pyramid is a temporary aberration; it is part of their culture. Secondly, there is a 'bulge' on the female side at age 10–14 which we don't understand. But the numbers of people are so small that I am sure there is a lot of stochastic flux.

Ohlman: Is there some deliberate selection in infanticide in favour of those girl babies considered most likely to survive naturally?

Neel: We know that the congenitally defective babies of both sexes are killed if they are recognized at birth. This is common all over the world in primitive communities. Beyond that, I am not aware that in killing more girl babies they try to pick out the weakest ones, because the mother has usually decided before the birth that if it is a girl she will kill the child; it is principally her decision, but subject to a certain amount of extraneous pressure. She is in the forest alone at the time of delivery, perhaps accompanied by her mother.

Truswell: Does a male child push an older female child off the breast?

Neel: I don't know.

Lozoff: Is the male–female birth interval in fact greater than the male–male interval?

Neel: We haven't studied that, but it's a reasonable suggestion that the interval might be related to the sex of the children.

White: There is some evidence, but I do not regard it as convincing proof, that in some Australian Aboriginal communities a mother may take less care of a female infant. In one community where I was able to study the birth and death figures for an 18-year period ending in 1972, the mortality rate for female infants was slightly higher than that for males. This could have been due to some neglect of girl babies, but I have certainly not observed any such behaviour.

Babies of both sexes appear to be treated with equally great amounts of love and care.

Neel: In the Yanomama it is actual infanticide.

Baruzzi: Traditionally it was unusual for the Indians to have more than two or three children. When they had one or two girls and another girl was born, they killed her. They did the same with twins and with handicapped newborn babies or when the father was unknown. This is one of the hypotheses proposed to explain why the Indian population was not larger at the discovery of the New World. Now there is cultural change, and the women sometimes have four or five children.

Neel: Formerly they were practising population control as best they could, namely by infanticide, but when they are contacted this practice is discouraged· As a result breast-feeding has been shortened from $3^1/_2$ years to two years.

Black: You made the point, with which I would agree, that the social disruption of an epidemic has an important effect on the outcome, and is something that can be dealt with. You avoided the genetic element, except that you did notice clinically that the cases of measles were more severe than usual. You left open the question of whether there are other factors as well.

Neel: As a geneticist I spend much of my life arguing *against* invoking genetic susceptibility to explain poorly understood situations, and I am not convinced that we need invoke any special genetic susceptibility in this situation, although I don't exclude it either. If I had to make a 'guesstimate' I would say that 80% of what we see in the way of 'excess' mortality from rubeola is non-genetic and maybe 20% is genetic.

Tyrrell: It was suggested earlier that there is no good evidence for a genetic role in susceptibility to tuberculosis, but you are claiming here that 20% of disease susceptibility might be genetic. This suggests that probably there is no real difference between us on this. There are two dangers: the first is to make sweeping generalizations, about infections or populations or situations, and a second is to expect to find that all the differences are explained by one factor. Very rarely must there be fewer than three factors operating, and immunological differences as a result of isolation from exposure are often the most important; secondly comes nutrition, particularly in bacterial infections, where the interaction between malnutrition and bacterial infection of the gut is a profoundly important and very dangerous combination. I would put genetic factors last in importance. One of the difficulties of demonstrating the genetic factors is that we are looking for them in the wrong way. If they have an important effect it must be over a period of years; a 5% survival advantage for an individual during his life could have a large effect genetically but would be difficult to measure in the situations we are discussing.

Neel: I agree; but there has been too much uncritical reference to genetic susceptibility which has not been demonstrated.

Gajdusek: There are many other ecological and epidemiological factors that can lead to differing susceptibilities to an infectious agent in different populations. We have been wondering about the enormous difference in neonatal tetanus between some parts of New Guinea, where a third of all liveborn infants die of it, and other parts where it has never been seen although extensively looked for (Schofield *et al.* 1961). We wondered if there is an acquired immunity to tetanus from skin infections without clinical disease, and we have now screened the sera of many adults and older children in New Guinea communities who have never had tetanus vaccine. Dr Geoffrey Edsall, at the London School of Hygiene and Tropical Medicine, found tetanus antibody in only two individuals of several hundred studied (G. Edsall, R. M. Garruto & D. C. Gajdusek, unpublished data).

Diphtheria, on the other hand, is another bacterial infection where there can be lasting immunity from undiagnosed cutaneous infection. This has also been found in New Guinea.

Then there is the further problem of rare, serologically negative older subjects for viruses such as herpes simplex, cytomegalovirus, Epstein-Barr virus, and even poliomyelitis, influenza, measles and adenoviruses in populations where the great majority of individuals are serologically positive. It is often harder to explain how such people remain negative if the viruses are really ubiquitous or if an epidemic has been through their area than to explain wholly susceptible populations. We have at times looked for anamnestic (secondary) responses in the 'negative' subjects by testing blood specimens collected a few days after immunization with influenza and measles vaccines from subjects with serologically negative pre-bleedings. Such specimens allow us to distinguish primary from anamnestic reactors. Only when there was a normally delayed primary immune response was the serologically negative pre-bleeding evidence of no previous exposure. When there is an anamnestic response we presume that the antibody level in the pre-bleeding had fallen below the level of sensitivity of our assay. The response to a given agent may vary in different populations and individuals, depending on their previous experience with other related viruses. This has led Fazekas de St. Groth to the concept of 'original antigenic sin' in his work with influenza viruses (Fazekas de St. Groth & Webster 1966). It could give rise to differences in responsiveness or susceptibility in different populations which would be fallaciously assigned to their genetic differences.

Weiner: What is your assessment, Professor Neel, of the value of the evidence on genetic susceptibility to disease obtained from comparisons of identical and non-identical twins?

Neel: The evidence there has the same standing as all evidence from twin studies, in that somewhat belatedly we are realizing how non-genetic familial factors have been confounded with genetic factors in studies of twins. Twin studies are a useful way of getting an idea of whether there might be a genetic component, but then comes the hard work. I think that the results of studies on poliomyelitis and on measles in twins are affected by the fact that identical twins are in subtle ways managed more similarly by their parents than non-identical twins. The differences in attack rates are not very different for measles in such studies, in any case.

Polunin: Given the likelihood that infections are important causes of death, and given the evidence for genetic variation in susceptibility to specific infections in inbred experimental animals, how do you explain this failure to demonstrate variations in susceptibility due to genes in man? Can you believe that it's true?

Neel: Part of the problem is this: we now realize that to demonstrate a selective differential of 1%, which would be an important difference, requires much larger numbers of individuals than almost any investigator has been able to assemble. Our series was not large enough to exclude a differential susceptibility of that order. It seems reasonable that there ought to be genetic susceptibilities but I don't think the case has been made for them.

Polunin: Even so, can you really believe that there are *not* genes that have a considerable effect on susceptibility?

Neel: What I *can* believe is that it is dangerous for public health administrators to believe this!

Harrison: I think you undervalue the large number of associations that have been found with known genetic systems, but to translate even a real association into selection effects is a very different matter. The numbers required to demonstrate any selection in a population can be enormous, as you say. If, for example, you attempt to detect selection by within-generation changes in gene frequency when the selection operates against a recessive gene at 10% frequency and the selection coefficient is 1%, you need two samples (before and after selection) each of about eight million to detect it. And to translate a particular association into selection it is necessary to establish accurately its effects on differential survival and reproduction. Nowhere do we yet have the demographic data for this in tribal societies. Further, although one tends to think of a selection operating in a rather acute form (an epidemic eliminating a large number of people, for example), selection also may act in more subtle ways, particularly in man, where someone who is, say, chronically infected, may feel constantly 'below par', doesn't rise in the social system as rapidly as someone else, cannot provide as well nutritionally for his children, or lacks access to as many women or marries late. These subtle features are probably impossible to detect in field work even as detailed and thorough as Professor Neel's.

Neel: Until the associations between particular diseases and histocompatibility (HLA) genes were found, which we still don't understand, the best case of association was that between blood group A and carcinoma of the stomach and the O blood group (and the non-secretor trait) with peptic ulcer. But neither of those diseases seems to have been very important to primitive man, and it is difficult to translate them into terms of selective values.

I believe we shall learn a lot from the HLA associations, but nevertheless I have to challenge you to translate any of these known associations into something that is important in human evolution.

Harrison: Admittedly associations with ulcer and gastric carcinoma do not appear to be of much selective significance, but a vast number of other associations with the ABO blood groups, including some with infective agents, have now been found. It is possible that the ABO system is playing some fundamental role in cell membrane structure which profoundly affects susceptibility to a whole host of pathogenic organisms.

Neel: A lot of this work has been challenged; associations reported in one series have not been reproduced in other series.

Harrison: Our recent analysis in New Guinea of an association between ABO and goitre is an instance where although I can't claim definitive selective significance, the facts are very suggestive (Harrison *et al.* 1976). There is also a lot of indirect evidence that the ABO genotype is subject to selection. And the fact that an association does not always hold is not surprising; we might expect situations to change according to total ecology. We are probably also naive in looking at selection as exerted on a single gene locus; we should be thinking of selection acting on the whole genome.

Tyrrell: Relationships between ABO blood groups and various virus infections have been confirmed (Potter 1969). Influenza and adenovirus infections are more likely in people with blood group O than in those with blood group A. But it can be confusing, because if the selection is exerted early in life, as it often is with these infections, children may have been infected more often if they were blood group O, at first exposure, and if later in life you draw from that population those who are getting, say, adenovirus infections, more of them are group A than group O because there are more group A people without immunity. But this is the sort of association which I suggest could have selective consequences, because respiratory infections in childhood make an important contribution to infant mortality.

Neel: One can have a very significant association of a disease with a genetic trait, with only modest implications for causation. We all know about the A/

gastric cancer and the O/duodenal ulcer association, and the association of the non-secretor trait with duodenal ulcers. But Fraser Roberts (1970) has shown that only some 5% of the tendency of brothers to be concordant for duodenal ulcer is due to their tendency to be similar with respect to O blood type and the secretor trait. Put that way, the genetic contribution looks rather small.

Shaper: For the chronic degenerative diseases as well as the infectious diseases, genetic mechanisms are sometimes evoked to explain different behaviour patterns when the evidence is really very weak. For example, the Masai and Samburu of East Africa, who are reputed to have a regular intake of milk, meat and blood, and therefore a diet that is high in fats, are found to have low concentrations of cholesterol in the blood (Shaper 1962; Shaper *et al.* 1963; Mann *et al.* 1964). People have attempted to explain this by a genetic mechanism whereby the synthesis of cholesterol in their livers is more readily suppressed than in other populations, but there is little evidence for this (Biss *et al.* 1971). There are also the diseases such as hypertension, coronary artery disease and gall bladder disease, which don't on the whole occur among the primitive communities, but begin to appear when these people alter their ways of life. The evidence in all these conditions is that the absence of the condition has nothing to do with genetic protection or susceptibility.

You mentioned obesity among some groups. What is beginning to emerge from epidemiological studies in western communities is that obesity by itself, separated from the associated problems of hypertension and diabetes, is a weak risk factor for many diseases, particularly coronary heart disease (Mann 1974; Keys 1975).

Neel: In the Amerindians whom we examined, the blood pressure does not continue to go up after the second decade as it does in western communities; it seems to reach a peak in the third decade and then to level out or even fall.

We also measure sodium chloride output in the urine over 24 hours; most of the Yanomama males are excreting less than one milliequivalent of sodium per 24 hours, which is almost nothing, and implies a very low salt intake. We don't know how the women manage to make babies with such low salt intakes! But—if one believes that salt *is* connected with hypertension—the reason that the North American Indians are developing hypertension may be that they have the same susceptibility to salt that we have but have never come into contact with salt in large quantities before, and *in addition* they are grossly overweight.

Shaper: I think the relationship between fatness and hypertension is a real one but that it is neither direct nor simple! And despite the fact that the salt intake is very low in all these isolated communities where blood pressure does not rise with increasing age, there seems to be tremendous individual susceptibility, within these primitive communities and in westernized ones, so that some people react to a lot of salt in much the same way as some rats will, namely with hypertension, whereas others will not (Freis 1976).

Woodburn: A peculiar observation is that where there are adjacent populations of hunters and gatherers and of agriculturists, the hunters and gatherers sometimes don't seek out salt and don't use it unless some is conveniently to hand, whereas the agricultural people both seek out and use salt. So it isn't just a matter of availability. There is a difference in the desire for salt which is presumably physiologically rather than culturally determined and may, I suppose, depend on some other dietary factor.

The Hadza, although they live close to a salt lake, do not gather salt there as their agricultural neighbours do. It is, however, possible in the Hadza case that they are taking in quite a lot of salt with their drinking water (Barnicot *et al.* 1972, p. 111).

Lozoff: Professor Neel, you mentioned female infanticide and war as causes of death; what other factors account for mortality in the community that you studied?

Neel: We were amazed how many people die from snakebites. It is an ever-present hazard. It may cause only one death every one or two years, but in a small village that cumulates to a sizeable fraction over a generation. And it particularly affects the women and children.

Shaper: Is it the treatment for the snakebite which is so lethal?

Neel: No. The snake is a viper, and there isn't much time for treatment.

Woodburn: Curiously enough, among the Hadza too, snakebite (and not treatment for snakebite) is a common cause of death.

Doctors in hospitals in East Africa see rather few cases of snakebite and tend to be sceptical about evidence that it is a common cause of death. I cannot talk about the situation in East Africa generally but in the special conditions of Hadza hunting and gathering, snakes kill.

Gajdusek: We also found that over many years snakebite was a major cause of death in some of the New Guinea communities.

References

ANDERSON, J., FUGLSANG, H., HAMILTON, P.J.S. & MARSHALL, T.F. DE C. (1974) Studies on onchocerciasis in the United Cameroon Republic. II. Comparison of onchocerciasis in rain-forest and Sudan-Savanna. *Trans. R. Soc. Trop. Med. Hyg. 68*, 209–222

BARNICOT, N.A., BENNETT, F.J., WOODBURN, J.C., PILKINGTON, T.R.E. & the late ANTONIS, A. (1972) Blood pressure and serum cholesterol in the Hadza of Tanzania. *Hum. Biol. 44* (1), 87–116

BISS, K., HO, K-J., MIKKELSON, B., LEWIS, L. & TAYLOR, C.B. (1971) Some unique biologic characteristics of the Masai of East Africa. *N. Engl. J. Med. 284*, 694–699

FAZEKAS DE ST. GROTH, S. & WEBSTER, R.G. (1966) Disquisitions on original antigenic sin. I. Evidence in man. *J. Exp. Med. 124*, 331–345

FRASER ROBERTS, J.A. (1970) *An Introduction to Medical Genetics*, 5th edn, Oxford University Press, London

FREIS, E.D. (1976) Salt, volume and the prevention of hypertension. *Circulation 53*, 589–595

GROVE, D.I., CABRERA, B.D., VALEZA, F.S., GUINTO, R.S., ASH, L.R. & WARREN, K.S. (1977) Sensitivity and specificity of skin reactivity to *Brugia malayi* and *Dirofilaria immitis* antigens in bancroftian and malayan filariasis in the Philippines. *Am. J. Trop. Med. Hyg. 26*, 220–229

HAMILTON, P.J.S., MARSHALL, T.F. DE C., ANDERSON, J. & FUGLSANG, H. (1974) Observer variation in clinical onchocerciasis. *Trans. R. Soc. Trop. Med. Hyg. 68*, 187–189

HARRISON, G.A., BOYSE, A.J., HORNABROOK, R.W., SERJEANTSON, S. & CRAIG, W.J. (1976) Evidence for an association between ABO blood group and goitre. *Hum. Genet. 32*, 335–337

KEYS, A. (1975) Overweight and the risk of heart attacks and sudden death, in *Obesity in Perspective* (Gray, G.A., ed.) (Fogarty International Center Series on Preventive Medicine 2), pp. 215–223

MANN, G.V. (1974) The influence of obesity on health. *N. Engl. J. Med. 291*, 178–185 & 226–232

MANN, G.V., SHAFFER, R.D., ANDERSON, R.S. & SANDSTEAD, H.H. (1964) *J. Atheroscler. Res. 4*, 289–312

POTTER, C.W. (1969) HI antibody to various influenza viruses and adenoviruses in individuals of blood groups A and O. *J. Hyg. (Camb.) 67*, 67–74

SCHOFIELD, F.D., TUCKER, V.M. & WESTBROOK, G.R. (1961) Neonatal tetanus in New Guinea. Effect of active immunization in pregnancy. *Br. Med. J. 2*, 785–789

SHAPER, A.G. (1962) Cardiovascular studies in the Samburu tribe of northern Kenya. *Am. Heart J. 63*, 437–442

SHAPER, A.G., JONES, K.W., JONES, M. & KYOBE, J. (1963) Serum lipids in three nomadic tribes of northern Kenya. *Am. J. Clin. Nutr. 13*, 135–146

The Kren-Akorore: a recently contacted indigenous tribe

R. G. BARUZZI, L. F. MARCOPITO, M. L. C. SERRA, F. A. A. SOUZA and C. STABILE

Departamento de Medicina Preventiva (Chairman: Professor M. Iunes), Escola Paulista de Medicina, São Paulo, Brazil

Abstract Primitive groups of people, living in complete isolation, are rarely encountered these days. In fact, the process of 'approximation', or contact, depends upon decisions made on both sides—that representing the civilized world and that representing the group called by us 'primitive'. The isolated group, however, can never perceive the tremendous risks its members will inevitably encounter once the barrier of isolation, by which they are protected, has been broken. Civilized man has the means of persuasion and attraction at his disposal and also knows the risks involved. It must therefore be his responsibility to protect and preserve the group right from the initial contact.

In spite of the medical resources available, primitive man has paid heavily in human lives through contact with the civilized world. This raises two equally important questions: (*a*) have medical resources been thoroughly applied to protect these groups? And (*b*) are the existing medical resources sufficient to ensure the survival of primitive man once his state of isolation has been broken? Without any definite answers to these questions, we are limited to describing our experiences with the Kren-Akorore Indians, recently contacted in Central Brazil. We also present data on the biological characteristics of these Indians, collected two years after the first contact.

It had been known for many years that a hostile Indian tribe was living in isolation in the region of the River Peixoto de Azevedo, tributary of the River Teles Pires, in the north of the State of Mato Grosso, near the State of Pará. The first reports had come from the Caiabi Indians in about 1949, when one of their villages had been attacked by that tribe. Later reports came from the Txukar-ramãe Indians who were contacted by Claudio and Orlando Villas Boas in the region near Von Martius Falls, Xingu River, in 1953. The Txukarramãe told of frequent skirmishes with the Indians of the River Peixoto de Azevedo, iden-tifying them by the name 'Kren-Akorore', meaning 'people with short, shaped hair', the name by which they have since been known.

Indians are accustomed to describing their adversaries as being fierce and physically superior. This was how the Caiabi and Txukarramãe described the Kren-Akorore. Among the Txukarramãe, the Villas Boas brothers encountered a young adult Kren-Akorore Indian who had been captured as a child. He was notable for his unusual height of 2.03 metres. From this had sprung the belief that the Kren-Akorore were much taller than all the other Indian tribes, and consequently were frequently referred to as 'giants'.

Although there was sufficient evidence that there were Indians living in isolation in the region of the River Peixoto de Azevedo, there were no particular reasons for entering into contact with them. This remained the situation until 1961, when Richard Mason, a young English doctor, was killed by the Kren-Akorore near the Cachimbo air base, in the south of Pará, close to the border with Mato Grosso State (Cowell 1974). Then, some years later, in 1967, when a group of Kren-Akorore suddenly appeared at the Cachimbo air base, this provoked panic among the personnel of the base, who fired shots into the air to disperse the Indians. The crew of an aeroplane which was about to land was alerted and the pilot flew low over the air-strip to scare off the Indians. The Kren-Akorore, alarmed at this reception, sought refuge in the jungle and disappeared.

As a result of this episode, Claudio and Orlando Villas Boas were given the responsibility of undertaking the search for the Kren-Akorore, in order to contact them. These dedicated men, with 30 years of experience with the Indian population of Central Brazil, had had considerable previous success in contacting isolated and hostile tribes. With the cooperation of Indians from varied linguistic groups from the Xingu National Park the Villas Boas brothers organized an expedition. The presence of the Xinguan Indians would be invaluable in the attempt to contact the Kren-Akorore, a tribe of unknown tongue. They would also prove their worth by their adeptness in moving through the jungle, their skill in building canoes and so on.

Past experience with hostile groups had taught the Villas Boas brothers to be cautious. Their expeditionary group was therefore relatively large, about thirty people. They hoped the size of their group would discourage the Kren-Akorore from attacking. A clash between the two groups would have disastrous consequences, not only because of the possibility of injury or death on both sides, but the flight of the aggressors, fearful of repercussions, would make the work of establishing contact even more difficult.

The expedition set off from the Xingu National Park, descended the River Xingu, penetrated its tributary the River Maritsaua, and continued overland through a jungle trail of 90 kilometres until it reached the River Peixoto de Azevedo. A Kren-Akorore village had been located by plane, and the expeditionary group went down the river to its vicinity. During this period, planes

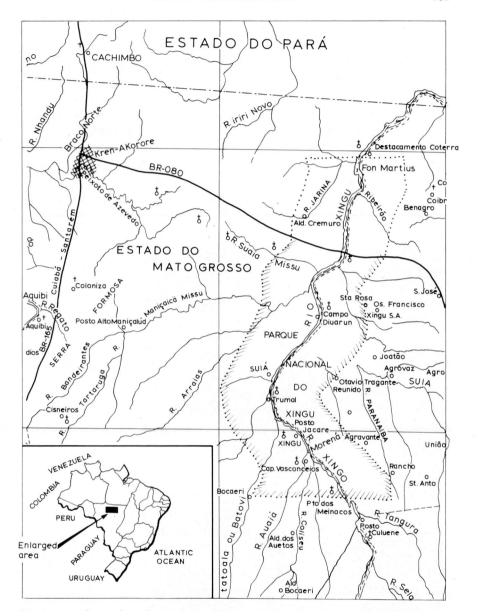

FIG. 1. Map of part of Brazil, showing the former Kren-Akorore territory, the Xingu National Park and the new roads.

dropped presents (such as large knives, hatchets, pans and aluminium bowls, and toys) in various parts of the jungle, to demonstrate to the Indians the conciliatory intentions of the 'invaders' and to attract them to a mutual encounter.

At last, when the Kren-Akorore village was reached, it was found to be deserted. Its inhabitants, faced with the prospect of encountering the intruders, had decided to take flight. They had abandoned their belongings and plantations and sought refuge in the jungle. Claudio Villas Boas and some companions stayed camped nearby for a further five months, even though it was the rainy season. They hoped that the villagers would return, but they waited in vain. The expedition, which began in May 1968, was terminated in January 1969.

Three years later, a new situation arose which would profoundly transform the life of the Kren-Akorore; namely, the preliminary plan of a project for the opening of a highway (BR. 165) to join Santarém in the north and Cuiabá, the capital of Mato Grosso State, in the south, showed that the road would cut through the area inhabited by the Kren-Akorore (Fig. 1).

FIG. 2. The first Kren-Akorore to be contacted, in February 1973.

A new expedition was organized. Another attempt was now imperative to prevent the disastrous effects of the impact of contact with 'frontiersmen'—the construction workers who would soon be penetrating the area. An expedition set off from the Cachimbo base at the beginning of 1972. Claudio Villas Boas and 28 Indians from the Xingu National Park undertook the arduous and precarious task of contacting the Kren-Akorore. After four months of cutting through the dense jungle they reached the River Peixoto de Azevedo and the first signs of the Kren-Akorore were found. A clearing was made in the jungle as an air-strip for small planes. The expedition camped near the river and set up an 'attraction post'.

At this point a setback occurred: a worker from the advance group constructing the BR. 165 was shot by an arrow of a Kren-Akorore and seriously injured. After this incident the Kren-Akorore retreated, stopped collecting the presents and, as was observed by plane, burned and abandoned one of their villages.

A further three months of patient watching and waiting finally brought fruitful results. Small groups of Kren-Akorore began to appear, shouting out, on the bank across the river from the encampment. Claudio, with a few Indians to assist him, crossed the river by canoe to meet the Kren-Akorore. However, the Kren-Akorore gradually backed away and once more disappeared into the jungle. Following these meetings 'at a distance', the Kren-Akorore began to pick up the presents once more.

Finally, on February 8th, 1973, about thirty Kren-Akorore Indians appeared on the opposite bank of the river and, going ahead alone, Claudio Villas Boas was able, after several attempts, to give presents personally into the hands of one man (Fig. 2). With this symbolic act, the rest of the Indians approached. The long-awaited contact was realized, brought about by the exchange of gifts. During the following weeks, new contacts took place as the Kren-Akorore, still rather apprehensive, appeared in small groups. One group visited the camp on the opposite bank and stayed several hours.

Throughout this period a doctor was always on hand and measures were taken to prevent the access of anyone suspected of having a contagious infection. Everyone going to the area was obliged to pass through the Xingu National Park and no one with the slightest symptom of infection was allowed to proceed on his journey.

The village of the Kren-Akorore Indians was made up of seven or eight irregularly placed huts of extremely primitive construction: broken branches, interwoven and covered with banana leaves. The Indians slept on banana leaves placed on the ground and used mounds of earth as pillows. During the night, each Indian slept near a small fire to keep himself warm. The lack of utensils was noted; they had no ceramic pots whatsoever. Water was carried in banana stalks and sections of bamboo. They used stone hatchets and pieces of sharpened wood to cut through the jungle and dig up edible roots. The most abundant food found was the sweet potato, baked, cut into slices and dried in the sun. Another food found in profusion was the banana, followed by peanuts, maize and manioc, the last two being more rare. Food was sometimes grilled over an open fire, but more often it was wrapped in banana leaves and baked between hot stones. They did not use salt to prepare the food. Near the village circular clearings were found surrounded by banana plants, forming a plantation in which crops were planted in symmetrical designs. For arms, there were bows and arrows, the latter made of bamboo with feathers attached. They had two types of clubs, one thick and heavy with the roots of the sicupira still attached to its end, and the other well-shaped from palm. Sometimes small monkeys and quatis (racoon-like animals) were seen among the Kren-Akorore. However, no dogs or cats were found. They did not possess any boats and they were poor swimmers, although they showed no fear of entering the water. Their paths, like those made by other tribes, were trails almost always made by hand (by breaking off branches) and defined through constant use.

The Kren-Akorore were nude and some were entirely painted with the blue-black juice of the genipapo fruit. There were symmetrical scars running length-wise down their trunks to their abdomen and thighs. Their height was comparable to that of other tribes.

After numerous contacts with groups of Kren-Akorore the Villas Boas brothers left the area, which then continued under the routine assistance of the Brazilian Indian Service (Fundação Nacional do Indio, FUNAI) whose members tried to find the best way of avoiding any lack of resources for the area. The relationship between the Kren-Akorore and the members of the expedition continued satisfactorily. The Kren-Akorore invited expedition members to visit one nearby village and later another situated more to the South.

In December 1973 the Santarém–Cuiabá highway was opened to traffic. The Kren-Akorore, attracted by the passing vehicles and by the presents they were being given, established themselves along the edge of the highway.

Personnel of FUNAI, assisted by some Kren-Akorore, constructed a new village in a region further away, beside a northern branch of the River Peixoto de Azevedo. The village consisted of four houses, one for each 'clan' or existing group of the tribe. There was also a 'men's house', situated in the centre, to be occupied by the bachelors, in accordance with tribal customs. Land was cleared near the village and the customary plantation made, to assure the villagers of sufficient supplies of food. However, this effort to re-unite the Kren-Akorore in a new village failed. The attraction created by the new highway was too strong, only ten months had passed since their first meeting with 'civilization', and the

Kren-Akorore were indiscriminately entering into contact with the frontiers-men penetrating into a new area of Central Brazil.

In the following year the situation gradually became more serious. It was evident that if the Kren-Akorore were to survive they had to be moved from that area. The Xingu National Park was chosen. This reserve was inhabited by fifteen Indian tribes, some that had been in the area since remote times (Von den Steinen 1894) and others that had been taken there when their lands had been occupied by 'pioneers' seeking to 'advance civilization'.

In January 1975, with the coordination of the Brazilian Air Force and FUNAI and orientation from Claudio and Orlando Villas Boas, the Kren-Akorore Indians were taken by aeroplane to the Diauarum Post in the Xingu National Park (see Figs. 3, 4 and 5). Seventy-nine Kren-Akorore Indians entered the reserve, three others having been taken to Cuiabá for medical treatment. Two years previously, when first contacted, between 135 and 140 Indians had been counted. However, according to data obtained from Richard H. Heelas (personal communication 1976), the decimation had been considerably greater. During 1968, when the first attempt at contact was made, the Kren-Akorore had abandoned one of their villages and plantations. They later suffered great hardship from the lack of food supplies, and when a flu epidemic attacked them

FIGS. 3–5. The removal of the Kren-Akorore to the Xingu National Park.

FIG. 4

their resistance was so low that many died. The memory of this tragic episode, plus the scarcity of food and privation that they were again suffering, must have been deciding factors which brought the Kren-Akorore to accept the process of contact used for the second time by the Villas Boas brothers.

On entering the Xingu National Park the Kren-Akorore were examined by a medical team from the São Paulo School of Medicine (Fig. 6). The clinical and laboratory findings will be presented later (p. 189). When a medical record of each Indian was being made, and his lineage established, it was confirmed that many people had died and that there were many orphans. This proved that the Kren-Akorore tribe had suffered great loss of life in coming into contact with the new world.

The Kren-Akorore remained at the Diauarum Post for only a day, during which they were inoculated with BCG intradermally and Sabin polio vaccine orally; they had almost all been previously vaccinated against measles. They were then transferred by boat to the village prepared for them. It was a small-holding, inhabited by a Caiabi family, on the right bank of the River Xingu, about two hours beyond the Diauarum Post.

Two big houses had been specially built to house the Kren-Akorore, who immediately showed difficulties in adapting to their new environment. Fishing was a problem, for canoes had to be used and the Kren-Akorore were inex-

Fig. 5

perienced boatsmen. The wide, formidable River Xingu contrasted too sharply with the narrow, clear, rapid streams of their home region and limited the movement of the Kren-Akorore. Hunting in the vicinity of the village was difficult, especially without rifles. When all the crops from the nearby plantation were exhausted, they needed to use canoes to fetch supplies. FUNAI had to intervene, by providing supplementary food. The delicate situation, aggravated by the deterioration in the health of the population and by the passive, resigned attitude of the members of the tribe, brought about the decision that the Kren-Akorore should be moved from this locality, only two and a half months after arrival.

Although the Txukarramãe had been legendary enemies of the Kren-Akorore, time had tempered their feelings. Under the moderating influence of the Villas Boas and with the acquiescence of the Txukarramãe, the Kren-Ako-

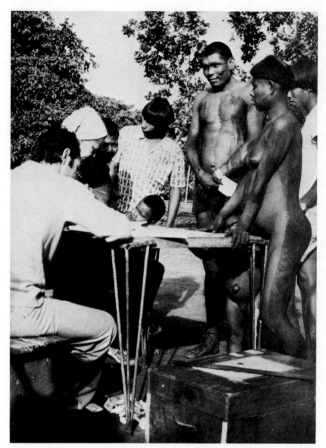

Fig. 6. Medical examination.

rore Indians were transferred to the Txukarramãe village of Kretire in March 1975. Kretire is on the left bank of the River Xingu, two hours by boat from the Diauarum Post. But only two small houses had been built for the visitors and as these were insufficient for all the Kren-Akorore, a number of them were distributed among the Txukarramãe.

In this region, rich in food, the Kren-Akorore could have recuperated from the chaotic situation into which recent circumstances had led them. However, as a result of the excessive paternalism which the Txukarramãe expressed in many ways, a state of growing apathy continued to spread among the Kren-Akorore. Because of the dispersal of the group and the discontinuation of its customs, tribal individuality was threatened. Once more FUNAI had to intervene, this time to preserve the group as an autonomous entity. It was decided to transfer the tribe again, eight months after their arrival at Kretire.

The new locality chosen for the Kren-Akorore was near the Suiá tribe, by the River Suiá-Missu, a tributary of the River Xingu, and only one hour by boat from the Diauarum Post. The Suiá were asked to welcome the Kren-Akorore but to avoid a paternalistic attitude towards them and to leave them to look after their own plantations and organize their own fishing and hunting. The Kren-Akorore village now has four houses where the inhabitants are distributed according to 'clan'. Because of the comparative nearness of the Diauarum Post, the Kren-Akorore are able to receive medical attention more regularly.

EVALUATION OF THE KREN-AKORORE INDIANS' STATE OF HEALTH ON ADMISSION TO THE XINGU NATIONAL PARK IN JANUARY 1975

1. Population data in January 1975

The data in Table 1 refer to the 79 Indians admitted to the National Park on January 12th, 1975. It was not possible to include three Indians who, as already mentioned, were in Cuiabá for medical treatment.

TABLE 1
Kren-Akorore Indians, by sex and age group, January 1975

Age (years)[a]	Male	Female	Total No.	%
0– 2	2	2	4	5.1
3–10	12	9	21	26.6
11–20	11	14	25	31.6
21–30	10	9	19	24.0
Over 30	6	4	10	12.7
Total:	41	38	79	100%

[a] Estimated age.

2. Height and weight of adults

The heights and weights of 27 adult Kren-Akorore Indians are shown in Tables 2 and 3.

3. Findings at the physical medical examination

At the general medical examination of 79 Indians, four appeared to be in a

TABLE 2

Height of Kren-Akorore Indians over 20 years of age according to sex, January 1975

Sex	Mean height (cm)	S.D.	Range
Male (n = 15)	167.9	5.06	161–180
Female (n = 12)	156.5	4.73	148–163

n, number of individuals; S.D., standard deviation.

TABLE 3

Weight of Kren-Akorore Indians over 20 years of age according to sex, January 1975

Sex	Mean weight (kg)	S.D.	Range
Male (n = 15)	64.2	8.61	50.0–84.6
Female (n = 12)	56.7	4.40	50.0–64.0

n, number of individuals; S.D., standard deviation.

fairly poor physical condition, one was in bad health and the rest were in satis-factory health. It was observed that 37% of the men, 23% of the women and 6% of the children under 12 years of age had deficient weight (more than 10% in relation to height). Skin examinations showed that almost all had symmetrical, raised scar lesions (made by sharp objects) on their trunks and thighs. Four Indians had hypochromic and irregularly shaped lesions with fine desquamation on their trunks and limbs. Jaundice was observed in one Indian who was in a poor state of health. Pallor of the mucous membranes was noted in 36 Indians, and 17 were found to have axillary temperatures above 37°C.

Lung auscultation showed crepitant and subcrepitant rales in 13 Indians. No abnormal heart sounds were found and blood pressure was not above normal in any individual (Table 4). Hepatomegaly was observed in 11 Indians and all but three of those examined had enlarged spleens; sometimes the splenomegaly was considerable (Table 5 and Fig. 7).

4. Laboratory tests

The results of biochemical analyses of the blood serum of Kren-Akorore Indians are shown in Tables 6 and 7. Blood haemoglobin measurements and mean corpuscular haemoglobin concentrations are shown according to age group in Tables 8 and 9.

TABLE 4

Arterial blood pressure (systolic and diastolic) of Kren-Akorore Indians over 20 years of age according to sex, January 1975

Sex	Systolic (mm Hg)		Diastolic (mm Hg)	
	Mean	S.D.	Mean	S.D.
Male (n = 16)	110.2	8.8	68.3	8.6
Female (n = 13)	97.2	8.2	61.1	6.0

n, number of individuals; S.D., standard deviation.

TABLE 5

Kren-Akorore Indians classified according to age group and splenomegaly index (Hackett's classification), January 1975

Spleen index	Age groups (years)					Total	
	0–2	3–10	11–20	21–30	> 30	No.	%
0–1–2	3	14	14	12	6	49	62.0
3–4–5	1	6	12	7	4	30	38.0

TABLE 6

Serum biochemical tests in 65 Kren-Akorore Indians, January 1975

Serum test	Mean	S.D.	Normal values[a]
Total protein (g/100 ml)	7.8	0.6	6.0–8.0
Albumin (g/100 ml)	3.3	0.3	4.0–5.0
Gamma globulin (g/100 ml)	3.0	0.7	1.2–1.8
Cholesterol (mg/100 ml)	99.5	20.0	150–250
Uric acid (mg/100 ml)	4.5	1.1	4.0–6.0

[a] For standard White populations.
S.D., standard deviation.

TABLE 7

Serum albumin levels in Kren-Akorore Indians, January 1975, according to the criteria of the Interdepartmental Committee on Nutrition for National Development (USA)

Albumin concentration (g/100 ml)	Number of individuals	%
Deficient: < 2.8	4	6.2
Low: 2.8–3.4	42	64.6
Acceptable: ≥ 3.5	19	29.2
Total:	65	100.0

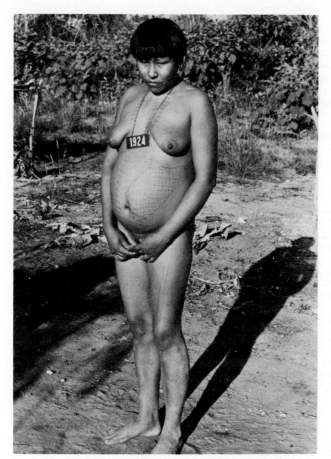

FIG. 7. A Kren-Akorore woman with a greatly enlarged spleen.

TABLE 8

Haemoglobin levels of Kren-Akorore Indians according to age group, July 1975

Haemoglobin concentration (g/100 ml)	Age groups (years)				Total	
	0–2	3–10	11–20	> 20	No.	%
< 8	1	2	2	4	9	14.6
8–10	1	13	14	14	42	63.6
⩾ 11	1	—	8	6	15	22.8
Total:	3	15	24	24	66	100.0

TABLE 9

The mean corpuscular haemoglobin concentrations (MCHC) of Kren-Akorore Indians according to age group, July 1975

MCHC (%)	Age groups (years)				Total	
	0–2	3–10	11–20	> 20	No.	%
< 30	—	7	10	6	23	39.6
30–33	1	8	10	9	28	48.3
34–36	—	—	3	4	7	12.1
Total:	1	15	23	19	58	100.0

5. Blood groups

The blood groups of 18 Indians were determined. All belonged to group O of the ABO system and all were rhesus (Rh)-positive.

6. Serological survey for evidence of infectious organisms

The Indians were tested for the presence of antibodies to a wide variety of viruses, as shown in Table 10. Titres of antibody to the antigen of *Plasmodium vivax* were measured as evidence of malaria (Table 11). Sixty-seven Indians were also tested for evidence of toxoplasmosis, as indicated by positive reactions in the fluorescent antibody test for immunoglobulin G (IgG) (Table 12).

TABLE 10

Serological survey for several virus antibodies in Kren-Akorore Indians, January 1975

Virus	Test [a]	Minimum positive titre	Number tested	Positive (%)
Hepatitis B	HP	—	68	23.5
Poliovirus I	NT	8	42	14.2
Poliovirus II	NT	8	42	0
Poliovirus III	NT	8	42	0
Epstein-Barr virus	FA	5	68	88.2
BK (papovavirus)	HI	10	68	36.7
Adenovirus	CF	8	47	44.6
Rubella	HI	8	68	0
Respiratory syncytial virus	FC	8	49	8.1
A/N.J./76[b]	HI	10	68	0

[a] HP, passive haemagglutination; NT, neutralization; FA, fluorescent antibody; HI, haemagglutination inhibition; FC, complement fixation.
[b] Influenza A/New Jersey/76 (Fort Dix 1976).

TABLE 11

Fluorescent antibody titres to malaria (*Plasmodium vivax as* antigen) in Kren-Akorore Indians, January 1975

Serum titre	Number of individuals	%
< 1:50	0	0
1:50	1	1.4
1:250	4	5.7
1:500	12	17.1
1:1000	22	31.4
1:2000	12	17.1
> 1:2000	19	27.1
Total:	70	100.0

TABLE 12

Distribution of IgG fluorescent antibodies to *Toxoplasma gondii* in Kren-Akorore Indians, by age group, January 1975 (Leser *et al.* 1977)

Age (years)	Number tested	Titres of reactions (1:)[a]						Positive reactions	
		16–64	256	1000	4000	8000	16 000	No.	%
2–10	15	1	6	—	1	2	1	11	73.3
11–20	24	—	1	3	6	5	7	22	91.7
21–30	18	—	—	1	3	7	7	18	100.0
Over 30	10	—	—	—	5	1	3	9	90.0
Total:	67	1	7	4	15	15	18	60	89.6

[a] Minimum positive titre, 1:16.

The 67 samples of serum were also examined by the haemagglutination technique. The results of the two reactions, fluorescent antibody and haemagglutination, were fairly similar, the titres coinciding in the majority of cases or with a difference of only one or two dilutions, and they indicated a high prevalence of infection by toxoplasma in the Kren-Akorore Indians.

The presence of IgM anti-toxoplasma antibodies was investigated using the immunofluorescence technique. The results were positive in 41 serum samples (61.2%), of which 35 gave high titres, of 1:256 or greater. These results suggested the presence of acute toxoplasmosis in 41 Indians. However, after adsorption of the sera with polymerized gamma globulin, the repeated tests gave negative results in 29 sera and a great reduction in the titres of the remaining 12. The false positive fluorescent reactions for IgM were therefore due to the presence of antibodies to human gamma globulin (rheumatoid factor) (Camargo *et al.* 1972). The latex test for these antibodies was positive in 61 Indians (91%), with high titres (1:64 to 1:512) in 34 sera.

7. *Examination of faeces*

The examination of the faeces of 35 Indians for protozoa and other parasites was positive for one or more intestinal parasites in 34 cases (97%). The results were as shown in Table 13.

TABLE 13

Incidence of intestinal parasites in faeces of 35 Kren-Akorore Indians, April 1975

Parasite	%
Ancylostomidae (hookworm)	97.1
Trichuris trichiura	75.7
Strongyloides stercoralis	29.8
Ascaris lumbricoides	15.1
Entamoeba coli	24.2
Iodamoeba bütschilii	24.2
Entamoeba histolytica	18.1
Endolimax nana	12.0
Giardia lamblia	9.0
Chilomastix mesnili	9.0
Negative examination	2.9

Comments on medical findings

Supporting the historical report that the Kren-Akorore suffered from some scarcity of food after the first contact was made, many were under-weight and had pallor of the mucous membranes when they were transferred to the Xingu National Park. Of those examined, 71% had low or deficient levels of serum albumin, and the level of haemoglobin was less than the normal value in 77% of the Indians. The anaemia could have been caused by malnutrition, possibly aggravated by hookworm which was present in 97% of the examinations, and by the occasional chronic haemolysis caused by malaria. Malaria antibodies were detected in 100% of the blood samples. By contrast, anaemia is rare among the Xinguan Indians although they have a high incidence of both ancylostomiasis and malaria infection (da Silva 1966).

The presence of a big spleen was verified in 38% of the 79 Kren-Akorore (Fig. 7, p. 192). This finding, together with the high level of gamma globulin found in the majority, and the presence of plasmodium antibodies in all, suggests the diagnosis of Tropical Splenomegaly Syndrome (Marsden & Crane 1976). This syndrome has recently been shown to occur in the Indian population of the Xingu National Park (Baruzzi *et al.* 1976).

The serological survey for antibodies against various types of virus in the Kren-Akorore group demonstrated an increased incidence of antibodies for hepatitis B virus, which were found in 23.5% of the serum samples examined. This is much higher than the 2.5% observed by Guimarães (1973) in the Xinguan Indians, and closer to that found in a group of Peruvian Indians (Blumberg *et al.* 1968).

The finding of high titres of antibodies against toxoplasma suggests infection of relatively recent acquisition, or more precisely in the post-acute stage, as was shown by the absence of IgM anti-toxoplasma antibodies and also by the similarity between the titres of immunofluorescent IgG and haemagglutinating antibody (Camargo & Leser 1976). We cannot therefore totally reject the hypothesis that infection by toxoplasma occurred after the isolated state of the Kren-Akorore had ended, two years previously. The 89.5% of positive serological reactions for toxoplasma in the Kren-Akorore Indians was greater than the percentage found in an earlier investigation of the population of the Xingu National Park, which was 51.6% (Baruzzi 1970).

FOLLOW-UP REPORT FROM JANUARY 1975 TO JULY 1976

Morbidity

Outbreaks of influenza in February and November 1975 and July 1976 affected practically all members of the Kren-Akorore tribe. Those affected had nasal catarrh, coughs and high temperatures for some days, sometimes with pulmonary complications. During the first outbreak pneumonia was diagnosed in 17 cases. The same symptoms were observed during the epidemic in July 1976, calling for greater medical vigilance and the administration of antibiotics, in view of the risk of pulmonary involvement.

The Kren-Akorore suffered frequent, severe attacks of malaria during the first weeks in the Xingu National Park. The transmission of malaria is intense in the Xingu region throughout the year, although there are seasonal fluctuations. A diagnosis of malaria must therefore always be considered whenever a high temperature is observed, as the malarial infection at times may superimpose on other clinical conditions, making the patient's state worse. On the other hand, the occurrence of acute malaria in those with the Tropical Splenomegaly Syndrome sometimes results in deterioration of the general state of health, prostration and jaundice, with a slow recovery. For this reason prolonged prophylactic treatment with antimalarial drugs has recently been started on six Kren-Akorore with considerable hepatosplenomegaly, and an improvement of the clinical picture is expected (Stuiver *et al.* 1971).

MORTALITY

Our enquiries into causes of death in indigenous tribes are generally frustrating and fruitless, because of the following facts:

(a) The absence of medical personnel when death occurs.
(b) Reluctance on the part of the Indians to discuss facts relating to death, even when asked to give information about the conditions in which the death occurred.
(c) The tribal habit of attributing death to malaria, as much because of the natural lack of specific knowledge as of the desire to terminate what seems to them to be a disagreeable subject.

Taking these limits into consideration, we have listed the deaths that have occurred since the Kren-Akorore entered the Xingu National Park (Table 14).

TABLE 14

Deaths among the Kren-Akorore since their entry into the Xingu National Park in January 1975, to July 1976

No.	Sex	Age (years)	Time-lapse between entry to the Park and death	Probable cause of death
1.	Male	38	20 days	Pneumonia
2.	Male	23	50 days	Pneumonia
3.	Female	9	60 days	Malaria
4.	Male	22	70 days	Malaria
5.	Male	15 months	75 days	Malaria
6.	Female	30	6 months	Not known
7.	Male	9 months	7 months	Not known
8.	Female	20	7 months	Malaria
9.	Male	22	8 months	Malaria
10.	Male	9	9 months	Accident
11.	Male	19	10 months	Drowning

The first five deaths occurred while the Kren-Akorore were in the Caiabi village, after arriving at the Xingu National Park. The other six deaths took place after this, when they had been transferred to the Txukarramãe village.

Births

Two baby girls were born after the tribe entered the National Park, but one died five days after birth. Only one woman has become pregnant since entering the reserve, but she had a miscarriage during the fourth month of pregnancy.

The situation in July 1976

In July 1976 the Kren-Akorore tribe was reduced to 64 members, living in their new village near to the Suiá tribe. Their number demonstrates that the tribe has suffered a great population loss, either if it is considered that they numbered between 135 and 140 in February 1973 (shortly after the first contact), or in relation to the total of 82 in January 1975. There are no details on their health, in terms of either morbidity or mortality, for the first period (February 1973 to January 1975). In the second period (January 1975 to July 1976) the Kren-Akorore tribe was reduced not only by death but also by the integration of some of its members with the Caiabi and Txukarramãe tribes. These members were afterwards rejected by the Kren-Akorore.

The general state of health of the Kren-Akorore Indians shows no appreciable difference from that of January 1975. A retrospective analysis verifies that in the space of eighteen months, since their admission to the Xingu National Park, the Kren-Akorore have had three epidemics of influenza, a serious illness for recently contacted groups. They have also had several serious attacks of malaria, suffered food scarcity for some months, and encountered difficulties in adapting to a new environment. In view of these repeated setbacks, the Kren-Akorore have presumably not had sufficient time to recover their health.

FINAL CONSIDERATIONS

It was expected that the Kren-Akorore, like other indigenous groups, would be considerably reduced in the course of encountering and making contact with non-Indian people. Owing to the drastic and unforeseen circumstances, this process of contact, once started, became uncontrollable, and led to the removal of the tribe to another region two years after the first contact. The Kren-Akorore group that entered the National Park had been decimated beyond the most pessimistic calculations. They were profoundly socially disorganized and there was not the necessary cohesion among them to resist the hostile forces of the new environment. A growing apathy affected their already weakened state of health.

In spite of this, there are now reasons to believe that the Kren-Akorore can enter into a medical and social 'convalescence' in the near future. This optimism is justified by their having their own village organized along the lines of the social structure of the tribe; by the facilities for agriculture, fishing and hunting; and by a return to their own cultural habits, now that they have the prospect of being established in a definite region. These conditions may reawaken the will to fight and live, indispensible for health. Regular medical assistance, now developed, will also allow better surveillance of the health of the population, which should minimize the risk of further deaths if epidemics threaten again.

ACKNOWLEDGEMENTS

We acknowledge the collaboration of Dr C. M. Torres and of Mr S. Pripas and Mr S. Dominguez Neto (senior medical students) in the field work, and thank Drs M. E. Camargo, P. G. Leser and A. Andriolo (Laboratorio Fleury, São Paulo), Professor J. A. N. Candeias (Departamento de Microbiologia e Imunologia, Instituto de Ciencias Biomedicas, University of São Paulo), Miss M. F. Sarmento and Dr I. Kameyama for the laboratory analysis.

We would like to record our gratitude also to Orlando and Claudio Villas Boas for their personal reports on the Kren-Akorore Indians.

These studies have been made possible with the cooperation of the Fundação Nacional do Indio, the Força Aérea Brasileira and the Ministério da Saúde do Brasil.

References

BARUZZI, R.G. (1970) Contribution to the study of the toxoplasmosis epidemiology. Serological survey among the Indians of the Upper Xingu River, Central Brasil. Rev. Inst. Med. Trop. São Paulo 12, 93–104

BARUZZI, R.G., FRANCO, L.J., JARDIM, J.R., MASUDA, A., NASPITZ, Ch., PAIVA, E.R. & NOVO, N.F. (1976) The association between splenomegaly and malaria in Indians from the Alto Xingu, Central Brasil. Rev. Inst. Med. Trop. São Paulo 18, 322–348

BLUMBERG, B. S., SUTNICK, A.I. & LONDON, W.T. (1968) Hepatitis and leukemia. Their relation to Australia antigen. Bull. N.Y. Acad. Med. 44, 1566–1568

CAMARGO, M.E. & LESER, P.G. (1976) Diagnostic information from serological tests in human toxoplasmosis. II. Evolutive study of antibodies and serological patterns in acquired toxoplasmosis, as detected by hemagglutination, complement fixation, IgG and IgM-immunofluorescence tests. Rev. Inst. Med. Trop. São Paulo 18, 227–238

CAMARGO, M.E., LESER, P.G. & ROCCA, A. (1972) Rheumatoid factors as a cause for false positive IgM anti-toxoplasma fluorescent tests. A technique for specific results. Rev. Inst. Med. Trop. São Paulo 14, 310–313

COWELL, A. (1974) The Tribe that Hides from Man, Book Club Associates, London

DA SILVA, M.P. (1966) Contribuição para o estudo do sangue periférico e da medula óssea em índios do Alto Xingu. Thesis, Escola Paulista de Medicina, São Paulo, Brasil

GUIMARAES, R.X. (1973) Frequência do Antígeno Austrália em indivíduos normais, índios do Parque Nacional do Xingu e portadores de esquistossomose mansônica. Thesis, Escola Paulista de Medicina, São Paulo, Brasil

LESER, P.G., CAMARGO, M.E. & BARUZZI, R.G. (1977) Toxoplasmosis serologic tests in Brazilian indians (Kren-Akorore) of recent contact with civilized man. Rev. Inst. Med. Trop. São Paulo, in press

MARSDEN, P.D. & CRANE, G.G. (1976) The tropical splenomegaly syndrome. A current
    appraisal. *Rev. Inst. Med. Trop. São Paulo 18*, 54–70
STUIVER, P.C., ZIEGLER, J.L., WOOD, J.B., MORROW, R.H. & HUTT, M.S.R. (1971) Clinical
    trial of malaria prophylaxis in tropical splenomegaly syndrome. *Br. Med. J. 1*, 426–429
VON DEN STEINEN, K. (1894) *Unter den Naturvölkern Zentral-Brasiliensis*, Berlin. Portuguese
    edition: *Entre os Aborígenes do Brasil Central*, Departamento de Cultura, São Paulo
    (1940), 713 pages

Discussion

Hamilton: With five deaths out of 11 due to malaria, the significance of this disease is obvious. Further, the distribution of Hackett gradings of spleen size which you demonstrated, with the very high proportion with persistent large grade-four spleens (below the umbilicus), is reminiscent of the distribution in the Watusi tribe of New Guinea. This distribution was associated with the syndrome known as Tropical Splenomegaly Syndrome, to which you referred. Its aetiology is not fully understood but exactly similar conditions have been found in many parts of the world, always associated with malaria. However, it is not due to one particular species of malaria parasite nor just to malaria *per se*, but to some other factor (Marsden & Hamilton 1969). Have you any comments on a possible change in the environmental or malaria pattern in these people, as a result of the move?

Baruzzi: The Kren-Akorore reported that they had malaria in the past but not very seriously compared to what has happened since they have been in the Xingu Park. I don't know if this was caused by another strain of *Plasmodium*. Certainly the presence of big spleens without any other aetiological factor being recognizable suggests that they had been exposed to malaria infection for a long time—that is, this disease was common among them in their original environment.

Hugh-Jones: Did the Kren-Akorore not receive antimalarial drugs?

Baruzzi: Yes, they did. They received antimalarial drugs when they suffered from malaria attacks. It was more difficult to provide prolonged prophylactic treatment against malaria. We had the opportunity to use depot injections of antimalarial drugs in the past, and we are not very enthusiastic about the results.

Hugh-Jones: The malaria in the Xingu seems remarkably vicious! I was on the Royal Geographical Society expedition and I was careful to see that everyone in the expedition took antimalarials, and I am certain they did, and yet two years later I got malaria. The load of parasites must have been enormous.

Lozoff: Were individuals with enlarged spleens symptomatic?

Baruzzi: When we examined the Kren-Akorore we found a high percentage of big spleens and most of them were asymptomatic. We had an autopsy on a man with a big spleen and the hepatic histological picture was described as Tropical Splenomegaly Syndrome.

Neel: Were these hard or soft spleens? Is this the picture of chronic splenic enlargement, or a recent development?

Baruzzi: The consistency of the big spleens was increased and the picture suggested chronic splenic enlargement.

Ohlman: What do you feel is the outlook now for the tribe, Dr Baruzzi? Will they decline, or are they going to survive?

Baruzzi: I believe that the Kren-Akorore are now for the first time beginning to achieve a state of better adaptation to their new environment. During the two years after the first contact the population was in decline because of deaths, but now this tendency has been arrested.

Ohlman: Was there any relationship between age group and morbidity and mortality? Or were these statistics distributed at random throughout the different ages?

Baruzzi: Death occurred at all ages but it was more frequent among the youngest and the oldest. When we did the medical examinations we tried to identify each family and it was possible to recognize frequent gaps in most of them.

Lightman: The abandonment of their homes and possessions by the Kren-Akorore at their first experience of contact emphasizes the extreme state of terror the situation must have held for them. I have no doubt that this terror and its resulting social disruption was a major factor in initiating the cascade of problems described by Dr Baruzzi.

Another very interesting situation is well demonstrated by the temporary sojourn of the Kren-Akorore with the Txukarramãe tribe. The rapid appearance of apathy and dependence if the shock of contact is followed by help and 'welfare' is a situation from which we can learn much. Unless the newly contacted group can continue to perform much of its own basic work-load, in terms of food supplies and other basic needs, it will lose much of its 'reason for existence'. The cycle of apathy, cultural dissolution and finally physical destruction will have gained momentum.

Baruzzi: It is interesting that the first attempt at contact was made by the Kren-Akorore, in 1967 when they appeared near the Cachimbo air base. Their sudden appearance provoked panic and they were repelled by the personnel of the base, as I described. When the 1968–1969 expedition reached a Kren-Akorore village, it had been burnt down and abandoned by its inhabitants, which suggests that the decision to avoid the contact was taken at the last moment, since the Kren-Akorore left bundles of food and utensils behind them. Their reaction to the second expedition some years later was at times contradictory: sometimes they showed themselves hostile, destroying the gifts left for them in the jungle; at other times they left friendly signs, which encouraged the expedition to continue.

Once contact was established it was necessary to decide whether the Kren-Akorore should be moved to another area or not, taking into account the risks involved in the opening of the new road through the Indian territory. This decision was taken two years later when it became evident that the only chance of survival for the Kren-Akorore was to move them to another area, and the Xingu National Park was chosen. One can ask now whether this should not have been done sooner, but one must remember that it was a difficult decision to make since the Kren-Akorore have lived in that area since ancient times.

The Kren-Akorore experience showed also that once a process of approach and contact is started, it becomes difficult to keep it under control.

Black: There are now three members of the Kren-Akorore living with the Mekranoti. In 1969 there was a raid and five Kren-Akorore children were brought in. I have no idea how many adults were killed. I think this is part of the reason for the decline in the Kren-Akorore population between 1969 and 1972 and the context in which they developed their great fear of outsiders.

Baruzzi: In fact the Txukarramãe, in 1966, attacked a Kren-Akorore village and killed many of them.

Gajdusek: I want, as a devil's advocate, to suggest two other approaches which might have been used in trying to help the Kren-Akorore to survive. The first might have been to have left them where they elected to be, right on the road, and instead of leaving the roadside exclusively to the exploitation of new immigrants, to have built a small hospital and school and an Indian protection service station, right in their own ancestral territory, with assistance and encouragement and, above all, legal protection to assure them freedom to build houses along the road and to work for government or private immigrants along the road, with extreme surveillance over their just reward. They would need legislation assuring that they would keep their own territory and giving them legal title to much of the land along the road in trust for a generation or two later when their offspring would come to understand the title and be able themselves to defend it. This would assure rapid acculturation (or retreat of those who did not want it into the remoter parts of their territory) with assistance from the government towards their integration into Brazilian society as quickly as they could.

The second approach is yet more daring. All 300 Kren-Akorore could easily have been taken to a modern centre of acculturation and education, with expert medical care, on the outskirts or even in the centre of one of Brazil's modern cities. The 'shock' and trauma would have been great—but perhaps less than the atrocities along the road and the disrupted culture and death toll at the reservation in the Mato Grosso. Surely there would have been far less loss of life and the young could easily have become, especially with extreme and 'unearned' indulgence, acculturated Brazilians, better able to defend the rights and heritage of their people than those now on the reservation.

Baruzzi: The Kren-Akorore history is very much like that experienced in the past by other native groups in many parts of the world. The process of development taking place now in the Amazonian jungle, leading to the opening of new roads, came upon uncontacted Indians tribes who lived in a state of complete isolation, just as in the Stone Age. Though it is difficult to know whether there are other Indians groups still isolated in the Amazonian jungle, it is important to understand the Kren-Akorore experience so that we can minimize the consequences of the process of approach and contact with any other remaining groups.

Cohen: There has been much interest in this particular group, but there are also many groups in different parts of the world with very much larger populations who are caught in similar situations. I will comment on a few groups which I know about in different situations and under governments with very different political thinking. Two groups who are liable to be affected, or are already being affected, in the Horn of Africa include firstly a group of 70–80 000 Afar nomads, living in the Danakil desert and Awash valley of Ethiopia. They have not been much studied by anthropologists. They are now being exposed to pressures like the Kren-Akorore in the interest of a road that would pass through their territory. Already their nomadic grazing grounds have been divided by a road up to an oil refinery in the north of Ethiopia and there are plans for another road to be built in the near future. This, coupled with extensive settlement of their area, means that there will soon be a major problem for this considerable group.

A second nomadic group, the Kereyou nomads living in the lower Awash valley of Ethiopia, have already been almost totally displaced from their lands for another related but different reason, namely tourism. Western tourists bringing capital into the country have been encouraged to use a natural park reserve which was these people's grazing ground.

These developments have been taking place in a paramilitary regime; one can point outside Ethiopia for an example from another type of regime, namely the moving of several ethnic groups in Mozambique under the influence of a Marxist–Leninist government, but probably with the same sort of effect on the people. A lot of nomadic groups in the north of Mozambique are being moved, or soon will be, into large village areas. I think this is likely to disrupt their life and to lead to the sort of changes that we have seen with the Kren-Akorore, but we may not be able to document them.

Baruzzi: One of the most impressive reports of the decimation of the Indians in Brazil was at the beginning of this century, at the border with Colombia, when the Indians were engaged in collecting rubber, working in very bad conditions and being cruelly punished when they didn't reach the level of production imposed by the commercial companies.

Woodburn: I want to stress the unusual nature of the Kren-Akorore instance. I don't think that the degree of disruption and mortality in the Kren-Akorore can be easily matched outside South America in recent times. It is important to recognize that previously uncontacted groups have been contacted in Australia, New Guinea and elsewhere during the past two generations without nearly so many deaths or so much disruption. We are not now in the nineteenth century: such destruction is not inevitable.

Baruzzi: In the past, numerous human primitive groups have almost disappeared completely after having been in contact with white people who invaded their territories. Nevertheless, during the last few decades such situations have not been reported in many areas simply because the remaining groups became very rare and had moved to distant and inhospitable areas. Of course, this has not been noted only in South America.

In the specific case of the Kren-Akorore we must remember that measures for their adequate protection were taken during the process of approach and contact. The task of approach was given to very experienced people, the access to the Kren-Akorore territory was under control, and once contact was established a new village was built far from the site where the new road would pass. There was no lack of material and human resources for the process of attraction and contact, at least in the early stages. However, when the road was opened to traffic the situation briefly became chaotic and in the following months the Kren-Akorore suffered considerable human losses. It would be very useful if we could establish what to do if another situation like this arose in the future.

Weiner: Is Dr Woodburn talking about episodes where people have been moved to new land, albeit left to fend for themselves, as something that hasn't happened to any extent anywhere else than in South America, or about people being dispossessed and losing their land? When simple communities lose their land, which has frequently happened, demoralization and destitution are almost inevitable.

Woodburn: But immediate loss of lands is *not* now the usual situation in the world. It is a peculiar situation that occurs in some instances in South America. Groups contacted in New Guinea, or in Australia in recent times, have apparently not in general lost all their lands. The fundamental question is why, in a country like Brazil, in which the population of Amerindians is now small and where there is, in the Amazon basin, plenty of land for them and for development, the roads couldn't have been built in different places and the Indians left in possession of their own land and with some chance of determining their own future.

Baruzzi: It is very difficult to answer this question. The road was planned to connect Santarém town, in the north, to Cuiabá, the capital of the state of Mato Grosso, in the south, and it runs between two big tributaries of the Amazon river. It is impossible to say whether the road could have been built further from the Kren-Akorore territory.

Hugh-Jones: In fact, the road could have gone north of the Falls of Von Martius, where it was originally intended to go. The reason it was built further south was a political one, which weakened the autonomy of the Xingu National Park.

Cohen: Clearly these are political questions. If we are talking about the resettlement of tribal groups we have to mention the situation in the Republic of South Africa, where there has been imposed the most massive resettlement of ethnic groups. In fact, resettlement of whole populations organized on such a scale has never been done before except in the USSR. South Africa overall has remarkably well-developed and prestigious health services, but of course these are hardly made available on any effective scale to the poor black populations that need them most. These people are in effect landless and their situation on a day-to-day basis must appear hopeless. The contrasts between the intensity of health care available to the Whites and the meagre resources put aside for the far larger black population is reflected in such basic statistics as appalling differences in mortality and morbidity from infectious diseases and infant mortality (Mahler 1975).

On an optimistic note, a successful move of nomads has been made in Somalia, where several tens of thousands of Issa pastoralists were taken by plane and fleets of trucks to live, as I hear fairly successfully, in fishing communities on the coast. So it can be done if the circumstances are favourable.

Haraldson: Some countries, including Iran, Somalia, and the Sudan, have accepted nomads and don't simply speak about 'sedentarization'—the settlement of nomads as farmers or ranchers. Sedentarization can be achieved in a number of ways, in theory at least: (1) voluntary, spontaneous settlement, mostly by marginal groups of nomads; (2) encouraged sedentarization, with advantages promised in connection with settlement, difficulties and obstacles created in feeding grounds, and so on; and (3) forced settlement.

There are a number of consequences of the sedentarization of nomads, many of them harmful. They can be summarized as follows. The nomad is leaving his tribal homeland for a new livelihood and economy. He often experiences social disruption, degrading through the creation of a lower class; disruption of tribal ties; and loss of cultural self-confidence. There is a loss of 'independence'. His diet is changed, from milk and meat to less protein-rich foods, with hungry seasons. A new pattern of diseases emerges, including degenerative disease and reduced resistance to infections and hardships. New harmful factors include the sedentary life, smoking, alcohol, and a cariogenic diet. Empty areas of land develop.

In some cases nomads have, after years of sedentary life, returned to nomadism, after experiencing new diseases and social discomfort.

Ohlman: There have been many such large movements of people. Dr Woodburn said there is no necessary loss of territory, but I think there is *always* some loss of territory; in other words, the group doing the moving takes territory away from the group subject to its whim. If you look at what has happened to the American Indians in the United States, some successfully 'adapted' like the Navajos, even increased in population, perhaps, but some have been wiped out completely, and those that survive are usually left with the least desirable lands.

Woodburn: Of course, I am not claiming that tribal groups in Africa and elsewhere have not in recent times been dispossessed of their land or part of it: they have been, very widely, and often with very damaging consequences. Rarely, however, has it been done as casually and as devastatingly as it has in areas occupied by Forest Indians in South America. What really is distinctive about the recent situation of Forest Indians is the loss of land on first contact, the scale of loss of land generally and, above all, the scale of avoidable death, disease and destruction probably unmatched elsewhere in recent times outside war zones.

Lightman: In addition to the problem of increased mortality, one of the major medico-social effects of contact is often a marked diminution in fertility. Dr Baruzzi has pointed out that there have only been two pregnancies during the post-contact years with the Kren-Akorore. It is interesting that in this same area in Brazil the Txicão did not have a single birth during the four years after contact.

Hugh-Jones: There is something extremely interesting about this. When Orlando Villas Boas was rebuilding the village of the Txicão they openly stated that they weren't going to have any more children, and nobody knows how this was done!

I am sure Dr Baruzzi would agree that now that the Kren-Akorore are near the Suiá, they are much more on home ground, in the sense that they are near a group who are linguistically similar. They are among culturally similar Indians, have large lands around them, and so in those terms they are not badly off now.

Baruzzi: For the Txicão it was a tribal decision not to have babies until they were well adapted to the Xingu National Park and had organized their own village and plantations. For the Kren-Akorore, I agree with Dr Hugh-Jones that in recent months since they have been living near the Suiá there has been some improvement in their general conditions.

Morin: Dr Baruzzi's paper clearly illustrates the ethnocide of American Indian populations, long recorded by many anthropologists (Jaulin 1972; Collectif De l'Ethnocide 1972) and by institutions such as Survival International, the International Work Group for Indigenous Affairs, and the Minority Rights Group.

In the name of economic development, modernization and progress, Brazilian policy for the development of Amazonia has resulted, since 1970, in major road construction projects. According to the estimates of FUNAI (the National Indian Foundation), these affect the territory of some 30 Indian societies which have until now escaped the 'ravages of civilization'. The Kren-Akorore are part of this population. At the Manaus–Brasilia/Santarém–Cuiabá cross-roads, they are, like many other groups, an obstacle to the colonization of this Amazonian area. Consequently they have to be integrated into Brazilian society. In the name of 'national security' and 'regional development in the national interest' (Article 36 of the Indian Statute) the deportation of a group becomes legal. It can therefore be assumed that the removal of the Kren-Akorore was not only for the medical reasons mentioned by Dr Baruzzi, but as part of this political integration.

As a result of this deportation—and in spite of thorough medical care—some ten Kren-Akorore died and the rest of the group is 'apathetic' and not adapted to their new environment in a village of the Xingu Park. As a social anthropologist I am not surprised by the reactions of the Kren-Akorore, for if, according to Dr Baruzzi, the displacement has allowed 64 members of the group to survive, he will also have witnessed the destructuring of their way of life and thought—in other words, the ethnocide of the Kren-Akorore. Two main factors are involved:

(1) Their relation to space, to the land and to the habitat. If these forest societies do not normally have a sense of land ownership similar to that of peasant groups in our societies, who think in terms of 'their land', they do have an image of the world, of space and of their own existence as a function of the environment in which they live. For the Tatuyo (Tucano Indians, Pirana; Bidou 1972), for example, the river is the centre of the universe, the point of communication between people, the place of culture, as opposed to the forest which is t1; wilderness and the world of the animals. Inside the Tatuyo tribe's territory, clans and lineages occupy specific areas according to a segmented and hierarchical structure; that is to say, high-ranking groups live on the main river and the tributaries are reserved for the lower ranks.

If the Amazonian forest is seen as uniform and wild (virgin forest) in western eyes, for the Indian it is highly differentiated, socially structured and symbolic in other cultural terms.

If we take the habitat as the yardstick, for the Bari (Motilones Indians, Venezuela-Colombia; Jaulin 1966, 1969; Pinton 1972) it is the main point of reference. Like many other Amazonian groups, the Bari live in large communal houses, shaped like the bottom of a ship turned upside down. Each house contains ten to thirty family units, arranged on the alliance principle, so that the neighbours of each family unit are people with whom it is possible for a member of that unit to intermarry. Within the living space of each unit the family's hammocks are suspended in a vertical pattern, ground level being for the women, the next level for their husbands and children, with the bachelors at the top. This is also in order to keep the latter as distant from the earth as possible, on the fertility principle. Within the communal house the Bari develop and define a whole system of social relations and it is from and around this system that the land for agriculture is patterned (every family exploits the piece of land which forms an extension of its residential area) and guides the individuals (the man goes hunting in the direction which is linked to his habitat). The house is thus the key point of the social structure and for the Bari the guiding principle of the world.

In view of these two examples, which illustrate the social and symbolic importance of the land and the habitat, it is easy to understand why the Kren-Akorore, moved to a village in Xingu Park—that is to say, to an environment and a habitat with which they can no longer identify—shows signs of psychopathological behaviour, including apathy and death.

(2) The second factor and a corollary to the first is one on which I will not elaborate, as it has been extensively studied by anthropologists during the last 20 years. I refer to the importance of the 'We' to the 'I'. The individual in this type of society exists above all as an integral part of the group. From early childhood he is socialized to the rules of the residence, kinship, and alliance, which the group has created for itself and which correspond to certain attitudes, taboos, and so on. The principles of identity are thus based on lineage, clan and filiation. The Kren-Akorore do not differ in this respect. What form of social organization did they have before they had contact with the outside world? Has the deportation affected men and women differently, or elders differently from the younger? Since more than half of the group died, the 64 survivors are not only obliged to face up to the shock of their displacement but also to the destruction and disintegration of their social forms. In the face of this ethnocide will they be able to reorganize themselves, and in accordance with which rules? These are the questions I asked as I studied the psychosocial effects of three centuries of ethnocide among the Shipibo of the Ucayali (Pano Indians, Peruvian Amazon; Morin 1972, 1973). (See also pp. 314–316.)

To sum up, it seems to me that the psychopathological disturbances of the Kren-Akorore illustrate that it is not sufficient to save the Indians from physical death, to vaccinate them and to regroup them in a national park. Their reactions indicate the price of the assimilation policy practised by a number of states, which necessarily leads to the ethnocide of these living cultures. In order to become a Brazilian citizen, the Kren-Akorore must cease being an Indian and give up his ethnic identity.

Baruzzi: Other tribes in the past, like the Kren-Akorore, suffered very much after making the first contact with white people. Usually, these tribes underwent a great population decrease in the months after the first contact. It took some time for them to reach a new state of relative equilibrium and only some years later was there slow population growth. We hope that the Kren-Akorore, in spite of the great population decrease they have suffered, will follow the same course.

An anthropologist, accompanied by his wife, has been living with the Kren-Akorore since December 1974; that is, a month before the transfer of this tribe to the Xingu National Park. From this anthropologist's report and our own observations we can add that the Kren-Akorore had periods of great apathy, with deterioration of their already poor state of health. Now they are living near the Suiá, a tribe with a culture similar to theirs, they show signs of better adaptation. Nevertheless, it is difficult to predict whether eventually they will be as well-adapted to their new environment as they were to their original one.

I do not know if men and women reacted differently to the effects of the transfer to the Xingu National Park.

Neel: There is something strange about the response of the Amerindian to first contact: after the early Conquistadors' contact, the Indian populations often died out quickly, and yet imported black populations did as well as a population can do under these conditions. There is some kind of cultural interaction here that we don't understand. The issue is extremely complex.

Hugh-Jones: As you say, it is too complex for us to compare conditions in New Guinea, say, with South America. I would also agree very much that we should study the psychological effects on this particular group.

Baruzzi: As a final conclusion, perhaps we can accept that the best course for an isolated people, previously uncontacted, is to let them remain in their state of isolation. Up to now, we have not been able to give them the necessary protection, even in medical terms.

Haraldson: I would like to follow up Dr Cohen's earlier comments (p. 203) on nomadic people with some points on their health and on what we can offer them medically. The majority of tribal people in the world today are nomadic (by which I mean people depending on migration for their livelihood and with no

fixed dwellings; semi-nomadic people make use of fixed houses to some extent).
There are about 50 million nomads in the world, which makes them the world's
largest minority! We usually count only the pastoral nomads as nomads. They
are all part of a scattered population, and this scattering and low population
density makes it necessary to think carefully when designing health services for
them.

It has to be remembered that nomadism is always an ecological consequence;
people are living in dry areas where there is no alternative to nomadism. It is
actually the animals who are nomads, and their owners must follow them. Under
the hard conditions with little rainfall, people cannot settle and farm. In some
cases nomads have not deliberately chosen the area where they live, but intertribal fighting may have forced them to occupy inhospitable regions, where they
have adapted to a unique ecology and developed nomadic cultures. Many
marginal groups of nomads are now leaving their migratory life and have settled
down, mostly as farmers or rangers.

One question asked about nomads is whether there are special nomad's
diseases, and we have found that there are not. Nomads as a whole are healthier
than the settled people around them, mostly because of better nutrition, with
milk and meat available. If they get trachoma it is milder than that of the settled
people, as seen in Kenya. Nomads have made themselves largely independent
of the outside world and have their own doctors, medicine men, healers and
herbalists; they are not always eager to have health services from us. Incidentally, there is no place in the world where people do not have some kind of
health system of their own, just as there seems to be no place where there is no
religion.

Many governments provide the most isolated pastoral areas with simple health
stations. They are primitive, and may not always do good although they may
be of psychological importance. They have antibiotics but the dresser often
misuses them. Furthermore, there is no communication and there are no transport facilities.

There are other less primitive ways of giving health services to mobile people.
The most important point in doing this is to have someone trained who has
double loyalty—to his or her own tribe, which selected him or her for training,
and also loyal to the people who trained him and who assist him continuously
in his work and back him up morally. This double loyalty solves half the problem, as has been seen in Alaska and in New Guinea. In Iran, a woman is selected
for short midwife training. In Alaska, one Eskimo girl is selected for training
from each village. Back in her village she is connected by radio telephone with
a doctor, so she is the prolonged arm of the health service. She is also visited
regularly by the district nurse and by the doctor. Communication of this kind

is a relatively expensive tool for health services. Air transport is even more expensive: health services cost 2000 times more per head for Alaskan and Canadian Eskimos than for the Ethiopian nomads. But infant mortality has been reduced from 100 to 20 per 1000 newborn among Alaskan Eskimos in 25 years, the same level as in the entire USA as an average. But one must ask whether there are places in the world where we suggest that people do not live, because the last link in dispersed health services, the air transport, sometimes costs more than half the total health budget.

As I mentioned earlier, the pattern of diseases changes with a more modern or westernized life. On the positive side, diseases like tuberculosis can be controlled, as in the Lapps and Eskimos; it is mainly a question of enough money being spent. Accidents take over to some extent in the disease and mortality pattern and also the chronic and degenerative diseases. Social diseases such as alcoholism and suicide are today increasing in isolated, tribal populations as symptoms of acculturation. Research wrongly and traditionally concentrates on physical factors such as height, and on genetics, but psychosocial problems and community planning are becoming increasingly urgent in these groups. (See Haraldson 1975.)

References

BIDOU, P. (1972) L'espace dans la mythologie Tatuyo. *Journal de La Société des Américanistes 61*, 45–105

COLLECTIF (1972) *De l'Ethnocide*, UGE, 10/18, Paris

HARALDSON, S.R.S. (1975) Socio-medical problems of nomadic peoples, in *The Theory and Practice of Public Health* (Hobson, W., ed.), Oxford University Press, London

JAULIN, R. (1966) La maison Bari. *Journal de la Société des Américanistes 55–1*, 111–153

JAULIN, R. (1969) L'ethnocide. *Atomes 24* (266), 358–365

JAULIN, R. (1972) *Le Livre blanc de l'Ethnocide en Amérique*, Fayard, Paris

MAHLER, H.T. (1975) Health implications of apartheid, in *Objective: Justice*, vol. 7, pp. 37–43, United Nations Office of Public Information, Geneva (See also *A Survey of Race Relations in South Africa* [1972] Section on health, pp. 405–410 and [1973] Section on health, pp. 350–358)

MARSDEN, P.D. & HAMILTON, P.J.S. (1969) Splenomegaly in the tropics. *Br. Med. J. 1*, 99–102

MORIN, F. (1972) Les Shipibo, trois siècles d'ethnocide, in *De l'Ethnocide* (Collectif), pp. 177–187, Fayard, Paris

MORIN, F. (1973) Recontre d'une civilisation amazonienne et de la civilisation occidentale—les Shipibo de l'Ucayali. Thèse de doctorat de 3ème cycle, Paris-Sorbonne, unpublished work

PINTON, S. (1972) La maison Bari et son territoire. *Journal de la Société des Américanistes 61*, 31–44

Diet and nutrition of hunter-gatherers

A. S. TRUSWELL

Department of Nutrition and Food Science, Queen Elizabeth College, University of London

Abstract The diets and nutrition of hunter-gatherers are discussed with the !Kung Bushmen (San) of the Dobe area, Botswana as the example.

In general they show no qualitative deficiency of specific nutrients though they are thin and may be undernourished (by our standards) at some seasons. They show little or no obesity, dental caries, high blood pressure or coronary heart disease; their blood lipid concentrations are very low; and they can live to a good old age if they survive infections or accidents.

Hunting and gathering were the only methods of obtaining food until 10 000 years ago or less. Many of the highly developed and densely populated countries in the world were once thinly inhabited by hunter–gatherers: we can get some idea of what they ate from archaeological evidence. In separate sites different patterns of animal bones and/or fish bones and shells are found. Some of the bones are of animals now extinct, and shells may be found away from the present coastline. Relics of plant foods are less substantial but nuts or seeds of fruits are found in some archaeological sites, and parts of legumes, roots or cereals in others, the last three often having been cultivated, not gathered (Brothwell & Brothwell 1969). The identification of plant remains is tedious and specialized. Other evidence comes from prehistoric art, especially rock paintings. In several parts of the world these show animals that were presumably hunted and even hunting techniques. Some show other types of food. A cave in Valencia, Spain depicts a man precariously collecting wild honey, as Kalahari Bushmen still do today (Thomas 1959). Some rock paintings in Southern Africa show women digging, presumably roots, with sticks, often weighted with round stones, and corresponding stones with a hole drilled through the centre (which must have taken a long time to make) have been found among the stone tools in the district. Bushmen and Hadza women (Woodburn 1970) still use digging sticks but these contemporary people do not use weights on them. In general there are great differences between separate areas in the dietary remains though there are often common elements.

Hunter–gatherers today constitute less than 0.001 % of the world's population (Lee & DeVore 1968); they live in areas remote from modern industrial technology and often in country which appears to be inhospitable. The diets of the separate groups differ considerably. In general they contrast with our modern western diets in the larger number of food items (though only some are consumed in large amounts) and in their dependence on season. For example, Lee (1965) found that the !Kung Bushmen at Dobe (in Botswana) eat 85 species of plants and 54 species of animals, though only nine of the plant species are eaten in large amounts and 17 of the animals are consistently hunted.

It is at first surprising that in contemporary hunting and gathering groups the gathering of vegetable foods provides more calories than hunting animals in over two-thirds of the 58 groups reviewed by Lee (1968). The exceptions live above a latitude of 50° and at these cold latitudes fishing or hunting provide most of the calories. Overall the average provided by hunting in the 58 groups worked out to only about 35%. Collecting the plant food is mostly women's work while the men do the hunting exclusively.

Food is shared among the other members of a band. When a large animal is killed it is shared out in an appropriate order. In a tropical environment, with drying the only possibility for food preservation but the band nomadic and not large, this is the obvious way to dispose of the meat, especially as hunting requires the cooperation of two or more men, depending on the animal and the method. When a large animal is brought in and eaten the !Kung Bushmen may then spend the night dancing. This sharing has very strong effects on the social organization within the group. Plant foods are not shared to the same extent. Lee (1973) describes how the !Kung Bushmen collect mongongo nuts and each adult woman keeps a pile of these for her household or family that cook together.

Chemical analysis of hunter–gatherers' foods is incomplete. In the !Kung Bushmen at Dobe several of the minor plant foods only have names in the Bushman (or San) click language. Their botanical names have not been worked out because they were dug up in the veld as a root, say, but the plant flowers at another time of the year when people may not be in the area. It was only quite recently that a high proportion of an unusual fatty acid (α-eleostearic) was found in mongongo nuts *(Ricinodendron rautanenii)*, the major source of calories in the !Kung (Engelter & Wehmeyer 1970). This means that it is more difficult in hunter–gatherers to predict nutritional state from dietary intake measurements than it is in sedentary cultivators.

Human nutrition has different features and different problems at four stages of technical development (Davidson *et al.* 1975*a*)—or five if we divide the second stage into two subdivisions. The types and distribution of undernutrition, malnutrition, overnutrition and food toxicity are thus quite distinctive in hunter–gatherers, primitive agriculturalists, nomadic pastoralists, urban slum or shanty dwellers, and the affluent society.

In our study of the !Kung Bushmen at Dobe, Botswana during three visits to the Harvard camp, in October 1967, April/May 1968 and July 1969, we made thorough medical examinations of over 100 adults and 60 children, some more than once. We took 99 blood samples and several 24-hour urine collections which we carried back in a coolbox with preservatives where appropriate to our laboratories in Cape Town (Truswell & Hansen 1968*a*; Truswell *et al.* 1969; Hansen *et al.* 1969; Truswell & Hansen 1976).

We confirmed that the Bushmen are generally short (men averaging 160.9 cm or 5ft 3.4 in) but not all, and some of the younger men were quite tall, up to 175 cm (5ft 9in) (Table 1). There is found to have been a secular change among

TABLE 1

Mean height in cm (and number of subjects) of Bushmen

	15–20 years	*21–40 years*	*41 years and older*
Men (79)	151.4	162.8	160.4
	(4)	(33)	(42)
Women (74)	150.1	150.9	149.5
	(8)	(30)	(36)

the Bushmen when modern measurements are compared with earlier ones (Tobias 1975). Those we examined were also thin and their weights were low for their height, except for occasional individuals who were living with sedentary Tswana agriculturalists in the area. The average weight/height ratio (Table 2) was only three-quarters that of US citizens and was about the same as seen in American men after six months' semi-starvation in the Minnesota experiment, which averaged 29.5 kg/m (Keys *et al.* 1950). We found that skinfold thicknesses tended to fall after the dry season. We consider that these people show mild seasonal undernutrition and that this can, at least partly, explain their short stature. Lee at first disagreed with this interpretation (Lee 1969). The difficulty arose mostly from the use of words and almost all who know the Bushmen agree that they are very thin, and they have been observed to grow taller when living on farms. It has been suggested that their relatively late age of menarche (about 15$\frac{1}{2}$ years) is because of their low body fat (Kolata 1974). On the other hand our western standards for body weight may be too high, and

TABLE 2

Weight/height ratios (100 × weight (kg) ÷ height (cm)) of Bushmen compared with ratios
calculated from average US weights

	Age (years)						
	15–19	20–29	30–39	40–49	50–59	60–69	70–83
Bushmen							
Men	24.2	30.0	30.4	31.1	28.8	30.2	24.2
Women	24.0	27.5	26.4	27.0	27.1	26.1	24.7
Average in US							
Men[a]	34.0	38.7	40.4	41.3	41.6	40.7	—
Women[a]	31.6	33.4	36.0	38.1	38.9	39.3	—

[a] calculated for men in shoes (1-inch heel), 5ft 4in and women in shoes (2-inch heel), 5 ft 1in.

there are advantages to being thin and light in weight when living in a hot, sandy
country. Their weight and food intake must vary with the time in the climatic
cycle that they are examined and their heights have been increasing in the last
generation.

While a mild amount of undernutrition was general there was very little
evidence of *qualitative* malnutrition even in children. Clinical examination and
biochemical tests on blood and urine (Table 3) showed good protein nutrition
and vitamin and mineral status with only a few exceptions in people who had
been ill or suffered from an accident. With a mixed diet and periodic large intakes of meat the supply of nutrients was well balanced. In this dimension
hunter–gatherers are better off than sedentary agriculturalists, who may have
plenty of food quantitatively speaking and may even become obese but are in
danger of qualitative malnutrition from concentrating on the one crop that
gives the best yield in the area.

Except for being a little short in stature—which causes no obvious incon-
venience—there was no evidence that these Bushmen were unhealthy because of
their diet. What is more, in several ways we found they were more healthy than
people in western countries.

1. They did not have obesity. There is no middle-aged spread (Table 2).

2. The !Kung Bushmen we examined and central Kalahari Bushmen (van
Reenen 1966) show very little dental caries, without having fluorotic mottling.
They have periodontal disease and the crowns of the teeth become worn in
older people. The only concentrated sugar available is from the occasional raid
on a wild bees' nest.

3. Their blood pressure does not show the usual average increase with ad-
vancing age (Fig. 1) and we found no one with hypertension (Truswell *et al.*
1972). The absence of obesity could be part of the reason for this phenomenon,

TABLE 3

Qualitative nutritional status in !Kung Bushmen in the Dobe region

---

Protein
Intake appears adequate; protein-calorie malnutrition exceptional in children, not seen in adults; urinary nitrogen, 5–18 g/day (10); serum albumin averages 3.77 g/dl (7/83, < 3.0 g/dl); plasma amino acid pattern normal in 11/12.

Vitamin A
Intake included animal livers; plasma vitamin A values all normal, 26–170 µg/dl (45).

Thiamin, riboflavin
Mixed diet; no clinical signs.

Niacin/tryptophan
Intake appears adequate; no clinical signs; urinary N-methyl nicotinamide low normal (8); plasma tryptophan low normal (10).

Folate
Intake appears adequate; anaemia rare; serum folate usually > 3.0 ng/ml (154) except in one in four of the pregnant and lactating women[a].

Vitamin B12
Good intake; anaemia rare; serum vitamin B_{12}, 250–1500 pg/ml (152)[a].

Vitamin C
Rich sources in diet, such as baobab and morula fruits; no clinical signs.

Vitamin D
Abundant sunlight; no clinical signs except craniotabes in three young infants who were kept completely covered.

Iron
Intake appears adequate; little parasitism; anaemia rare; serum iron average 117 µg/dl (38 men), 92 µg/dl (80 non-pregnant women), and 112 µg/dl (nine pregnant women); only six out of 154 had subnormal transferrin saturation[a].

Calcium
Present in well water; urinary Ca, 60–152 mg/day (10), same range as controls.

Phosphorus
Urinary phosphates low, average 157 mg/day (10), possibly because their diet lacks cereals.

Sodium and chloride
Salt not available in environment; blood pressures low; urinary Na low, only 30 mmol/day (10).

Potassium, magnesium, zinc and copper
Urinary excretions normal: 86 mmol, 3.7 mmol, 650 µg and 100 µg/day respectively (10).

Iodide
Goitres uncommon and only seen in Bushmen from central Kalahari (Ghanzi), 150 miles south of Dobe.

Fluoride
Fluorotic mottling of teeth rare.

Numbers in parenthesis indicate numbers of samples.

[a] Metz *et al.* (1971)

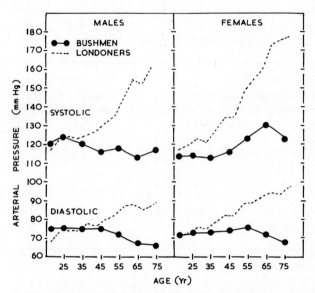

FIG. 1. Variation of Bushmen's blood pressures with age, compared with standard figures for a group from London (obtained by Hamilton *et al.* 1954). (Reproduced from Truswell *et al.* 1972 by permission of the C. V. Mosby Company.)

which has been reported in a few other isolated communities such as in the New Guinea highlands, some Pacific islands, the Orang Asli in Malaysia and East African pastoralists. I believe the unusually low salt intake may be the main protective factor in the Bushmen we examined: their urinary sodium concentrations correspond to NaCl intakes of 2.0 g per day. I am sceptical about lack of mental tension as an explanation. Living on a Hebridean island (Hawthorne *et al.* 1969) or on the edge of the primeval forest in the Congo basin (Miller *et al.* 1962) does not protect against hypertension.

4. Serum cholesterol concentrations were very low, averaging around 120 mg/dl (3.1 mmol/l) (Truswell & Hansen 1968*b*) and triglycerides were low too, around 100 mg/dl (1.12 mmol/l), although individuals were not fasting when blood samples were drawn. These serum cholesterol values are nearly at the bottom of the international league table of average values in healthy adults, which range from around 100 mg/dl in New Guinea Highlands and Congo pygmies up to 286 mg/dl in East Finland.

The low serum cholesterol concentrations can be explained by the combination of a moderate fat diet, high in polyunsaturated fats, the absence of obesity, and plentiful exercise. Mongongo nuts, their major source of vegetable fat, are rich in polyunsaturated fat (Engelter & Wehmeyer 1970). The meat of wild bovids in Africa has much less fat on and between the muscles fibres, and this fat is less saturated than our own butcher's fat, containing appreciable amounts of polyunsaturated fat (Crawford 1968). We found high proportions of linoleic acid in the Bushmen's serum triglyceride fatty acids (Truswell & Mann 1972). The meat is eaten only intermittently and there is a high fibre intake, which may also contribute to lower plasma lipids. I regard the Bushman's cholesterol values as healthy, possibly ideal, and it is the perspective from groups like this which makes us believe now that levels in Britain are in general unacceptably high (Royal College of Physicians and the British Cardiac Society 1976).

5. Dr B. Kennelly, a cardiologist, looked with me for symptoms or signs of coronary heart disease. We took histories, listened carefully to the hearts, took 105 electrocardiograms on a portable, battery-operated machine, and did effort tests (Kennelly *et al.* 1972). We encountered occasional cases of rheumatic heart disease but could find no evidence of coronary heart disease in the community.

6. Provided they do not die from infections or accidents the !Kung in the Dobe area can live to a good old age. The oldest we examined was a man of 83 years. The proportion of people over 65 years was 7% (11 out of 154) which compares favourably, say, with the proportion in Scotland in 1901 (Davidson *et al.* 1975*b*) which was 4.8% (and 9.9% by 1951).

Many of these features are reported in other hunter–gatherers.

Contemporary communities that obtain their food from hunting and gathering are not necessarily all living as their ancestors were. They may have been driven away from more fertile land; they may be regressive societies. But the diet of hunter–gatherers seems in general to be associated with little nutritional deficiency and no evidence of nutritional excess. Studies from such societies provide an important perspective to guide modern man who has so much technical control over his food supply and yet has more nutrition-related disease. Of course we cannot go back to living the life of hunter–gatherers. There isn't enough space and we should find the life uncomfortable and unstimulating. But there are indications that we should aim to model our dietary constituents and eating patterns more on those of hunter–gatherers. This is an important contribution which a few studies of a few small bands have made to nutritional science and preventive medicine.

ACKNOWLEDGEMENTS

This work was done in collaboration with Professor J. D. L. Hansen, Dr B. Kennelly, the late Professor V. Schrire, Dr and Mrs. I. DeVore, Dr R. B. Lee, Dr Nancy Howell, Dr H. Harpending, Dr Pat Draper, Dr J. Yellen and others, to all of whom I am grateful for help of very varied kinds and friendship.

References

BROTHWELL, D. & BROTHWELL, P. (1969) *Food in Antiquity*, Thames & Hudson, London

CRAWFORD, M.A. (1968) Fatty acid ratios in free-living and domestic animals. Possible implications for atheroma. *Lancet 1*, 1329

DAVIDSON, S., PASSMORE, R., BROCK, J.F. & TRUSWELL, A.S. (1975a) *Human Nutrition and Dietetics*, 6th edn, p. 3, Churchill Livingstone, Edinburgh & London

DAVIDSON, S., PASSMORE, R., BROCK, J.F. & TRUSWELL, A.S. (1975b) *Human Nutrition and Dietetics*, 6th edn, p. 654, Churchill Livingstone, Edinburgh & London

ENGELTER, C. & WEHMEYER, A.S. (1970) Fatty acid composition of oils and some edible seeds of wild plants. *Agric. Food Chem. 18*, 25

HAMILTON, M., PICKERING, G.W., ROBERTS, J.A.F. & SOWRY, G.S.C. (1954) The aetiology of essential hypertension. 1. The arterial pressure in the general population. *Clin. Sci. 13*, 11

HANSEN, J.D.L., TRUSWELL, A.S., FREESEMAN, C. & MACHUTCHEON, B. (1969) The children of hunting and gathering bushmen. *S. Afr. Med. J. 43*, 1158

HAWTHORNE, V.M., GILLIS, C.R., LORIMER, A.R., CALVERT, F.R. & WALKER, T.J. (1969) Blood pressure in a Scottish island community. *Br. Med. J. 4*, 651

KENNELLY, B.M., TRUSWELL, A.S. & SCHRIRE, V. (1972) A clinical and electrocardiographic study of !Kung Bushmen. *S. Afr. Med. J. 46*, 1093

KEYS, A., BROZEK, J., HENSCHEL, A., MICKELSON, O. & TAYLOR, H.L. (1950) *The Biology of Human Starvation*, vol. 1, p. 146, University of Minnesota Press, Minneapolis

KOLATA, G.B. (1974) !Kung hunter-gatherers: feminism, diet and birth control. *Science (Wash. D.C.) 185*, 932

LEE, R.B. (1965) The subsistence ecology of !Kung Bushmen. Ph. D. Thesis, University of California, Berkeley

LEE, R.B. (1968) What hunters do for a living, or, how to make out on scarce resources, in *Man the Hunter* (Lee, R.B. & DeVore, I., eds.), p. 30, Aldine, Chicago

LEE, R.B. (1969) !Kung Bushmen. (Letter.) *S. African Med. J. 43*, 47

LEE, R.B. (1973) Mongongo: the ethnography of a major wild food resource. *Ecology of Food and Nutrition 2*, 307

LEE, R.B. & DEVORE, I. (eds.) (1968) *Man the Hunter*, Aldine, Chicago

METZ, J., HART, D. & HARPENDING, H.C. (1971) Iron, folate and vitamin B_{12} nutrition in a hunter-gatherer people: a study of the !Kung Bushmen. *Am. J. Clin. Nutr. 24*, 229

MILLER, D.C., SPENCER, S.S. & WHITE, P.D. (1962) Survey of cardiovascular disease among Africans in the vicinity of the Albert Schweitzer Hospital in 1960. *Am. J. Cardiol. 10*, 432

ROYAL COLLEGE OF PHYSICIANS OF LONDON AND THE BRITISH CARDIAC SOCIETY (1976) Prevention of Coronary Heart Disease, Report of a Joint Working Party. *J. R. Coll. Physicians 10*, 213

THOMAS, E.M. (1959) *The Harmless People*, Secker & Warburg, London

TOBIAS, P.V. (1975) Stature and secular trend among Southern African Negroes and San (Bushmen). *S. Afr. J. Med. Sci. 40*, 145

TRUSWELL, A.S. & HANSEN, J.D.L. (1968a) Medical and nutritional studies of !kung Bushmen in north-west Botswana: a preliminary report. *S. Afr. Med. J. 42*, 1338

TRUSWELL, A.S. & HANSEN, J.D.L. (1968b) Serum-lipids in Bushmen. *Lancet 2*, 684

TRUSWELL, A.S. & HANSEN, J.D.L. (1976) Medical research among the !Kung, in *Kalahari Hunter-Gatherers: Studies of the !Kung San and their Neighbours* (Lee, R. B. & DeVore, I., eds.), p. 167, Harvard University Press, Cambridge, Mass.

TRUSWELL, A.S. & MANN, J.I. (1972) Epidemiology of serum lipids in southern Africa. *Atherosclerosis 16*, 15

TRUSWELL, A.S., HANSEN, J.D.L., WANNENBURG, P. & SELLMEYER, E. (1969) Nutritional status of adult Bushmen in the northern Kalahari, Botswana. *S. Afr. Med. J. 43*, 1157

TRUSWELL, A.S., KENNELLY, B.M., HANSEN, J.D.L. & LEE, R.B. (1972) Blood pressures of !Kung Bushmen in northern Botswana. *Am. Heart J. 84*, 5

Van Reenen, J.F. (1966) Dental features of a low-caries primitive population. *J. Dental Res.* *45*, 703
Woodburn, J. (1970) *Hunters and Gatherers: The Material Culture of the Nomadic Hadza,* British Museum, London

Discussion

Hugh-Jones: Your last point is the real crux of the argument that the study of so-called primitive man makes one wonder just what are the desirable physical standards—it is not so much a matter of what is 'normal', but of what is desirable. It is not only those who want to move about on sand who might benefit from being a good deal lighter than we are; all the evidence on longevity suggests that the only factor increasing it is to be thin rather than fat and to have a small amount of subcutaneous fat. There is also the whole question of world nutrition: large people take up space and they take up food! There are two phases of human life where protein nutrition is of extreme importance, at the end of uterine life and during the first months when a lot of neurological development is going on, but apart from that there is not much evidence that we need as much as we do eat in the westernized countries.

I wondered whether you were going to discuss the relation of illness to nutritional state in the Bushmen, or are there not enough statistics?

Truswell: We saw, and their histories indicated, very little infantile gastroenteritis, which is the main killer of children in the third world. This could be explained by the very small groups and by the wise sanitary arrangements, which reduce the chance for contamination.

Weiner: I am surprised to hear that, because in the Kalahari in 1958 there was a big outbreak of gastroenteritis among the Bushmen in our vicinity. There was also evidence of other infections, including tuberculosis.

Truswell: I wasn't dealing with infections specifically in my paper. We did see seasonal malaria; unfortunately gonorrhoea; streptococcal infections—tonsillitis and rheumatic heart disease; and some eye and skin infections and respiratory infections (including tuberculosis). Gastroenteritis was unusual, and others have reported similar experience among other groups of Bushmen (Bronte-Stewart *et al.* 1960).

Weiner: Every one of the older men that I saw in the central Kalahari had extraordinary loose folds of skin over the abdomen and buttocks. This was in remarkable contrast with the young men in their prime (just after puberty). It seemed to me that this might be evidence of seasonal shortage of food. This apparent emaciation increased with age, and gave an impression of premature ageing. It made it difficult to tell peoples' ages, in fact.

Truswell: The ages were provided by the anthropologists, who were there continuously and knew the relative ages and also birth dates in relation to external events such as storms, visitors, a meteorite, the year of the influenza, and so on. They had assembled the information using a computer method (Howell 1976) and knew the ages of adults probably to within a year (and of children more accurately). The finding was that this appearance of wrinkled skin started at about forty and not much before. Why did it develop then? The Bushmen are not black, and perhaps their skins are insufficiently protected against the intense solar radiation and the radiation off the sand; in addition, they sleep around fires.

Cohen: Your studies on seasonal variation are important because they have a practical application for people looking after children in maternal and child health clinics in the poorer countries. Some years ago studies in The Gambia (McGregor *et al.* 1968) showed that the seasonal variation in weight-for-age could account for one-third of the difference in weight-for age standards published throughout all of Africa at the time. We have looked again at this phenomenon in Lesotho, using a measure that is independent of knowing the precise age of the child—the incidence of weight loss. There was a marked bimodal monthly variation throughout the year in the incidence of weight loss, a finding which has important implications not only for the epidemiology of growth-faltering in Lesotho but for the workloads in the clinics. In The Gambia there was an effect of season of birth on weight-for-age with differentials in weight up to the age of two years. In Lesotho there was a persistent effect of birth season on weight-for-age up to 4–5 years. Did you look for this phenomenon in the Bushmen?

Truswell: The weights of the young children certainly tended to go down during the dry season. I don't think the numbers we examined would be large enough to subdivide them by birth season.

Lozoff: Could you comment on infant-feeding practices among the Bushmen and their possible relation to the lack of hypertension and cardiovascular disease?

Truswell: The predominant food for well over the first year is breast milk and breast-feeding continues usually for three years (Konner 1976). Supplements come in later in the first year: certain roots, melons, and perhaps nuts; but almost all the foods are tough and difficult to chew, so there is a 'calorie gap' from about six months onwards, although the quality is good.

We saw early rickets, incidentally, surrounded as they are by sunlight. As you also see in Ethiopia, the babies are completely covered in the first few months before they start crawling.

Lozoff: In spite of the presumed caloric deficit, the Bushmen growth curves do not appear to show a falling-off in weight late in infancy.

Truswell: The dots representing individual children in our growth curves are crowded by the percentile lines in the first year of life and we have separate graphs for boys and girls. The majority of the eight we examined who were six months of age had weights very close to the 50th percentile of the Boston standard. Above this age, the majority of children had weights just below the 3rd percentile of the Boston standards (see Truswell & Hansen 1976, p. 176).

Pickering: The failure to find a rise in blood pressure with age has been the experience in many populations; one of the most interesting studies was Professor Shaper's in East African tribes, where blood pressure didn't rise in age but if the men joined the army it did go up, suggesting that this was not genetic but an environmental effect (Shaper 1972; Shaper *et al.* 1961, 1969). I don't myself believe that it's due to sodium chloride; this is far too facile and it doesn't hold for the population of the UK. When Miall and Oldham did their monumental survey in South Wales, Miall (1959) took 24-hour urine collections from women in the upper and lower ranges of blood pressure and found very little difference in the rate of excretion of sodium chloride; surprisingly, sodium excretion was higher in those with systolic pressures under 150 mmHg than in those with systolic pressures over 200 mmHg.

In a recent survey of employees at the Atomic Energy Research Establishment at Harwell and some general practices in the neighbourhood, E. W. Thomas & J. C. G. Ledingham (unpublished work, 1976) measured blood pressure and selected those with some of the highest and some of the lowest diastolic pressures (> 100 and < 85 mmHg). The rates of excretion of sodium chloride over 24 hours were almost identical in these two groups.

I wonder what you think of the idea that perhaps the decisive difference between the 'civilized' way of life and the tribal way of life is that in the former, people constantly have to make decisions, whereas in a tribal society decisions are not so frequently necessary, because so much is laid down by custom and taboo?

Truswell: How could that explain the results obtained on the Isle of Tiree (Hawthorne *et al.* 1969)?

Pickering: The islanders there take decisions of all kinds—whether to listen to the wireless, to go to church, to allow your daughter to marry someone! The trouble about 'stress' is that it means nothing.

When you analyse what is meant by stress in civilized societies, it consists of conflicts of one kind and another.

Truswell: I wonder if there is a threshold effect of sodium chloride. It apparently makes no difference if your sodium intake is 7 grams or 15 grams, but perhaps below a certain intake the whole population is, as it were, going into the equivalent of a low-sodium diet. Below that intake, sodium intake may be correlated with blood pressure.

Joossens *et al.* (1972), in Belgium, repeated the blood pressure measurements many times and also the urinary 24-hour sodium excretion measurements (ten times). They claimed to find a 'within-population' correlation. But clearly sodium is not by any means the whole explanation.

Lightman: I feel sure that the aetiology of hypertension is multifactorial. Among the Bushmen whom you have studied there are four major factors that differentiate their situation from that of our industrial populations: their salt intake; their nutritional status; their blood cholesterol concentrations; and their unquantifiable, but presumably lower, levels of stress. It is impossible to single out one of these factors, since control groups are unavailable. In addition, many people feel that hypertension itself produces hypertension in a vicious circle, so that it might only be the initial abnormality at an early stage that is significant. In spite of these caveats, your findings are fascinating, particularly since hypertension is already one of the greatest public health problems of western society.

Hamilton: Professor Shaper showed that the nomadic warriors of Northern Kenya, when they entered the army, did show a rise in blood pressure with age compared to those who remained in the tribal area, but unfortunately no one has yet been able to study the effects on blood pressure or other variables among those who went back from the army to live in their original tribal areas. Such studies among army recruits from the tribal areas of Kenya and perhaps the Nepalese who joined the British army might be rewarding, particularly in relation to environmental factors and nutrition.

Woodburn: Among hunters and gatherers rather widely one finds the same difficulty that you noted in this group, of a shortage of suitable available solids to put infants onto at an early age—the lack of cereals and a shortage of other suitable foods to supplement the breast and to wean them onto—and a consequent very heavy dependence on breast milk for the first year and more. What interests me is whether you have any information about prolonged post-partum amenorrhoea, which I suppose one might expect if the nutritional strain on the mother is heavy. (Unfortunately I don't myself have any useful evidence on how long post-partum amenorrhoea lasts among the Hadza in East Africa.)

Truswell: R. B. Lee (1975) is now suggesting that the fact that the women have to breast-feed for longer means that they are likely to take longer before they conceive again. Possibly there is an intercourse taboo also; certainly G. B. Silberbauer (1965) reported this in the Gwi Bushmen. Bushman women living a sedentary life, with cattle and cow's milk available in the Dobe area, had a mean birth interval of 36 months, as against 44 months in women living the hunter–gatherer way of life with longer lactation. It may also be that because the women are thin, there is a relative insufficiency of the pituitary gonadotropic hormones, which would reduce fertility.

Woodburn: Isn't it the case that if they are not much above the malnutrition level, this is the particular point at which one would expect to find strain?

Truswell: Yes. And I am sure that if these children were to be crowded together in some re-settlement scheme with dirty sanitary arrangements and a communal water supply, they would be very vulnerable. But as hunter–gatherers, they must be in small groups, and so there must be relatively less circulation of intestinal pathogens, and most of the children seem to survive this period. H. C. Harpending (1976) made an extensive survey of all the Bushmen in a wide area round Dobe: the infant mortality appeared to average 120 per 1000.

Black: I am impressed by the nature of the terrain on which the Bushmen live. When you find a degree of malnutrition here, is it fair to generalize to all hunters and gatherers, or are these the hunters and gatherers who have been left with the worst of the land, and hence are likely to be most deprived?

Truswell: I believe that the earlier hunters and gatherers had an easier time than the present-day Bushmen. After all, there were hunters and gatherers even here in England at one stage!

Black: If these people now survive so well in these extreme conditions, does this imply that through most of our history we were somewhat better off as a species?

Truswell: That is right. I think that early on, all hunters and gatherers were not necessarily short in stature, for example.

Woodburn: We now do know from archaeological and also anthropological evidence that surviving hunters and gatherers probably resemble our hunter and gatherer ancestors in some ways and differ from them in others. Until 10 000 or 12 000 years ago, man lived solely by hunting and gathering. That does not mean that everywhere he was nomadic. The evidence suggests that in the pre-agricultural period there were some sedentary or semi-sedentary populations of hunters and gatherers, perhaps like the North-West coastal Indians of North America in recent times. It is also true that there is persuasive evidence for more extensive collective hunting and trapping among some ancient hunters than exists among any recent groups except perhaps for the Plains Indians whose economy depended on the European horse. Among hunters and gatherers in the period just before the development of agriculture there must, I think, have been a wide range of somatic and nutritional differences between populations, greater probably than one finds between hunting and gathering peoples today.

Gajdusek: The majority of earlier hunter–gatherers were surely fisher folk as well. This is a major source of food which is generally overlooked.

References

BRONTE-STEWART, B., BUDTZ-OLSEN, O.E., HICKLEY, J.M. & BROCK, J.F. (1960) The health and nutritional status of the Kung Bushmen of South West Africa. *S. Afr. J. Lab. Clin. Med. 6*, 188–216

HARPENDING, H.C. (1976) Regional variation in !Kung populations, in *Kalahari Hunter-Gatherers: Studies of the !Kung San and their Neighbours* (Lee, R. B. & DeVore, I., eds.), p. 158, Harvard University Press, Cambridge, Mass.

HAWTHORNE, V.M., GILLIS, C.R., LORIMER, A.R., CALVERT, F.R. & WALKER, T.J. (1969) Blood pressure in a Scottish island community. *Br. Med. J. 4*, 651

HOWELL, N. (1976) The population of the Dobe area !Kung, in *Kalahari Hunter-Gatherers: Studies of the !Kung San and their Neighbours* (Lee, R. B. & DeVore, I., eds.), pp. 138–151, Harvard University Press, Cambridge, Mass.

JOOSENS, J.V., WILLEMS, J., CLAESSENS, J., CLAES, J. & LISSENS, W. (1972) Sodium and hypertension, in *Nutrition and Cardiovascular Diseases* (Fidanza, F., Keys, A., Ricci G. & Somogyi, J.C., eds.), pp. 9–109, Morgagni Edizioni Scientifiche, Roma

KONNER, M.J. (1976) Maternal care, infant behaviour and development among the !Kung, in *Kalahari Hunter-Gatherers: Studies of the !Kung San and their Neighbours* (Lee, R. B. & DeVore, I., eds.), pp. 218–246, Harvard University Press, Cambridge, Mass.

LEE, R.B. (1975) The Kalahari Research Project 1963–1975, paper at *Burg Wartenstein Symposium, No. 67 (The theoretical and methodological implications of long-term field research in social anthropology)*, Wenner-Gren Foundation, New York

McGREGOR, I.A., RAHMAN, A.K., THOMPSON, B., BILLEWICZ, W.Z. & THOMSON, A.M. (1968) The growth of young children in a Gambian village. *Trans. R. Soc. Trop. Med. Hyg. 62*, 341–352

MIALL, W.E. (1959) Follow-up study of the arterial pressure in the population of a Welsh mining valley. *Br. Med. J. 2*, 1204

SHAPER, A.G. (1972) Cardiovascular disease in the tropics. III. Blood pressure and hypertension. *Br. Med. J. 3*, 805–807

SHAPER, A.G., WILLIAMS, A.W. & SPENCER, P. (1961) Blood pressure and body build in an African tribe living on a diet of milk and meat. *E. Afr. Med. J. 38*, 569–580

SHAPER, A.G., LEONARD, P.J., JONES, K.W. & JONES, M. (1969) Environmental effects on the body build, blood pressure and blood chemistry of nomadic warriors serving in the Army in Kenya. *E. Afr. Med. J. 46*, 282–289

SILBERBAUER, G.B. (1965) *Report to the Government of Bechuanaland on the Bushman Survey*, p. 79, Bechuanaland Government, Gaberones

TRUSWELL, A.S. & HANSEN, J.D.L. (1976) Medical research among the !Kung, in *Kalahari Hunter-Gatherers: Studies of the !Kung San and their Neighbours* (Lee, R. B. & DeVore, I., eds.), p. 167, Harvard University Press, Cambridge, Mass.

Beliefs and behaviour in disease

G. A. LEWIS

Department of Social Anthropology, University of Cambridge

Abstract Isolated tribal communities depend on the resources available where they live and on knowledge to use them well, which is passed on by education and training in cultural skills. Anthropological studies have recorded the successful adaptations achieved in some societies. This paper discusses notions akin to those of contagion and infection as they are understood by people in a community in New Guinea. Do they show in these ideas the accurate observation and deduction apparent in their other adaptive achievements? The people have approved patterns for behaviour to maintain health and heal illness. Is the behaviour seen to be effective by them? It may not seem so to the outside medical observer but it is not rejected by the people, who must use it in coping self-reliantly with their circumstances. The question of prognosis is discussed from their point of view so as to show problems which they face in responding to opportunities of modern medical care and in judging the efficacy of treatment.

An isolated tribal society is a relatively closed community of knowledge and experience. The knowledge and experience must be passed on by word of mouth. Ways to survive are likely to have first place in the economy of what must be learned, memorized, and passed on to succeeding generations. The people may relate such knowledge, or some of it, explicitly to health; and it may also have consequences on their health which they are unaware of. They may stipulate risks to health different from ones we understand; for instance, that a hunter must not eat game he has killed himself for fear that his own blood will wither and dry up—such a rule, connected with ideas about success in hunting, its value and prestige, has consequences for sharing meat and its wide distribution. Notions of health and normality (whether they involve mere freedom from illness, some average state of ordinary well-being, or an ideal more perfect than the common lot of men) are bound up with dominant themes and ideas about how to survive, and the forces people believe are active in the world they know.

The limitations of memory restrict the diversity and detail of knowledge that can be preserved without writing. The number of people who may contribute their abilities and experience to the common fund of knowledge is small: at least, this is likely to be the case in the few communities which still remain isolated. Clearly it is not possible for them to accumulate and store experience of the elaborate, descriptive kind we in our society have used in recognizing the variety of ways of being ill, and the regularities diseases show in their development and outcome. The scale is quite different. No doubt some kinds of illness are frequent and perhaps distinctive, but much other illness must remain peculiar, undifferentiated, and anomalous.

Because of pain and incapacity, because of possible death or persisting damage, illness provokes distress, uncertainty, and anxiety. Serious illness is hard to accept as an incident with no meaning, like the passage of a cloud across the sun, indifferent to the man who notes it. The illness involves a particular person. The view is rare that nature works quite impersonally in the production of disease. Instead, people brought down by illness, frustrated in what they would have hoped to do, made to suffer, sometimes destroyed, search to make it intelligible in human terms. They look for answers in justice, right and wrong conduct, malice, motive and purpose. In these they may find a reason for their sense of suffering and harm. Such an answer about why it happened may also suggest a way to control or correct the situation.

In our western medicine we turn our clinical attention chiefly to the patient's body. Observations of how it is disordered may guide the choice of appropriate treatment. Whether the patient is a generous, God-fearing man, or a disreputable slanderer, makes no difference to how disease and treatment will work on him. The processes, we think, are bound by natural laws indifferent to his moral state. They show intrinsic regularities that follow their course regardless of whom they afflict. We can rarely say why it should have happened that week, and not the next, or why he fell ill, and not his brother or his neighbour. Illness singles someone out. The view that illness does not come casually and unmotivated, but serves to harm, punish, or warn, usually requires a diagnostic frame wider than that given by the patient's body with its intrinsic signs. The sick man's conduct and social relationships must be looked into to find the circumstance or action that provoked his illness. Familiar experiences of human intentions and motives provide analogies for understanding why illnesses came about, though they may be ascribed to men or to spirits or to responsive natural forces. Such analogies may imply that the causes of illness can act capriciously and irregularly, as human beings sometimes do.

I happened to work in a small Gnau community in the West Sepik Province of New Guinea. The people there paid little attention to the clinical signs of illness. The causes that they recognized for illness were not supposed to produce specified symptoms or signs of illness. As they did not think the cause could be told from clinical signs, exact observation of these was not relevant to diagnosis in their terms. Cause and remedy were to be revealed by other evidence than that of the body's state. They had to find something that the patient had done to expose himself to the cause or provoke it. What had he done? What had he eaten? Where had he been? With whom had he had dealings lately? Recent events, activities, social relationships were scrutinized to pick out actions that were wrong or rash, coincidences that could be seen to be significant with the hindsight of illness. In actual illness they selected from among their ideas of cause and articulated them to the events of ordinary life, giving special attention to invisible powers which they thought dominated over the work of making a livelihood (Lewis 1975, Chapter 7).

When we think of the medicine of exotic peoples, we usually ask what they know of disease and how they treat it; we tend to neglect what they know of health and its maintenance. Illness is the marked subject for concern: its absence or opposite—health—is relatively unremarked upon. Knowledge relating to health may be subject to stronger corrective and selective pressures than those which act on a people's knowledge of illness and its treatment; error and harmful practice in illness may the more easily persist. Knowledge to guide normal practice must work for survival and serve to maintain most people in reasonable health. This is obvious with regard to food and how to get it. The achievements of some societies in harsh environments show remarkable resourcefulness in discovery, in powers of observation and deduction about natural processes, and about the animals and plants where they live.

Rules harmful to the healthy (say, those concerning food or water) would be disastrous for a population in ways that similar rules applying only to the ill might not be. Only a relatively small part of people's lives is passed in illness. Illness is an occasional event. The rules which concern normal life—most people most of the time—these, at least, must be successfully adapted to their needs. This is a first reason why corrective and selective pressures may act on knowledge for health more stringently than on that for illness.

People may observe difficult or complex customs which sometimes benefit their health. They may offer what seem to us strange reasons for following the customs. Rules forbidding sexual intercourse to parents during the infancy of an existing child occur in many tribal societies, but the explicit reasons given in different societies for avoiding it are varied. Because of the prohibition, succeeding births are spaced at roughly two or three year intervals. Despite what we might see as the natural impulse favouring its failure, many societies make the prohibition effective. The advantage of the prohibition has presumably helped to establish it successfully in many disparate societies (Saucier 1972, but also see Heider 1976).

Would customs survive if they often made well people seriously sick? After I had been living six months with the Gnau, most of their domesticated pigs fell ill. They do not keep many. The owners cossetted them but they died. The cause was anthrax. The epidemic coincided with my wife's arrival with our son, aged one year. I was appalled to see the people cut the dead pigs up, share them out, and eat them. Dr R. J. Sturt, with long experience in the area, told me that the only case of human anthrax he knew of had occurred to a veterinary surgeon who did a post mortem on an infected pig. Anthrax in their pigs was a recurrent blight for the Gnau but, so far as I know, they were not wrong to suppose that they could eat the diseased pigs' flesh without harm.

Epidemic illness poses certain problems for people who look for explanations for why illness singled someone out. The Gnau sometimes see many cases of pig anthrax at once; the illness is distinctive; the outbreaks recur. And so the Gnau name the pig illness and its cause, *wolape*. They say that the spirit causing it kills domestic pigs that they shall go in place of men and save them from the spirit's elder brother, Taklei, demanding people's deaths. If men should die in large numbers, so they say, the domestic pigs would not, but the wild forest pigs would too. If the domestic pigs die, then men and the forest pigs go free. In effect the theory does something to reconcile them to the loss of their pigs. The Gnau domesticate the wild piglets that they catch.

I came across Taklei as a cause of death when recording Gnau genealogies. In pre-contact times, about 36 years ago, close to half the population then in the village had died in an epidemic of bloody diarrhoea. My estimate comes from recording all the lineage genealogies of the village, and asking about causes of death. The epidemic took about three months to complete its ravages. For the first month, people remained in the village. Finding no respite, they abandoned the village. Families scattered separately to live apart in garden bush. The survivors told me how obtaining food became difficult then because so many were affected and feeble; how too many died to do the funeral rites for each dead person and how instead one man had to drag two or sometimes three bodies together and let them roll down a cliff or rubbish slope. In narratives of the epidemic, which I tape-recorded, they mention how some decided they must drink only stream water and from upstream of where they stayed; how fathers, as the illness came on them, begged their sons to abandon them, or at least not to share the same sleeping place, the same food, the same house. These decisions stemmed not from prevailing accepted notions of infection but, like their dispersal from the village, from the urgency of their plight, the impotence of what they knew to control the situation, and also, possibly, from accurate observation and inference. Ideas about infection have a marginal place in the usual Gnau understanding of illness and its causes, though they recognize contagion in the spread of scabies and the fungal disease, tinea imbricata. Gnau ideas about spirit presence and attention, its varying concentration and localization, might be faintly likened to our notions of infection, but it would misrepresent the character of Gnau ideas to develop this aspect further here for the sake of finding a similarity.

Trial and error may show up advantage or disadvantage in some course of action if the effect is distinctive enough, or the number of attempts suffices to make the answer plain. In epidemic illness, such answers may show up. Though everyone in the community maintains the conventional Gnau explanation for pig anthrax, many of the women who have to care for the pigs and mother them try hard to keep sick pigs away from the well ones, knowing from experience that if a well pig can be kept apart it may not fall ill.

Individualized, particular reasons for each person's illness are not suited to epidemics. Influenza struck the village while I was there. Among the first people to fall ill, some could find precise reasons for their illness. For instance, Purkiten had taken me with him when he planted a garden and had spoken so that I could hear his planting spells. He said he thought that his subsequent illness came from his lineage ancestors who were cross with him because he had done this for me. But, as more people came down with it, most accepted that it was a general malady which required no special explanation to account for why they had it. If I pestered them to tell me whether a spirit or a shade of the dead caused it, some answered that it clearly could not be one because so many were affected; it was not as though just one or a few individuals had fallen ill. It was like a wind passing through the village, they said. The usual course of the illness was seen and expected. It was just *tu melawug* (phlegm—literally, throat snot). The hamlets were littered with people lying about, miserable and apathetic, waiting to feel better. So many were affected that the daily fetching of food and water was a small problem for a time—but those who felt all right were able, with the sturdy help of children, to sort it out. The brief though unpleasant illness had an expected course. The fact that many others were also sufferers removed for most people the anxiety to account for why any particular person was ill.

If an illness has an expected course, it is easier to detect whether some treatment makes a difference. If, as with the Gnau and other peoples like them, most illness is not differentiated by clinical signs into kinds having expected prognoses, it becomes difficult to distinguish between those treatments that help and those that do not, even if some of them do objectively alter the course of an illness. The form the prediction of outcome takes must alter how one views success or failure in treatment. If a man supposes that most illness may untreated lead to death, then whatever he does and for whatever reasons, he will conclude that his treatments often help—for so much of all illness is (we know) recovered from spontaneously and not lethal. A pessimistic view that almost any or every illness may prove fatal in the end, would tend to confirm belief in the value of what one can do in treatment. The hope of cure, the optimistic bias shown in the high regard which most people seem to have for their own ways of treatment, has probably prevailed at most times in history and in most places. A tranquil scepticism like Montaigne's, which doubts the skill of doctors to better an illness, and leaves the illness as something to be patiently endured until it works itself out or kills, is rare.

One suffers worse, it seems (Beecher 1959), from a pain that cannot be accounted for and is thought untreatable, than from the same thing when it is explained and the hope of cure or control granted and maintained. Perhaps, even without pharmacologically effective means to treat, a system of ideas and practices offering convincing explanation and the hope of remedy can alleviate that part of suffering in illness which derives from dread and uncertainty. In this sense, the tribal patient (and his family and friends) may derive real benefit from the knowledge and treatment provided by his culture, though to us it seems grounded in error, false knowledge, and ineffective or even harmful practices.

We may, as outsiders, be quick to see what we regard as errors or false knowledge in their explanations and practices. But we see them according to the knowledge which we share with members of our own culture. We do not have to take a view that isolates each of us as an individual with an understanding no one shares. Within an isolated, closed community, private doubts or scepticism about what other people publicly and generally assert regarding the causes and treatment of illness may well occur. But to bring them forward, the individual must be prepared to separate himself from what everyone else says he believes. That is hard, especially with ideas concerning illness associated with dominant themes of wider significance for understanding the world and how it works, or associated with moral issues generally agreed on.

In fact the Gnau do little directly to the patient in their way of treatment. Actions to control the illness are directed at spirits and things outside the patient's body. In effect sick Gnau people mostly abstain from certain foods and lie waiting miserably for the illness to pass. It might be argued that such measures are safer in the general run of illness than the clysters, purges, potions, and bleedings that Montaigne and Molière spoke out against, and our medical predecessors so stoutly advocated.

The knowledge and technical skills that led to our present means of treating illness lie quite outside Gnau grasp. They appreciate the benefit of some things we offer them for sickness. Without yet abandoning their own assumptions about illness, they will try our treatment, and want it if it seems to work. Why it works does not much concern them; the benefit is what does. As they do not much differentiate clinical kinds of illness or patterns of outcome, they face difficulties in deciding when, or for what illness, it is worth searching out modern medical treatment. They must make a journey to find it. They make less use of the facilities available to them than we might hope for. Since they lack clinical guides and clear prognostic signs, failure of their own treatment is not easily discerned; judgement about the urgency of doing something else or seeking outside help must depend on their general assessment of severity and on their impression of whether the patient is improving or worsening. They do not expect that a treatment will necessarily effect a sudden or rapid improvement. They must therefore wait to see, but the problem is: how long?

The pressure in present illness is to know what to do about it; desire to bring about the healing of the sick person leads them to try the remedy if there are grounds for thinking it might work. Since many treatments may be given in one illness, and as the prognosis and the speed of action of a treatment are unspecified and uncertain, the conditions of proof or disproof for some particular explanation or remedy are not clear. The eventual view of what really caused an illness or what made it better is often left open to opinion. Thus, if to get modern treatment means a journey, even though the wish for such treatment be clearly there, the decision whether to go and when can be a difficult one in practice.

In western medicine we have managed to find ways to alter the course of many bodily diseases and to stop many infections, but most of them are very recent discoveries. They came only with advance along countless chains of systematic inquiry into natural processes, and the development of multifarious technical skills inside and outside medicine. For nearly all man's time on earth, he has had almost no power to combat disease in the way we do now. Largely lacking effective somatic treatments, lacking microscopes and chemistry and knowledge of the intimate, intrinsic characteristics of disease, most people's decisions about treatment have made probably little, or random, difference to the natural outcome of their ailments. In terms of evolution, disease was mostly left to work on human populations like the wolf among the caribou, taking the infirm, leaving the rest—the healthy—to run free. Few had the means to take decisions about the treatment of disease which could really alter its effects on the structure of their populations—that is, until almost now. Discovery and improvements in ways of producing food, storing and distributing it, of getting water, warmth, shelter, and security, have played a far greater part in the differential success and survival of different human populations than what they thought worth doing for manifest disease. Now, positive measures, like those for the treatment and eradication of malaria, may quickly increase the density and size of the population surviving in a place. The long-term effects of our recent advances in the treatment and control of disease are on a different scale from what went before. Who can predict them?

But the evolutionary scale is inhuman. The Olympian stance we may be tempted to take of looking down on the attempts of tribal peoples to treat illness and seeing in them but a curious collection of practices, based on false knowledge, often random or negligible in its effects, lacks understanding of the human dimension in managing illness. We can see why error is easy in medicine. In serious illness, people find it hard to wait and do nothing. It is difficult to take decisive action if one thinks one has no knowledge by which to choose one course of action rather than another. Divination may have practical advantages (Moore 1957). Belief of total ignorance and incapacity can paralyse action. Inaction is the last outcome, after striving, of despair. Trial of something may lead to discovery when exhausted or brute passivity would not. Given the uncertainty of illness and the absence of sound knowledge, beliefs which strengthen a resolve to action and enable decisions to be taken, may have played some part in the advance of learning about illness, though I have emphasized why this is difficult. But, apart from that, the essential aspect of disease which makes it a human, social, and psychological problem of suffering, is what it does to the individual—to myself or to people I know and care for—and not what disease in general, or in the long term, will do to mankind or a population. If part of the suffering surrounding illness is not simply physical, but is bound up with concern for individuals, affection between people, their personal values, with uncertainty about the significance of what is experienced, and with dread of the outcome, then the management of illness in tribal societies shows us some ways to meet and overcome that suffering, to give support and some comfort, both to the patient and to those who suffer in sympathy with him, by drawing skilfully on social and psychological strengths in people, which we ourselves now perhaps forget.

ACKNOWLEDGEMENT

I would like to thank the Social Science Research Council for financial support of my research in the Lumi Subdistrict, West Sepik Province, New Guinea, during 1968–1969 and in 1975.

References

BEECHER, H.K. (1959) *Measurement of Subjective Responses*, Oxford University Press, New York
HEIDER, K.G. (1976) Dani sexuality: a low energy system. *Man 11*, 188–201
LEWIS, G.A. (1975) *Knowledge of Illness in a Sepik Society*, Athlone Press, London

MOORE, O.K. (1957) Divination: a new perspective. *Am. Anthropol. 59*, 69–75
SAUCIER, J.-F. (1972) Correlates of the long post-partum taboo: a cross-cultural study. *Curr. Anthropol. 13*, 238–249

Discussion

Cockburn: On this question of the knowledge of contagion among tribal people, I have a parallel example, which also concerns anthrax. In 1943 I was with the British army in West Africa, loaned to the colonial government to deal with huge epidemics of meningitis. I was called to a village which was found to be surrounded by men with spears from neighbouring villages, stopping people leaving the village. When I was reluctantly allowed in, I found that a cow had fallen sick; it was attributed to a snake bite, and the cow had been eaten. It was anthrax. Thirty-six people were ill. About five or six of them had bellies swollen up with abdominal anthrax and these died. All I had to treat with was for the meningitis—sulphadiazine—and arsenic drugs for sleeping sickness. We filled the survivors with what we had and they all got better. The point was that the people did not know what was wrong with the cow, and the surrounding people didn't know what was the matter but could see them all sick, so they quarantined the village, allowing no one in or out. Incidentally, the word 'epidemic' means literally 'upon the people' and the Africans had accepted the incident in this meaning.

Woodburn: Dr Lewis, you are suggesting that having explanations of illness is a source of reassurance. To me the fact that commonly in tribal societies the explanation of illness lies either in the malevolence of others (that it is due to witchcraft or sorcery) or in one's own guilt (that one has breached some taboo or moral rule) suggests that explanations may be very far from reassuring; in fact they may be very distressing for the individual concerned. He has somehow to accept the malevolence of close kin or his own guilt. What may be reassuring is surely not the explanation but the procedures then adopted for coping with the situation, for remedying disharmonious relationships and for shedding individual guilt.

Lewis: That is an important point: an explanation as such is not necessarily reassuring. It may be so if it points clearly to a way to correct or control the situation. What is assumed or implied by a particular type of explanation needs to be known in detail. If you know the underlying premises or assumptions, it may be easier to understand why particular explanations are brought forward as they are in someone's illness. For example, in the progress of the illness, the proposed explanation may be non-threatening or one that suggests a means of treatment. Treatment fails; the man gets worse; then, when it is thought that he may die, or after his death, the explanation may turn to sorcery from which there is no hope, or little hope, of escape. The explanation then is highly threatening, and its effect is to move people's feelings towards anger and thoughts of revenge. Explanations vary; some may imply that the patient is responsible for his own illness or guilty of some moral offence.

The general point I was after was that an explanation may help someone distressed by pain, or a sense of bodily ill-ease, by anxiety about what may follow, associated perhaps also with feelings of inadequacy, or doubt about how he stands with regard to other people. It may help by defining the problem, its cause, and a way to cope with it. In divination or the process of diagnosis and treatment, diffuse distresses may be localized and identified for the patient and shown to fit into a scheme of things that he understands. It may offer him some hope of escape or of 'domesticating' or coming to terms with, say, the spirit or the people held to be afflicting him.

This can be done with authority by the diviner, the social group or the cult in an approved way. Some people present or express by somatic complaints diffuse distress associated with social and psychological tensions or conflict. Authoritative diagnosis or identification may help to focus such diffuse distress by explaining it in culturally acceptable terms, recognizing the presence of problems in terms valid for that society (they may be phrased as problems of relationship with a spirit or ancestors, etc.). Explanation which defines the cause and situation may then help to make such problems manageable, or at least make them known or understandable ones, whereas before they were obscurely felt or not explicitly recognized, and therefore perhaps more distressing and harder to resolve. But I agree with your point that some explanations can be upsetting and threatening.

Hugh-Jones: There is a difference between satisfaction in an explanation and comfort in an explanation; you may have both, and because you have satisfaction that may be comforting, but it isn't always so. A good example is the Auca in Ecuador; these people were afraid of the evil spirits in the forest, and so fearsome was the explanation, that they were burying people alive if wounded, to get away from the evil spirits! On the other hand, the comfort they received by the medicine man getting rid of the evil spirit was enormous.

Polunin: I would like to take up a point raised by James Woodburn. The situation you were describing is one in which disease has an important social role as a kind of social sanction, in maintaining social norms.

Woodburn: If we are going to make any generalization we could say that explanations of disease in tribal societies are commonly related directly to people's social relations with each other, and to moral notions of people's individual behaviour. Such explanations and the actions which follow from them constitute an important part of the system of social sanctions generally. It is, however, unsatisfactory trying to generalize, because of the extent of cross-cultural variation.

Lightman: Much of what Dr Lewis has been saying is more universal than he has indicated. The effect of expectations on the outcome of disease is a reality in all societies including our own. In hospitals we consistently see the slower recoveries of patients who do not expect to get better. The general practitioner is involved in the same type of situation. Sometimes, however, this may present quite a dilemma to the doctor. The queues of patients requesting antibiotics for their viral sore throats are only responding to an unquestioned belief in the magical abilities of these products of technological research. Taking the pills will thus make them feel better although the ingredients themselves have no effect on their viral infection.

Our approach to incurable disease also has much in common with the work of the witch-doctor. The last thing one should say to such a patient is 'there is nothing we can do'. The assertion that there are ways we can help, although not necessarily cure, a condition, can provide considerable uplift to a patient during the most difficult time of his life.

I think, perhaps, that Dr Lewis's paper demonstrates particularly well how much easier it is to look objectively at other societies rather than at one's own, and thus how we can learn much about ourselves by looking at others.

Lewis: My aim was in part to direct our ideas in these directions. If we look at treatment in tribal societies, hoping to learn from it, it is in their skill at meeting expectations and at providing social and psychological support and care during illness that the primary interest lies, I think, rather than in the possibility that we may find useful healing plants or drugs that we do not know.

Jones: It is interesting that tribal people who have had some contact over a generation or so make use of *both* systems, the diviners and traditional healers referring people to modern practitioners or in some cases using techniques developed in the western world. This can lead to confusion. Modern practitioners don't like having their patients 'monkeyed about' by people whom they call witch-doctors. In fact, if one is able to follow through the course of an individual's illness, he is being treated usually for acute symptoms at a clinic or hospital or by a general practitioner, and at the same time by a traditional healer, not for the acute symptoms but for the things Dr Lewis has been talking about and also perhaps for chronic complaints—like backache or lumbago or rheumatism. It is rather difficult in western medicine to cope with all these things but they are handled marvellously in a traditional system. It seems that in simpler societies many people have the best of both worlds, where we in modern societies only seem to have the best of one.

Ohlman: The theme of optimism and the expectation of always benefiting from medical practice has started to backfire in California, where medical malpractice suits have reached such a stage that doctors have gone on strike. We build up the expectations of people, with our 'supermedicine' and life-support systems which often merely prolong the process of dying. We also have a counter-irritant close by in Mexico in the person of Ivan Illich, who seems to be an heir-apparent of Montaigne and Molière in his campaign against organized medicine (Illich 1975).

Cohen: Dr Lewis, you said that a relatively small part of these people's lives in New Guinea is spent ill and for the most part they are healthy. In a previous symposium here Leonardo Mata reported studies done in a Guatemalan village which showed that, on the contrary, illness episodes were remarkably frequent in a similar community, at least in the earlier years of life (Mata *et al.* 1976). I wonder if you might change what you said to the comment that though there may be substantial episodes of illness in their lives, they are seldom regarded as sick? In other words, they don't go through the social process for legitimizing sickness.

Lewis: I had in mind the relative proportion of time spent ill compared to that spent not ill, when the decision about whether illness was there or not was made by the people themselves. What is recognized as illness by the people themselves may not correspond exactly with what the modern medical expert would regard so. People anaemic by our standards, or infected with roundworms, for example, may not consider themselves ill. It would be interesting to know more of the variations tolerated in different cultures as to what counts or may not count as illness, and the kinds of condition or disease that go unrecognized or unaccepted as illness by the people concerned.

I did attempt to count how many days the people in the village I lived in spent confined by illness. They spent between four (for women) and nine times (for men) as many days restricted by illness as English men and women have been found to spend (see Lewis 1975, pp. 115–120). The New Guinea people I lived with lost much time because of illness compared to us, but in terms of total person-days, the days spent ill are a small proportion of their lives.

Stanley: I have been amazed at the load of illness that children in some Australian Aboriginal groups have been able to cope with, compared with white children. The Aboriginal child copes remarkably well with an amazing number of infections at one time, whereas the white child would be extremely ill. It is not until the Aboriginal child is 15% dehydrated that he starts to look ill. We have done many biochemical and bacteriological investigations of these Aboriginal children, and studied the parasite numbers, and we were amazed that they weren't physically much more ill, from the amount of infection they carried.

Cohen: I am making a social distinction, not a medical one. I think it is a very important difference. If you look at the parasite loads and infestation of children in different villages in different countries they may well be the same, though in one place the child is regarded as well and in the other sick. What determines the 'label' given depends on the mores and attitudes of the particular society.

Pereira: Dr Lewis mentioned an influenza outbreak. Influenza in New Guinea is of particular interest because it has shown a curious pattern, with two big epidemics caused by the same virus in the last eight years. In the Lowlands the epidemic had a normal pattern like that in many parts of the world, but in the Highlands there was apparently an enormous mortality. Have you an explanation?

Lewis: No. My experience was confined to one very small area. I was working in Lowland New Guinea.

Gajdusek: I have done research during several influenza epidemics in New Guinea, the two referred to and the previous Asian flu epidemic in 1957 which spread throughout the island, and a more limited A_2 influenza epidemic in 1964–1965, and the influenza B epidemic in 1965 (Barnes 1966). We had sufficient warning in 1969 and 1970 to be able to have laboratories standing by; many isolations of the virus were made and it was always identified as 1969 Hong Kong (A/New Guinea/1/69 H_3N_2). To our great surprise we found that it was the same strain of influenza which in Mende, in the Southern Highlands, produced a very high attack rate and mortality of 3% or 5%, but which later 'crept like a lamb' through the adjacent Tari Valley, killing no one and causing a very low attack rate. It passed through some areas in the Eastern Highlands with an attack rate of nearly 100%, every school-child coming down with clinical disease and every person in some villages; yet the same virus behaved very differently in other villages and other areas in the Eastern Highlands. In some villages and schools the virus arrived and left with only 5% and 10% attack rates. We isolated the virus, and since we had bled people before it arrived and after it left, we could measure the antibody response to infection. The low attack rate had nothing to do with the presence of only a few susceptibles. Most people were susceptible, without previous contact with a closely related influenza strain, and yet they remained unaffected although they were in close contact in classrooms or in village houses with the few affected patients. When the virus returned several months later, with a new introduction, it now 'picked up' *some* of those previously missed, but, again, not all of them (Garruto & Gajdusek 1975).

Our conclusions were complex, but we were sure from isolations and serological findings that only one strain of influenza was involved in the 1969/1970 epidemics. There was no strain difference detected in the laboratory that could account for the clinical and epidemiological variations. The deaths in some areas were largely from diarrhoea, in other areas from pneumonia, and in others from meningitis. Around Lumi, where Dr Lewis worked, there was, I believe, a high rate of meningitis complicating the disease. We found that the carrier rate for *Pneumococcus, Haemophilus influenzae* and *Neisseria meningitidis* (meningococci) in the community before the arrival of influenza had much to do with the kind of complications that occurred: the attack rate and type of complications were markedly affected by the kind of infections passing through the population at the time. The weather correlated very closely with the attack rate and the incidence and severity of complications. We soon realized that in Highland villages, as in the Lowlands, the child or adult with a high fever or headache would be out of doors under a tree or on the grass—usually lying in the sun— instead of attending school or sitting in a house. Even when the patient came indoors in the evening he often came to sleep alone and withdrawn. On the other hand, in cold and wet weather the same child patient would crowd into a tightly packed classroom or home or the adult into a crowded house. The number of secondary cases per primary patient can increase over ten-fold with such dense human packing. In hot, dry weather only one, two or three children in a classroom might get influenza.

Later, if the same agent came back to the same school in cold and wet weather, all those who had escaped the first time would now be sick.

We found that the concept that some individuals were intensive spreaders or shedders of the virus and others, although clinically very ill, were not, could account for much of the observed variation in epidemiological behaviour. This seemed to correlate well with the observation that some victims had no coryza (catarrh) or cough, or started to cough only late in their clinical course, while others had much coryza and severe cough very early. Also, laboratory evidence indicated very much more virus in throat or nasal washings in some early patients than in others. This varying 'spreading' capacity of different patients coupled with severe dependence of crowding on the weather and the established variability of carrier rates for many pathogenic bacteria (as well as different prevalence rates for other endemic respiratory and enteric infections which influenced the frequency and nature of complications) could account for all the epidemiological variability that we saw (Garruto & Gajdusek 1975).

References

BARNES, R. (1966) Epidemiology of the 1964–65 influenza outbreak in the Sepik district. *Papua New Guinea Med. J. 9*, 127

GARRUTO, R.M. & GAJDUSEK, D.C. (1975) Unusual progression and shifting clinical severity, morbidity and mortality in the 1969 Hong Kong (A/New Guinea/1/69 H3N2) influenza epidemic in New Guinea. *Am. J. Phys. Anthropol. 42*, 302–303

ILLICH, I. (1975) *Medical Nemesis: the Expropriation of Health*, Calder & Boyars, London

LEWIS, G.A. (1975) *Knowledge of Illness in a Sepik Society*, Athlone Press, London

MATA, L.J., KRONMAL, R.A., GARCÍA, B., BUTLER, W., URRUTIA, J.J. & MURILLO, S. (1976) Breast-feeding, weaning and the diarrhoeal syndrome in a Guatemalan village, in *Acute Diarrhoea in Childhood (Ciba Found. Symp. 42)*, pp. 311–330, Elsevier/Excerpta Medica/North-Holland, Amsterdam

Medical practice and tribal communities

A. DAVID JONES

Department of Social Psychology, London School of Economics and Political Science

Abstract   Recent studies are discussed of societies in which medical procedures, involving injections and other modern techniques, are carried out by unqualified practitioners. These practitioners are discussed from the point of view of the sociology of health care.

I became aware of the problem of contact between modern medical personnel (who practise within a scientific, technical and largely Western European and North American framework), and tribal healers (who seek to care for health in a distinctly different manner but who nowadays look to modern medicine for certain things), when I was investigating the diffusion of new farming techniques among the Plateau Tonga of Zambia in the early 1960s (Jones 1966, 1974). Scotch (1963) in his review of medical anthropology at that time indicates that there had been little systematic study of the use of modern medicine made by indigenous clients and indigenous healers in the underdeveloped world. I, myself, was at first surprised and alarmed to find that the small percentage (between 1% and 5%) of men who had received some four to six years of education and had previously, or still had, jobs as teachers, extension workers, clerks and orderlies and who had travelled to South Africa or elsewhere for work or had been in the army (in other words, showed signs of the 'cosmopoliteness' diagnosed by Lerner [1958] as necessary for transformation from traditional to modern society) tended to own hypodermic syringes. I made no systematic study of this or of other modern medicine used by the Plateau Tonga, but I observed that the diffusion of innovations in agriculture seemed to be paralleled by a diffusion of innovations in medicine. In other words, trying out new techniques to see if they could be 'made to work' had already begun among certain members of the community. The number of people who used their syringes was probably very low. The only person, out of about two dozen owners known to

243

me, who definitely gave injections was known as *musilisi* (i.e. a man skilled at curing invalids of their pains and physical discomforts with herbs, roots, infusions, dressings and so on, as distinct from *nyanga*, who deals with people when they are disturbed by misfortunes associated with spirits). He injected saline into some clients whom he also treated with herbs etc. and whom, in some cases, I was interested to discover, he counselled to go to the government-run hospital two days' walk away. So much for my initial impressions of contact between modern medicine and people who until the turn of the century had been living in a late Stone Age or early Iron Age culture—a people isolated almost completely from the rest of the world and of whom Livingstone (1865) wrote, when he 'made contact', that they appeared to be a disorderly rabble.

Nearly a decade after Scotch (1963), Fabrega (1971) is more explicit in stating that: 'Rigorous studies of how folk modes of treatment link with Western medical modes are needed so that a widely applicable model of medical treatment can be constructed'. There have been a few studies which mention the use of some modern methods of treatment (notably injections and antibiotic pills) by healers who practise in a traditional setting and who are not licensed to practise by any state authority, and these studies can, perhaps, lead us towards the construction of such a model. Maclean (1966; W. Africa), Cunningham (1970; Thailand) Chen (1975; Malaysia), Bhatia *et al.* (1975; India), Leeson & Frankenberg (1972; Zambia), and Imperato (1976; Mali) report findings which suggest that there may be some common trends. This literature is perhaps the more persuasive as the authors tend not to be aware of the others' work. In discussing it I will have to ignore much of what, in a fuller discussion, would be crucial, namely the various systems of beliefs, practice and institutional setting within which the diffusion of new medical techniques is occurring. I am also ignoring the fact that some countries, such as China and India, have considered embodying some practitioners, such as Ayurvedic, Sidha and Unani in India and the practice of acupuncture and moxibustion in China, in their health care services (Bhatia *et al.* 1975) and that others exclude them. The authors referred to above only provide a minimum of this type of contextual information.

The following, then, gives an indication of the characteristics of the adoption of new medical techniques in communities which rely very largely on 'traditional' medicine, and includes 'injection doctors' in Thailand who manifest the least traditions, Indian practitioners with a very large body of tradition, and other practitioners somewhere in between these extremes.

THE SPREAD OF NEW TECHNIQUES

Leeson & Frankenberg (1972) state that 'traditional healers are more numerous and more readily available than any other source of medical care' in the townships of Lusaka. Bhatia *et al*. (1975) studied the rural population in three Indian states and reports one qualified modern doctor per 4700 people, used by about 10% of the population, and one full-time traditional healer per 1300 people. Chen's (1975) figures suggest that traditional Malayan healers outnumber modern practitioners by 10 to 1. Cunningham (1970) found a similar ratio, in a district of nucleated settlements in Thailand, between modern and 'injection' doctors (i.e. healers who administer injections but who are not medically qualified) though 55% of households seeking care had used modern doctors and 76%, 'injection doctors'. (Some of course used both.) The total number of treatment sessions was, however, about the same which suggests that, in Thailand at least, although there are far fewer modern doctors they see, overall, two-thirds as many patients and have more treatment sessions with them than do the 'injection doctors'. Maclean (1966) found '12 native doctors in a group of 400 men' in Ibadan, indicating that there were probably more than that. The ratio of modern doctors per head of population was 1 to 3170 town dwellers and with a rural catchment as well. In all these studies, then, we find that traditional healers are more numerous than modern doctors. They also tend to live and practise a shorter distance from their clients. They may, however, have a smaller case load than a modern doctor.

All the authors point out that some patients may visit more than one 'traditional' doctor in addition to a modern doctor. Imperato (1976) found this to be particularly common in his investigations in Timbuctoo. Leeson & Frankenberg (1972) found that only 10% of patients of 'traditional' healers were young children whereas they represented between 25% and 45% of the patients of modern doctors (in private practice, as hospital out-patients and at a clinic). About two-thirds of 'traditional' patients were adult women, who represented a little under half of the patients of modern doctors. The authors point out that men are more mobile and less intimidated by modern doctors and, along with children, more likely to appear at a doctor's with an acute condition whereas women are more likely to seek a 'traditional' treatment for a chronic condition and its disturbing social effects, such as problems about conceiving children.

Patients frequently pay more for treatment by a healer than by a modern doctor. Cunningham (1970) found that villagers who used 'injection doctors' spent about 7–8 times more per treatment than the amount spent at a modern health station. Leeson & Frankenberg (1972) point out that treatment by indigenous medical practitioners can be very expensive, especially if the treatment involves dancing and other ceremonies.

In some cases healers have other occupations as well. Cunningham (1970) reports that most 'injection doctors' only have other work as a side-line (although 'teachers, other civil servants, policemen, traders and some farmers may give occasional injections') and although Bhatia *et al.* (1975) only investigated those who were full-time healers it seems likely that alternative occupations existed. About 90% of the *bomoh* or traditional medicine-men among Malays are farmers who practise only when the need arises (Chen 1975). About a third of Leeson & Frankenberg's (1972) sample in Zambia were in full or part-time employment.

Treatment of patients includes a range of practices which owe their origin to modern medicine. Leeson & Frankenberg (1972) report one healer who 'used only chemists' medicines and dressings' and none of the herbal preparations commonly used by the other healers in Lusaka. Another had lost his job as evangelical minister because he had given injections. It is not really clear how widely diffused is the use of modern medicines among Lusaka healers. Leeson & Frankenberg (1972) record a significant number (about 25%) of healers observed using objects derived from modern technology, such as magnets and mirrors, in making diagnoses. As they were not averse to referring certain clients to hospital it seems likely that the use of modern medicines might be a little greater than is implied in Leeson & Frankenberg's (1972) account. In the Indian sample of 93 healers studied by Bhatia *et al.* (1975) 90% reported using some modern western medicines and techniques. (87% had syringes, 77% thermometers, 68% stethoscopes.) More than 80% had given at least one injection during the previous week. 'Injection doctors' in Thailand, by definition, give injections—mainly of penicillin, streptomycin, camphor vitrol, sulpha drugs, vitamins and infusions of saline or glucose water. Vitamin and other pills are also used and patients are sometimes referred to modern doctors and even taken there by the 'injection doctor' himself. Referral to modern clinics and hospitals seems to be a widespread practice among traditional healers for some of their patients. There is an irony in this aspect of their practice for although, as Cunningham (1970) states, 'injection doctors may play a significant role in the total referral system which culminates in use of a modern government facility,' he goes on to refer to senior government health personnel who 'view the idea of "injection doctors" as anathema'.

The differences between various types of non-modern medicine have so far been ignored in this discussion. Clearly there are important differences between the Indian and Chinese traditional systems which have existed in written form for a long time and which demand scholarship and learning and command respect, including, in India, the respect of modern doctors, according to Bhatia *et al.* (1975), and 'injection doctors' in Thailand who practise a simplified form of modern medicine, injecting antibiotics on an entrepreneurial basis and often practising from a site in a market place. There are differences between the

Yoruba healers in Ibadan who are essentially herbalists and those priests of the Ife cult who, according to Maclean (1966), specialize in a form of psychotherapy. Leeson & Frankenberg (1972) distinguish between herbalist and witchdoctor. Whether or not the functions of herbalist, healer, diviner, priest or a specialist such as an 'injection doctor' are carried out by separate people or by one type of person in a community, they all share important qualities which differentiate them from modern medicine. Their mode of operation is essentially personal and their approach is inclusive of any personal human concern which client or patient may have. Thus, although non-modern medical practices may take very many forms in different communities and even within one community, such that a good description of them would require pointing out their differences, they seem to have some important things in common which set them apart from modern medicine from which they have nevertheless borrowed some techniques and to which they refer some of their patients. It is to this that I shall now turn.

TRADITIONAL AND MODERN PRACTICES COMPARED

In order to explore the relationship between modern and traditional medicine and to understand the consequences of isolated people making contact with modern medicine it is useful to note what they might and might not have in common. Polgar (1962) pointed out in his *myth of the empty vessels* that it is not true that primitive groups are lacking ideas about health and how to care for it which can then be supplied by modern medicine. All communities have a system of health care which, if the community has survived, must be judged as adequate at least for that purpose. Such systems may be difficult for outsiders to comprehend. In the course of the following comparison I will deal with two of these difficulties which seem to lead to misunderstanding, namely the difficulty in comprehending the processes of thought underlying practices which, discussed out of context and repeated second-hand, appear to be bizarre, and the difficulty in respecting the integrity of practitioners who appear to be using superstition and even sleight of hand instead of deferring to scientific evidence. But this is to anticipate the details of a more general discussion which stems initially from the seminal writing of Parsons (1951) and the use and criticism of it and of similar authors. (Leeson & Frankenberg 1972; Freidson 1975; Young 1976.)

The functions served by the people who care for health in a community may be described under three broad headings.

(a) Amelioration and prevention of discomforting symptoms associated with 'disease' and with physical functioning; i.e., curing.

(b) Defining the rights and obligations relating to people who are diagnosed as 'ill'; i.e., legitimizing the 'sick roles'.

(c) Providing a conceptual framework within which sense and meaning may be discovered about social relationships and activities of which the patient and his 'condition' is a part and within which he hopes to improve; i.e., healing.

Modern medicine as it is construed in its ideal form is focused on *(a)* and non-modern medicines are focused on *(c)*. Both are involved in *(b)*. Western medicine embodies a concept of sickness as conditions which are biologically and physically determined. The person who is sick is seen as being the object of the sickness (a host to microorganisms, a victim of circumstances, the inheritor of an unfortunate set of genes) and at the same time he is the object of the physician's or surgeon's procedures. His condition and responses are essentially considered as mechanical and as passively dependent on the expert. His participation in and initiation of action in deciding the treatment prescribed by the doctor is given relatively little emphasis. Non-western medicine emphasizes the person as being an actor, to be counselled, prompted and brought to a viable state in a network of social relations. Rituals and ceremonies of dance, drumming, fasting and the use of narcotic or psychedelic substances and the use of trance states are frequently a part of this and, nowadays, so is the use of modern drugs for the removal of acute symptoms.

The different focus of modern and traditional medicine requires elaboration. The emphasis in modern western medicine is on the disease process within the sick organism, or more particularly the diseased organ, which is thought of along mechanical and physical lines. The person, while being important in the moral sense of having rights, is expected to surrender himself to the inspection and expertise of a medical practitioner. His domestic, social, political and career interests are considered irrelevant to the disease process proper—or almost irrelevant. Epidemiology, theories about stress-linked illness, psychosomatic symptoms and placebo effects are linked to a set of ideas about the interlocking nature of all the features of a person's social and physical existence in producing health and sickness. Nevertheless modern physicians are not trained, and nor can they consider it proper, to attempt much in the way of treating their patients' personal problems at work, at home and in the community. Giving advice about this sort of thing is considered secondary in modern medicine. In non-modern medicine intervention at that level is often the main activity and is carried out by ritual, ceremony or in statements about breach of taboos and disturbances caused to supernatural spirits. This intervention can, and perhaps usually does, affect the network of relationships which the patient has with other people in the community (e.g. Turner 1964) and its effects may be judged as beneficial by those who are involved in it. Modern doctors, especially psychiatrists, know that although they are often exhorted to learn from witch-doctors (Turner 1964; Torrey 1972) it is not possible in an urban area to bring together sufficient members of family lineages and other relevant people, employers, workmates, rivals, neighbours, officials, 'the law', and so on, for a day or two in order to heal the disturbed network of relationships associated with a patient. Social gatherings, notably office parties, family celebrations, or reunions may sometimes have a similar effect. So can plays and films, sports events and involvement in local and national crises. But none of these potentially therapeutic diversions and recuperations can come under the control of experienced and accepted healers of the stature of the Ndembu doctor described by Turner (1964) in an isolated region of Zambia. The best we can do is family and marriage counselling and the various 'group' therapies. But I digress.

The scientific and professional stance or ideal of modern medicine, as compared with the social and emotional stance of traditional medicine, invites the following contrasts, each one of which requires some qualification concerning the training, deportment and practice of medical personnel.

1. Modern: Emphasis on formal and lengthy training and apprenticeship, although, as Becker (1961) points out, informal influences shape the judgement and practice of general practitioners to a high degree, for example in the distrust of theory and emphasis on intuitions based on experience.

Traditional: Skills acquired informally and by observation. Apprenticeship is quite common. Formal training is limited to those systems of medicine which have been written down and are sometimes associated with monastic life.

2. Modern: Professional body legislated for by government regulates practice and code. But, as Carr-Saunders & Wilson (1933) pointed out, the greatest regulator of practice is reputation. Those with a poor one cease to be used by their colleagues and by patients.

Traditional: Consensus and reputation determine practice.

3. Modern: The practitioner is not expected to have undergone treatment himself (except in the case of psychoanalysis), though he is expected to be 'healthy'.

Traditional: If the practitioner is a member of a cult he will have undergone treatment himself.

4. Modern: The practitioner is expected to maintain normal, unimpaired consciousness. His patient is sometimes encouraged not to, through the use of anaesthetics and analgesics and even through hypnosis.

Traditional: The healer or his client may go into a trance.

5. *Modern:* The practitioner is respected, liked, sought after, with aspiration for his offspring, sought after for non-medical positions and, contrary to Parsons' (1951) ideal of professional specialization, there is a tendency to believe that doctors are specially equipped to be wise about the non-medical side of human behaviour (Freidson 1975).

Traditional: Held in awe. Feared. Disliked. Avoided.

6. *Modern:* Consultation is accepted as private and the information gained by the practitioner is considered to be highly confidential, even secret. It is considered proper that the doctor ask direct questions, though only a relatively narrow range of topics are considered relevant. Ley & Spelman (1967) have shown that the amount and accuracy of information which passes between doctors and patients is low.

Traditional: Consultation is public (exceptions being where financial or astrological affairs are discussed). In some contexts, such as among the Yoruba (Maclean 1966) and the Mayan Indians of Tenejapa (Metzger & Williams 1963), direct questions are taken to be a sign of incompetence. The practitioner is expected to know the situation and to show a calm confidence in his mastery of it. Among the Ndembu, Turner (1964) tells us, 'the clients try to trip up the diviner by feeding him false information, and it is the mark of a "true diviner" if he avoids this pitfall'.

7. *Modern:* Consultation and the procedures carried out by the practitioner are done in a special place: consulting room, clinic or hospital. This has developed in western countries from a period when the emphasis was on the general practitioner visiting his patients in their homes and thereby seeing and knowing their circumstances. Modern medical practitioners in underdeveloped countries have never had this emphasis. They tend, according to Chen (1975), to be brief and impersonal. They don't visit their patients and they lack an understanding and a respect for their circumstances. Frequently they do not speak a common language fluently and sometimes are identified as racially different.

Traditional: Consultation and practice are carried out in the home of either the healer or of his client. Although the practitioner may be 'marginal' in one sense—for example, his development in the community may be problematic, due to his ancestry (Turner 1964) or he may have an aura of having come 'from afar', from a mysterious and potent source (as Leeson & Frankenberg's (1972) material seems to imply)—practitioners usually are very familiar with the history, social and family structure, customs, habits and problems of the locality in which they practise.

RELATIONSHIPS BETWEEN MODERN AND TRADITIONAL PRACTITIONERS

Traditional healers do not show the same degree of hostility towards modern practitioners as the latter do to them (Cunningham 1970). The reasons are probably complicated but two aspects of the antipathy should be mentioned. The traditional healer appears to think in a different way and he is likely to do things which suggest that he is a charlatan exploiting his clients unfairly by sleight of hand. I shall deal with these in turn.

Horton (1967) is the main exponent of the idea that there are some essential differences between the thought processes common in traditional or 'closed' cultures and those common in scientific or 'open' cultures. There is only space here to point out that, like the idea expressed by Aristotle in the first book of *Politics* about slaves ('they participate in reason to the extent of apprehending it in others though destitute of it themselves', a view which was discarded when sufficient numbers of people known to be able to reason had been enslaved), any theory about inherent differences between communities of people which is based on what they usually do cannot tell us what they can, and probably occasionally do, when they find themselves in a different context. For example, in typifying the western European as having a mastery of things in contrast to the African's mastery of social relations, a distinction of Horton's (1967), it could be argued that comparing a scientist thinking about his research with a traditional healer illustrates the contrast. If, however, we compare the thought processes of the rural general practitioner, who is described by Freidson (1975) as being sceptical of theories, pragmatic, sometimes less than frank, even uttering a white lie if it is necessary, and shrewd about handling relationships in the community, the contrast with the thought processes of the Ndembu doctor disappears. Likewise the scientific mode of thought, though not pre-eminent in the daily life of primitive man, is not absent from his thought processes, for it is trial and error, the appraisal of effects and a flexible approach to explanations, discarding those which don't work, and an inclination to experiment, which have led to the diffusion of innovations, including innovations in curing.

The following are some observations about the integrity of indigenous practitioners likely to be found in isolated communities. There are probably practitioners everywhere who are guilty of deliberate deception in furthering their own interests. Indigenous practitioners live in the communities which they serve and are less able to hide behind institutional arrangements to protect themselves from their clients' evaluations than are modern practitioners. The reputation of a practitioner in a traditional community is paramount in determining his activity, whereas a modern doctor may be able to use 'qualifications' in order to obtain some sort of practice even if his reputation is poor. Retribution against a person who lacks integrity can be devastating in a simple community. Even if the individual escapes with his life his subsistence is threatened if he is simply ostracized and, unlike his modern counterpart, he has no formal appeal that he may make. Perhaps the biggest problem a modern doctor has, however, in evaluating his traditional counterpart is in focusing on one, bizarre deception and concluding that its perpetrator is a fake. Turner (1964) handles this very well, for the integrity of one of the practitioners which he studied is not impaired when we are told that he produced a tooth, presumably by sleight of hand, from the body of a patient. A point which Turner (1964) does not make but which bears on the point of integrity is that such an act does not require the other participants to be taken in by it. So long as they collude with the practice, as real, the integrity is maintained. It seems likely that some will firmly believe the extraction is genuine, others know it is not. The question of whether trickery has occurred does not arise any more than it does over the nature of the sacraments in a Roman Catholic communion service. It is quite possible to feel doubts and qualifications about a practice when discussing it and not feel them when doing it. I noticed this contrast at rain-making ceremonies in Zambia when the rains had not come, and in discussion when they had.

One argument by which modern doctors are sometimes persuaded is that traditional healers and witch-doctors do more harm than good—or even all harm and no good. This is a less well-founded argument than Illich's (1974*a*, *b*) view that the major barrier to health is the practice of modern medicine, because of the iatrogenic conditions associated with it. He means this in two senses, both of which are relevant to contact with people who have previously been isolated from the rest of the world. Firstly, although infant mortality can fall and life expectancy can increase as a result of modern techniques and cures, the application of modern medical techniques has side-effects, or simply effects, which injure people physically. Secondly, as a result of the practice of a form of medical care which is adapted to the scientific and industrial mode of production, typified by construing people as objective resources playing a part in production, servicing and consuming in a modern economy, people become alienated. Instead of one network of relationships, typical of a hunting and gathering group or of early agricultural and pastoral people, most of whom can meet for a day or two to sort out envies and jealousies, the individual is treated by different categories of other people in different ways and there is nothing to create harmony in the set of pigeon-holed relationships in which he exists. Modern medicine, according to Illich (1974a, b), is a product of this and a perpetuator of it as soon as it takes healing away from the community group and attempts to practise cures on people without their full participation and control in caring for each other.

Modern doctors in treating patients from traditional backgrounds sometimes find that the simple perceptual, emotional and behavioural aspects of falling sick differ in different communities. Any new community which is discovered is likely to have its own peculiarities. For example, the classification of disease and the labelling of illness is important. Modern doctors use different categories from their patients. Ackerknecht (1947) tells of an extreme case where a community viewed as normal what in modern medicine is a disease (of the skin) and shunned those who lacked it as sick. Young (1976) points out that some conditions, bilharzia for example, are categorized in modern medicine as one disease. Those afflicted may look upon themselves as having a sequence of unrelated episodes of illness. There is the very real possibility that a set of biophysical causes will manifest itself in patterns of symptoms which are notably different in different communities. Gelfand (1966) reports that bilharzia in black Africans is more associated with abdominal pains and in Europeans with lassitude. This type of difference, of importance to clinicians, could arise because expectations gained from experience and from other people influence the sensations which people have in objectively identical circumstances (Schachter 1964; Barber 1969; Jones 1975). The processes whereby people decide that they, or others, require treatment, and the decisions as to what sort of treatment it is appropriate to seek, are also relevant. Zola (1966) demonstrated that communities differ in these respects. A backache after physical exercise will be seen as a sign in one community that something is wrong, which ought to be treated by a doctor, and in another community it will be seen as an indication that the person was really working hard.

POSTSCRIPT

Traditional practitioners whether or not they have adopted some modern practices are serving a need. In part the need is for cures for acute conditions which are not provided by modern practitioners, who are located mainly in towns and who become even less accessible in crises such as warfare, famine, and other natural disaster. Also the need is for healers who not only cope with acute symptoms but also satisfy what psychologists used to call 'an effort after meaning'—that is, the need to understand incidents in our lives in terms of the overall pattern of life and of the moral principles involved in it. This is related to the roles which people as ill, or as invalids, convalescents or handicapped people, are cast into by other members of their community, including doctors. Modern doctors use roles developed in industrial societies. Traditional healers use those developed in the underdeveloped world—the bewitched, the possessed, the unclean or polluted. These are becoming redefined as new roles are emerging in developing countries. One of the effects of making contact with isolated people is that they will begin to redefine their roles. They provide us with a setting for investigating how this happens. I sometimes wonder if Livingstone, who was a great believer in the good effect of having commerce with primitive people, could have foreseen the extent to which the people with whom he made contact would change.

References

ACKERKNECHT, E.W. (1947) The role of medical history in medical education. *Bull. Hist. Med.* *21*, 135–45

BARBER, T.X. (1969) *Hypnosis: A Scientific Approach*, Van Nostrand Reinhold, New York

BECKER, H.S. (1961) *Boys in White*, Chicago University Press, Chicago

BHATIA, J.C., DHARAM VIR, TIMMAPPAYA, A. & CHUTTANI, C.S. (1975) Traditional healers and modern medicine. *Social Science and Medicine 9*, 15–21

CARR-SAUNDERS, E.M. & WILSON, P.A. (1933) *The Professions*, Clarendon Press, Oxford

CHEN, P.C.Y. (1975) Medical systems in Malaysia. *Social Science and Medicine 9*, 171–180

CUNNINGHAM (1970) Thai 'injection doctors'. *Social Science and Medicine 4*, 1–24

FABREGA, H. (1971) Medical anthropology, in *Biennial Review of Anthropology* (B. J. Siegel, ed.), pp. 167–229, Stanford University Press, Stanford

FREIDSON, E. (1975) *Profession of Medicine*, Dodd, Mead, New York

GELFAND, M. (1966) The general or constitutional symptoms in *S. mansoni* infestation: a clinical comparison in two racial groups. *J. Trop. Med. Hyg. 69*, 230–231

HORTON, R. (1967) African traditional thought and western science. *Africa 37*, 50–71 and 155–187

ILLICH, I. (1974*a*) Medical nemesis. *Lancet 1*, 918–921

ILLICH, I. (1974*b*) *Medical Nemesis: the Expropriation of Health*, Calder & Boyars, London

IMPERATO, P.J. (1976) Traditional medical beliefs and practices in the city of Timbuctoo. *Bull. N.Y. Acad. Sci. 52*, 241–252

JONES, A.D. (1966) Plateau Tonga farmers, in *New Elites in Tropical Africa* (Lloyd, P., ed.), Oxford University Press, London

JONES, A.D. (1974) Social and psychological factors in teaching farming. *Human Relations 33*, 27–35

JONES, A.D. (1975) Cannabis and alcohol usage among the Plateau Tonga: an observational report of the effects of cultural expectation. *The Psychological Record 25*, 329–332

LEESON, J. & FRANKENBERG, R. (1972) Traditional healers in a Lusaka suburb (mimeographed). Association of Social Anthropologists, University of Kent

LERNER, D. (1958) *The Passing of Traditional Society*, The Free Press, Glencoe, Ill.

LEY, P. & SPELMAN, M.S. (1967) *Communicating with the Patient*, Staples Press, London

LIVINGSTONE, D. (1865) *Narrative of an Expedition to the Zambesi and its Tributaries*, Murray, London

MACLEAN, C.M.U. (1966) Hospitals or healers? *Human Organisation 25*, 131–139

METZGER, D. & WILLIAMS, G. (1963) Tenejapa medicine. *Southwestern J. Anthropol. 19*, 216–234

PARSONS, T. (1951) *The Social System*, pp. 615–630, The Free Press of Glencoe, Glencoe, Ill.

POLGAR, S. (1962) Health and human behaviour. *Curr. Anthropol. 3*, 159–205

SCOTCH, N.A. (1963) Medical anthropology, in *Biennial Review of Anthropology* (Siegel, B. J., ed.), pp. 30–68, Stanford University Press, Stanford

SCHACHTER, S. (1964) The interaction of cognitive and physiological determinants of emotional states, in *Advances in Experimental Social Psychology*, vol. 1 (Berkowitz, L., ed.), Academic Press, New York

TORREY, E.F. (1972) What western psychotherapists can learn from witchdoctors. *Am. J. Orthopsychiatry 42*, 69–72

TURNER, V.W. (1964) An Ndembu doctor in practice, in *Magic, Faith and Healing* (Kiev, A., ed.), Collier Macmillan, London

YOUNG, A. (1976) Some implications of medical beliefs and practices for social anthropology. *Am. Anthropol. 78*, 5–24

ZOLA, I.K. (1966) Culture and symptoms. *Am. Sociol. Rev. 31*, 615–630

Discussion

Shaper: I don't think the difference between traditional and modern doctors is as great as you tended to suggest, and as you emphasized with your seven points. It is a problem of stereotypes. In looking at traditional doctors and traditional medical practices, we are armed with the stereotype of what *our* practice is like and we reinforce it by looking at traditional doctors and saying how different they are. This comes out in almost all your seven very judgemental statements about modern doctors, where you give a stereotyped image of what modern doctors do. However, you admitted that we aren't as scientific as we think we are and that we tend to do very much what traditional doctors do, when you described our rural general practitioners.

It is interesting to see the effect of the local situation on so-called modern doctors when they work in underdeveloped countries and often adopt traditional methods. In East Africa and West Africa there are 'injection' practices run by western-trained doctors who load up their cars with boxes of penicillin or saline (often it's an antibiotic rather than saline, which would be better) and visit the villages. The doctor, trained in western methods, doesn't even get out of his car but gives injections to everyone who cares to line up and pay. The stereotype of the caring traditional doctor with a feeling for his culture and the modern doctor who is less willing to care about his community is simply not true. Anybody who has sat with a group of active, modern young general practitioners, even in London, will realize that they have a conception of the cultural and social situation of their patients as much as the traditional doctor has in your stereotype.

Ohlman: It seems to me that the seven points could be summarized by saying that in western societies we have individual or specialized practice, as against a group or tribal pattern of consultation, where there is complete interplay between those practising medicine and those receiving it.

Shaper: One must look on the modern doctors' waiting room as part of his practice, however; there you have a large group of people interacting with each other. One of the functions of a waiting area is this interaction.

Ohlman: And is the trick to bring the waiting room and the consultation room together? The fact that they are segregated *is* the difference, perhaps?

Dr Jones, when we contrast western and traditional medicine, this implies an objective measure of effectiveness. If we say that the traditional way is in some ways better than the modern, we need a measure of this.

Jones: In principle it should be possible to measure changes occurring as a result of treatment, whether it is called traditional or modern treatment. In practice it's often impossible to make those measurements. We have to use our judgement and say that some things seem to work for some people in traditional medicine.

Ohlman: This seems rather weak.

Jones: Yes; but a lot of modern medicine is also very weak on the demonstration of its efficacy.

Lightman: Your seven differences are based on a western view of medical practice, without consideration of the different premises under which western and tribal doctors practise. As soon as one goes into these premises in detail it becomes apparent that the different forms of treatment are related to different ideas of aetiology (Lightman 1976). Once you realize that the so-called traditional doctor often considers disease to be caused by irregularities in the patient's environment, his method of treatment would seem as logical as that of our own general practitioners, and your seven differences would evaporate.

Stanley: What interests me is the way your generalizations apply to tribal people. I am not so much interested in comparing the two types of medicine as in comparing the effect of the modern doctor on the aboriginal population with the effect of the traditional doctor on that population. One of the major differences is that the modern doctor—for example, me, flying around in a flying-doctor plane—has only occasional contact. He goes in for a day and then flies to the next place, whereas a traditional doctor is there all the time. In Australia the person who has taken the place of the traditional doctor is the public health nurse, who has a tremendous amount of respect; people willingly bring their problems to her. I stress her importance in the medical care of nomadic or other tribal societies. The public health nurse becomes very much a 'traditional doctor', in fact.

Hugh-Jones: Yes. Although I agree with Dr Jones about the tendency to concentrate on the system or organ that is 'wrong' in modern medicine, it depends to some extent on the way you analyse the problem and the degree to which you *do* analyse the problem. In somewhere like the Musandam peninsular of the Oman, when I had perhaps 400 patients to see, all you *can* do is say 'hands up all those with headaches', 'hands up all those with diarrhoea', and separate them on that basis; or you can go further in diagnosis. In many places one uses methods of analysis that are inappropriate to the local situation; for example, there is a modern doctor in a hospital to which the patients may or may not come. The public health nurse is often much better suited to going round the community.

Stanley: The doctor also tends to be curative in almost all situations, whereas the public health worker and the traditional doctor are more preventive: 'this will help you', 'this will stop you getting the disease', 'use this particular charm, or this umbilicus', etc.

Gajdusek: There is one medical situation in which even a Stone Age population quickly recognizes the advantages of western medical practices. This is with severe yaws—infection with the *Treponema pertenue*, as was encountered in high prevalence throughout New Guinea on first contact with new groups. One injection of three million units of depot penicillin resulted in cure. Nothing done by their own practitioners had ever helped much. One to two weeks after the injections of penicillin there was no question in the minds of the New Guinean as to which therapy worked and which did not. No New Guineans ever contended that traditional healers were also necessary in curing yaws; no one refused penicillin injections once its efficacy had been so dramatically demonstrated. We should see where our modern medical methods have most clear-cut advantages over traditional procedures. New Guinea Medical Aid Post orderlies were quickly trained, even from unschooled young men, and they carried on the use of penicillin injections for yaws. There are many examples of situations where the primitive population has immediately seen that modern medicine has something to offer in certain situations.

Hugh-Jones: Did the people distinguish between the contents of the syringe and the syringe?

Gajdusek: Yes, very quickly. Throughout New Guinea it is not the doctor who 'pushes' the use of injections, but the people. The doctors fight for the greater use of oral medication; the people prefer injections—they demand injections! There is a resistance against antibiotics in the form of pills, on the other hand. Most Melanesians are against pill-taking.

Jones: There is certainly no comparison as far as curing goes. When one speaks about *health* rather than curing, one is on different ground. The traditional healer indeed can help, although he cannot cure yaws. Traditional healers often act as clearing-houses referring people to modern medical care. They help to decide who goes to have an injection and who shouldn't. They also give people comfort, and help to reduce their anxiety. They explain what is going to happen to them.

Gajdusek: The situation I described showed how essential it is now for the traditional healer, or at least a member of the community, to be trained so that the peoples' own therapeutic repertoire becomes larger. Traditional healers are often very willing to cooperate; very few of them resist supplementing their therapy with additional treatments available from the modern hospital.

Woodburn: Dr Jones' stereotype of the traditional healer needs further correction. In almost all African societies there were many different sorts of traditional healers operating simultaneously: there were bone setters, herbalists and diviners of a variety of sorts. We have to be careful that, in looking at these societies, we are not selecting out a particular type of traditional healer that fits our own stereotype of what traditional healers are like. In most non-western societies and certainly in Africa there are a range of different healers, only some of whom fit reasonably closely with the types you have selected for discussion.

Jones: I am aware of this variety, and I was deliberately trying to generalize!

Tyrrell: Even when people are trying to practise what we call scientific medicine, it is a fact of logic that you can never *know* whether what you did to the patient made him better; the real difference between the scientific and the non-scientific practice of medicine is in the basis for choosing the treatment you give. If you choose a treatment because it is what everyone thinks is good, that is not scientific. If you choose it because of the diagnosis made as accurately as possible and previous, scientifically evaluated studies of what treatment works and doesn't work in that condition, you are practising scientific medicine. But when it comes to whether your patient gets better, or doesn't, you cannot strictly 'know' whether what you did was good or bad.

Hugh-Jones: The late Alan Gregg, President of the Rockefeller Foundation, pointed out to me that curative medicine is like Roman morality: you do what the patient expects and what everybody expects in a given circumstance; whereas preventive medicine is like Greek virtuosity: you do what you know to be right in the community even though the patients loathe it!

Lewis: The problem raised about the distribution of doctors is a practical one. There are more local healers or practitioners than trained modern doctors. The local healers may have useful skills and might be involved more than they are in providing some health services. Although the majority of illnesses may come to these healers for treatment at some stage, we have largely neglected to find out what it is they do, how far they select their patients, how well they treat them, how they might be brought into cooperation with health services in a constructive way. There is not much published for any particular place that I know of which really makes clear the extent and nature of their practice in terms that might allow one to decide whether they do harm or good, or make no difference, and for what kinds of illness. If they have skill in the management of some illness, in treating mild and chronic illness, in distinguishing between serious and other medical situations, they might be more positively and usefully involved in the health services of their countries and provide what they are good at or are willing to learn, and so save the time of the fewer other medical care workers who have different specialized skills.

Shaper: In trying to break down the stereotype of the tribal practitioner one should also keep re-examining the concept of what modern doctors do, because it has changed tremendously in the last 20–30 years and is still changing. One must not simply accept a stereotype, not think about it any more, and then make comparisons with other groups.

Jones: All practitioners of course *care*, whether they are of the varied types that have existed and still exist in African tribes, or are modern and a rapidly evolving and changing type, but such is human motivation that is is untrue that the health and well-being of their clientele is their only care. It is right for a practitioner to want to develop his own career and to consider his rivals and his reputation and sometimes be assertive in doing so. But western-trained doctors certainly care. There is much anxiety among some modern practitioners about what they are doing to people in the underdeveloped world when they don't speak their language, even though they visit them often and try to like and understand them; you cannot expect someone from a different culture to really understand the local scene. In my paper I was attempting to emphasize what is feasible and what is not. Traditional healers have their own limits of feasibility within which to work, and a modern doctor in an underdeveloped country works within other limits. These two systems are simply different; neither is better than the other; they have different pay-offs.

Ohlman: There has been an increasing emphasis at WHO on trying to make use of traditional healers, with the idea of persuading them to add certain practices from western medicine to their own practices. Has anyone any experience with trying to do this?

Gajdusek: In the Anga Linguistic Area of the Eastern Highlands of New Guinea the Simbari people are smoke-healers who acquire great prestige. They evoke spirits, they talk with the dead (Mbaginta'o 1972, 1977); they have moved into the kuru area and, somewhat like the itinerant patent medicine men in the West of the United States, roam around dispensing their cures. They have obtained high prices for their services for an attempt—although unsuccessful—to cure kuru and they seek to treat many other ailments more amenable to their ministration. The Fore people, who have no traditional belief in the Anga spirit or ancestor world of magic, have accepted these shaman as healers even though they are from a different linguistic family and culture. They are most wanted for vague chronic complaints and anxieties. One of these Anga smoke and trance healers insists that the people first take the patient to the hospital and secure there an injection of penicillin and other medication which he considers the proper preliminary treatment for his magic, particularly in the case of acute febrile diseases. No westerner has suggested this to him. The people attribute to western medicine one necessary ingredient of the cure, but credit the smoke and trance ceremony with a major part of the recovery and their feeling of well-being.

In another situation, a sophisticated Chimbu from the Central Highlands brought a complex healing ritual to the less sophisticated Fore and Gimi people, allegedly for the cure of kuru. He came from a foreign cultural and linguistic group over 100 miles away, and in one year of practice amassed vast numbers of pigs and other wealth in payment for his services. Finally the people became worried about his continuing failure to alleviate or cure kuru—their kinsmen were still dying of it—and they drove him out. Kuru has thus produced the same phenomenon that in all western countries arises with incurable disease: a series of ritual healers who move in to provide support to the helpless and often to extract a sizeable reward themselves. When we of western medicine failed to cure kuru, *outsiders* from other New Guinean cultures came in with 'traditional' methods modified both for the 'new' disease and to extract advantage from a new situation.

Cockburn: I was a WHO advisor in epidemiology with the Ceylon government for two years. The Minister of Health, Mrs Wimala Wijewardene, instructed me to teach the Ayurvedic physicians how to use antibiotics. At that time, 1956–1957, there was one western-trained doctor for ten Ayurvedic doctors. The latter had done very nicely up to the end of World War II, but then antibiotics flooded in and they found themselves at a disadvantage; they began to lose their patients and started losing money. So I was given the order to teach them how to use antibiotics. The WHO Regional Office in Delhi said I was under no circumstances to teach them this, but these doctors were using antibiotics anyway, with or without training.

The incident had a strange sequel. In 1961 the Prime Minister, Mr S. W. R. Bandaranaike, was assassinated. The six persons arrested included the Minister of Health, a lecturer from the newly formed Ayurvedic College, and a herbalist who actually committed the murder. The latter, Talduwe Somarama, gave evidence that he did it because the Prime Minister favoured western medicine over the traditional native Ayurvedic form. He was hanged (Cockburn 1963, p. 238). (See also *Time*, July 13, 1962, p. 36).

Baruzzi: It is extremely useful to work with the traditional doctor, avoiding any restrictions on his work and his own prestige. It is even relatively easy to establish a satisfactory *modus vivendi* between them and us. The task becomes much more difficult when we try to choose someone in each village to help in providing medical care within his own community. The presence of such an attendant is very important for the best results of medical care, but he must be well accepted by the whole tribe and especially by the traditional doctor. Perhaps anthropologists with some experience with these tribes could be very helpful here.

Gajdusek: The so-called Native Medical Assistants in Papua New Guinea were at first trained by the Australian territorial Medical Service from illiterate young men, who were then assigned to Aid Posts as medical orderlies back in their own community. However, in some groups they could not survive in their own community in the quasi-European role they were trying to assume; at their own request they were sent to other villages or language groups. In these foreign communities they could safely dress up and masquerade a bit like Europeans, a performance which they could not get away with at home. They also often had problems over who would help them with their gardens, since much of their time was taken up by work at their Aid Posts. In some foreign villages the people were ready to help them in return for their medical service and the prestige of having an Aid Post; in their own villages more often than not they had problems in getting gardening help. In the kuru region of the Eastern Highlands Aid Post orderlies with only one or two years of Pidgin English schooling often did well in Aid Posts away from their home villages; few survived for long as medical assistants in their own villages. In other parts of Papua New Guinea, as in Chimbu, Aid Post orderlies have survived better in their own villages. One should keep the possibility of such problems in mind in training and placing indigenous paramedical workers.

Haraldson: WHO has considered this question (WHO 1975*a*, *b*). I belonged to an expert group concerned with alternative ways of meeting the basic health needs of populations in developing countries, and we recommended that the local communities, the presumptive consumer population, should participate in the planning and operating of their own health service. We said that local people should be selected by their communities for short periods of training as auxiliary village health aides (primary health workers), and that there should be an intensified supervision of rural health service units, including regular periods of in-service training, stimulating advice, and assistance with complicated cases. Reliable communication systems (radio-telephone) should be developed as well as all-weather-proof transportation systems for emergency and referral cases, personnel, drugs and equipment.

Rather independently of each other, systems of this kind have been launched in several places: the 'simplified medicine' in Venezuela, the Ujamaa village system of Tanzania, Eskimo 'village health aides' in Alaska, Aid Post orderlies in Papua New Guinea, and the bare-foot doctors of China. These systems appeared in these places not to be compromises, but realistic solutions of the problem. And there are no alternatives.

Polunin: The stereotyped view, on which many western children are brought up, of a war to the death between the modern doctor and the 'witch-doctor' is the opposite of the situation we are familiar with in Asia, where we *expect* the village traditional physician more often than not to ask our help and to offer us help. This is encouraging if we have the hope that looking at traditional systems can help us to see what patients in the modern world are missing.

Let me recall an example of how experience of tribal medicine has helped my understanding. I described earlier (p. 18) a rather trivial incident. I had just reached an isolated tribal village after an exhausting journey. I felt nauseated, and accepted my tribal assistant's offer to make an incantation to cure me. Under his ministration I quickly became aware of a considerable 'settling of the mind'. The realization struck me like a shaft of light that I felt better because someone who really cared was trying to help me. Although social support of this kind is a valuable potential component of all therapeutic situations, I had not been aware of it as I had not seen it in isolation.

Hugh-Jones: We noticed working with coal-workers with pneumoconiosis in South Wales that when doctors went in and did something in relation to the miners, and we could show quite conclusively that there was no objective evidence of improvement, they felt much better. I am sure this is extremely real. One is tempted to ask how this relates to hypnotic and other such experiences.

Polunin: I discarded the idea that I felt better because of the power of suggestion. I cannot frankly remember whether I was less nauseated or not; what I remember is that I *felt* psychologically quite different in my mental state.

Shaper: Does you own general practitioner give you the same feeling?

Polunin: Yes, to some extent, but I hadn't thought of it this way before. You might say that I was describing a natural experimental situation where I was being given therapy which I thought was not effective. I didn't think I was subject to suggestion, as I did not expect to be improved by it, but I *was* subject to a great deal of social support by someone who cared.

Pickering: A former house physician of Sir Derrick Dunlop told me that that was exactly what Derrick Dunlop did to his ward patients. It wasn't the medicine that he prescribed: it was the way he conveyed to his patients that he really cared, and they all felt better.

Gajdusek: In the Western Caroline Islands of Micronesia much of the traditional medicine depends upon massage. All children, male and female, are taught to become expert masseurs and masseuses. They are expertly instructed by their older family members and some become better at the practice than others by the time they are adolescents. Instead of only gossiping, cooking and eating snacks, and grooming and searching for lice in each others' hair—activities which dominate the relaxed social setting in many houses elsewhere in the Pacific—here many people lie about with a small boy or girl or an older friend or kinsman massaging every real or imaginary muscular ache or pain, headache, belly-ache or cramp. The training in massage that all young people receive from grandmothers, grandfathers and other elders for the relief of every pain is extensive. It is so skilful that physicians with headaches come to my home in the US to request such massage from my adopted Micronesian boys. An interesting matter is that in these skills there are no shaman. Everyone is trained from childhood so that in every household or gathering there is someone who is expert at the techniques.

Ohlman: This gives a whole range of physical treatment, but Sir George was alluding to bedside manner, which is completely mental. Perhaps what you were experiencing, Dr Polunin, was something in between, because you mentioned an incantation. Might there have been an effect akin to the masking phenomenon? (Namely, when you want to concentrate you wear earphones and are fed 'pink noise', which is like the sound of the sea.) There is perhaps something physiological going on, not just suggestion.

Polunin: My guess is that my experience had nothing to do with suggestion, or with pink or any other colour of noise, but rather with my awareness of my social situation and my assistant's social contribution or influence, or 'bedside manner'. It was a social situation of being cared for by another human being, in a situation in which one would otherwise have felt very isolated.

Truswell: Among the Kalahari Bushmen the older men do the healing. They go into a hypnotic trance, often during a dance, but it doesn't seem to start at such a young age as in New Guinea. It is as if when a man ceases to be good as a hunter he acquires this skill, so that he still has a valuable social role.

Hugh-Jones: This form of care is of course a form of dependency, and a psychiatrist would say that dependency is reasonable in childhood, and when you are ill you automatically want dependence on someone who can help you. I think that is the sort of phenomenon Dr Polunin described, in which he felt dependent on somebody who was careful and was literally mothering him.

Shaper: I have been struck by the fact that although we are talking about the tribal context, this whole discussion is relevant to our own society. For example, we don't hear of many young doctors who qualify in our western society and go back to live in their own villages; the flight from one's own village is almost a universal phenomenon.

The attitude of caring, again, is a universal one. I begin to wonder what we really are talking about and what is so special about these so-called 'tribal' groups, other than their isolation.

Hugh-Jones: You are right about the basic similarities of what we like to think of as modern man and primitive man, and it is of course a continuous spectrum. But one reason for this symposium is to see how much we can learn from such people, and what are the best ways of looking back in human evolution to try to understand our present state in 'modern' societies. It is the mistake of many amateurs going into the field that they think they are dealing with human beings different from themselves.

Shaper: A vital similarity is the question of ethnicity, the strength of the small group in maintaining traditions and not wishing to become part of larger nation groups or federations, and one wonders whether in attempting to assimilate tribal groups, which some people feel is important, we are doing the right thing.

Morin: I agree fully with this criticism of the assimilation policy which is being applied by a number of African and Latin American states at the present time to tribal societies. In the name of national unity and civilization they impose a dominant, western type of culture, creating a uniformity and homogeneity which spells the cultural death of the minority groups. It is our duty as research workers to point out the importance of their preservation, not as a vestige of the past, but as an example of social organization and political and economic structures which could, as Dr Hugh Jones pointed out, teach us a number of values which are lacking in our 'civilized' societies. They could also help us to better understand the crisis which our civilization is experiencing and the conflicts it engenders.

I believe we must stop looking at tribal societies from an evolutionary point of view and equating them with prehistoric man. On the contrary, we should regard them as *different* societies. I had a chance to do my fieldwork a few years ago living in a South American tribal society and I am at present studying the French minority of Occitans as well as the Bretons and Corsicans. What strikes me is that both the Indians and the Occitans contest the notion of the state, reject centralization, and lay claim to and identify with an area, language and culture different from those imposed on them by the national society.

Hugh-Jones: What interests me is the conflict between the individual, the sub-society and the general society. The unification of countries like Germany and Italy is of course relatively recent. This desire to unify because of its obvious benefits, economically and in terms of defence, comes into conflict with a desire to be free and to be separate, and this conflict is always going on.

Morin: I believe, as does Professor Shaper, that there are many similarities between tribal societies and our modern world, as for example the need to identify with a specific area. Post-industrial societies which are in a process of change have a tendency to erase economic frontiers and to favour international exchange. The material acculturation, which imposes a certain uniformity of culture, is not accompanied by an equivalent 'formal acculturation' (Bastide 1970)—in other words, a metamorphosis of the psyche. There is a divorce and contradiction between the economic universalization and the social regionalization. The collective identity of the individual is neither that of the planet, nor of an international language such as English, nor the culture of the supermarket or blue jeans. The revival of ethnic or regional identity is therefore some kind of answer to the change in industrial societies and the rejection of a certain set of values linked to this change, which reflects the form of progress represented by intense urbanization, transforming the way of life and social relations and encouraging individualism at the expense of family life.

Woodburn: We shouldn't see this as an either/or situation, however. The alternative is not a simple one between segregation and assimilation. We shouldn't forget that probably the majority of the world's population is bilingual and willing to identify, in appropriate contexts, with more than one group; it is extremely common for people to identify with one home language and culture and with a different national language and culture. There will not necessarily be any fundamental conflict. In particular places, however, conflict between local linguistic and cultural loyalty and national loyalty is only too obvious and such conflict is often increased by discriminatory government policies, but we should not assume any inevitable conflict.

Morin: Dr Woodburn is right to emphasize the development of bilingualism on a worldwide scale. But bilingualism does not mean political, social or economic pluralism. In other words, a country can accept the use of two languages but this does not necessarily mean that the two corresponding cultures share economic and political power in similar proportions, nor is the social stratification necessarily perceived as egalitarian. It must be remembered that the state exerts a form of coercive power ('one against many') to achieve the formation of a national consciousness, more often than not eliminating other forms of ethnic group identity existing within the state. This power is exerted at administrative level by electoral and educational systems which aim at a national consensus, excluding other forms of consensus (ethnic, communal, parental, territorial, and so on). The kind of bilingualism, which does not necessarily signify that both languages are official but only one of them (which permits access to political and economic power), gives this language the value of a cultural code which is not necessarily linked to the indigenous language. It is therefore possible for bilingualism to coexist with a policy of assimilation spelling eventual 'ethnocide'.

Gajdusek: An interesting point on territoriality: an example of clinging to ground and acknowledging prior ownership that is seen as well in America and Australia with European settlement as in Melanesia and elsewhere in the Pacific before European arrival, is found in the persistence of place names used by former owners, who may be extinct and whose language may be extinct. We repeatedly find place names that do not stem from any living group but have nevertheless been maintained by the new occupants of the territory. Sometimes in Melanesia we are able to trace the origins of such names even when the original name stems from prehistory. There are two phenomena here working against each other: the importation of new names from the area of origin, as in the United States with names such as New Amsterdam, New York, Harlem, New Hampshire, Rome, Ithaca, and similarly throughout Canada, South and Central America, and Australia; and the keeping of the name used by the original owners, as in the widespread use—sometimes misuse—of Indian place names in North and South America and of Aboriginal place names in Australia. Throughout New Guinea place names are rarely those given to the land by the people who are there. We have found that they are valuable tools in reconstructing the prehistory of a group. I wonder, since this phenomenon of preserving names is so universal, whether it reflects a respect people have for land ownership, *even* that of people they exterminate or displace? People have in general permitted even the names used by an obliterated people to remain associated with the places they occupied. It is only recently that, with arrogant nationalism, the replacing of a former name has seemed important.

Polunin: Benjamin (1966) has described for the Temiar tribe of Malaya a situation where parts of the culture, such as ritual observances, and even the ethnic group to which a person answers, are more a matter of place than of ancestry. If you are born and brought up as a Temiar person in Temiar territory, but move into the Semai tribe's country, you must behave like a Semai. This perhaps is a more developed example of the same thing.

Shaper: Isn't that merely the problem of joining another social group and identifying with it, rather than anything to do with the territory?

Polunin: Apparently it is not so. A group can move into Semai land and assume culture and behaviour appropriate to Semai even though there are no longer any Semai in the area. Of course they are already familiar with Semai culture.

Jones: I think there is an anxiety in people's minds (and it may be an illusion, based on a romantic idea; I don't know) that large numbers of people whom we might call tribal, in many if not all parts of the world, are in for a bad time in the future. They seem likely to suffer more from hunger than they would have done if they hadn't become acculturated, and likely to get into a position where we who are acculturating them have given them the feeling that inherently they are of less value and less able to do things because their culture has no identity, and hasn't the potency to it, and somehow they become bereft of value inside themselves. One can conjure up an image of South America being populated by people living packed together in terrible urban conditions, and in fact settlements like this have already begun to spring up. If as a result of attempting to help people by studying them and to help people by curing them we are adding to this situation, I think we have grounds to feel anxiety.

References

BASTIDE, R. (1970) *Le Prochain et le Lointain*, Cujas, Paris

BENJAMIN, G. (1966) Temiar Social Groupings. Kuala Lumpur. *Federation Museums Journal 11*, NS, 1–25

COCKBURN, T.A. (1963) *The Evolution and Eradication of Infectious Disease*, p. 238, Johns Hopkins University Press, Baltimore

LIGHTMAN, S.L. (1976) The inter-relationship of tribal and scientific medicine. *Survival International Review 1* no. 13, 20–24

MBAGINTA'O, I. (1972) Les esprits guérisseurs chez les Dunkwi Anga. *Journal de la Société des Océanistes 28*, 337–343

MBAGINTA'O, I. (1977) Medicine practices and funeral ceremony of the Dunkwi Anga. *Journal de la Société des Océanistes*, in press

WORLD HEALTH ORGANIZATION (1975a) Meeting basic health needs in developing countries: alternative approaches. *W.H.O. Chron. 29*, 168–187

WORLD HEALTH ORGANIZATION (1975b) *Health by the People* (Newell, K. W., ed.), WHO, Geneva

Pitfalls to avoid: the Australian experience

ISOBEL M. WHITE

Department of Anthropology and Sociology, Monash University, Clayton, Victoria, Australia
(Since February 1977, Visiting Fellow, Department of Anthropology, Research School of Pacific Studies, Australian National University)

Abstract   In this paper the major health problems facing Australia's Aboriginal population are reviewed and an attempt is made to assess the genetic and environmental, social and cultural factors to which they may be attributed. Among Aborigines living in remote areas under semi-tribal conditions, recent improvements in health, though considerable, have not been commensurate with the greatly increased expenditure on health and welfare services. This disappointing outcome is due partly to loss of control by Aborigines over their own lives, including matters concerning health, and partly to failure of white medical and welfare personnel to communicate with people holding different beliefs about health and disease. The bad health of Aborigines living in cities and rural areas can be attributed largely to their poverty, which in turn stems from discrimination in employment, housing and community services. In both the remote and the settled areas health services for Aborigines are increasingly coming under the control of Aborigines themselves and producing encouraging results.

PERSPECTIVES AND PROBLEMS

The occupation of Australia by the British, beginning at Sydney in 1788, spelt disaster for the Aboriginal population, whether by outright killing, by introduced disease, or by destruction of their livelihood, their culture and their identity. Tables 1 and 2 show the fatal effect of white settlement; the denser the settlement the more deadly it proved (Curr 1886, p. 209), so that communities of full descent Aborigines remain only in those areas most recently and most thinly settled. In the south-east and south-west of the continent the present Aboriginal population consists almost entirely of descendants of liaisons between white men and Aboriginal women.

In the early days the most fatal disease was undoubtedly smallpox, which spread from tribe to tribe right across the continent and killed many thousands. More insidious killers were also introduced, for example tuberculosis, syphilis,

TABLE 1

Aboriginal population of Australia, 1788–1971 (Includes Tasmania and Torres Strait Islands)

	Population	As % of 1788 figure
1788	314 500[a]	100.00
1861	179 402[a]	57.04
1871	155 285[a]	49.38
1881	131 366[b]	41.77
1891	111 250[b]	35.34
1901	94 598[b]	30.08
1911	80 613[b]	25.63
1921	69 851[b]	22.21
1933	67 314[b]	21.40
1947	70 465[b]	22.41
1954	75 567[b]	24.03
1961	85 685[b]	27.24
1966	101 978[c]	32.43
1971	115 953[c]	36.87[d]

Source: Figures extracted from Tables XII.1 and Table XII.2 (vol. 2, p. 478) of *Population and Australia: a demographic analysis and projection* (First Report of the National Population Inquiry ('Borrie Report'), Australian Government Publishing Service, Canberra, 1975)
[a] Estimated.
[b] Includes enumeration for some states, estimates for other states and for Northern Territory. From 1861 onwards the figures include an increasing proportion of part-Aborigines.
[c] Census figures, approximately half representing Aborigines of full descent.
[d] If only those of full Aboriginal descent had been counted the figure would have been less than 20% of the estimated original population.

gonorrhoea and alcohol, all unknown before. The childhood diseases could decimate a community, and as late as 1948 at Ernabella Mission, in the Western Desert, measles caused at least twenty-three deaths. Even today influenza kills a much higher proportion of Aborigines than white Australians. In June this year (1976) there were five deaths in a Northern Territory community out of a population of about 900, a rate which would have caused well over 10 000 deaths, with consequent major panic, had it occurred in Melbourne.

It seems that the previous long isolation of the Australian continent and the low population density had kept it free of most of the great scourges of mankind (Moodie 1973, p. 29). There was no leprosy until it was introduced from Asia into Darwin and Broome in the 1880s. It killed and maimed many Aborigines before medical discoveries made possible its control, with the hope of complete eradication in the near future. But until quite recently the discovery of a case called forth most cruel procedures, with those infected being torn from their families and communities and put into what were called 'lock-hospitals'.

Most of the infectious diseases which used to be killers have now been con-

TABLE 2

Aboriginal population of Victoria and the Northern Territory 1788–1971

	Victoria		Northern Territory	
	Aboriginal population	As % of 1788 population	Aboriginal population	As % of 1788 population
1788	15 000[a]	100.00	50 000[a]	100.00
1861	2384[b]	15.89	48 500[a]	97.00
1871	1700	11.33	44 000[a]	88.00
1881	900	6.00	38 500[a]	77.00
1891	731	4.87	33 500[a]	67.00
1901	652	4.35	28 000[a]	56.00
1911	643	4.29	23 500[a]	47.00
1921	586	3.91	19 500[c]	39.00
1933	865	5.77	16 500[c]	33.00
1947	1277	8.51	16 147[c]	32.29
1954	1395	9.30	17 163[c]	34.33
1961	1796	11.97	19 707[c]	39.41
1966	2715[d]	13.10	22 312[c]	44.62
1971	6371[d]	42.47	23 381[c]	46.76

Source: As for Table 1.

[a] Estimates. The 1788–1881 estimates for the Northern Territory might well be somewhat high.

[b] Smallpox, brought into the Sydney area with the first fleet in 1788, spread rapidly across the continent, and killed many Aborigines in what is now Victoria; the full impact of white occupation was not felt until after 1835, the year Melbourne was founded.

[c] The European population of the Northern Territory is very small compared with that in the southern coastal areas of Australia. The 1961 census was the first in which the European population exceeded the Aboriginal, but in 1971 Europeans outnumbered Aborigines by more than two to one.

[d] The sharp rise between the 1966 and 1971 censuses does not represent a real rise in numbers. There was a change in the policy on race, so that mixed race persons could for the first time in 1971 *choose* the race to which they considered themselves to belong. Moreover, between these dates increasing government help to Aborigines began to make it financially beneficial to claim some Aboriginal descent, and increasing political solidarity won many part-Aborigines back to pride in their Aboriginal heritage. None of the Victorian Aborigines is of the full descent, the last having died in the mid 1960s, though there are a few who have moved from other states.

quered or at least controlled, but still Aboriginal mortality and morbidity is a cause for shame, in an affluent country proud of its health standards.

Though more publicity tends to be given to deaths of children, deaths of older Aborigines also show higher rates than for other Australians (Moodie 1973, chapters 4, 5 and 6; Kirke 1974, pp. 81–83). Moodie (1973, p. 62), using figures from the early 1960s, writes that 'The median age at death (the age at which half the deaths occur at younger ages, and half at older ages) was approximately 25 years for Northern Territory Aborigines, 40 years for Maoris, 45 years for Ameri-

can Indians and 71 years for Australia'. Even when we discount the high infant
and toddler mortality, we find that for the years 1964–1971 the life expectancy of
Central Australian Aborigines was 40.2 years at one year of age and 47.3 at
two years, compared with an expectancy for all Australians, for 1960–1962, of
71.5 and 70.6 years at the ages of one and two respectively (Kirke 1974, p. 82).
For Central Australian Aborigines the crude death rate for 1964–1971 averaged
19.4 per thousand, while that for Australia as a whole in 1969 was 8.7. (Note
that it is not possible to give comparative birth and death rates for the whole of
Australia, because birth and death certificates do not distinguish between Aborigines and other Australians. Figures quoted here have been collected by
medical personnel for certain areas and communities.)

Dr P. M. Moodie (1969, p. 180) estimates that in the early 1960s 'Aborigines,

TABLE 3

Infant mortality rates (deaths per thousand live births). Rates for Northern Territory Aborigines compared with rates for total population

	Northern Territory Aborigines				Total Population		
	Northern Region	East Arnhem Region	Southern Region	Whole Northern Territory (Aborigines)	Northern[a] Territory	Victoria[a]	Australia
1901–1905					149.4[b]	95.9	196.9
1965	89.9	145.6	196.9	142.7	25.2[c]	17.5	18.5
1966	130.6	86.0	204.3	147.3	19.6[c]	17.4	18.2
1967	107.1	101.3	92.3	100.0	63.5	16.8	18.3
1968	69.6	83.7	90.1	80.9	48.5	14.4	17.8
1969	88.7	110.6	88.8	94.8	45.3	15.0	17.9
1970	76.2	62.2	181.8	115.1	48.0	14.5	17.9
1971	86.1	99.2	219.3	142.9	60.0	14.7	17.3
1972	37.5	113.2	117.0	87.0	41.5	14.6	16.7
1973	38.7	89.4	107.1	79.7	35.6	14.3	16.5
1974	54.5	50.5	59.7	55.6	36.7	14.9	16.1

Sources: For Northern Territory Aborigines: Australian Department of Health, Canberra
(Courtesy of Dr Elspeth Seagrim). For Australian Population: Australian Bureau of Census
and Statistics.
[a] I have selected Northern Territory and Victoria for comparison because (1) N.T. has the
highest proportion of Aborigines and Victoria the lowest (except Tasmania), and (2) N.T. is the
least urbanized, Victoria the most urbanized, of the States and Territories.
[b] The 1901–1905 N.T. figure excluded Aborigines. Note that this rate is higher than the rate
for Aborigines 70 years later.
[c] The 1965 and 1966 N.T. figures exclude Aborigines of full descent, and some part-Aborigines.

TABLE 4

Age distribution of Aboriginal deaths in the Northern Territory 1964–1971

	Number of deaths
Stillborn	71
Infants	449
Toddlers	123
Two years and over	596
Total:	1239

Source: D. K. Kirke (1974, p. 83), using Northern Territory Medical Service Records.

TABLE 5

Age distribution of Aboriginal infant and toddler deaths in the Northern Territory 1965–1969

Age at death (months)	Number of deaths
Under 1	68
1– 5	101
6–11	101
12–23	93
Total:	*363*

Of these deaths 119 were due to respiratory infections, 96 to diarrhoeal disease, 33 to other infections, and 61 to malnutrition.
Source: D. K. Kirke (1974, pp. 83–84).

comprising about 1% of the Australian population contributed at least 2% of the births, 10% of infant deaths, at least 28% of deaths in the second year of life and about 9% of deaths of two to four-year olds'. Similar figures calculated for Western Australia show that in the 1960s Aborigines were 2.5% of the population, but provided 20% of infant deaths and 27.5% of deaths of one- to four-year olds (Edmonds *et al.* 1960, p. 79). Tables 3, 4 and 5 show some figures for the Northern Territory, with Table 3 indicating that greatly increased expenditure on health services in the early 1970s had a significant effect on the infant mortality rate. For the Southern Region (the desert region centred on Alice Springs) the rate fell dramatically from 219.3 in 1971 to 59.7 in 1974; this represents a reduction from fifteen times to four times the rate in the affluent state of Victoria. Infant and child mortality rates are high for the part-Aborigines of the cities too: a 1968 survey of Sydney revealed that 28 mothers had lost 128 of their live-born children under the age of one year and a further six under five years (Lickiss 1971).

Moreover, high morbidity rates for both adults and children have been recorded for Aborigines in many parts of Australia in numerous recent books and journal articles (for example, Moodie 1973; Hetzel *et al.* 1974; Kalokerinos 1974; Doherty 1974; Kamien 1976*a*, *b*). These note the prevalence of respiratory and chest disorders, parasitic infestation, venereal disease, gastroenteritis, and other ailments at much higher rates than in the white community.

THE RECORD OF ONE ENDEMIC DISEASE: TRACHOMA

Though one authority on the disease, Dr Ida Mann (1957), believes that trachoma is an introduced disease, I would side with Professor Abbie (n.d., pp. 86–87) in regarding it as endemic in the arid areas of Australia, where the words for *blind* and *old* tend to be used almost interchangeably. Indeed almost all the old people I have met in the Western Desert have been blind by about the age of sixty. White Australians in these areas are affected too, but to a lesser extent, almost certainly for environmental rather than genetic reasons.

Dr Mann (1954) reported that in 1953, in the Kimberley Division of Western Australia, of 1678 Aborigines of full descent, 948 (56.5%) were affected by trachoma, of whom 109 were blind and 82 had impaired sight. Of 507 part-Aborigines, 205 (44.4%) were affected, three were blind and two suffered impaired sight. Of 423 white persons only 26 (6.1%) were affected, none was blind, one had impaired sight. She found similar figures for other parts of Western Australia and Dr Flynn (1957) in examining 4876 Northern Territory Aborigines found 3051 (62.6%) showing effects of trachoma, of whom 359 had impaired sight, with the worst effects in the driest areas. A report in June 1976 by the recently instituted trachoma eradication unit (see below) found that in desert areas half of all Aborigines over sixty years old are blind and that most children showed some signs of the disease, indicating that up to now treatment has been relatively ineffective, because one attack gives no immunity, and each individual may suffer many re-infections.

In 1967, when I was one of a group of women research workers studying Aboriginal women's secret ceremonies, while we were recording at Indulkana in the Western desert an infection of acute and extremely painful conjunctivitis, probably trachoma, spread rapidly amongst the Aboriginal women and children, and to one of our team. There were clouds of bush-flies whose favourite resting-places were the corners of human eyes. Our team member recovered with the aid of the antibiotic ointment we carried, but on her return to Melbourne she was advised by an ophthalmologist to have frequent eye examinations and to take special precautions when on subsequent field-trips. We reported this outbreak to the health authorities concerned and learned later that a nursing sister had been sent to Indulkana and that the prescribed treatment had brought this particular outbreak under control.

I have reported this incident at some length because it reveals that speedy cure with antibiotics has been possible for some years, but that the fragmented nature of treatment has made our experience typical. However, this year, 1976, has seen a new and hopeful attack on the disease, at the instigation of Aborigines themselves. Under the direction of Mr Gordon Briscoe, of the Australian Department of Health, with the support of other Aborigines and the Aboriginal communities involved, a ten-year trachoma eradication campaign has been mounted and there is now working in the desert areas a team consisting of two white doctors and six white supporting staff, together with five Aborigines to act as interpreters and educators.

THE CHANGE IN LIFE STYLES AND ENVIRONMENT

Since European occupation of the continent the amount of change to the environment has varied with the density of human settlement, and the surviving Aborigines can be divided into three categories according to which zone of density they occupy (Rowley 1970):

1. Aborigines of full descent, those last contacted by Europeans, living in the least densely settled areas, mostly living on reserves and cattle stations in the desert areas and the northern tropics (Rowley's *Remote Aborigines*, 1971*b*). (Fig. 1.)

2. Mostly part-Aborigines, living in rural areas or on the outskirts of small towns.

3. Part-Aborigines, living in the poorest areas of the cities.

Categories (2) and (3) together make up Rowley's *Outcasts in White Australia* (1971*a*).

The first category still live in or near their old tribal areas, but have had their life styles profoundly affected. Even on the so-called reserves, there has been continuing interference and intrusion by various outsiders, such as government officers, missionaries, explorers, prospectors, surveyors, telegraph linesmen and, more recently, international mining companies. The northern Aborigines were profoundly affected during World War II by the counter-measures to the threat of Japanese invasion.

Outside the reserves their land was taken for grazing, they were expropriated from their hunting grounds and they became more and more dependent on the expropriators. The wonders of white technology gave them false hopes of an easy life, and they came to depend more and more on hand-outs. Many were soon destitute and starving, so ration depots were set up and a diet consisting

FIG. 1. Aboriginal children of the full descent from the Western Desert of Australia. (Photographed by I. M. White in the early 1970s).

mainly of white flour, white sugar and tea was substituted for the old wild foods. Policies were instituted for christianizing, educating and generally domesticating the Aborigines. Soon large groups of several hundred were living in permanent camps, occupying only a fraction of their ancient territories, over which they used to forage in small scattered bands of a dozen to fifty people.

Reasons for today's morbidity are evident if we compare the old way of life and the new. I will use the example of the desert people because it is amongst them that I have done almost all my fieldwork, and because their health seems to have shown the most severe deterioration since contact.

The physical conditions of the desert areas are rigorous: hot, dry, windy and dusty for much of the year, with a short winter season when the nights are bitterly cold. Rainfall is not only low on average, but also extremely unreliable, and there are long cycles of drought. Nevertheless, in regions where many white travellers and explorers have perished, the Aborigines survived for thousands of years and maintained a complex and satisfying social, cultural and religious life.

Early travellers describe them as healthy and vigorous, while photographs, notably those of Sir Baldwin Spencer, show slim, graceful and active women, well-fed babies and children, strong, agile men. In such rigorous conditions there would have been a weeding-out of those least fit to survive, giving high death rates at all ages compared with white Australia today, and possibly even compared with today's Aborigines.

A CHANGE IN FAMILY SIZE

Archaeologists and pre-historians believe that Aboriginal populations remained relatively constant over many millennia (Mulvaney 1975, p. 240). Though, as we have seen, the first result of European occupation was a dramatic fall in Aboriginal numbers, since about 1921 this tendency has been reversed. A significant increase appears to have taken place in the birth-rate. The oldest Aboriginal women I know (born before European contact) remark on the fact that their daughters conceive more frequently than they themselves did when younger. (This is confirmed for other areas of Australia.) The older women had five or six conceptions at most, whereas there are younger women today who conceive every year or eighteen months.

Explanation is not easy, but I can suggest two of the main factors at work here*. One is a lengthening of a woman's fertile years and the other is the introduction and use of suitable infant weaning foods. In the community in which I did most of my research, genuine surprise was shown when babies were born to schoolgirls, aged fourteen or fifteen, and to women in their forties. In fact I know three women well who had babies when they were well over forty and all told me that they refused to believe it when the nursing sister assured them that they were pregnant. This would reinforce findings from elsewhere that a change to a western diet may not only lengthen the time between menarche and menopause, but also increase the likelihood of conception in the first and last few years of this time-span.

Among the desert people in traditional times there were no suitable weaning foods, so that babies were completely dependent on their mothers' milk until they were nearly two years old, and partly dependent for another year or two. Thus ovulation may have been inhibited in most women for two to three years, and only if a new pregnancy followed too soon on the previous birth were abortion or infanticide practised. (Research in Australia has failed to discover the use of any reliable native medicament for abortion or contraception; abortions appear to have been induced by mechanical methods.) The supplementing of infant diets by well-intentioned welfare and medical personnel may often trigger ovulation in nursing mothers and cause the closer spacing of births today. Whatever the cause of this closer spacing, there is no doubt in my

---

* For ideas on the change in birth rates I am indebted to the many hours of discussion I spent with Dr Roger deRoos and his wife Carolyn deRoos, of the Division of Biological Sciences, University of Missouri, USA. They spent some months in 1975–1976 as guests in the Department of Anthropology and Sociology, Monash University, engaged in a critical study of available literature about human fertility among Australian Aborigines and other pre-industrial societies. Their extensive knowledge of the role of hormones in controlling ovulation made an important contribution to my understanding of Aboriginal fertility.

mind that it is partly to blame for much infant mortality and morbidity. The Aboriginal mothers I know are so evidently devoted to their children's welfare that it is tragic to hear that their babies are suffering from malnutrition—even in some cases, neglect. Only quite recently have the women been offered adequate family planning, which has been accepted gladly, and is now used by many to space their children.

A CHANGE IN DIET

When we collect all possible information about the traditional diet of the desert Aborigines, we find that it is high in protein, roughage, and vitamins, but low in fats and carbohydrates. Observing one of the last self-sufficient groups of desert hunter–gatherers in 1966, the anthropologist Dr R. A. Gould and his wife noted that the main staples in their diet were varieties of solanum fruit and that for each man, woman and child, the women were collecting about three pounds a day of these so-called 'desert tomatoes' (Gould 1969, pp. 261–262). A recent analysis (Peterson 1977) of three species of solanum shows that all rate better than tomatoes in protein, fat, calories and ascorbic acid. Thus the daily intake of vitamin C by the group studied by Gould would exceed by many times that recommended by most dieticians in western society.

In addition to these fruits the women's contribution to the diet of desert Aborigines consisted of ground seeds, a considerable number of other fruits in smaller quantities, various bulbs and roots, and edible green leaves. The women and the children caught lizards, snakes, small birds and mammals, and collected birds' eggs. The men hunted large game such as kangaroo and emu, and of these nothing edible was wasted. For example, the blood and bone marrow were consumed and, in times of extreme drought, even the stomach contents were eaten*, thus providing some half-digested green vegetable food.

Today at some settlements the whole population, men, women and children, are fed in big communal kitchens, but this practice is gradually being abandoned. In other settlements until the mid-sixties rations were given out to the whole population. Rations used to consist of flour, sugar and tea only, in the expectation that the Aborigines would continue the old practice of hunting and gathering. They still hunt everywhere—with varying success—but gathering of 'bush tucker' is steadily declining and has long since ceased at many settlements. (Only a regularly moving group can depend on wild food.)

* For this information about eating the stomach contents, together with the information used later (p. 284) about 'strong' and 'weak' foods, I am grateful to Miss Margaret Bain, who has worked as a missionary among Aborigines for many years, and is now a graduate student in anthropology at Monash University.

Instead of handing out rations the settlements now have quite well-stocked food stores and the people buy what they like. In order to assess the diet I served in a food store at a mission for a couple of weeks. For a family of five people the weekly purchase would be 25 lb of white flour, $^1/_2$–1 lb tea, 6 lb white sugar, two 12 oz cans meat, $1^1/_2$ lb jam, one large 30 oz can of fruit (peaches or pears), 6 lb lean mutton, $^1/_2$ lb butter, 8 lb white bread, six oranges or apples (if available), 1 lb full cream dried milk, 1 lb semi-sweet biscuits, 12 eggs. The meat would probably be supplemented in most weeks by a quarter of a 60 lb kangaroo or of a 40 lb wombat, or perhaps by two rabbits. *No* native fruits or vegetables were collected in most weeks. (There were a few fruits which would be collected in season, but none in considerable amounts.) During the week each child over two years old would get three 13 oz cans of soft drink and three packets of potato crisps, and each adult six 13 oz cans of beer. In addition, a considerable number of flagons (half gallons) of sweet port would come into the camp. I was told one evening that at least sixty flagons had arrived. These would have been shared that same evening by perhaps sixty or so persons.

The only food that might last the whole week would be the flour which, when the bread had been consumed, would be made into three or four large dampers, to be eaten with butter and jam (if any were left) or dunked in sweet tea.

The mission provided some supplementary foods for babies, toddlers, school-children and old-age pensioners. Even so the contrast between traditional and modern diet speaks for itself. In the old days Aborigines hunted and gathered the food that nature offered and this provided a healthy diet, so that there was no need to be diet conscious. Today they still take what food is most readily available, and cannot easily understand that the cheapest foods offered by the white man in his store provide such a poor diet.

GENETIC FACTORS

Some clinical symptoms have been observed in Aboriginal patients suggesting that genetic factors might be affecting Aboriginal health. At least ten thousand years of genetic isolation is long enough for some adaptations to have occurred and for mutations lacking selective advantage to have become established. Dr R. L. Kirk (1972, p. 99), one of Australia's foremost human geneticists, suggests that there might be differences in susceptibility to particular diseases and in physiological and biochemical function, both between black and white Australians and between different groups of Aborigines.

The possibility of differing susceptibility to introduced infectious diseases is suggested by the high death rates already noted. Instances of difference in physiological and biological function are the high rate of *diabetes mellitus* in older Aborigines (Moodie 1973, p. 178) and the high incidence of lactase deficiency (Elliott *et al.* 1967; McCracken 1971; Harrison 1975). But there is some disagreement as to whether the lactase deficiency is genetic or an 'acquired factor due to long-standing chronic dysentery in the Aboriginal babies and children' (Clements 1970, p. 141).

In their nomadic condition it is doubtful if the Aborigines suffered from degenerative diseases such as atherosclerosis and hypertension, though they seem to follow the same course as white Australians if they adopt similar life-styles (Moodie 1973, p. 212). However, there is one observation I would like to make from my own experience: there seem to be more centenarian Aborigines of full descent than one would expect. I myself have met two of them and know of at least one more. Their ages are not certified by birth certificate and some detective work needs to be done, as a colleague and I did in the case of Jack Long (Hercus & White 1971). In 1970 when we wrote his biography we were sure that he was born no later than 1872, but probably several years earlier. In 1976 he is still fit and well, still able to walk, see, hear and (unusual for an Aborigine of his generation) read. An old man, whom we know to be in his late eighties, says of an old woman, still alive but now becoming senile, 'She was a married woman, settled down, when I can first remember her, when I was a real little fellow'. There is a kinship terminology in Aboriginal languages for great-grandparents, and in the camp I used to work in there was an old man, now dead, who had great-great-grandchildren.

At the other end of life, Annette Hamilton (1971) has suggested that there was a selective advantage for those infants and toddlers who could survive a period of malnutrition between about twelve months and three years. This is the period during which breast milk alone tends to be insufficient for the child's nutritional needs, but at the same time suitable weaning foods are not available in a hunter–gatherer economy. Among traditionally oriented Aboriginal communities there is considerable resistance on the part of mothers to accepting new ideas about weaning. Moreover, since Aboriginal mothers carry their young children most of the day, they prefer them not to grow too quickly. Recently when some Aboriginal mothers at Alice Springs were shown some well-nourished white babies, as an example of the results of a recommended weaning programme, they asked 'but how would we carry them?' So not only the availability of food but also the mothers' well-being might select for those who could survive a period of malnutrition.

Whatever the true facts about this particular pattern of selection, we cannot doubt that in the rigorous conditions of a hunting and gathering life in the desert there was considerable selection for resistance to alternations of famine and plenty.

It should be noted that none of the genetic factors I have discussed would seriously affect mortality and morbidity if recognized and treated. Moodie (1973, pp. 281-284) sums up the situation with regard to the more serious genetic diseases thus: 'traditional and present-day full-blood populations have not produced any evidence of serious recessive defects (under 'inbreeding' conditions which test for their presence) which are not already present in the white Australian population'.

THE CHANGE IN LIFE-STYLE AND ITS SOCIAL CONSEQUENCES

Aborigines had traditionally lived in small nomadic bands, containing from twenty-five to fifty persons, which only came together occasionally. The new life-style differs from the old not only in occupation and diet but also in the social environment.

As Aborigines moved into mission and government settlements, more and more white administrators arrived to take care of them. On the whole they have been treated kindly but as if they were children rather than adults. They have become more and more dependent on this alien paternalist authority, so that group decisions have been taken out of their hands. These settlements have become total institutions, with many of the attributes of Erving Goffman's asylums. Though present policy is to make these communities autonomous, the long period of dependence has made it hard to develop new decision-making processes or to revive the traditional ones.

Compared with the active, vigorous life of their hunter–gatherer forebears, most adult Aborigines today live a somewhat inactive existence. Estimates today are that half the total Aboriginal work-force is unemployed. In general Aboriginal women have always found it so hard to get jobs at all that most are not even registered in the work force. In the tribal settlements the women sit around much of the day doing nothing except play cards. The change to a very fattening diet has already been described, so that it is no surprise that they have changed from the slim graceful figures of the Spencer photographs to the overweight figures of today. The men are more active but tend to drink more alcohol than the women and most are overweight too.

Similarly in rural and urban Aboriginal communities, unemployment, poverty and discrimination have brought inactivity, apathy and depression, and here too it is hard for community leaders to arise.

Research, notably that of Dr Cawte (1974), has shown a high rate of psychiatric disorders in several communities studied. The outward symptoms of a deeper social malaise all pale into insignificance by comparison with the most widespread symptom, the abuse of alcohol.

Today, with the exception of the most remote settlements and missions, all Aboriginal communities are within reach of outlets for alcoholic beverages, and most experience more or less frequent incidents of drunken violence, sometimes leading to destruction of property, personal injury, even death. Moreover expenditure on alcohol adds to unemployment, diverts money from food, and causes ill-health among heavy drinkers, while drunkenness and its consequences send many Aborigines to gaol.

Amongst various counter-measures suggested or tried, the two most hopeful are recent experiments by Aborigines themselves. At Finke, N.T., the local Aboriginal Council has bought the hotel (with the help of a government loan). Rules are made by the Council, one being that no flagons are sold and that no alcoholic drinks are to leave the premises. Near Alice Springs the Central Australian Aboriginal Congress has opened a country property, a fruit and vegetable farm, as a rehabilitation and treatment centre for alcoholics. Neither of these experiments has been going long enough to assess their effects.

Another symptom of psychosocial disorder is the frequency of outbreaks of petrol-sniffing amongst young men and boys in a few Aboriginal communities. Several deaths and some permanent brain-damage has resulted. Nurcombe (1974) suggests that solutions might be found 'in the educational system and through the mobilization of existing traditional authority'. He found need for Aborigines' own self-respect to be enhanced and for new community structures to be evolved.

Yet another manifestation of social disorder is continuous and obsessive gambling by many adults in most Aboriginal communities. But then they have little else to do.

ABORIGINAL BELIEFS ABOUT BIRTH, DEATH AND SICKNESS

Beliefs about birth and death show great differences from ours. Sexual intercourse is a necessary but not sufficient cause for pregnancy. The woman must also be entered by a spirit to animate the fetus. If a child dies young then its spirit will return to the spirit store and may enter the woman again when she again conceives. But if a baby dies away from its home country then the spirit may not be able to find its way back and may be lost entirely. So a group suffers double grief if a baby dies in a white hospital far from home. On the other hand, grief at the death of a baby who dies at home is not quite as acute as it might otherwise be, since the mother believes it will be born to her again. It has been said that Aboriginal infant mortality is a white not an Aboriginal problem, since it seems that white intervention has reduced the rate below what it was before contact and the mothers are brought up to accept their children's deaths with stoicism.

Good health is considered the natural state and is not directly connected with food and living habits. Food is eaten for pleasure and to satisfy hunger, though in the old days there was knowledge that one should eat both meat ('strong food') and vegetable food ('weak food') and that without food and water one would die. The older women and men had some concepts of what foods were good for babies and children, in addition to breast milk, but they find it very hard to translate this knowledge into the foods available today. Because adults show hunger and look for food, a mother applies the same principle to her children and in consequence a child may not be *offered* food if he does not demand it. This is all very well for the healthy child, but the child who is listless through a minor health problem may fall into a state of malnutrition through not demanding food. This is perhaps one of the most important contradictions between the two belief systems, and makes it hard for Aboriginal mothers to understand what doctors, nurses, health educators are trying to tell them. Moreover, since no connection is seen between dirt, infection, and ill-health, teaching about cleanliness is also not understood.

Traditionally oriented Aborigines still believe that disease and death are caused by evil spirits or human sorcery, not by bacteria, viruses or other agents listed in the western medical system. A death may be followed by an 'inquest', which in turn may lead to a revenge expedition if human sorcery is discovered. However, deaths of the very old and the very young are regarded as in some way natural and need not be avenged.

Each Aboriginal group has at least one medicine man, the native healer, who has an intimate knowledge of his fellows and their interrelationships. For specific ailments and injuries there is a compendium of herbs and treatments, known to all adults, men and women. For patients whose ailments are not so easily diagnosed the medicine man may use massage and other magical acts to reverse the supernatural cause or to remove foreign bodies. The women specialize in performing ceremonies with the sick person at the centre. The patient thus becomes the focus of the group's attention and activities and feels not only comforted but once more at one with his neighbours. At least this creates the proper climate for recovery and may be expected to work in most cases.

If a person becomes gravely ill, then the native healers, with wisdom and experience behind them, may recognize their inability to effect a cure, and warn the patient and his family that death is imminent. Those of us from the western world who have tried to understand something of Aboriginal culture have the greatest respect for the attitude to death, whether it is his own death or that of a near kinsman that an Aborigine must face. Contrary to Dylan Thomas's command, they 'go gentle into that good night'. Unnatural procedures, such as hospitals use, to give the patient a few more days of painful or unconscious existence, are deeply resented. In 1974, while visiting an Aboriginal community, I went with a friend to the hospital some miles away, to pay a farewell visit to one of the big men of that community who had suffered a severe stroke. Knowing full well that he could not recover, about fifty of his kin had moved to the vicinity of the hospital, and were camped there in the middle of the new white mining town, waiting for the appropriate moment to start the great mourning ceremonies. We found the patient completely unconscious, in an intensive care ward with every kind of life support, surrounded by his three wives who appeared to be more upset because he was alive than because he was dying. That night he died and I believe, though I did not enquire too closely, that the hospital staff had complied with the wishes of his wives and kin to let him die. He had after all left them when he fell into unconsciousness, but custom forebade them to mourn for him until he had indeed died.

HEALTH EDUCATION FOR TRIBAL PEOPLE

A number of programmes have been organized by medical and welfare organizations (government and independent). For over three years Sandra Stacy was the health educator for a health education programme organized by the Institute for Aboriginal Development, an autonomous body based in Alice Springs. She learned the language of the people she worked with, she lived with them in the camps and also had a few of them at a time for a series of three-week courses in Alice Springs. She made the most impressive efforts to communicate with Aborigines, and to understand their belief system regarding health and hygiene. She has recently summed up her work as follows (Stacy 1976/77):

'The aim was to change the health practices of the Aboriginal people in the areas of nutrition and hygiene, thereby contributing to the efforts of other health workers in lowering the incidence of Aboriginal infant morbidity and mortality. It was hoped to give knowledge in a way that could be understood by the Aborigines and help them to realize the implications of their changing life style so they would see a need to change their health practices. Each phase of the programme was built on, or adapted to Aboriginal culture and needs as perceived by the planners. These people wanted behaviour to change not because of force or compliance, but because the Aborigines involved saw the actions as a means to an end which they themselves desired....

'Towards the end of 1974 the programme was formally evaluated and an attempt was made to both describe what was happening and explain why it was happening....

'It was found that knowledge about European food and hygiene practices taught was retained by the participants in the programmes and in some instances this had been passed on to other members of their group. When asked to do so these people could repeat accurately the nutritional needs of an infant or the germ theory. They were also able to perform actions necessary to apply this knowledge and on occasions did so for a limited period, e.g. one group bathed babies for three weeks after their return home. There was no evidence of lasting change.

'These results indicated that the desired changes had not occurred....

'It appears however, that Aboriginal people view the high incidence of infant mortality and morbidity in much the same way as Europeans view the mounting road injury and death toll. Europeans express concern about vehicular accidents, they are distressed when lives are lost, but on the whole they accept that these are part of our way of life....

'There was no change because they did not see the health teaching as being relevant to them. They saw participation in the programme as being a means to an end which they themselves desired, which was to build relationships with Europeans.

'The reason the programme was not relevant was because until those conducting it understood the meanings the Aborigines gave to their actions, and realized the significance of understanding these meanings, they were not able to make it relevant.'

THE RURAL AND URBAN ABORIGINES: THE OUTCASTS IN WHITE SOCIETY

Most of the discussion so far has been concerned with the Aborigines of full descent, living in their own communities (even if these are dominated by white administrators) and clinging to traditional language, custom and belief as much as they possibly can. In contrast, in the areas of Australia completely taken over by the Europeans, the Aborigines, mostly of part descent, live as fringe-dwellers, suffering discrimination in employment, education, housing, and all the welfare services, including health.

The majority of dwellings occupied by the part-Aborigines are substandard by Australian standards. Outside some small towns are reserves where the houses are made of corrugated iron, cardboard and any other available material, with poor water supply and little or no sanitation. In the cities Aborigines live in overcrowded slum housing with plumbing unsatisfactory and inefficient. Though the women work hard to keep their families properly clothed and fed, the diet tends to be inadequate for growing children. The birth-rate is higher than in the white Australian society, though here too, as with the tribal people, family planning is now available and used.

The patterns of ill-health are those of any population living in such condi-

TABLE 6

Aboriginal housing, June 1971 Census

	Aboriginal dwellings (%)	Total Australian dwellings (%)
Improvised dwelling	25.6	Below 0.5
No gas or electricity	30.3	1.0
No kitchen, no bathroom	19.4	0.4
No sewage disposal	31.1[a]	4.0[a]
No television	51.6	9.4

Source: Census of Population and Housing (Bulletin 9.).
[a] Includes 'method of disposal not stated'.

tions, with poor housing and sanitation, overcrowding and low incomes. Discrimination on account of race makes it much more difficult for them than for whites in poverty. It is hard for one individual, one family or the whole community to make even small gains. Those few individuals and families who achieve success can only do so at the expense of losing friends, and even if they manage this step they face a continual battle to maintain their position.

HEALTH SERVICES FOR ABORIGINES

The tribal people may suffer from bad housing, unemployment and poverty, but they have various medical services provided for their benefit. A typical settlement of 400 people is likely to have a reasonably well-equipped clinic and hospital, manned by two resident nursing sisters, and two or three Aboriginal nursing aides. The Flying Doctor visits the settlement perhaps once a month and in emergency a plane can leave the Flying Doctor base at short notice to bring a patient from the settlement to a large hospital and if necessary carries a doctor and nurse on board. (This service is of course available to all people, white and black, over the whole of outback Australia.)

The resident sisters make a visit to the Aboriginal camp every day, particularly to check the old people and the pre-school children. They visit the school too to see the school children. Either a sister or a welfare officer provides daily supplementary foods—cereal, milk, vitamins, fruit—to babies and toddlers. They usually have some programme in operation to teach the mothers about weaning foods, though, as described above, such programmes have not so far been very successful.

The school children are provided at a small charge with a midday meal at school, which is dietetically planned to yield at least 50% of the daily requirement of food and vitamins.

In contrast to these home-based institutions, the Flying Doctor flies sick people to the unfamiliar and sterile surroundings of a big hospital, which are hostile and frightening to the Aboriginal patient, thus separated from his or her social group. It has even been the practice to fly out quite small babies without their mothers. They are then necessarily weaned and finally returned to the camp with a bottle and formula. With the realization that a bottle in the camp conditions is equivalent to a death sentence for a small baby, this practice is now declining; if possible the mother is flown out with the baby, or the required treatment is given in the local hospital, which may not be able to offer the full range of services, but presents a less traumatic experience.

For the Aborigines in the rural and urban areas, hospitals, and even doctors' surgeries, may become places to fear and to avoid, if they have experienced ethnocentric and authoritarian medical treatment, and if white patients have made them feel unclean. Many outback hospitals are segregated, with quite inferior facilities for Aborigines. This practice is now disappearing, with attempts to give equal treatment to Aborigines. While medical treatment for tribal Aborigines has been virtually free, until recently rural and urban Aborigines had to pay for it or accept charity. This made them delay seeking treatment and bear stoically many ills that would send white Australians to the doctor immediately.

Where they are available, the Aboriginal Medical Services have done much for Aboriginal health (see below).

CONCLUSIONS

Now I come back to the title of this paper—*Pitfalls to avoid*. Though measures are being taken, at least in some areas, to avoid such pitfalls I will list them nevertheless:

1. Taking away from the Aborigines all responsibility for their own health.
2. Ethnocentric and authoritarian attitudes of medical personnel.
3. Little attempt to communicate with patients. Shouting at them in English rather than attempting to learn their languages or to use interpreters.
4. The building of large impersonal hospitals long distances from the patients' homes, rather than up-grading existing local facilities.
5. An attitude of curing illness rather than encouraging good health.
6. Failure in attempts to understand Aboriginal attitudes and beliefs about health and disease. Ridiculing these beliefs as 'primitive superstitions' and treating the medicine men with contempt, rather than trying to integrate the two systems and to work *with* the medicine men and the wise women. As it is, Aboriginal patients take medicine without understanding its implications, and view advice given by doctors and nurses as irrational.

7. Instructing patients to carry out procedures which are impossible for them to perform. An example is to instruct a mother to carry out a procedure by which she will cause her child to cry (such as cleaning a wound). She will not do it, because an Aboriginal mother must never cause her child to cry (Hamilton 1974).

8. Because Aboriginal health problems tend to arouse guilt feelings in white Australians, the idea has arisen that all that is needed is unlimited finance and problems will be solved. Much money is needed, but if it is spent without careful planning and insight it may not cause commensurate benefit (the large impersonal hospitals are an example).

9. A final pitfall is the belief that medical measures alone will bring Aboriginal health up to white standards—that is, a failure to realize that health problems arise more from low social and economic status, from poor housing, food and education, than from lack of health care. Many medical men do in fact fully realize this. Drs Cawte & Kamien (1974) in particular have advocated that a doctor must act as a community change agent and, without being authoritarian, must encourage the people themselves to act for their own social and economic advancement. Dr Moodie (1974, p. 276) stresses the need to restore 'some of the quality of life which one feels was appreciated by Aborigines in their traditional environment'.

Finally, lest it be thought from some harsh words that I have written that all doctors and nurses are thoughtless and arrogant when dealing with Aboriginal patients, let me add that in my experience most of them are deeply concerned, and dedicated to Aboriginal welfare. However, a lack of mutual understanding with consequent failure in communication may lead to frustration and even hostility on both sides. For this reason I have stressed the necessity for understanding and communication.

SOME POSITIVE MEASURES: THE ABORIGINAL VIEWPOINT

In the last few years, in spite of new hospitals, orientation courses for doctors and nurses, education programmes for Aborigines, and other reforms, babies continue to die, children's sight and hearing is still damaged, many adults are chronically sick. In many areas improvements in health have been made, but at a much slower rate than the expenditure of money and effort would warrant. Some of the necessary measures were stated forcefully to me in an interview with Gordon Briscoe, an Aboriginal leader who works in the Aboriginal section of the Australian Department of Health, Canberra. The following paragraphs are a summary of his statement.

The different problems and needs of tribal, rural and urban communities must be recognized. He stressed point (1) above, that responsibility must be handed back to the Aborigines themselves and their communities. Already such a step has been taken by the Central Australian Aboriginal Congress, which has set up a health service in Alice Springs. This now employs three white doctors and a white administrator, but has Aboriginal directors. The Congress also runs the alcoholic rehabilitation centre already mentioned.

Rather than building large European-oriented hospitals (for example, a new $ 5 million, 21-bed hospital at Yuendumu, N.T.) it might have been better to put these resources into strengthening the tribal infrastructure, training medicine men and women so that their intimate knowledge of the community and its psychological, as well as merely physical, needs could be reinforced by basic knowledge of when and how European medicine could best be called in.

The traditional self-management of health problems within the extended family groups needs to be revived.

From the Aborigines' point of view this means taking from the European system what they feel they need and want to reinforce their own system. But they will only feel involved in the system if European health personnel are genuinely the *servants* of the Aboriginal communities, replacing the old authoritarian attitude of European doctors and nurses.

Aborigines living in the towns and rural areas have suffered even more than in the tribal areas from discrimination by the medical establishment. In the urban areas, where Aborigines live in poverty, we can at last see some hopeful signs. All the big capital cities now have Aboriginal Medical Services, directed by Aborigines, and employing European and Aboriginal medical personnel (Briscoe 1974).

Aborigines living as fringe-dwellers in the rural areas and small towns present a different problem again. Here the communities are stagnant and depressed. First, possible leaders must be chosen and trained in community skills such as finance and administration. Only when the communities regain identity and motivation will the organization of community health become possible.

ACKNOWLEDGEMENTS

In addition to Gordon Briscoe I am grateful to many friends and colleagues, Aboriginal and non-Aboriginal, who have helped me with facts and ideas. Unfortunately, space has not permitted me to make as much use as I would have liked of the thoughtful comments I received on the first draft of this paper.

References

ABBIE, A.A. n.d. *The Original Australians*, Reed, Sydney

BRISCOE, G. (1974) The Aboriginal medical service in Sydney, in Hetzel *et al.* (1974) *(q.v.)*

CAWTE, J. (1974) *Medicine is the Law: Studies in Psychiatric Anthropology of Australian Tribal Societies*, Rigby, Australia

CAWTE, J. & KAMIEN, M. (1974) The doctor as a social change agent in Bourke N.S.W., in Hetzel *et al.* (1974) *(q.v.)*

CENSUS OF POPULATION AND HOUSING (30th June 1971) Bulletin 9, *The Aboriginal Population*, Commonwealth Bureau of Census and Statistics, Canberra

CLEMENTS, F.W. (1970) Comment in *The Impact of Civilisation on the Biology of Man* (Boyden, S.V., ed.), pp. 140–141, Australian National University Press, Canberra

CURR, E.M. (1886) *The Australian Race*, vol. 1, Government Printer, Melbourne

DOHERTY, R.L. (1974) A microbiologist looks at Aboriginal health. *Med. J. Aust.* 2, 149–155

EDMONDS, R., ROBERTS, R.W. & SCHLAFRIG, G. (1960) The morbidity of young children in Western Australia: the Aborigines' contribution. *Aust. Paediatr. J. 6*, 76–80

ELLIOTT, R.B., MAXWELL, G.M. & VAWSER, N. (1967) Lactase maldigestion in Australian Aboriginal children. *Med. J. Aust. 1*, 46–49

FLYNN, F. (1957) Trachoma among natives of the Northern Territory. *Med. J. Aust.* 2, 269–271

GOULD, R.A. (1969) Subsistence behaviour among the Western Desert Aborigines of Australia. *Oceania 39*, 253–274

HAMILTON, A. (1971) Socio-cultural factors in health among the Pitjantjatjara: a preliminary report. South Australian Department of Health (Typescript)

HAMILTON, A. (1974) The traditionally oriented community, in Hetzel *et al.* (1974) *(q.v.)*

HARRISON, G.G. (1975) Primary adult lactase deficiency: a problem in anthropological genetics. *Am. Anthropol. 77*, 812–835

HERCUS, L.A. & WHITE, I.M. (1971) The last Madimadi man. *Victorian Naturalist 88*, 11–19

HETZEL, B.S., DOBBIN, M., LIPPMANN, L. & EGGLESTON, E. (eds.) (1974) *Better Health for Aborigines* (Report of a National Seminar at Monash University), University of Queensland Press, Brisbane

KALOKERINOS, A. (1974) *Every Second Child*, Nelson, Melbourne

KAMIEN, M. (1976a) The physical health of Aboriginal children in Bourke, N.S.W. *Med. J. Aust. (Special Suppl.) 1*, 33–37

KAMIEN, M. (1976b) The physical health of Aboriginal adults in Bourke, N.S.W. *Med. J. Aust. (Special Suppl.) 1*, 38–43 (see also Cawte & Kamien 1974)

KIRK, R.L. (1972) Genetic diversity among Aborigines, in *The Australian Aboriginal Child (Report of the First Australian Ross Conference)*, Ross Laboratories, Cronulla, N.S.W.

KIRKE, D.K. (1974) The traditionally oriented community, in Hetzel *et al.* (1974) *(q.v.)*

LICKISS, J.N. (1971) Aboriginal children in Sydney: the socio-economic environment. *Oceania 41*, 201–228

McCRACKEN, R.D. (1971) Lactase deficiency: an example of dietary evolution. *Curr. Anthropol. 12*, 479–517

MANN, I. (1954) *Ophthalmic Survey of the Kimberley Division of Western Australia*, Perth, Government Printer

MANN, I. (1957) Probable origins of trachoma in Australasia. *Bull. W.H.O. 16*, 1165–1187

MOODIE, P.M. (1969) Mortality and morbidity in Australian Aboriginal children. *Med. J. Aust. 1*, 180–185

MOODIE, P.M. (1973) *Aboriginal Health*, Australian National University Press, Canberra

MOODIE, P.M. (1974) The part-Aboriginal community, in Hetzel *et al.* (1974) *(q.v.)*

MULVANEY, D.J. (1975) *The Prehistory of Australia*, Penguin, Ringwood, Australia

NURCOMBE, B. (1974) Petrol inhalation in Arnhem Land, in Hetzel *et al.* (1974) *(q.v.)*

PETERSON, N. (1977) Aboriginal uses of Australian Solanaceae, in *The Biology and Taxonomy of the Solanaceae* (Hawkes, J., ed.), Academic Press, New York, in press

POPULATION AND AUSTRALIA: *A demographic analysis and projection* (1975) First report of the
    National Population Inquiry ('Borrie Report'), vol. 2, Government Publishing Service,
    Canberra
ROWLEY, C.D. (1907) *The Destruction of Aboriginal Society: Aboriginal Policy and Practice*,
    vol 1, Australian National University Press, Canberra
ROWLEY, C.D. (1971*a*) *Outcasts in White Australia: Aboriginal Policy and Practice*, vol. 2,
    Australian National University Press, Canberra
ROWLEY, C.D. (1971*b*) *The Remote Aborigines: Aboriginal Policy and Practice*, vol. 3, Australian
    National University Press, Canberra
STACY, S. (1976/77) What do we mean by subjective data? An analysis of a health education
    programme in Alice Springs. *Australian Nurses' Journal*, December–January 1976/77

Discussion

Stanley: I would like to describe briefly the present situation in Western
Australia, which I know best. As one goes from desert areas to the rich coastal
area the condition of the Aborigines changes. The desert tribes, who are mostly
still full-blood Aborigines, have a lower birth rate and better health than the
fringe dwellers and squatters round the towns. These areas contain the real
tragedies of assimilation. The Aboriginal population is one of the most rapidly
growing populations in the world, with many families of seven, and a high
fertility rate.

In the urban ghettos of the west, Aborigines are very badly off. On the East
coast they are now organizing themselves, but in, for example, metropolitan
Perth, the Aborigines' condition is far worse. Infant mortality is very high.
The age-specific mortality rates as compared to those of whites, Maoris and
Cape coloureds in South Africa are shown in Table 1.

TABLE 1 (Stanley)

Age-specific mortality rates for Northern Territory Aborigines and others, 1959

Age group	Aborigines	Australia	Maoris	US Indians	South Africa Coloured
< 1 year	142.0	22.0	52.9	56.6	155.2
1–	64.7	2.0	5.8	—	—
2–	12.5	1.2	2.2	—	—
3–	5.8	0.9	2.6	—	—
4–	4.8	0.7	1.4	—	—
1–4 years	21.6	1.2	3.0	3.8	23.4

(From Moodie 1973, p. 50.)

The reserve and mission people live in appalling conditions, on what are no
more than rubbish heaps. The next stage up is round the towns (the peri-urban
areas). Here I found high levels of infection in the children, with suppurative

otitis media in 60–80%, often with deafness resulting. The health of the full-blood Aborigines is not so bad as that of the part Aborigines.

There are *no* hunter–gatherers left in Australia now; everyone has become assimilated to some degree, and the assimilation problems are extreme: venereal disease and alcoholism are prevalent everywhere, although there are no accurate incidence rates. The Aboriginal population declined drastically in the late nineteenth and early twentieth centuries but is now increasing again (Lancaster Jones 1970), as Isobel White showed in her Tables 1 and 2 (pp. 270, 271). It is predicted that there will be a million Aborigines by the end of the century (Lancaster Jones 1970). There is already a 50% unemployment rate, and the unemployed are supported by social security cheques. The problem is also that of the apathetic Whites, who exploit the Aborigines. Compensation for mineral wealth found on Aboriginal land was given in cash, not in land or in some more permanent way. There has been little concern for including Aboriginal opinion in the running of the health and social services.

Morbidity is actually rising, despite the provision of health services, for some conditions such as venereal disease, including congenital syphilis, and trachoma. Migration in and out has increased and VD is now found far out among the desert people.

Alcoholism leads to social disruption; the women now do everything, while the men drink. For example, the women collect the welfare payment cheque and also spend it. On the fringes of Perth the women are now starting to drink and are commonly prostitutes. This hastens family breakdown, with children being born annually, each to a different father.

The rates of gastroenteritis in children and of tuberculosis are also rising, and so is the incidence of psychiatric illness, including among adolescents.

Although the 'Aboriginal problem' is a serious one it is numerically a *small* problem, by comparison with those of other countries like India or South America. There has been a lot of change in awareness of the Aboriginal people by white Australian society recently. Guilt may have something to do with it; considerable publicity was brought about by the Aboriginal Rights movements around Australia. Promises were made by the Labour government which came to power in 1972 and much money was set aside for Aboriginal health and welfare. This, however, to a great extent was abused. One of the plans of that government was to form a consultative council to which Aborigines from all over Australia would be elected. The council was to advise the government on Aboriginal matters. But the result was that the educated and vocal Aborigines who had done so much for Aborigines locally were removed from their own communities and sent to Canberra. This was devastating in Western Australia, where there were so few educated and articulate Aborigines. In Canberra they got huge salaries but no power; they spent most of the three years of that government on strike, fighting the Minister for Aboriginal Affairs for more money so that they could do something. In the recent election (1975) the Aborigines were less of an issue and interest has faded. In some places civil rights leaders are being surreptitiously removed from public awareness by being forced into compromising positions and then arrested, as happened recently in Queensland.

Harrison: What do you think could and should be done now, supposing you had a committed white population?

Stanley: The first thing is unquestionably land rights; any Aborigine will tell you that. They want land, where *they* want it and so that they can do what they want with it.

Harrison: You mean some form of separate development, rather than assimilation?

Stanley: Yes, definitely.

Hugh-Jones: In Australia, visiting Aboriginal communities, like everyone else I was horrified by what I saw until I reached Arnhem Land. There was a vast difference between the Aborigines here and those in central Australia. It seemed to me that the difference lay in what their lives meant, what they were doing and why they were doing it. In Arnhem Land the people had occupations —hunting, for example; they were therefore thinner and in better physical condition. This is a fascinating example of the problem I tried to state at the beginning of the symposium, a problem that occurs in our own society, namely dependency. Once a group of people is dependent, in this case on the white population, there is nothing in life for them.

As a specific question, do you think that a lot of the obesity seen in Aborigines is simply the indirect result of boredom?

White: It is a product of their diet of flour, sugar and tea, *plus* the fact that most of the women sit gambling most of the day; the men join in at 5 p.m. when they come in from work (if they have it), and the gambling goes on till about 7 p.m. It happens in Arnhem Land too, incidentally. Yes, it is essentially boredom, and the lack of more constructive things to do.

Stanley: That includes lack of exercise.

Shaper: I hope the resemblance to our own society, with obesity among the bingo-playing female population, will be brought home to us!

Truswell: You mentioned lactase deficiency—the lack of the enzyme in the intestine that splits milk sugar. In fact, Whites are the exception in the world; most of the world's population—in Asia and most of Africa—develop a partial lack of this enzyme after infancy (Cook 1973). They can therefore drink only a small amount of milk. So the Australian Aboriginals are more or less the same people elsewhere in having this enzyme deficiency.

White: The deficiency used to have disastrous effects, but until recently the white nurses and doctors who treat Aboriginal children could not know about it. Previously, the child who was already undernourished, and came for treatment for diarrhoea, was cured of the diarrhoea but was then filled up with milk, with the result that diarrhoea was likely to recur if the child happened to be lactase-deficient. Now alternatives to milk are given to treat the malnutrition.

Truswell: Is much hunting done now by the Aborigines? You showed us some illustrations of women hunting, which seems unusual for such communities by comparison with the rest of the world, where the hunting is normally done by the men. Is this part of the breakdown of the society?

White: I think it may be change but not breakdown. I asked the women if they were allowed to hunt and kill the kangaroo, which has great ritual as well as economic importance. They told me they were allowed to hunt and kill it if they could. In the old days only the men would have had suitable weapons, spears, spear-throwers, and clubs or boomerangs. Today, in that area, the Nullarbor Plain in South Australia, introduced European breeds of hunting dogs are used, and appear to be more effective killers than the traditional weapons or the semi-domesticated dingo. These hunting dogs are valuable possessions, which can belong to men or women, and can also be borrowed for a hunting expedition. Hunting parties can be all men, all women, or mixed. (I have written an article on the subject of change in hunting practices: see White 1972.)

Hamilton: The conditions you have described are remarkably similar to those of the slums of Glasgow fifty years ago or the overcrowded poverty areas of many large cities, particularly with rapid urbanization in the third world. The most striking picture for me was the amount of gastroenteritis in communities with very poor water supplies and even single standpipes. If money is to be poured into health centres and health facilities, it would seem more practical and cost-effective to spend it on water, and piped water, to each house, and good sanitation, rather than to bother with health services and doctors. That water and sanitation are the innovations most productive of good health is axiomatic, but it requires education. Do you believe that you can instil the habit of washing the clothes or bodies of children among the Aborigines? This would depend on the change of attitude. Would such a programme work?

Stanley: I think it is starting. This is where the public health nurse is so important, because she is the preventive arm of the health service. Our recommendation to the West Australian Government was to increase the number of public health nurses (Alpers *et al.* 1972). They educate the mothers to keep their children clean, but of course the mothers can't do this if they lack the facilities. This is where the government is being so misdirected in its efforts. It installs expensive health services; it tries to get doctors to work in these areas by offering them large salaries and houses. It should be looking at the situation in a practical way and asking what the real needs are. This is where we, the epidemiologists, come in; we have to point out to the government and to the public health service what is required.

Hamilton: The West Indies are now doing exactly this with their public health nurses and the nurse-practitioner as a concept, but the problem is to persuade the public to accept it.

Hugh-Jones: I wrote a report (unpublished) for the Sultan of Oman making precisely this point that hospitals are of least importance to the community and that you must start at the other end. But there is an emotional desire among the public in general to 'look after' people and give them medicine, rather than to really look at the problem and start with the most basic needs. This wish to pour in money and hospitals is partly based on guilt and also on finding an easy way of appeasing that feeling.

Tyrrell: In Taiwan it was shown that where there was running water from a standpipe, the incidence of trachoma fell. This is another disease that would be ameliorated by providing facilities for washing.

Cockburn: In Bangladesh in 1958 there were smallpox and cholera epidemics, with 1500 deaths from smallpox and 500 deaths from cholera every week. Our solution for cholera was to put in pure water, although it took a year to get pipes. We sank 12 000 two-inch pipes in 12 000 villages, but this was not enough. We needed twenty times that number. The cholera rate diminished until it was brought back from other endemic areas in the country.

In Australia, I was told that the fall in the birth rate of the Aborigines was caused by gonorrhoea which sterilized the women, and now that you are wiping out gonorrhoea, there is a population increase.

Stanley: But we are not wiping out gonorrhoea: we are not doing anything about it; that is what is so serious. The incidence is increasing.

Cockburn: You discussed trachoma, Mrs White. I was told that it was imported by traders from New Guinea (Mann 1957). Dampier, the first Englishman there, said the natives threw back their heads to look straight ahead. This has been interpreted to mean that they had trachoma.

White: I agree that my evidence for trachoma as an indigenous disease is not at all strong. It is the evidence that blindness is accepted as part of the aging process—for example, the use of the words for 'blind' and 'old' almost interchangeably—but blindness might have had another cause.

Cockburn: Cataracts may be a more likely explanation of that association.

Hugh-Jones: The problem of alcohol can't be avoided when discussing the Australian Aborigines. Dr Gajdusek, is there any evidence that if alcohol is introduced into a community that has no previous experience of it, there is any change in the metabolic pathways?

Gajdusek: I know of no evidence for adaptation in man to a small toxic molecule like alcohol. The problem seems to be more in the lack of social controls set upon the use of alcohol than in specific genetic susceptibility to its effects. There is now the same problem in many Canadian and American Indian and Eskimo communities. There would be much the same problem, but for rather strong government control, in Papua New Guinea in townships where the Australians were joined by their Papuan New Guinea colleagues in the bars once the prohibition on 'the native consumption of alcoholic beverages' was lifted. It is a huge problem. Some Canadian Indians on the reservations have themselves asked that the government ban alcohol on the reservations, to deal with the supposed exploitation of the Indians by liquor salesman. It turns out that most of the purveyors of alcohol are Indians themselves, and they are the first to object to controlling legislation aimed specifically at them.

White: In a study on an equal number of Aboriginal and white volunteers in Fremantle Gaol, the Aborigines were found to have better tolerance for alcohol than the Whites. However, not all the Aborigines were of the full descent and in any event a sample of a prison population may not be representative (Marinovich *et al.* 1976). A hopeful development that I referred to (p. 283) is that the Aborigines near Alice Springs are now running their own rehabilitation centre, where people go who would earlier have gone to prison. The local Aboriginal council is now running the hotel at Finke, with a new rule that no alcoholic liquor is to be taken out.

Stanley: One of the bad side-effects of the Australian government's recognition of Aborigines as 'people' in 1967, by giving them citizens' rights, was that Aborigines were then entitled to drink. Aboriginal rights meant in fact alcohol rights. Alcohol was suddenly made available to every Aborigine. The same thing has now happened as Dr Gajdusek has described: Aborigines in the Northern Territory have demanded that alcohol be withdrawn from the reserves, but the white publicans who are selling the drink are refusing to stop doing so.

Jones: I am struck by how quickly we move from talking about metabolism to talking about social control, and I am impressed by the fact that one cannot talk about health without talking about politics. If we are going to talk about attitudes towards washing babies and washing the body, this is only one small part of a person's attitudes, and it becomes legitimate to ask about other attitudes that people have.

One thing that has happened in the US and in Africa is that among groups of people who haven't enjoyed much in the way of health, wealth or education, living in peri-urban communities, the idea has been spreading that you must be responsible for yourself in your own community and that one cannot expect any improvement once people have become dependent on a strong, powerful, affluent group of other people who with good, paternalistic ideas want to spread good health and increased wealth to other people. I am reminded here of Conor Cruise O'Brien's definition of paternalism as 'kinship without affection'. It seems that that has been echoed in the Aboriginal setting. My question is this: in the change in attitudes among Aborigines, is there evidence of the consciousness-raising idea, which Black Power and women's movements have used as an attitude-changing device?

Stanley: Yes. I have been involved with the Aboriginal Advancement Council's campaign; there are groups of active people in all the states, and in visiting them I was severely criticized for my ideas, which did me a tremendous amount of good! There was however a vast difference between the Western Australian Black Power movement, which was very ineffective, and that of the eastern states. In the east there is much more awareness of how they can achieve changes politically by pressure, in all sorts of subtle ways.

Cohen: One should not be too pessimistic about the problem of dependency, if the political context turns out right. I am impressed with an essay by Franz Fanon (1967) called 'Medicine and colonialism' in which he describes the dramatic change in the attitudes of the Algerian people towards health and disease during the war of liberation. During the fight against the French, Algerian people were not allowed to obtain medicines on their own nor could they be treated except by doctors recognized by the French authorities. This was done so that it would be impossible to hide and treat wounded freedom fighters. Nevertheless both medicines and bandages and help from sympathetic doctors were obtained. The need to cooperate with treatment and, for example, to take drugs such as antibiotics regularly, which had always been resisted, was suddenly understood and even women, previously so strictly segregated, joined in with the treatment of wounded men brought into their houses. Once the feeling of psychological dependency had gone, the change from the attitudes of alienation of the patients which had persisted for so long under the colonial regime took only six months or a year.

Stanley: Attitudes are changing very fast in Australia also, on the east coast particularly. One of the most brilliant moves before the 1972 election was the idea of setting up an Aboriginal Embassy in the form of a tent, in the grounds of Parliament House in Canberra. This was widely filmed and reported and the 'embassy', which was a terrible eyesore, became acutely embarrassing to the government. It remained there for 18 months, eventually being removed by rather violent police efforts, which were televised and beamed around the world.

Gajdusek: In these Aboriginal communities, are there school buses taking the children in to the best schools in town, or not? In every disadvantaged community in the US, the people themselves have discovered that they do not want just their local community schools for their own children; they want their children in the best schools available in the greater urban area. They are prepared to send their children even at pre-school age across the city by bus because they understand what this experience may do and what it brings home. This has, of course, occasioned huge dissent in the US. Distances in Australia are great, but it is possible even to fly children to schools each week; it has been done in other parts of the world. Is anything like this happening?

White: The bright Aboriginal children are flown to good high schools in Adelaide, or other cities, but the missions and settlements have their own primary schools which most of the children attend up to the age of fifteen. Many of these now use the local Aboriginal language as the medium of education for the younger children, while English is being taught as a second language.

Stanley: I don't think the very young Aboriginal children could cope yet with the drastic transition which Dr Gajdusek is advocating. They don't even speak English in many areas.

Gajdusek: The problem was overcome by Micronesia; you start their education at the age of five or even earlier in a major language like English with good elementary teachers fluent in English and keep at it.

Woodburn: If you start children in an English-speaking school system at five or under, particularly if it is a boarding school system, and if you don't provide real opportunities for them to develop their knowledge of their own local language and culture, they will no longer have local loyalties remotely resembling their parents' ones. Maybe that is the right philosophy, maybe not, but we have to be clear that this sort of policy is essentially one of assimilation.

Hugh-Jones: One has only to recall the recent (1976) riots in South Africa, when Afrikaans was to be imposed as the language of education on the black people, to understand that people soon realize that in order to succeed in a community you must have the know-how of that community, which is the problem of the integration of tribal people into a larger society. Everyone has to have a fair start.

Jones: An additional and essential ingredient in making improvements seems to be therapeutic optimism. If everyone had Dr Gajdusek's optimism, the problems might be solved, but I sense that in Australia there is an enormous amount of pessimism about the future of the Aborigines.

Woodburn: I would like to introduce an even greater feeling of pessimism, which I think we must accept before we can look at these situations sensibly. We should remember that the Australian position of the Aborigines is in various ways *better* than that in many other places. Consider the newly independent countries of Africa, in several of which there are highly authoritarian governments, *in practice* committed to a limited section of the community—in some cases to a particular tribe or set of tribes, in others to the intelligentsia or the literate population as against non-literates, in yet others specifically to members of the army—with many groups in the country having no political power, especially if they do not share a common language with the other Africans administering them. Politically weak, isolated, non-literate groups in poor countries are extremely unlikely to get any of the substantial increases in finance which the Australian Aborigines are now receiving.

Relating this specifically to pastoral nomads, almost all African governments have an unenthusiastic attitude about them. They tend to regard them as basically rather undesirable and say that if they are to continue to exist as cattle or camel herders they must change from a system of producing for themselves to a system in which they are contributing food to the population as a whole by becoming ranchers. But, if they do that, the cruel consequence may be that they can't support the same numbers of people on the same area of land as they could when they depended on milk production for home consumption rather than on meat production for the national market. So what happens to the surplus population? They may well be in a situation that is as bad as that of Aboriginal Australians on the fringes of urban society. Usually no provision is made for displaced nomads. Development agencies are investing large sums in the development of meat ranching without in general making provision for those displaced. While the Australian situation is undoubtedly appalling, in much of the third world the situation is worse, and numerically greater also.

Haraldson: Yes, you are right. If we exclude the Sudan, African governments are certainly hesitant to discuss their nomads, whom they often consider 'inferior' and undesirable. Thus, large pastoral districts in Africa, for example in Kenya, Ethiopia and Botswana, have been gravely neglected in the planning and development of health and other social services. Tribalism has contributed to a sometimes drastic geographical maldistribution of health service facilities. Over 50% of all physicians in Ethiopia are working in Addis Ababa, which has 3% of the population of the whole country.

Much international influence and assistance may be needed to correct this imbalance in the accessibility of health services, especially as new and nontraditional kinds of services and new types of personnel are needed for 'pastoral medicine'. Services in these areas with scattered populations and low population density are bound to be expensive, and may therefore be regarded by authorities as of low profitability and low priority. This is understandable when we consider the extremely low health budgets with which most of the concerned nations are actually working. Because of low access to services in sparsely populated districts, the utilization rate will be low and the profitability, if calculated as cost per treatment or person served, will in many cases seem prohibitively high to the granting administrative bodies. (See Haraldson 1973.)

References

ALPERS, M.P., ALLBROOK, D., McCALL, M.C., ALEXEYEFF, S., STANLEY, F. & ARMSTRONG, B.K. (1972). Summary Report of the Aboriginal Studies Group, School of Medicine, University of Western Australia. *Aust. Nurses' Journal* 2(6),20

COOK, G.C. (1973) Incidence and clinical features of specific hypolactasia in adult man, in *Intestinal Enzyme Deficiencies and their Nutritional Implications* (Borgstrom, B., Dahlqvist, A. & Hambreus, L., eds.) *(Symposium of the Swedish Nutrition Foundation no. 11)*, pp. 52–73, Almqvist & Wiksell, Uppsala

FANON, F. (1967) Medicine and colonialism, in *A Dying Colonialism*, pp. 121–145, Grove Press, New York

HARALDSON, S.R.S. (1973) Health problems of nomads. *World Hospitals 7*, no. 4

LANCASTER JONES, F. (1970) *The Structure and Growth of Australia's Aboriginal Population*, Australian National University Press, Canberra

MANN, I. (1957) Probable origins of trachoma in Australasia. *Bull. W.H.O. 16*, 1165–1187

MARINOVICH, N., LARSSON, O. & BARBER, K. (1976) Comparative metabolism rates of ethanol in adults of Aboriginal and European descent. *Med. J. Aust. (Special Suppl.) 1*

MOODIE, P.M. (1973) *Aboriginal Health*, Australian National University Press, Canberra

WHITE, I.M. (1972) Hunting dogs at Yalata. *Mankind 8*, 201–205

The responsibilities of intervention in isolated societies

STAFFORD LIGHTMAN

Department of Medicine, Middlesex Hospital, London and Survival International, London

Abstract Development pressures are pushing industrial society into the remaining refuge areas of the world. As it spreads it destroys much of the biological and cultural variety that has evolved over millions of years. Not only is mammalian life diminishing, but also the genetic pool of plants and cultivars, as well as the culture-specific knowledge of their use. Even culture itself, the highest attribute of mankind, is being rapidly erased, often before any attempts are made to record it.

The medical problems of remaining tribal groups are severe. Western medicine has developed to deal with western problems and is often poorly equipped to deal with the many-sided health hazards of tribal man.

The effects of contact upon disease status are discussed with particular reference to North and South American Indian history. Infectious disease is only one of many causes of ill-health, and the problems of nutritional change and social disruption are also considered.

The approach to health care in tribal communities is discussed and axioms for the initiation of health care programmes are proposed.

The problems of health and disease in isolated societies cannot be considered as isolated biomedical situations. This multidisciplinary symposium, with its inclusion of doctors, anthropologists, virologists, nutrition experts and social scientists, stresses the multiple interrelationships involved when isolated communities become assimilated by our dominant culture. Not only are these isolated communities themselves often shattered by their process of acculturation, but the whole face of our planet's physical and cultural diversity is irreversibly altered, often in a way that is deleterious for the majority of its present and future inhabitants.

Cultural man has existed for two million years, for more than 99% of this time as a hunter–gatherer. In fact it is only during the last ten thousand years that man has learnt to domesticate plants and animals, discovered the use of metals and fossilized fuels and finally emerged into the industrial and atomic age. More than 90% of men who have ever lived have been hunter–gatherers.

Our view of tribal man is dictated by the particular age we live in. This is an age of pressures which are now being felt globally. Population expansion, agricultural and industrial development, the utilization of fuels and resources and finally the political pressures of developing nationhood all act to push the boundaries of our dominant culture even further into all remaining refuge areas. Already the tribal groups who lived in the more hospitable areas of this planet have been removed, leaving a false impression of the way most groups of hunter–gatherers formerly lived. Thus over 70% of Eskimos used to live south of the Arctic circle, and the Kalahari and Australian desert aboriginal populations represent but a fraction of the original inhabitants who lived in much more fertile areas of these continents. The North American Indians are an even better example of people who have been dispossessed of their fertile and rich lands and whose present way of life has been dictated by their enforced existence on reservations in inhospitable areas.

We live in a world of exploitation. Resources are finite and soon even our all-powerful society will be forced to be conservationist. No human population shows voluntary conservation and thus people who live in areas where conservation is a necessity have much to teach us. These people to a large extent are represented by the remaining tribal groups, who have managed to avoid cultural and physical destruction by living in areas of the world which the ecologist calls 'marginal', and which include the extremes of temperature and moisture gradients with their correspondingly more delicate balance of nature. Now, however, we with our newest technological feats are ready to conquer this final frontier.

GENETIC, CULTURAL AND ECOLOGICAL LOSSES

Industrial man may in many respects be considered an aggressive and successful weed strangling other species and even the weaker members of its own. Odum (1959) describes the 'Diversity Index' as the ratio between the number of species and the number of individuals per species. Adverse environments such as high altitudes and areas of low rainfall will lower this index. This too is the effect of modern man—an effect that is most powerfully felt in the marginal environments where the index is already low.

The highly adapted flora and fauna and the continued culture of the local population must be balanced against the search for new sources of fuel and other raw materials. Appell (1974) has highlighted the alarming rate at which both the resources of our eco-system, and the culture-specific knowledge relating to these resources, are rapidly being lost. The most commonly quoted example is that of our fellow mammals. During the last 2000 years 110 species have ceased to exist while, in the last 200 years, 600 species have reached the point of extinction. Rather less obvious, but of great importance, has been the contemporaneous drastic loss in species of flora. Of particular concern is the rapid decline in the world's genetic pool of indigenous cultivars. These crops, which have adapted to local conditions of climate and disease, provide a huge genetic pool from which better species could be produced by cross-breeding. In spite of this, the introduction of highly specialized varieties developed in western countries supplants local varieties that are lost for ever. The loss of varieties of dry rice in South-East Asia alone must be colossal.

Closely related to this loss of environmental knowledge is the loss of the knowledge stored up in the fragile form of tribal culture. Culture is learned, and cessation of the learning process leads to cultural death within the duration of one generation. In contrast to insect societies where knowledge is genetically programmed, the human must spend about one-third of his total lifespan undergoing a process of 'enculturation'. *Herein lies the particular frailty of the smaller non-dominant societies.* The powerful appearance of the dominant and apparently more promising society can temporarily wreck the basic traditions, beliefs and perceptions of the contacted groups. This immediately slows or stops the learning processes of the younger members of the population. The sudden appearance of an apparently superior society and its dazzling luxuries places tribal groups in a 'Catch 22' situation which they themselves could not possibly be expected to have the insight to avoid. When they eventually discover that the elysium of the new foreign culture offers no place for them, they no longer possess their own environmentally cohesive culture to fall back on. Meanwhile social organization may have collapsed and society degenerated into existence and torpor. Thus man by this possession of culture as his most recent evolutionary achievement is the most unstable creature upon the whole evolutionary tree. It takes only a few decades to lose all that has been gained in thousands of generations.

I am not calling for cultural isolation. Gross cultural contact is and always has been an enriching process. However, the problem now is that there has never before been a dominant culture with such immense power and resources, together with its ethnocentric self-justification and total lack of interest in contrary cultural patterns.

Not all tribal groups have been equally susceptible to this cultural disruption, particularly where a culture is strong and the population large. However, the majority of our remaining tribal groups are both small in population, and culturally and physically isolated from other groups, thus being devoid of the broad cultural roots necessary for protection from the initial shock of contact. This is particularly true among the Amazonian Indians where contact has proved especially destructive.

The drive towards cultural conformity is definite policy in many countries from both the capitalist and socialist blocks, where cultural independence is often thought of as deviation or a threat to national security. To an extraterrestrial observer our dominant culture must appear as a spreading cancer that is seeking and strangling its rival, or just cohabitant, ways of life.

POSITION OF WESTERN MEDICINE

How then does medicine fit into this one-sided cultural levelling process? Western medicine is a product of western culture with a discrimination aimed at western problems. An historical approach to our medicine gives us some perspective within which to understand the contrasting priorities of tribal and western medicine. Hippocrates thought of health as an expression of the harmonious balance between the environment, human nature and the individual's way of life. He described a good physician as one who 'has a due regard to the seasons of the year, and the diseases which they produce; to the states of the wind peculiar to each country and the qualities of its water; who marks carefully the localities of towns, the surrounding country, whether they are low or high, hot or cold, wet or dry; who, moreover, takes note of the diet and regimen of the inhabitants and of all the causes which may produce disorder in the animal economy'. These ideas held sway for a considerable time until their rejection by Renaissance scientists. However, it was only towards the end of the last century that our medicine took its violent plunge towards specialization. The wide spectrum of medical humanism shrank into a technological interventionist science that forsook the wider problems of man's relationship with his environment, thus illustrating the cliché of knowing more about less. We are only now beginning to realize that our preoccupation with the microbiologia of disease is too limiting, with the recent growth of the specialities of community medicine and perhaps medical anthropology. We have almost had to discover psychiatry and sociology for a second time.

Medicine encompasses the complex relationship of man, his environment, his culture, and physical and social pathogens. It is well to bear in mind the recent convolutions undergone by our own ideas of medicine before we seek to apply our version of this art to other societies.

What then should be the role of medicine in our approach to tribal people? Our two major problems are perspective and application. Limitation of perspective ensures a tendency for doctors to think that the problems of all societies revolve primarily around their own special field of health care, rather than being one aspect of the much wider cultural environment of the recipient which is being assaulted by the process of acculturation.

These problems of acculturation are felt on many fronts, and are certainly medical in the hippocratic meaning of the word. Thus new social, nutritional and disease patterns are introduced into a previously stable society, resulting in a complex alteration in the life processes of the people. The World Health Organization defines health as a state of complete physical, mental and social well-being, and acculturation has profound effects on all three of these areas.

PROBLEMS OF PHYSICAL HEALTH

History clearly relates how contact with our society can produce severe deleterious effects on the physical health status of tribal communities. Available information allows us to generalize that hunter–gatherers are usually people with a good nutritional status, a low incidence of chronic disease and, by virtue of their isolation and small populations, relative freedom from epidemic disease. They have in fact attained a high degree of adaptive stability that our society has only been able to maintain by the use of complex public health and vaccination programmes. Once the local ecology is upset by the intrusion of our society, however, this stability is disturbed and without enlightened aid the group is liable to destruction.

Evidence of this destructive influence of foreign presence is not difficult to find. The problem of epidemic disease was reported as early as 1552 when the Jesuit Francisco Pires noted how disease struck his first batch of converts near Bahia, Brazil: 'almost none of them have survived and did not die'. This was but one of many outbreaks in which tens of thousands of Brazilian Indians died. Since then similar disastrous epidemics have been described in many parts of the newly discovered world. The measles epidemic in Fiji in 1875 is a particularly well-documented tragedy which resulted in 30 thousand deaths, while much more recently Centerwall (1968) has dramatically described the rapidity with which an epidemic of the same disease created a catastrophic situation in a virgin-soil population of Yanomama Indians in South Venezuela.

The introduction of disease does not only result in these great epidemics, however, but more often creates an extended picture of chronic disease interspersed with acute episodes. Cook (1973) has managed to collate much of the data available on the significance of disease in the extinction of the Indians of the north-east of the United States of America. North-west of the Hudson river alone there was a loss of 93.5% of the Indian population in the three hundred years up to 1907, most of which took place in the first one hundred years of European settlement.

After contact with settlers from the early 1600s, the mainland suffered two major epidemics; first of 'plague' between 1610 and 1619, and then of smallpox from 1637 to 1641. The significance of these epidemics in terms of population decline, however, is clearly questioned by a study of the populations of the two off-shore islands of Martha's Vineyard and Nantucket, areas without either intertribal raiding or fighting with settlers. From the mid-1600s until the mid-1700s, assuming population loss to be an exponential function of the population, the yearly population loss from Martha's Vineyard was a colossal 1.85% and for Nantucket, 1.61%. This was a time free from epidemic illness! If these figures are applied to the mainland Indians it becomes apparent that chronic disease was a considerably greater factor in population decline than the epidemics themselves.

It should not be forgotten that this chronic disease was not a condition in isolation but was greatly exacerbated by the factors of malnutrition and despair inflicted on the Indian by restriction of his territory and the inhibition of his traditional way of life. Disease was but a condition expressing the destruction of his way of life.

NUTRITIONAL ASPECTS OF DISEASE

Nutritional deficiencies are very important factors in the process of acculturation with its concomitant changes in diet. Many people still subscribe to the misconception that hunter–gatherers have nutritionally poor diets. In the main this could not be further from the truth. Unfortunately, very little work has been done in which diet has been assessed before and after acculturation. Moisés Béhar (1968), however, has made use of the available information to compare the dietary problems and nutritional conditions of the Mayan population before the Spanish conquest and now. Corn was a staple diet in both groups, but the pre-Columbian species were better adapted to local ecological conditions. There was also a greater availability of game, more land available for cultivation, and no competitive markets, as well as prolonged breast-feeding and a lack of industrialized products. The subsequent socio-cultural and economic changes resulted in considerable nutritional problems, especially protein deficiency, which is most marked in the children.

The Mayans live in a reasonably abundant part of the world, and it is therefore useful also to look at a group of people who live in particularly harsh surroundings. The !Kung bushmen of the semi-arid north-west Kalahari desert are such a group who have been well studied by Richard B. Lee (1968). Professor Truswell has already provided details of their dietary status (pp. 213–221), but I would emphasize here that these people (1) have a varied diet, using 85 species of food plant, including 30 roots and bulbs, as well as meat, (2) only need to work a $2^{1}/_{2}$-day week and six hours per day looking for food, and (3) have an excellent balanced diet with an average protein intake only exceeded by six countries in the world. This was observed during one of the most severe droughts in South Africa's history when in Botswana more than 100 000 cattle died and the world food programme initiated famine relief for 180 000 people— over 30% of the population.

Similar findings of good nutritional status with only a small work-load have been made in Australian Aborigines (McCarthy & McArthur 1960) and the Hadza of East Africa (Woodburn & Hudson 1966). It is interesting to note that in the latter group we again see the deleterious effects of acculturation, with the appearance of new dietary habits, particularly the introduction of corn meal. Breast-feeding and the use of bone marrow and pre-chewed meat had previously ensured that children obtained a well-balanced diet, and had added protection from maternal immunity. After the rapid change from this traditional diet, protein calorie malnutrition and pellagra were reported for the first time (Jelliffe *et al.* 1962).

An extreme situation is seen when more entrenched acculturation results in the introduction of cash crops. This immediately leads to neglect of the production of traditional crops, and dependence on imported convenience foods. Income becomes subject to price fluctuation. Lump sums are used to buy status symbols, and often not enough money is saved to ensure food supplies through to the next harvest. Good examples of this can be seen in the agricultural areas of West Africa that have taken up cocoa growing (Collis *et al.* 1962). Similarly, protein-calorie malnutrition was almost unknown to the Chagga of Tanzania before the local cultivation of coffee and cotton (Marealle *et al.* 1965). These are certainly extreme samples, but tribal societies are even more sensitive than others to the introduction of new feeding habits which are seen as superior to their own, and they are thus immediately precipitated into a dependent position.

SOCIAL ASPECTS OF DISEASE

As well as the primary health and nutritional consequences of rapid acculturation, the social changes brought by a sudden alteration in tribal belief and taboos can have an extremely destructive effect on a culture. Even when all possible medical care is taken of any small group, history has repeatedly shown that attempts at rapid integration often lead to apathy, alienation and dependency. One starts with a community which has an accepted structure of authority, a people with a sense of identity and mutual respect. The very process of integration puts them into a position of inferiority. There is a loss of authority and pride disappears. This results in stress and new patterns of disease.

We are thus left with a fairly gloomy picture of the effects of acculturation, and it is instructive to review the picture produced. We have (1) poor nutrition; (2) overcrowding with consequent increase in droplet and faecal–oral contamination; (3) the introduction of new chronic and epidemic diseases; and (4) the devaluation of society with the consequent production of new stress patterns and stress-related disease. These features may not all be found in every case, but the point must surely be made that our offer of a new way of life is scarcely an attractive proposition, and if such a change is to be enforced just by our presence, the least we can do is to protect tribal people from the worst excesses of this contact.

RESEARCH

Assuming, as we surely must, that it is now inevitable that increasing contact with our remaining isolated communities will occur, we should look back and try to apply what can be learned from past experience.

First, and perhaps incongruously, I must mention the value of research. Carleton Gajdusek (pp. 69–94) has already clearly outlined areas where the study of tribal people has allowed great advances in our understanding of medical problems, not to mention the sociological information obtained by the anthropologists. However, I would stress that the spin-off from this research, important as it surely is, is of no use whatsoever to the people on whom the research is done. Considering the concurrent harm that our contact usually causes, I feel that unless this research is coupled with a programme of medico-social aid to the group concerned, it is ethically unjustifiable. Although I would accept that research is a vitally important component of work among our remaining tribal groups, two facts must be borne in mind: (1) these people are an extremely precious and vanishing resource, so that priorities for research should be established and our remaining 'material' not be wasted; (2) there should be a significant *quid pro quo* for all work done.

POSITIVE ACTIONS

When positive actions are considered that might be taken to alleviate the problem of acculturation, it should not be forgotten that specialist knowledge in this area is available, particularly in the form of non-governmental organizations, whose knowledge and expertise is largely untapped. As a representative of one of these organizations, I want to end this paper with an outline of the basic principles which seem to me to be important in the pursuit of positive medical intervention.

Many of the medico-social problems of integration are based on the ethno-centric aim of the contacting society to hurriedly integrate its new citizens. This in itself is a misconception of the possible effects of contact. It is not that change in itself is wrong; only that if this is engineered from outside rather than developed from inside, it is doomed to failure. In the resulting institutionalized and dependent populations any altruistic theories of social integration and increased living standards become buried in a morass of cultural destruction. Speed is often the main culprit; Leighton & Smith's interesting study (1955) of social and cultural change in eight different parts of the world confirmed the relationship between the rapidity and extent of change on the one hand, and the serious disorganization of society on the other.

What then should be the guidelines for anyone hoping to deal with the medical problems of this process of acculturation? The necessity for rapid and basic preventive medicine is of course of supreme importance after the period of first major contact, but after this it is unreasonable to lay down strict instructions, since no two situations are the same. There are, however, basic principles that are paramount in the successful initiation of medical services in these areas. Maurice King (1966) has already drawn up the major axioms for medical services in the developing world, and in a similar way I shall adapt these to the particular problems of tribal people.

Basic learning

It is impossible to set up an effective and appreciated medical system before one has a basic understanding of the people one is working with and for. If there are any anthropological books or papers on the local culture these should be read, and if possible the anthropologist himself consulted. Failing this the health worker himself must do some basic anthropological field work. The knowledge so gained should be basic to his practice of medicine and his understanding of local problems. Nutritional taboos, for instance, may be the basis of a malnutrition problem which no amount of logical argument will otherwise overcome. Similarly, the relationships between witchcraft and disease may explain reluctance to seek treatment. Even on a more western epidemiological level, the control of imported venereal infection requires considerable insight into social relationships. With these types of problem in mind, and the fact that acceptance of any change must usually be initiated by the more respected members of the community or a powerful grouping within the community, there are seven major areas for learning by the health-care worker:

    1. Identification of the respected leaders.

2. The basic working of family structure and obligations, marriage and inheritance.
3. The existence of other groupings—religious, sexual or political.
4. Basic attitudes to health and disease.
5. Methods of practice of local medical practitioners.
6. The existence of taboos, particularly nutritional.
7. Accepted symbols of wealth and happiness.

Initiation of medical programme

After the urgent medical work of first contact, a medical programme must be built on the associated pillars of self-reliance, good nutrition, land rights, legal rights, education and an increased consciousness, by the people concerned, of themselves, their culture and their rights. Only if these factors have been considered is one in a position to build up medical care. There are five basic principles upon which this medical care should be based.

1. Medical care should be developed within the context of the local culture, and without debasement of local knowledge.
2. There should be local participation in the health-care programme, including the involvement of local practitioners.
3. The wants and needs of the community should be monitored.
4. Organization should be from the bottom up, primary health care taking precedence over more technological secondary care.
5. Maximum coverage of the population should have precedence over more comprehensive medical care.

Lack of money is often cited as the major obstacle to the development of effective health services in tribal communities. This statement usually reveals a lack of understanding of the correct priorities in the setting up of such medical schemes.

There is much to learn from the richly endowed attempt by Cornell University Medical College, the United States Public Health Service and the Navaho Tribe to set up a comprehensive delivery of high-technology medicine among a non-technological group of Navaho Indians (McDermott *et al.* 1972). This entailed the initiation of a system of health care which was hospital based and 'delivered' by outside physicians and nurses, with help from Navaho auxiliaries.

This five-year programme was limited to a community of 2000 Navaho, among whom the clinical impression obtained was of 'a disease-ridden people whose disorders would be largely preventable within a modern society'. In spite of this appraisal of the situation the results of the doctor-intensive medical care programme could scarcely be classed as a great success.

In western terminology, there was a 'possible slight' reduction in crude mortality and the infant death rate remained three times above the national average throughout the programme. There was no reduction in the pneumonia and diarrhoea syndromes, which remained the commonest cause of mortality and morbidity, and the prevalence of trachoma was unchanged. There was, however, a significant reduction in the transmission of tuberculosis, and in the fifth year only in the incidence of otitis media.

The conclusions are largely obvious. It is not lack of doctors, money and equipment that are the major problems in the implementation of this type of health care. Even the large resources of the Navaho project could not make western concepts of curative medicine suitable for use in the tribal situation. The basic problems lie at the preventive level and do not require the expensive assets of primary health care delivered by western physicians. Some form of community health care with perhaps a physician in a consultative role would have been more rational and certainly much cheaper. Care of this kind should entail a long-term programme involving the basic principles of identification with the community and the sharing of ideas and decisions. Unless a medical programme develops from within the body of the community, it cannot be expected to succeed.

References

APPELL, G.N. (1974) Partial social models and their failures to account for the pernicious effects of development. *Fields within Fields*, World Institute Council, New York

BÉHAR, M. (1968) Food and nutrition of the Maya before the conquest and at present time. *Pan Am. Health Organ. Sci. Publ. 165*, 114–119

CENTERWALL, W.R. (1968) A recent experience of measles in a 'virgin soil' population. *Pan Am. Health Organ. Sci. Publ. 165*, 77–80

COLLIS, W.R.F., DEMA, J. & OMOLOLU, A. (1962) The ecology of child health and nutrition in Nigerian villages. Part II: dietary and medical surveys. *Trop. Geogr. Med. 14*, 201–229

COOK, S.F. (1973) The significance of disease in the extinction of the New England Indians. *Hum. Biol. 45*, 485–508

FRANCISCO PIRES to brothers in Portugal. Bahia 1552, Poixoto, Cartas Avulsas 129 (Personal communication from John Hemming)

JELLIFFE, D.B., WOODBURN, J., BENNETT, F.J. & JELLIFFE, E.F.P. (1962) The children of the Hadza hunters. *J. Pediatr. 60*, 907–913

KING, M. (1966) *Medical Care in Developing Countries*, Oxford University Press, London

LEE, R.B. (1968) in *Man the Hunter* (Lee, R. B. & DeVore, I., eds.), Aldine, Chicago

LEIGHTON, H. & SMITH, R.J. (1955) A comparative study of social and cultural change. *Proc. Am. Philosoph. Soc. 99* (no. 2)

MAREALLE, A.L.D., KAZUNGU, M. & KONDAKIS, X.G. (1964) Cross-sectional studies on protein calorie malnutrition in Tanganyika. *J. Trop. Med. Hyg. 67*, 222–229

McCARTHY, F.D. & McARTHUR, M. (1960) The food quest and time factor in aboriginal economic life, in *Records of the American Australian Scientific Expedition to Arnhem Land*, vol. 2: *Anthropology & Nutrition* (Mountford, C.P., ed.), Melbourne University Press, Melbourne

McDERMOTT, W., DEUSCHLE, K.W. & BARNETT, C.R. (1972) Health care experiment at Many Farms. *Science (Wash. D.C.) 175*, 23–31

ODUM, E.P. (1959) *Fundamentals of Ecology* (2nd edn), Saunders, London

WOODBURN, J.C. & HUDSON, S. (1966) *The Hadza. The food quest of a hunting and gathering tribe of Tanzania* (16 mm film), London School of Economics, London

Discussion

ETHNICITY AND THE PSYCHOSOCIAL EFFECTS OF ACCULTURATION

Morin: Dr Lightman has shown us to what extent the domination of industrial society can break down the structure of tribal societies. I would like to illustrate certain aspects of this process with a specific case which I studied some years ago in the Amazonian region of Peru. I refer to the Shipibo, an Amerindian group living along the Ucayali. This group has been exposed to economic, territorial, social and religious pressures from western society for over three centuries. In order to appreciate the extent of the ongoing ethnocidal process resulting from the contact of the two civilizations, one has to construct an inventory of the values which rule tribal existence and those which the dominant society wishes to impose, whether it be colonial or national.

The Shipibo, like all Amazonian groups, map out for themselves an area in which they fish, hunt, and practise slash and burn agriculture. But these areas do not belong to them in the sense of heritage or individual ownership. The territory is held collectively by the tribe. Their economy is based on a form of domestic production with a division of labour by sex. It is a 'society of abundance' (Sahlins 1972) in so far as it satisfies the needs of the group; they produce to live but do not live to produce. In other words, they refuse to market the surplus. It is a classless society in that it is set up on the principle of reciprocity. It is also a stateless society devoid of coercive political power. The chief of the tribe only directs a limited number of economic and ceremonial activities of the group. He can neither decide nor command, as the Shipibo, like all Indian chieftaincies (Clastres 1974), is based on communal consent. The real seat of power is the entire tribe. The residential structure is centred on the matrilocality and the lineage is matrilineal, so that the woman is the key figure of the communal home. The men hold the political and religious power. The Shipibo practise a form of shamanism and their vision of the world derives from animist beliefs. They establish a certain number of 'links' with nature and with the spirits and the individual associates intimately (Bastide 1953, 1966) with one and the other.

In 1660, when the Franciscan missionaries were ordered by the Viceroy to go down the Andes to pacify the unfaithful and explore the wealth of the Peruvian Orient, the Shipibo, who are open, tolerant and curious by nature, were not hostile and even tried to establish contact by offering hospitality under their roof and a share of their food. In return they accepted the machetes (choppers), axes and knives which the missionaries offered—presents which were really traps set by the Whites to convert the 'savages' of the Ucayali; in other words, to impose a set of Christian morals to dominate and shape their universe and to destroy what is different. Belonging to a faith of triumph and representing a civilization of conquest, the missionaries considered the Shipibo 'barbarian, capricious and lazy'. Consequently they had to be 'civilized'. To achieve this they forced the Shipibo to leave their communal houses and to regroup themselves in villages, in order to support the church. In face of this policy of constraint the Shipibo began to understand that an alliance was not possible and they rebelled at various times. For two centuries there was a clash of two value systems and two visions of the world: on the one hand the practice of tolerance, multi-ethnicity, and the refusal of coercion, of the appropriation of land or the community as a whole which decides on economic and political structures—and on the other hand the refusal to accept that which is different, following a policy of homogeneity and uniformity, conquest and annexation of 'virgin lands' and the centralization of power, first by the Spanish Crown and after Independence by the Peruvian state representing a policy of coercion and assimilation, the development of a capitalist economy and the introduction of a system of social stratification. In other words, politics and economics dictate the laws to be followed by society. The western 'carnivorous' pattern (Jaulin 1970, 1974) knew from the start how to sap the very foundations of the Shipibo society by the type of dependence it created. Having discovered iron from gifts of the missionaries, these Neolithic men developed a thirst for more (Metraux 1952) and in order to get more they accepted the modification of their way of life, their social structure and their beliefs; they became 'rubber slaves' in the nineteenth century and remain to this day in a state of life-indebtedness. Although they lost their own value systems, which had shaped their ethnic identity, the Shipibo have not really absorbed western thought and do not share the national identity. As objects of a three hundred year-long process of ethnocide and enforced assimilation, some find refuge in myth (messianism) or in mental illness (neurosis, women refusing to fulfil their sex roles of maternity, cooking, etc.). I would stress two principal explanations for this state of affairs:

1. The acculturation process has touched a certain number of levels (econ-

omic, social and political). It has radically changed their way of life, but there remains a gap which Bastide (1970) would call *'formal acculturation'*—that is to say, the acculturation of the psyche. It is not enough to change one's way of life, food habits, clothing, handicrafts, household structure or group filiation, to see one's territory recede, and theoretically to be a Peruvian citizen, in order to change one's mentality. The Shipibo continue to think and to perceive the world and space in terms of 'participation' and 'relationships' (Bastide 1953, p. 66). They do not share our Cartesian logic. 'Men' and 'the Gods' for them form part of one and the same mythical space.

2. The second reason for this 'anomic' situation is that the structure of ethnic identity includes both a number of objective factors (land, language, culture) and a number of subjective factors which are a result of the interaction of the image the group has of itself and of others, and the images which others impose on them. Three centuries of contact with the other world have weakened the Shipibo's sense of identity. The steamroller of 'civilization' has tried to teach them that their culture is savage and barbarian, that they should be ashamed of their customs and their way of life. In their eyes the 'others' are synonyms of force, power, technology and progress. The picture with which the nation is presented of the forest tribes, on the other hand, is filled with prejudices and exotic images (Indians with feathers) and paternalism (since the last revolutionary government was established one no longer refers to '*Indio*', but to '*campesino*', which means peasant). The subjective elements constituting the Shipibo's identity are therefore charged with negative factors and illustrate the difficulties of assimilation.

In this symposium there has been much discussion of physical disease and very little of the psychological effects of assimilation of tribal societies to a modern state. One should ask oneself whether the creation of a national consciousness must necessarily be accompanied by the negation of an ethnic identity. Are nationalism and pluralism really incompatible? 'From tribe to nation' seems to be the royal road to modern civilization for the political scientist. In view of the ethnic revival movements in present-day Europe, I do not believe that the road is necessarily so single-tracked. Finally, if these tribal societies must really disappear physically and culturally, a study of the way they function may help us to understand the present crisis in our civilization and could help us to identify a certain number of values which may be indispensable if man is to feel an adequate member of his society.

Hugh-Jones: Are you saying that although small groups may become parts of big groups, you want them to be able to maintain themselves within the big group?

Morin: I would hope that ethnic and cultural pluralism—the right to be different—could exist within a national structure. But in our western societies as well as in African and Latin-American nations (who in fact copy the western pattern), nation-building seems to spell assimilation, unity and the negation of plurality.

Woodburn: There appears to be an assumption that diversity is declining, and perhaps in general it is, but we should remember that, in parts of Western Europe, and in the USSR and in some other places, there seems to be, as Dr Morin says, a real resurgence of local ethnic awareness accompanied, in some cases, by a spread of local language. Far from a united march to 'melting pot' assimilation and a single national language spoken by everybody, to the exclusion of local ethnic loyalty and local languages, there does seem to be evidence of some increasing differentiation or at least of a desire for greater differentiation.

The recent experience of country after country has been that policies attempting to deny people the opportunity to use their own local language in favour of a national language simply have not worked. In France over a long period there has been a specific national policy of stressing French at the expense of local languages but it has not succeeded in suppressing the use of local languages. The idea that the whole population of a country must demonstrate their unity and their loyalty by speaking just one national language doesn't work well in practice. As I pointed out earlier (p. 265), most of mankind now seems to be bilingual. Interestingly enough, probably fewer intellectuals are genuinely bilingual than are less literate people, and the paradigm of an assimilated homogeneous, undifferentiated, monolingual population is, perhaps, an intellectual's ethnocentric stereotype.

Surely people could accept that there is no inherent conflict between speaking one language at home and maintaining one set of cultural values in your own locality, and also subscribing to a national ideology in which you speak the national language and function within the wider national cultural unit.

White: Unfortunately, in many countries one language, usually the one spoken by the majority, is considered superior to others. All languages are equal in their ability to express the speakers' thoughts, but in the real 'melting pot' countries, such as Australia, the Italians, Greeks, Turks and so on cling to their own languages, while the English-speaking Australians try to persuade them that their languages are inferior to English. The older people may resist this idea, but school-children are more susceptible to the prejudices of their peers, and indeed of the teachers too in many cases. The teachers should instead feel responsible for conveying to the children that their native language is as 'good' as English, while at the same time helping them to learn English. In Australia this applies not only to the languages of the immigrants, but also to the Aboriginal languages. These were described by some of the early settlers as little more than a series of grunts, but now that they have been studied they turn out to be some of the most beautiful and complex languages in the world. However, the minority group has to contend with the pervasive idea that the majority language and majority culture are somehow superior. As I mentioned (p. 299), many of the schools on the reserves are now using the local Aboriginal language as the teaching medium for the youngest children.

Ohlman: One could almost say that when a language disappears, or where the original language group stops speaking it in favour of the majority language, their culture is in the process of disappearing, and this is probably irreversible. The people will either be assimilated or they will remain to themselves, but I don't think you can have both.

Woodburn: I disagree. There are many cases where even without a separate language, cultural distinctiveness remains.

Gajdusek: One of the largest and oldest languages and one spoken by tens of millions of people, Javanese, is being voluntarily abandoned—as was Latin. In the new Indonesian nation many Javanese intellectuals have chosen, in order to maintain political power for Java and the unity of their nation, to synthesize in less than 20 years a new national language, Bahasa Indonesia, based on Malay. They stopped teaching in Javanese in the schools, and now in many homes of young educated Javanese they no longer speak the Javanese language. Many young Javanese know little of this wonderful and complex language. They knew that they could not maintain an Indonesian Republic of many different peoples and races based on Javanese. Little as we may like it, here is a gigantic language group, of 80 million people, who have the political majority and power, and have been willing to stop using their own language in the schools and even with their own children at home.

VALUE OF RESEARCH ON TRIBAL GROUPS

Harrison: I feel, unlike Dr Lightman, that research has a merit in itself and that, whether it is practical or not, mankind derives benefit from it. In the symposium we have not touched on many areas of research, often assuming instead that we have the facts already and can make broad policy decisions from them. I would like to question some of the so-called facts. I would, for example question whether the hunter–gatherer state is such an idyllic one as it has been presumed to be. There are almost certainly penalties in being a hunter–gatherer, which we ought to know about.

A view is developing now in human biology that we should adopt a total, or holistic approach to the examination of human populations, not only isolated or tribal groups but our own type of group as well. In this view we don't focus specifically on the genetics or the medicine or the demography or the sociology but examine the group as a total system in which there is a complex set of inter-actions between many factors, which can conveniently, but often arbitrarily, be classified as cultural or biological. This approach does make great intellectual as well as practical demands on research, but I suspect it will provide us with quite new and penetrating insights into the organization and functioning of human societies.

Hugh-Jones: I think the feeling is that these isolated people are in balance with their environment; whether they are happy or not is something different. But there is a tendency for outsiders to go into such societies and to try to improve them.

Harrison: I would question the value implications to the proposition of their being 'in balance'. That itself is a sophisticated concept. In a sense the hunter–gatherer state of economy appears to be a maximum equilibrium situation with the natural environment but, had you come along in distant geological periods, most of the organisms at those times would have appeared in balance with their ecology. Evolution produces new forms which necessarily disturb the balance and a series of adaptive processes lead to another equilibrium. The essence of evolution can in fact be thought of as coming *out* of equilibrium. By 'in balance' you also imply that there is no fundamental pressure on the persistence of the group from the environment. I think that at least at the hunter–gatherer stage you can apply the ecological maxim derived from the study of all other animals and say that directly or indirectly food supply is a limiting factor, and conclude from the fact that numbers were so small for so long indicates that in the broad term there was nutritional control of the population. There may have been a social amelioration of this control; nevertheless there was almost certainly a natural limiting factor in the environment—some form of periodic if not chronic shortage of food.

I would also like to question the implication that infanticide and death in general are 'better' than survival in a condition of persistent and severe mal-nutrition. We do know that the change in the economy that came with agriculture and the domestication of animals led to an enormous population expansion. Today we look unfavourably on this but at the time the people, who had previously been hunter–gatherers, probably saw this as the idyllic state in which they could have a lot of children who would survive.

Haraldson: Dr Lightman spoke about the need for research in tribal groups being of some immediate benefit to the group. There has been much discussion on whether one should do research in developing countries and what sort of research should be done. The Swedish International Development Authority tried to formulate rules for such research. It was said that research in developing countries must focus on high priority problems, and must be likely to give results within a reasonable time. The results, moreover, should be used immediately, and in the area where they were obtained. I think these ideas are in accordance with WHO thinking too.

On the question of health services, it is important that we should work for lasting effects, and curative medicine has not offered much in the way of lasting effect in the past century. It is surely time to change to a public health approach. It has been said, rightly, that we have been looking through the microscope for a hundred years; it's time to look through the windows. We are dealing with macro problems to a great extent and trying to solve them with micro methods. There is also the fact that in many nomadic groups the pattern of diseases is switching rapidly from physical diseases to social and mental diseases for which we are not trained and where we don't know much about treatment, and have not many resources. Nevertheless we have to tackle these problems, which are caused mainly by acculturation and by too rapid development.

Stanley: Stafford Lightman stressed that research done on tribal people was not benefiting the population under study. I would go further than Dr Haraldson and say what is needed is the *application* of what we already all know. We have diagnosed many things we think are wrong, and it is now a question of applying our knowledge. In Australia the Aborigines themselves have told us that they don't want further studies made, and that we should try to apply a little of what we have learned and benefit them! Why are we so incapable of applying what we have learnt?

Woodburn: This is an extremely important point. One can see it clearly in relation to the tiny minority of the world's population who are hunters and gatherers. The studies made over the past 25 years have demonstrated that in virtually every case of forced settlement of hunters and gatherers (as opposed to voluntary settlement, which is quite a different situation), there have been devastating consequences—death, disease and demoralization. My view is that most of these settlement schemes have been put into operation not by people of ill-will but by people of good-will who, when they initiated the policy of forced settlement, believed that they were acting directly in the interests of the people being settled. There is something terrible about a situation in which basic knowledge of this kind is so little known, or, if known, is so easily discarded by the people responsible for the policies. This is surely something we should try to do more about. We may not be able to do much about people of ill-will, but we can surely try to persuade people of good-will to think more carefully about the probable consequences of their policies (see Woodburn 1972).

Tyrrell: Some people would say that one thing we know for certain is one or two ways of doing a job *badly!* We know a lot about what goes *wrong*, but not enough about how to do it in the right way. Therefore, perhaps not in a very academic sense but in an applied, practical sense, there is need for studies of how things go, and what helps them to go right and what makes them go wrong. Methods of monitoring, not just of what people think but of what actually happens, are needed so that things can be learnt which can be applied more widely.

Hamilton: The danger is that we are often trying to be too clever too fast in medicine and forgetting that it is the very simplest level of public health involvement which matters. This is not 'medically' oriented, but is a straightforward public health, engineering and sometimes agricultural question. It is basic economic growth and engineering practice that has really brought about changes in public health.

Stanley: We haven't a lot of *time* to do yet more detailed research into the relevant factors for people such as the Aborigines, because they are not going to let us do it. We tried to evaluate the only consumer-run medical service that I know in Australia, the Aboriginal Medical Service in Perth, and they wouldn't allow us to do it.

Shaper: They have enough insight to know that this is totally irrelevant to them and that health is a matter of political and economic factors.

POVERTY, MEDICINE AND THE RIGHTS OF MINORITY GROUPS

Shaper: I presume we are becoming aware in this symposium that we are not discussing tribal societies so much as using tribal societies indirectly to discuss our *own* problems! What Dr Lightman and Dr Morin said about the problems of tribal peoples really describes our own western society. When Dr Lightman talked about the principles of medical care, in fact every one of his principles applies fully to our own medical situation, in Nottingham or Oxford or London.

Hugh-Jones: Tribal societies *have* become so interesting partly because we can look at their problems from outside; we are not caught up in them. The danger is in thinking in terms of 'us' and 'them', when in fact there is a continuous spectrum, with different stages of development.

Lightman: I would certainly agree with you, Professor Shaper, that basic principles of medical care are universally applicable. I have, however, been trying to pinpoint some of the specific problems of isolated tribal societies that are of particular importance in their unique situation. I would add, moreover, that once the process of acculturation has begun, there is often a rapid progression to dependency and poverty resulting in a new situation where the major medical problems are now the problems of poverty. The problems then are the same as in other impoverished areas of the world, with poor sanitation, hygiene and housing, with all their associated sequelae.

Shaper: Your principles, however, are as applicable to the UK or any other highly developed technical society for establishing priorities in medical care as they would be for the most impoverished.

Lightman: I do not deny that, but the priorities of medical care in acculturated or acculturating tribal communities are not the same as our own, and are to a large degree governed by the socio-economic status of the group concerned. Children with malnutrition and chronic debilitating infections have a higher priority for food than for antibiotics.

Shaper: It's a transfer situation: we are trying to achieve in small groups what we are totally unable to achieve in our own large group!

Lozoff: Sahlins (1972, p. 37) has argued that hunter–gatherers are the 'original affluent society' who live in a 'kind of material plenty'. He notes that they 'have few possessions *but they are not poor*. Poverty is not a certain small amount of goods, nor is it just a relation betweens means and ends; above all it is a relation between people. Poverty is a social status'. Thus our contact with these people *makes* them poor.

Lightman: I agree. That is why I have tried to distinguish between recently contacted groups and those already in a situation of acculturation.

Gajdusek: I think we can agree that it is the impact of outsiders that leads to the extreme poverty and if so, the question becomes one of how one can have the contact but ensure that such people end up wealthy, not poor. If we have anything to offer we should address ourselves to the matter that if they are wealthy people when we meet them, in spirit and in pride and in human dignity, there should be some attention to the indulgence which may keep them in that aristocratic, privileged position. We know that if they slip into the category of the hundreds and millions of poor, they will be unlikely to survive as a culture, coming from small, fragile groups with little preparation for such competition.

Hugh-Jones: The question is of the best way of doing this.

Gajdusek: For a start, I would challenge the thesis of slow acculturation; this to my mind is a direct route into poverty. We graduate such people by slow acculturation to competition with the poorest and least privileged in huge cosmopolitan societies, and to competition with people who have the least sympathy and understanding for them. They are surely then the poorest equipped of the poor to withstand such competition. What they need is 'undeserved' and 'unearned' indulgence.

Hugh-Jones: Why do you think slow acculturation is disastrous? If a community is in balance and people from outside come in and disturb it, the community needs time to acquire the know-how for it to fit into a new society.

Gajdusek: But we and they do not *have* the decades in which they can slowly abandon hunting and gathering, while slowly acquiring some economic substitute. If the process is slow they are automatically in poverty. If for example a legal organization could put their homeland into trust for them, for a generation or a century, even if all the people left it, the fact of having it in legal trust as their *own* land would be an unrivalled anchor for both group identity and economic advantage and eventual competitive survival through their own efforts.

Hugh-Jones: This is what Survival International has been trying to do, to help such people enter our legal systems, so that they can have their own rights.

Lightman: Land rights are the sheet anchor for the maintenance of cultural identity and self-respect. The problem is that the people must acquire the knowledge of *how* to get their land rights. This is certainly a situation where outside help is invaluable, and a high priority area for Survival International.

Ohlman: Perhaps we should be looking at the effect of the combination of minority position and power. You can be a minority and maintain yourself as long as you have power, which could be defined in terms of wealth per head, the kind of resources you have at your disposal. If you are in a minority, but lack power, you probably will disappear as a group.

Woodburn: You cannot equate personal wealth with power. An exploited Aboriginal artist in Australia, say, might have a greater money income than I do, but he may also be politically impotent and is in a situation in which he has no way of investing in the future. The social security income of an American Black is probably greater than the income of 99% of people in developing countries; the problem is their *political* impotence, and this is not a matter of wealth.

Ohlman: If wealth cannot be equated to power in these circumstances, what is power?

White: Power *is* control over resources. A lot of groups all over the world are being expropriated and exploited because they own a particularly desirable piece of land—because someone wants to put a road through or because, like the Australian Aborigines, they are sitting on the world's biggest uranium deposit. If they themselves can get together, and win the support of enough white people who see the justice of their claim, then they may be able to maintain control over their traditional land and its resources. But it depends partly on whether Aborigines can unite, and this is very difficult for what were traditionally a number of small, separate societies.

Ohlman: It requires a certain guilt feeling, perhaps, on the part of the majority which prevents them exercising their own power, before minority rights will be recognized.

Woodburn: This comes back to the point that dependency and political impotence tend to have a corrosive effect on those who become dependent. You can be dependent in a situation in which there is a well-meaning government, or where the government bears you much ill-will, but the effects can be similar. It isn't just a matter of establishing the good-will of the central government.

Hugh-Jones: Mrs White says that the Aborigines are sitting on the uranium. We know to our cost in the UK the effect of the Arabs sitting on oil supplies and gaining so much wealth; yet the Aborigines, although sitting on the uranium, don't get anything. I was told in Irian Jaya that the Dani and Damal people are sitting on a copper mine, so they ought to be immensely wealthy! The reason they are not is that they have not had the time or the experience to assert themselves within the community, and so it comes back to the question of running one's own life.

Lozoff: Well-meaning people have given land rights to individuals, according to the legal system of the dominant culture. This has led to unintended abuse and disenfranchisement of these isolated communities. In order to ensure that the land is actually protected, land rights need special legal arrangements that reflect an understanding of the community's structure and cultural patterns.

Lightman: This is an important consideration. If, for instance, land rights are given to people in their own names, they may well be induced to part with it for money or alcohol! It is no less important to consider how to protect such people from losing their rights once they have been gained.

White: In the state of South Australia this problem has been recognized both by the Whites and by the Aborigines, and all Aboriginal land has been put into the Aboriginal Land Trust. It needs a certain number of signatures to sell one acre, and even then the money cannot go to an individual. This isn't a case of the Whites behaving paternalistically; the Aborigines are very much aware of their own weakness and support moves to protect themselves against it.

Lightman: Does the government still maintain the power to alter the Aboriginal Land Act if there is, say, a uranium find?

Stanley: They have done so in the past when minerals were found—whole tribes were just evacuated and resettled elsewhere.

White: South Australia was the first state to legislate for land rights for Aborigines, but the original draft for the legislation was altered in the state's Upper House. The government had intended to give the Aborigines rights over the minerals below the surface, but the opposition contended—successfully— that since throughout the whole continent all such minerals belonged to the Australian people as a whole (through the Crown), no exception should be made for Aborigines. Thus rights to land for Australian Aborigines do not include rights over minerals.

Lozoff: The problem is whether it is realistic to expect any country to put into trust enough land to ensure the survival of such groups.

Haraldson: There is a declaration of human rights for tribal people which is little known. It was drawn up by the International Labour Organization in 1959 (Convention No. 107), and much of what we are now discussing is there. In Article 12 it states that tribal people should not be forced to leave their tribal area or to become sedentary, except 'in accordance with national laws and regulations for reasons relating to national security, or in the interest of national economic development or of the health of the said populations'. When removal is necessary, they shall be provided with lands of quality at least equal to that of the lands previously occupied by them, suitable to provide for their present needs and future development'.

Polunin: How many countries have ratified this convention?

Haraldson: In 1971 four had done so—Pakistan, Egypt, Syria and Tunisia. There may be more now.

On the basis of information collected on field visits in Africa and Asia which I made for WHO, a seminar with representatives mainly from Arabic countries was organized in Shiraz in 1972 (see Haraldson 1973). Twelve recommendations were made to governments of countries with large groups of nomads, and point six reads as follows:

'Whenever sedentarization is considered realistic, it must be voluntary, well planned, and gradually introduced to avoid failures and unnecessary acculturation. The establishment of model villages demonstrating settled conditions, such as improved agriculture and animal husbandry, health services and education, housing, etc. might attract marginal groups of nomads to sedentarization. These model villages would also stimulate nomads to improve their own conditions'.

Ohlman: A rather different kind of policy statement, specifically on the Tasaday people, was issued by PANAMIN, the Private Association for National Minorities, in the Philippines. PANAMIN was founded by a single person with his own wealth, but has received considerable government support. It is interesting to contrast the specificity of this statement of attitudes towards minority peoples with the more general statements of the ILO Convention (Nance, 1975, pp. 219–221).

Cohen: I don't think there is any *one* best way of handling these things, but it is worth considering cultures that have re-settled successfully. One is Israel, where a large number of people re-settled themselves very successfully, probably because they had such strong ideological beliefs and also sufficient wealth behind them. One interesting feature of that culture has been its inability to tolerate minority opinions within it; perhaps to re-settle successfully you must be extremely resistant to other groups around you? This is relevant for the ethnic minority groups in the UK, some of whom have established themselves fully and others, the more recent arrivals, are attempting to do so. A threat to them comes from the fact that some people, with whom they may appear to compete or at least mix, cannot bear the fact that some of these groups have been already or look likely to be successfully re-settled; it appears to excite envy. This is the other side of the coin: how will the majority population group come to accept the situation?

Ohlman: People have various ways of entering the mainstream of a society. In the USA, entertainments and sport have been main routes of entry of minority groups. From these power bases, they can advance into other fields. It is interesting to see how people in different countries work their way up into 'respectability'.

Jones: There are some practical facts that have to be faced in this whole matter of assimilation. It is true that settled agriculturalists and pastoralists are a threat to foragers and hunters and gatherers, because they disturb the ecology, but industrial man is a threat both to hunters and gatherers *and* to settled agriculturists and pastoralists for the same reason, that he disturbs the ecology. If we are discussing what we would like to see happen, it has to be within the bounds of the possible, and the characteristic of industrial man is that he is made up of being a labour force and being a consumer force. We cannot detach ourselves from these two perhaps rather unpleasant concepts, in discussing the future of small groups.

Lewis: We have brought up land rights and a variety of political, social and economic problems in this discussion. Surely our job is to show, if we can, what are the connections between the patterns and outcome of illness and some of the social changes we have discussed, and to show how these changes come to have, or may come to have, those consequences on health. I doubt that our views on the rights and wrongs of some situation will carry weight unless we can make clear how they are based on medical knowledge and not only on our general views and sympathies.

Woodburn: The issue of land rights *is* not only an issue of morality or politics, but is a medical issue. Land rights are only one way but by far the most obvious way in which people obtain some focus, some security, some confidence in working for their own future, and some clear identity—identity both as individuals and as members of a whole succession of groups, including a particular local group and a wider national group. Such a social framework is basic for effective medicine and more particularly for effective public health and preventive medicine.

Stanley: If we wait for more direct evidence of how land affects health, we shall be here for 150 years, and meanwhile the Australian situation, at least, will become steadily worse.

Polunin: What Dr Woodburn says may well be true but we are faced with the situation where it is unlikely that many of the people we are primarily talking about will get an adequate land base. We *have* to speak from the point of view of our respective professions, and in terms of our professions. For instance, nobody will listen to doctors if they suddenly start saying that the basis of health is having a land base. This is outside the field where we are thought of as being competent.

Ohlman: No government is going to give, in perpetuity, land to a minority group. Governments can always use the right of eminent domain—which every government maintains—to take the land back. It may be a military reason or a health reason (as the ILO convention allows for). One can easily find an excuse, and a 'reasonable' one, to take land from people. Constitutional protections only delay this. Secondly, in the US we have many Indian tribes who were granted reservations for a century or more, but this does not really give them absolute rights. The only thing that enters the public consciousness is when they become politically active, which gets them attention in the media. The media have had a great deal to do with mobilizing Indian consciousness; they have learned this from the Black movement in the US. They realize that even if you are a minority you can demand certain rights if you are militant enough.

Morin: I do not believe that the media are the mobilizing factor of the revival of the Indian movements in the US in recent years. The Indians do not discover the exploitation and prejudice which they meet in the national society in their reserves but in the cities. It is in the urban setting that they demand a new ethnic identity, often very different from the one they had known in the reserves. For the urbanized Indian this changed demand represents a defence against environmental pressures. It is worth noting that one finds urbanization as the mobilizing factor for the revival of other ethnic groups, such as the Bretons and the Occitans in France. In their rejection of a world of anonymous and isolating cement blocks they rediscover language, culture and history to provide the sense of belonging for which they feel a need.

Cockburn: I have been dealing with health, so-called, and medical care among poor people for thirty years, and for the past ten years among the poor Blacks in Detroit, who are just as despairing and as depressed as some of the tribal people we are discussing. What is significant to me is that when a people settle down for the first time or make first contact, they get the diseases of the white man and are reduced down to a third of their number. Then, as white culture influences them, especially in the past few years with penicillin and other developments, the population begins to go up again. This is so for the Australian

Aborigines, the Navaho Indians, the Arabs in Israel, the Eskimos of Alaska, and others too. It produces pressures and tensions of all kinds. If you expect a million Aborigines in Australia in A.D. 2000, most of them not working and on welfare, you will have tension. Perhaps twenty or thirty years after that, it will be two million. Population is a crucial matter.

Shaper: What Dr Cockburn and others have been saying seems to be telling us that the whole health business is a confidence trick, and is not of major relevance to the problems of either our society or tribal societies. Perhaps one of the worst things WHO has done is to define health, by giving an expectation of perfect health and well-being which nobody can ever achieve and yet everybody is asked to match up to. We don't only walk into remote places and make the people poor, we also make them ill, because we give them a definition of health which renders all populations sick. I suggest that the health aspect of this reflects our conscience in society and is one of the ways in which society can avoid major re-structuring. Health is almost a peripheral involvement which keeps many of us professionally happy and interested, because we have a vested interest in disease.

Gajdusek: We are moving into vast sociological issues, yet we met as a group with an interest in what, if we were botanists, would be rare orchids: the small, still primitive and culturally intact groups of mankind. The real problem here is how to preserve the fragile orchid habitat. We see that this we cannot do, so we search for a conservatory or greenhouse where they may survive. We are all interested in the strange cultural and genetic selection that has produced a few small groups in various parts of the world. Only the soil of incredibly special privilege will enable them to survive. To give such fragile cultures 'an equal chance' will not allow their survival. If they are to survive in a way that will permit them to defend and maintain their uniqueness, we must invest in them many times the amount of money per head that we are willing to put toward the education and maintenance of the masses of poor in huge suburban slums and in impoverished, overpopulated peasant economies. If the members of these unique primitive groups are not granted special privilege and consideration there is little likelihood of their survival far into the next century.

Lightman: The problem is not whether we should be in the business of *preserving* people like rare orchids. The situation to which we should be seeking a solution is how to manage the inevitable process of contact and cultural transfer so as to prevent the subsequent social and medical disasters that have been discussed in this symposium. We have, I think, agreed on some medical priorities; for example that preventive and social medicine are more important than hospital-based medical practice. We have not, however, discussed *who* should be delivering this primary health care and whether they might be nurses living in the community, bare-foot doctors, village midwives with additional training, or—as I feel is usually inappropriate—outside doctors.

Hamilton: When we think about what we as doctors have to offer, really we can only offer (1) clinical intervention on a small number of specific conditions, yaws treatment being the classic example, and (2) the possibility of monitoring and perhaps predicting epidemics. In order to do that a health 'presence' may be required in each community; this may simply be somebody with a satchel on his arm, who knows when to call on more expert help. But if we *are* to offer anything medically, we have to offer the confidence that if something goes seriously wrong, someone will take effective action if possible, and this means a good back-up clinic and hospital facilities.

Lightman: The isolated groups we have been discussing in this symposium have survived a long time without access to large hospitals.

Hamilton: But we are now talking about going into these societies and what we can offer them. We can offer a limited amount of clinical knowledge to deal with specific problems, as well as the public health side, but also confidence in knowing that if they are seriously ill, something will be done about it.

Cohen: We should not be too fatalistic. This symposium comes at a time when it is predicted that the World Health Organization will shortly announce the complete elimination of smallpox from the world—a disease which has done more than most to decimate primitive isolated societies. We should think in terms of the positive measures that we can offer to people—measures based on known, effective and, one hopes, fairly simple remedies that have been tested and have proved to be successful. These are what people want and expect. It is unreasonable that we should base *all* our work with isolated societies on preventive rather than curative medicine. There has to be a balance, and that sort of equilibrium is not even what we are able to achieve for ourselves. When facilities exist and they become known, people's hopes rise and at least a little of what they believe needs to be given to them! If therapies and some form of institutional facilities are not provided in these situations as policy, then sooner or later we shall be in trouble. We have to achieve a balance, but the balance should be on the optimistic side, using the limited basic resources but also including some of the unarguable technological advances. We are, after all, living towards the end of the twentieth century.

Gajdusek: The medical profession, in trying to reach out with healing into the villages, using facilities of low calibre, when many of the conditions that can be remedied can only be handled in large cities in specialized facilities, is making a serious medical and psychological error. In Papua New Guinea the government has not hesitated to fly people for cardiac surgery to Brisbane from the Stone Age and back to the village, without greatly upsetting the individual or the culture. If we as western doctors, able to treat compound fractures, depressed cranial fractures, placenta praevia, ruptured ectopic pregnancies, cancers and cardiac anomalies, decide to practise bush medicine, reserving our most advanced medicine for those of our own culture, we have betrayed the trust that members of primitive groups are willing to give to us. I suggest that for any small, still primitive group the cost of flying a few individuals to the major city for medical treatment of serious correctable conditions is minimal and that we shall waste money by giving them a costly intermediate, low-grade facility nearby. When it comes to such small groups as those in the Xingu National Park, I cannot accept that a compound fracture or osteomyelitis should be dealt with in the village setting when the occasional patient can be taken to Rio for proper treatment, even with a year of physiotherapy if need be. To do less is to be hypocritical. We are short-changing primitive man if we think the young person in any primitive culture cannot leave the Stone Age, go to the city for two years, and come back to his culture. It is being done all the time in the modern world.

Lightman: You are talking about treating one person, however.

Gajdusek: Yes, because that is where we come into the problem. In this meeting we are talking of special, exotic populations of very small numbers. We are not sociologists trying to solve the problems of the overpopulated cosmopolitan world; and, above all, we are doctors!

Lightman: You are suggesting the use of expensive interventionist medicine aimed at the sick individual rather than at the diseases of the community at large. Certainly the psychological advantages of curative medicine are great, and are often the basis for successful health programmes, but it is the consequent community health care that achieves the results. The Navaho Indian community experiment that I quoted (p. 312) demonstrates the overall ineffectiveness of hospital-based interventionist health care.

I also feel you are skating over the obvious problems of expense. Most tribal societies come low down on the priority scale of their respective governments, and are usually within countries that are poor and have insuperable health problems of their own. These countries cannot be expected to make their tribal groups a special case of greater importance than the rest of the population.

Ohlman: Unfortunately, ministries of health are not usually the most powerful ministries. With unlimited resources you can afford to treat people by flying them round the world for an operation, but with finite resources, is it right to spend $ 100 000 on one person, when you could immunize 100 000 people at a dollar each instead? It is an economic question.

Black: In dealing with these isolated and tribal societies, perhaps we have some hope. Dr Baruzzi's data on the Kren-Akorore make the situation seem bleak, but the Xikrin also went through a four-fold reduction in their population, and although they are not completely out of the woods yet, they are on their way up. By taking one step at a time—smallpox eradication, measles immunization, yaws treatment—we may get such peoples through the first stage, of declining population. On the psychological problems we can also do something; let us not fail to do that.

*   *   *

Polunin: At this stage, may I try to draw together some points that have come out of the symposium and suggest where we go from here in the way of further studies? I would like to suggest that a tribal group is thriving if it shows the following characteristics:

1. Comparatively stable populations. The population should not decline nor should it show a rapid increase.
2. Reasonably low morbidity, both for physical and mental disease and for conditions reflecting disordered social relations like drug dependence, delinquency, and suicide. Mortality rates should be reasonably low at all ages.

Only a general, tentative statement can be made about the conditions under which a tribal group will continue to thrive, but I would expect them to include:

(a) An adequate subsistence base (permanent rights to the occupation and use of lands, waters, etc.).
(b) Generally harmonious relationships with neighbours and with the national government. This involves recognition by the government of the validity of the culture of tribal nationals and recognition that it is not incompatible with national ideals. It also involves awareness by the tribal people of their rights and duties as nationals, together with their feeling that they have a say in determining their own future.
(c) The maintenance of group identity and self-respect.
(d) The ability to adapt to change.

What studies should be undertaken? Studies on any aspect of tribal health and disease will probably be useful and are likely to be determined by the special circumstance prevailing among the tribal people and our interests and resources as investigators.

There is a considerable need for monitoring the situation by long-term follow-up studies, and a considerable lack of such studies. I suggest that the decennial censuses of population undertaken by nearly all countries are particularly suitable times for starting such studies, which could be repeated at, say, ten- or five-year intervals. The censuses provide useful information on tribal population.

Populations for follow-up study could be selected to represent the range of circumstances in each country or because the people have special problems. A limited number of characteristics should be regularly studied which throw light on disease and living conditions. Special attention could be paid to children born since the previous survey, as they *largely* reflect conditions since then.

References

BASTIDE, R. (1953) Contribution à l'étude de la participation. *Cahiers Internationaux de Sociologie 14*, 30–40

BASTIDE, R. (1966) Conclusion d'un débat récent: la pensée obscure et confuse. *Le Monde non-chrétien*, 75–76, 137–156

BASTIDE, R. (1976) *Le Prochain et le Lointain*, Cujas, Paris

CLASTRES, P. (1974) *La Société contre l'Etat*, Editions de Minuit, Paris

HARALDSON, S.R.S. (1973) *Seminar on Health Problems of Nomads, Shiraz/Isfahan* (Report), World Health Organization (duplicated)

JAULIN, R. (1970) *La Paix Blanche*, Seuil, Paris

JAULIN, R. (1974) *La Décivilisation, politique et pratique de l'Ethnocide*, Editions Complexe, Paris

MÉTRAUX, A. (1952) Jésuites et Indiens en Amérique du Sud. *Revue de Paris 59*, 102–113

NANCE, J. (1975) *The Gentle Tasaday: a Stone Age People in the Philippine Rain Forest*, Harcourt Brace Jovanovich, New York

SAHLINS, M. (1972) *Stone Age Economics*, Aldine, Chicago

WOODBURN, J.C. (1972) The future for hunting and gathering peoples. *!Kung: the Magazine of the London School of Economics Anthropology Society*, 1–3

Chairman's closing remarks

PHILIP HUGH-JONES

King's College Hospital Medical School, London

As always, in scientific endeavour, we have raised more questions than we have been able to answer. But their formulation alone has been most valuable. Our conference has achieved what I always thank the Ciba Foundation for, namely the fertilization of ideas between those who work in different disciplines.

At the start of this symposium I set out with the idea that we might end by making some recommendations, but I think this was an arrogant thing to suggest. At this point it would be better to look back on the intentions that we originally had when the symposium was conceived and see to what extent we have covered the ground and what conclusions we can draw.

We began with three questions: first, how best to make contact with isolated people; secondly, the related question of the assimilation of such communities into the rest of society; and, thirdly, the question of what the rest of the world could gain by studying these communities.

On the question of contact, we initially had in mind the problems of where to look for isolated people, how to protect them, and what information to collect and how to collect it, to which I would now add the problem of why we should study such people at all. For me, the reason is what we gain from them. They are of extreme interest from the point of view of their isolation, both psychological and physical. Also, such people are inevitably going to be contacted, probably by those who will do a good deal more harm than we will, as scientists and doctors, provided we exercise our social consciences.

On the question of where to look, it has become clear that there are almost no totally isolated groups left, but if there are even one or two, they could be very important for critical information which we need to have and can get in no other way. Perhaps developments such as the earth satellites will help in the looking, particularly advance looking when it is known that, say, a road is going into an unknown area. This would enable research workers to get together and decide what they want to find out at the time of primary contact. When we do go to meet such isolated people, we have the duty to protect them after the breakdown of their isolation. All that we have heard about virus studies makes us fairly confident that we could do something to protect them from exogenous microorganisms, by giving antibiotics and by isolating investigators before they make contact. We can certainly protect them from the destruction of their livelihood and from outright killing and forced settlement.

Having said that, and being honest with ourselves, it is we who want information. What are we going to collect, and how shall we collect and record it? In the symposium we have not, unfortunately, decided what should be collected. Certain information has to be collected at the time of first contact; many other items can wait. It is important that we think out what must be collected immediately after contact. Interesting and promising recording systems such as Dr Lozoff's have been mentioned which will help us to record a mass of information, including behavioural information.

We are then faced with the problem of assimilation. My general feeling is that, before contact, primitive isolated people are in balance with their environment, and we do not wish to reduce them to a much poorer state, for either their sake or our own. For their survival means that we can continue to learn from them—from their myths and legends, their past life, and all the other things they have to offer. So in the process of assimilation we should try to convince those directly involved that it would pay them to assimilate such people into society in a satisfactory way. To do this, we must analyse what things are so damaging. We talked about the introduction of infection and we think we can do something to prevent that. But the greatest dangers appear to be the psychological ones, chiefly the dangers of imposing, rather like a parent, a dependent state upon people and making their lives pointless. Once such a state of dependency is induced there really isn't any reason to go on living, and it becomes a question of half-living rather than really living. That is perhaps why many uninformed members of apparently civilized communities tend to look down on Indians. They see them away from their own environment before they have had a chance to learn new skills, whereas when I go into the jungle it is the Indians who, very reasonably, laugh at me!

I would agree with Carleton Gajdusek to the extent of saying that one needs, in the process of assimilation, to ensure enough legal protection against exploitation while people are learning to fend for themselves in the new larger community. I see no reason why that cannot be given.

Something that should also be emphasized is that it is chronic ill-health that decimates these peoples and ultimately leads to their destruction, rather than the more obvious causes such as infections, which can in fact be dealt with.

When we consider assimilation, therefore, it is not only how to assimilate tribal people but the rate at which it is done, if indeed you ever do fully assimilate people. I am not certain that it is good to have complete fusion anyway or whether people always want to remain identified. Thus we should be concerned with the ultimate identity of tribal people, at balance in a new society, but forming a new group within it. This sounds a reasonable state to aim for, but considering that the world at the moment is not prepared to give even 1 % of the income of the developed countries to the third world, one feels doubtful whether it will happen.

Instead of making recommendations of what we think ought to be done, we have stated in this symposium what could be done, so there may be a chance of some notice being taken of it by governments who do not like adverse criticism.

The third point was what do we, in 'westernized' societies, learn by examining isolated communities. It is obvious that we learn an enormous amount. Our discussion has shown that we are all part of a continuous spectrum of human beings, and one of the advantages of looking at isolated groups is that we are also looking at ourselves, both psychologically and physically, at a stage we were once at, in a more clear-cut and simplified form than we see in our own complex societies. It seems clear, therefore, that such studies can be extremely valuable, provided they are done effectively.

The whole problem of nutrition is fascinating. What are the real nutritional standards? Are large-sized people in modern communities really desirable or is the balance achieved in hunter-gatherer society a good deal better than the recommendations that are often made as to what is perfect human nutrition?

The study of primitive people clearly gives us a key to many physical diseases of our society: the work we have heard about on cysticercosis, scabies, epilepsy, kuru or measles shows just how much can be gained from studying disease in isolated populations.

A further point that came out is the dissatisfaction felt in our modern world with what modern medicine is giving us. It is fairly clear that we as doctors look at the disease of an organ, or we look at the system in biochemical terms, and we do not always act in the best way from the point of view of the patient. We can learn a lot on the emotional problems in disease by studying the medicine of primitive people, in contrast to the way modern medicine operates. Does something like our National Health Service in the UK increase dependency, and is this desirable? The demand for medicine has increased continuously, and I think we may be able to see better why this is so by studying isolated and primitive societies.

We have discussed the question of exploitation and how cultural diversity can be lost as a result. This is important. Although I don't think we have really tackled this question, I particularly liked the idea of the setting up of an Aboriginal Embassy in Canberra, and I agree with Dr Katherine Elliott, who has suggested that if we could move the headquarters of WHO to Calcutta, that also might have some effect!

A further problem that has arisen from the symposium, about which people are not always intellectually honest, is that many of our 'ideals' are not necessarily valid. There is no doubt that as doctors in the modern community we are working against natural selection; we are imposing our attitudes in favour of always saving life, without thinking about the quality of the consequent life. We might learn something from seeing what people in isolated groups have done where the same tenets are not necessarily held.

It remains for me to thank the contributors for their lucid papers and comments and especially to thank the Ciba Foundation and its staff. One thing is certain from this symposium, that there is so much to be gained by the study of isolated groups. I hope that those working among primitive communities do freely interchange ideas so that information is not lost before change makes it irrevocable. We may have but a decade to collect much information that needs to be collected and we should think hard and quickly how we are to collect it!

Index of contributors

*Entries in **bold** type indicate papers; other entries are contributions to discussions*

Indexes compiled by William Hill

337

Subject index